The Middle Ages:

An Encyclopedia for Students /

William Chester Jordan, *Editor in Chief*
for the
American Council of Learned Societies

Volume 3

CHARLES SCRIBNER'S SONS
Macmillan Library Reference USA
Simon & Schuster Macmillan
New York

SIMON & SCHUSTER AND PRENTICE HALL INTERNATIONAL
London   Mexico City   New Delhi   Singapore   Sydney   Toronto

Developed for the American Council of Learned Societies by Charles Scribner's Sons and Visual Education Corporation.

PRINTING
3 4 5 6 7 8 9 10

Library of Congress Cataloging-in-Publication Data

The Middle Ages / William Chester Jordan, editor in chief for the American Council of Learned Societies.
       p.   cm.
   Includes bibliographical references and index.
   ISBN 0-684-19773-1   (hard/libr. bind. : alk. paper)
   1. Middle Ages—Encyclopedias, Juvenile.   I. Jordan, William C., 1948– .   II. American Council of Learned Societies.
D114.M54 1996
909.07´03—dc20   95-49597
                                                                          CIP

ISBN 0-684-80483-2 (vol. 1)
ISBN 0-684-80484-0 (vol. 2)
ISBN 0-684-80485-9 (vol. 3)
ISBN 0-684-80486-7 (vol. 4)

Incense

* **resins** solid or semisolid substances obtained from various plants

Incense is a substance that produces a sweet-smelling smoke when it is burned. The smoke itself is also called incense. In the Middle Ages, various substances—including seeds, bark, wood, and resins*—were burned as incense.

Before Christian times, incense was used as a perfume, to relieve weariness, to mask unpleasant odors, as a sacrificial offering, and as a mark of honor to important persons, places, and things. The early Christians used incense in their homes, at funerals, and in cemeteries. It was not used in early church worship because it was associated with pagan rituals. As Christianity developed, however, incense became an important part of church rituals as well. As early as the 400s, it was used in various church processions, including funeral marches and the entry of important dignitaries into the church. Incense played an important role in the MASS, especially during Communion. For medieval Christians, incense symbolized sacrifice and prayer, and it was associated with joy and the forgiveness of sins. It was also thought to have the power to heal and the power to exorcise, or drive out, evil spirits.

* **censers** vessels used to hold incense; also known as thuribles

Within the church, incense was burned in ornate censers* of gold, silver, bronze, or iron. Some censers were stationary, while others were hung on chains and swung to spread the aroma of the burning incense. In the late Middle Ages, the swinging of the censer, known as censing, became a highly complicated and intricate procedure. (*See also* **Cosmetics and Beauty Aids; Herbs and Herbals; Magic and Folklore; Mass, Liturgy of; Medicine.**)

Indulgences

* **purgatory** place of temporary suffering or punishment after death and before entering heaven

In the medieval Roman Church, forgiveness of sins was a two-step process. First, the sinner had to confess his or her sin to an ordained priest, who then granted absolution (forgiveness). The second step required a penance (punishment) to make amends for the sin, either in this life or after death in purgatory*.

During the Middle Ages, church authorities had the power to grant indulgences, which permitted a sinner to substitute something else for all or part of the penance. Substitutes included visiting a church, making donations for the poor, or going on a crusade. Indulgences varied from those which canceled only a small part of a penance to those which canceled the penance for all the sins the individual ever committed prior to receiving the indulgence. This second kind of indulgence was called a plenary indulgence.

* **heretic** person who disagrees with established church doctrine

* **infidel** person who does not accept a particular faith

Plenary indulgences were of two kinds: jubilee and crusade. Popes issued jubilee indulgences during special HOLY YEARS to those who traveled to Rome to seek them. Pope BONIFACE VIII issued the first jubilee indulgences in 1300. Popes also issued plenary indulgences to those who joined crusades against heretics* and infidels*. In 1095, Pope URBAN II promised full remission of penance to those who joined the first CRUSADE against Muslims in the Holy Land. He further granted eternal life to those who died in battle during the crusade. (*See also* **Papacy, Origins and Development.**)

Inheritance Laws and Practices

I nheritance laws and practices reveal much about a society and its values. In addition to establishing rules about how an estate—property, money, and other items—is to be passed from one generation to another, inheritance practices show how a society regards the legal status of men, women, and children.

Western European Inheritance. Inheritance laws and practices in medieval Europe took many different forms, depending on time and place. The laws of inheritance that developed in Italy were based on Roman civil law, on the customs and traditions of the Germans who settled there after the fall of the Roman Empire, and on canon law*.

The Roman orator and historian Tacitus (ca. 56–ca. 120) described Germanic inheritance customs with the remark "And no last will." To his Roman audience, this meant that Germans died without a formal written will. This practice differed markedly from Roman practice, in which a man gave his property to anyone he chose by means of a formal testament, or will. The only restriction on a Roman citizen was the legal requirement that at least one-fourth of the estate be guaranteed to his children or other heirs.

The German father, on the other hand, lacked the opportunity to control the fate of his property after death. The property passed to all his children or legal heirs in a fixed order of succession. Underlying these practices were different ideas about family and property ownership. Romans believed that the father was the guiding force in a family and therefore should determine the fate of the family property. For Germans, however, the family group was more important, and property remained within the group and was transferred automatically and divided among its members.

Economic expansion during the Middle Ages generated more wealth in the form of cash money, titles, offices, and honors. Powerful interests—such as the church, the nobility, and urban associations—affected inheritance laws and practices. Under the influence of the church, for example, the inheritance rights of illegitimate children were diminished. Some early Germanic inheritance laws had recognized illegitimate children almost as equal to legitimate children. But in the 1000s, church reformers were determined to put an end to adultery and to sexual activity among clerics. Their reforms included prohibitions in canon law on inheritance to illegitimate children.

Changes in inheritance practices during the Middle Ages also affected women. The rights of women to inherit had been severely restricted, and even denied, by early Germanic laws and by some Roman laws. With the revival of the dowry* system, however, certain inheritance practices were modified. The dowry transferred a considerable portion of a woman's father's estate to her husband. The dowry was intended to provide adequate support for a woman in marriage and widowhood, and it eventually passed to her children. The dowry, therefore, was a kind of advance inheritance for a woman, although it came with several restrictions. Often a woman was required to renounce any further claims to her father's estate on payment of the dowry.

Inheritance laws and practices in England differed from those in Italy. Land in England could not be willed, as it could be in other parts of west-

* **canon law** body of church law

* **dowry** money or property that a woman brings to the man she marries

ern Europe. Under the laws of primogeniture, the exclusive right of inheritance of land went to the eldest son. Other children in the family were provided for in other ways. The English will, therefore, was not used to pass property within the family but to endow outsiders, especially the church, or to provide for children other than the eldest son. Primogeniture allowed the English nobility to preserve the unity of its landholdings and not to have them divided among numerous heirs. However, primogeniture did not apply to peasant land or to land in towns, which could be left by will. With regard to fiefs*, in the absence of a son, daughters inherited equally.

Islamic Inheritance.   The QUR'AN contains 12 verses dealing directly with the laws of inheritance. Prior to the revelation of the Qur'an, Islamic tradition limited the right to inherit property to the adult male members of a tribe. The Qur'an, however, extended the inheritance rights to females. In the so-called inheritance verses of the Qur'an, specific shares of an estate may be awarded to daughters, mothers, wives, and sisters, among others. A person is not permitted to designate one or more heirs. Instead, a minimum of two-thirds of the estate is divided according to specific rules stated in the Qur'an.

Islamic inheritance laws have been subject to numerous—and widely differing—interpretations over the centuries. Often the application of the rules of inheritance created unanticipated problems. For example, if a man dies leaving his parents, wife, and two daughters, the shares of his estate to which each is entitled by law adds up to more than 100 percent. Therefore, the surviving family members are unable to inherit the fractional share of the estate specified in the Qur'an. Recent scholarship has suggested that the system of inheritance revealed to Muhammad was quite different from the system that developed after his death.

Byzantine Inheritance.   Byzantine practices regarding inheritance were derived almost entirely from the principles of Roman law. Such laws distinguished between inheritance specified in a will and that which could be passed on without a will. Byzantine property could be divided among several heirs. The primary item of an inheritance was land, although personal property and other rights and obligations might also be included. When no will or testament existed, Byzantine laws and practices gave preference to children, then to relatives on the male side, followed by relatives on the female side. Only in the absence of other heirs could property be willed to a spouse.

The emperor JUSTINIAN I transformed the Byzantine system of inheritance by removing the distinction between heirs related through the male and the female lines. His reforms made inheritance practices less complex and gave adopted children rights along with biological children. In the Byzantine world, the estates of the parents were usually divided equally among the children, with the daughters receiving their share as a dowry. This practice was in direct contrast with the primogeniture practiced in England. The Byzantine system led to land divisions that produced small and uneconomical holdings. (*See also* **Family; Law.**)

* **fief** under feudalism, property of value (usually land) that a person held under obligations of loyalty to an overlord

What Did It Mean to Inherit?

To be someone's heir in the Middle Ages amounted to more than being a property owner. An Italian merchant, for example, who inherited his father's estate also inherited the family name, honor in the community, and the responsibility for upholding family traditions for the next generation. Likewise, a peasant inherited more than his father's ties to a lord. He also inherited a position in the community and the esteem built up by his father. Although these symbolic elements of inheritance did not appear in the law, they were important to people in the Middle Ages.

Innocent III, Pope

ca. 1161–1216
Lawyer, diplomat, and pope

* **theology** study of the nature of God and of religious truth

* **excommunication** formal exclusion from the church and its rituals

Innocent III was one of the most influential popes of the Middle Ages. He sought to extend papal authority in political matters as well as spiritual matters. He encouraged missionary activities, advised rulers, and provided encouragement and support for the crusades. The Fourth Lateran Council in 1215, over which he presided, was one of the most important church councils ever held.

Innocent III was one of the most powerful and effective medieval popes. During his papacy, he instituted a number of important church reforms. He was renowned for his personal piety and devotion, his commitment to spiritual reform, and his skills as a preacher, theologian, lawyer, and diplomat.

Born Lothario dei Segni to a powerful Italian family, Innocent received his early education at a Roman monastery. He later studied arts and theology* in Paris and law in Bologna. Innocent's education served him well, and he rose rapidly within the church because of his expertise in church law and his reputation as a theologian. He was appointed cardinal in 1190. When the elderly pope Celestine III died in 1198, Innocent was elected pope by other cardinals eager to have a young, learned pope who would provide strong leadership.

Innocent believed that papal authority extended beyond spiritual matters and that secular rulers were subject to that authority. Immediately following his election as pope, he set out to establish his role as a spiritual ruler with secular political power. He reorganized the government of Rome and asserted his authority over the PAPAL STATES. Throughout his papacy, Innocent's vision of papal authority involved him in secular politics within the HOLY ROMAN EMPIRE and various European countries.

Motivated by his sense of papal responsibility, Innocent encouraged missionary activities, advised monarchs, and granted royal titles. Among his highest priorities were regaining JERUSALEM from the Muslims and stamping out heresy. He provided financial support for the Fourth Crusade and helped plan the Fifth Crusade. He also launched a victorious, but bloody, crusade against the Albigensians, a heretical sect centered in southern France.

The height of Innocent's papacy was the Fourth Lateran Council, a large church meeting held in Rome in November 1215. One of the most important church councils ever held, it approved 70 canons, or decrees, that defined church doctrine, reformed the clergy, organized church government and finances, and regulated such matters as excommunication* and INDULGENCES. One of the canons established measures for suppressing heresy, which became the basis of the INQUISITION. (*See also* **Cathars; Church–State Relations; Crusades; Papacy, Origins and Development.**)

Innocent IV, Pope

ca. 1200–1254
Medieval pope, legal scholar, and diplomat

* **laity** those who are not members of the clergy

Pope Innocent IV was considered a great legal scholar and a master diplomat. His best-known work, the *Apparatus*, is a masterpiece of medieval law. Innocent was concerned with rights and protections against unjust and cruel authority. Yet, the tactics he used to achieve his goals were sometimes abusive of rights, and they made him unpopular among both clergy and laity*.

Born Sinibaldo Fieschi in Genoa, Italy, Innocent was promoted rapidly within the church. He became a judge of the papal curia, or court, in 1226 and was appointed cardinal in 1227. On June 25, 1243, two years after the death of Pope Gregory IX, he was elected pope and proclaimed Innocent IV.

Innocent's papacy was dominated by the struggle against Holy Roman Emperor FREDERICK II and his successors. Since the time of Pope INNOCENT III, the papacy feared that a strong, German-controlled empire would overrun Italy and the PAPAL STATES and weaken the authority of the church. During the first months of his papacy, Innocent tried, unsuccessfully, to negotiate with Frederick. When a revolt erupted in Rome in 1244, Innocent feared that Frederick was behind it. He fled to France and remained there until 1251.

While in France, Innocent tried everything possible to break German power. He excommunicated* Frederick and placed penalties against the German church officials to try to force their loyalty. He also preached a crusade against Frederick and his imperial power. After Frederick's death in 1250, Innocent continued the struggle with the emperor's successors. He was ultimately unsuccessful in limiting the power of the German emperors. Moreover, the policies he used in his struggle, including the levying of higher taxes and attempts to control church appointments, made him very unpopular.

Innocent's best relations were with religious orders. With his support, FRANCISCANS and DOMINICANS conducted missionary work as far away as Mongolia in Asia. Innocent also had a more tolerant attitude toward Jews than many of his contemporaries. In 1247, he helped protect Jews in Germany and France from acts of revenge after the alleged murder of a Christian child by Jews.

Innocent's legal decrees were concerned mostly with legal procedures and the administration of justice. His most famous legal doctrine was the idea that a collective group of people, such as a city, could not be excommunicated when the innocent would be punished along with the guilty. (*See also* **Church–State Relations; Papacy, Origins and Development.**)

* **excommunicate** to exclude from the rites of the church

Inns and Taverns

Since ancient Roman times, travelers had depended on private hospitality for lodging and food. For many years in western Europe, free hospitality had been more prevalent than the commercial form. Wealthy and powerful people had had a right to lodging, and the most modest of households had regarded it as a duty—and in some cases a legal responsibility—to welcome weary travelers. MONASTERIES and hospitals had been sufficient to provide for the needs of pilgrims traveling to the Holy Land. The situation changed early in the 1000s, as hosts began to charge for their hospitality.

Rise of Commercial Hospitality.   With the increase in the number of traveling merchants on roads, free hospitality became scarce. In France and Italy, the types of lodgings from PROVENCE to ROME included hostels* in the cities, private homes in villages, and inns in outlying areas.

Not all of western Europe was so well provided. In England, inns seem to have been found only in cities. One could quench one's thirst in alehouses, simple places that sometimes served food but did not provide lodgings. In Spain, the situation was even worse. Inns were few and expensive, and a traveler even in a middle-sized town could not be sure of finding a place to stay for the night.

* **hostel** lodging place or inn

Inns on well-traveled roads and in thriving regions prospered. They were usually located near markets, near business centers, and along roads that entered towns. Hostels were often located in the suburbs because the cost of land there was lower and because fields were nearby to provide fodder and pasturage for the travelers' animals. In Aix-en-Provence in southern France, the leases of inns covered both the hostelry and one or more meadows for pasturage. It was common for an inn to show its importance by the size of its stables.

Structure and Furnishings. Two distinct types of inns were common in England until the 1700s: block inns, which were separated from the courtyard and the surrounding service buildings; and inns that surrounded a courtyard. The latter were also typical of southern Spain, where inns were built on the model of the caravansaries* of the Arab countries. In France and Italy, most hostels opened directly onto the street, even if they were located outside the city walls.

Inns were often ordinary houses that their owners furnished for commercial use. In Italy, the owners of such a house might place pitchers and plates in the window to show that they were running an inn. Elsewhere, innkeepers used signboards in front of the door. Sometimes a long pole with a thick bunch of leaves in the shape of an enormous broom extended over the road, in place of a signboard. In some areas, signs were legally required. In Florence, for example, innkeepers displayed an eight-pointed red star to show that they were members of the innkeepers' guild*. The fleur-de-lis, or lily, the national symbol of France, graced the inns' signboards in many French villages. Other symbols for inns included animals, fruit, mythical signs, saints, and symbols from HERALDRY.

The buildings used for lodging ordinarily had three types of rooms: the bedrooms, the main hall, and the kitchen. In the poorest inns, the chimney of the hall served as the hearth where meals were prepared. Bedrooms usually contained several beds, and often several people slept in the same bed. The beds were made of wooden frames lined with straw or mattress pads. Most were large and could fit two people comfortably. Bedrooms might also have benches, chests, and, sometimes, tables and chairs. Some rooms were even named, such as "Room of the New Bed." Inns varied in size from 1 to 12 bedrooms.

Ownership and Management. The person who ran the inn, the innkeeper, was not always the owner. A paid staff (a man or a couple) was hired, usually for a one-year period. The staff was fed and clothed and allowed to keep any gifts the guests might offer. The salary—about 12 florins* a year for a man and 20 florins for a couple—was about the average for domestic servants.

Owners frequently leased their inns to innkeepers, signing a contract similar to those for rural properties, small shops, or street stalls. Many innkeepers were from out of town, and some were even foreigners, such as Italians in southern France or Germans in Italy. Innkeepers who were foreigners could accommodate travelers who spoke their language, act as intermediaries in the travelers' business affairs, and offer their fellow citizens a place to meet and conclude business dealings.

For some time, innkeepers were members of the same guild as butchers, bakers, and wine makers. By 1324, they had their own organization.

* **caravansary** lodging in the East where caravans stopped to rest, usually surrounding a spacious courtyard

* **guild** association of craft and trade workers that set standards and represented the interests of its members

* **florin** gold or silver coin used in some European countries, equivalent to two shillings, or ten pennies

Taverns and Trouble

Some people thought of taverns as dens of sin, but the writers of the *Carmina Burana*, a collection of medieval Latin secular songs, praised them as sanctuaries with the following words: "When we are in tavern, we care not for thoughts of the grave. . . . There none fears death, but rolls the dice for Bacchus's (Roman god of drink) sake."

State or guild regulations governed the rules of inn keeping. For example, the door of the inn had to be closed when the last bell was rung at night, and entrance was forbidden to jesters, prostitutes, and thieves.

Clientele and Literary Reputation. Guests at inns were not only merchants or pilgrims. In university towns—such as Bologna, Italy—students boarded by the year. Carpenters, stonecutters, and bell casters needed lodgings during periods of intensive construction. Bishops visiting their dioceses sometimes stayed at inns, and ambassadors were required to stop at certain prominent, well-kept inns. The account books of innkeepers show a great variety of lodgers, from mule drivers to priests and nobility.

Inns and innkeepers appear in medieval literature. In the *Canterbury Tales* by CHAUCER, the Tabard Inn serves as the setting and provides a sense of realism to the plot. However, in BOCCACCIO's *Decameron*, the sly and deceitful innkeeper is more of a stereotype.

Medieval Taverns. One of the meanings of the word *taberna* was cabin. It was a simple place where people came to meet, eat, and drink together or do business. Merchants met at taverns to conduct business until the end of the Middle Ages. Students especially sought out taverns, so much so that in one university city the large convent school of the DOMINICANS had to open one within its walls to keep students from spending their time in taverns in the town. The record of a student meeting at a tavern called La Mule perhaps best expressed the general feeling about taverns: After the students had met in church, one of them said, "It seemed best to go to a tavern, where there was a fire, for it was a cold day." (*See also* **Guilds**.)

Inquisition

* **heresy** belief that is contrary to church doctrine

* **friar** member of a religious brotherhood of the later Middle Ages who worked in the community and relied on the charity of others for his livelihood

The medieval Inquisition was a tribunal, or court, established to investigate and prosecute heresy*. It lasted about 150 years, except in Spain, where an Inquisition was instituted in the 1400s and continued until the early 1800s. The Inquisition was a legal process known in Latin as *inquisitio,* meaning inquiry.

Trials for heresy traditionally were under the authority of religious courts. There was, however, little uniformity in the prosecution or punishment of offenders. Beginning in the late 1100s, several popes tried to standardize the procedure. In 1231, Pope Gregory IX instituted a formal and orderly investigation of heresy conducted by specially appointed judges.

Conrad of Marburg, a priest, and Robert le Bougre, a Dominican friar* were the first inquisitors appointed by Pope Gregory IX. They traveled through Germany and France, respectively, prosecuting suspected heretics. The two men were eventually charged with acting on baseless accusations. Conrad was murdered in 1233, and Robert was suspended for his excessive zeal. Other tribunals were established in Europe and outlying areas, such as Norway, Morocco, Tunis, and Armenia, but they had no real importance. The Inquisition was never established in England. The Spanish Inquisition was used by monarchs for their own ends and was outside papal control.

The Inquisition began in order to suppress heresy and to strengthen religious unity. In the early 1200s, St. Dominic was sent to southern France to preach to the heretical Cathars (Albigensians) in the hope of converting them. This illumination shows St. Dominic overseeing the burning of heretical books.

Two inquisitors generally presided over an investigation. They began by stating their authority and purpose in a sermon, and then they called for the accused to confess. Interrogation had some serious disadvantages for the accused. The identity of the accusers was kept secret for fear of retaliation. The most a defendant could do was to provide a list of his or her personal enemies, whose testimony in the case was to be discounted. No lawyer or advocate acted for the accused person, for to do so would risk the charge of aiding a heretic. Many people believed inquisitors used verbal traps to trick people into confessing. Evidence was accepted from confessed heretics, criminals, and even children.

Anyone could accuse another of heresy. There were even professional "heretic hunters" eager for the rewards that were offered. Admitted heretics often accused others in the hope that such information would reduce their punishment.

Inquisitors could impose only those penalties that were authorized by the church. The mildest penance was to visit church on specified days over a period of time. Forced pilgrimages were also a form of penance, and they could be ruinously expensive and amount to years of exile. These penalties were for those who confessed and repented.

Heretics who did not repent were handed over to secular authorities along with a plea for mercy that was certain to be ignored. The punishments imposed by secular authorities were much more severe. They included heavy fines, confiscation or destruction of property, exile, life imprisonment, torture, and death, often by burning at the stake.

Despite their reputation for harshness, the early judges were capable of leniency. Sentences were reduced or commuted for persons who were especially cooperative, and exemptions were allowed in cases of unusual hardship. It is estimated that for every hundred who received penalties in the mid-1200s in France, one was burned, ten were imprisoned, and the rest had lighter punishments. (During the Spanish Inquisition, the death penalty was applied much more freely.)

The Inquisition functioned actively for 150 years. Although it was begun as an aid to the clergy in suppressing heresy and strengthening religious unity, the Inquisition eventually became an independent tribunal with increasingly severe methods. (*See also* **Cathars; Dominicans; Heresy and Heresies; Languedoc; Toulouse; Waldensians.**)

Insanity, Treatment of

During the Middle Ages, attitudes toward insanity were generally tolerant, and mad people were not excluded from society. When they were confined in cells and chains, their confinement was meant to protect the community and to prevent the violent ones from harming themselves, rather than as torture. In rural areas, most of the insane led productive lives in at least some capacity.

As people moved from the countryside to the cities, however, the presence of increasing numbers of mentally ill people in one area caused concern. Although the majority of the mentally ill remained with their families, poor and homeless mad people were usually hospitalized. After about 1400, hospitals began to separate the demented from those with

* **asylum** place of refuge and protection

* **sacrament** religious ceremony of the Christian church considered especially sacred, such as Communion and baptism

* **civil law** body of law that regulates and protects the rights of individuals

* **relic** object cherished for its association with a martyr or saint

infectious illnesses. The mentally ill people were confined in cells or lodged together in asylums*. These shelters were regulated and received financial support from the government. Authorities could forcibly hospitalize an insane person unless the person's family objected; then the courts decided.

The law generally favored the common good but considered the welfare of the patient and the degree of illness. Usually the family was responsible for the insane person's well-being and actions. An insane person could receive the sacraments* but could not join the clergy. Civil law* prevented insane people from transacting business, but not from owning property. In criminal law, insanity often ruled out guilt, except in Celtic and Germanic regions, where the accused was guilty until proven innocent, even if the accused was demented.

Two main forms of mental illness were recognized during the Middle Ages—mania (frenzied excitement) and melancholy (extreme depression). Physicians believed that excessive "heat" had upset the brain's normally cool, moist state. Treatments included various "cold" herbs, purges, and even skull surgery to allow harmful vapors to evaporate. Some treatments were aimed at strengthening mental processes, such as memory and reason.

In search of relief, many mentally ill people journeyed to shrines of saints connected with mental ailments. As a result, the towns around some of these shrines became treatment centers where patients stayed for several weeks while being blessed, touched with relics*, bathed, and led in processions of chanting and dancing. (*See also* **Hospitals and Poor Relief; Law; Medicine; Pilgrimage.**)

Iran

* **dynasty** succession of rulers from the same family or group

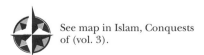

See map in Islam, Conquests of (vol. 3).

Iran, sometimes known as Persia, is situated on a rugged plateau that lies between the Caspian Sea and the Persian Gulf. During the Middle Ages, Iran was an important part of the Islamic world, a place where Arab traditions blended with ancient Persian traditions to form a distinct Islamic culture.

By the early Middle Ages, Iran had already seen a thousand years of civilization. This proud heritage included a period when Iran was one of the largest and most powerful empires in the ancient world. From 224 to the mid-600s, Iran was ruled by the SASANIANS, a dynasty* whose kings attempted to restore the glories of the ancient Persian culture. The official religion of the Sasanian Empire was Zoroastrianism, an ancient faith founded in Persia between 600 and 500 B.C. Sasanian rule came to an end in the mid-600s, when the empire was conquered by Arabs during the early period of Islamic conquests.

Arab Conquest. The conquest of Iran by the Arabs changed the course of Iranian history in several ways. First, for the next 850 years, Iranian politics were overshadowed by the politics of the Arab Empire, and Iran lost its separate geographical identity. Second, the ancient Zoroastrian faith was gradually replaced by Islam, the faith of the Arab conquerors. Third, the Persian language gave way to Arabic, which became the official language of government. Only in the late 900s did the Persian language reappear, primarily in poetry. Fourth, Persia's ancient tradition of king-ship was displaced by the Islamic institution of the CALIPHATE. Under the ABBASIDS, however, the caliphate began to resemble the Persian monar-chy, especially in its majestic ceremonies and large body of government officials. The Arab conquest of Iran also had a significant impact on the social structure of Iran. Iran's Persian inhabitants, even after they con-verted to Islam, did not achieve social and economic equality with the Arabs. Many Persians adopted the Shi'ite* form of Islam rather than the predominant Sunnite* form, and their beliefs about the IMAM were used to assert the superiority of the Shi'ite imams over the Sunnite caliphs. These beliefs have remained a distinctive feature of Iranian Islam to the present day.

By the early 800s, Iran was fully absorbed into the Islamic world. Much of the Persian population had converted to Islam, and the Arab set-tlers were largely absorbed into the population. However, when the power of the central Islamic government in BAGHDAD weakened in the late 800s as a result of internal struggles, the Persians reclaimed some of their former power. Between 820 and 1055, a number of local Persian dy-nasties ruled in Iran through regional governors and local officials. Al-though generally appointed by the caliph, these rulers maintained a great

* **Shi'ites** Muslims who believed that Muhammad chose Ali and his descendants as the rulers and spiritual leaders of the Islamic community

* **Sunnites** Muslim majority who believed that the caliphs should rule the Islamic community

From 224 to the mid-600s, Iran was ruled by the Sasanian dynasty, which strove to restore the glories of the ancient Persian culture. Sasanian rule ended when the Arabs conquered Iran and introduced Islam. This silver plate from the early 600s shows the hunt of Sasanian king Khosrow II.

* **patronage** the support of an artist, writer, or scholar by a person of wealth and influence

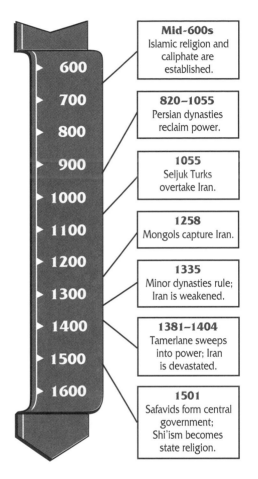

| Mid-600s |
| Islamic religion and caliphate are established. |

| 820–1055 |
| Persian dynasties reclaim power. |

| 1055 |
| Seljuk Turks overtake Iran. |

| 1258 |
| Mongols capture Iran. |

| 1335 |
| Minor dynasties rule; Iran is weakened. |

| 1381–1404 |
| Tamerlane sweeps into power; Iran is devastated. |

| 1501 |
| Safavids form central government; Shi'ism becomes state religion. |

deal of independence. Some of the dynasties played an important role in the rebirth of Persian language and literature through their patronage* of Persian scholars and writers.

At the beginning of the 1000s, Turkish nomads moved across Iran from the east. These peoples had moved into the Islamic Empire the century before and had converted to Islam. One branch of these Turks, the SELJUKS, established themselves as rulers in Baghdad in 1055 and reunited much of the Islamic world. The Seljuks ended the local Persian dynasties that had ruled in Iran for more than 200 years. They also supported the Sunnite form of Islam in Iran. This caused a temporary setback to the spread of the Shi'ite faith, although Shi'ism continued as an underground movement.

Mongol Rule. Beginning in 1219, the Mongols invaded Iran under the leadership of GENGHIS KHAN and his grandson, Hulagu. The Muslims were unable to resist the Mongol invasion, and over the next 50 years, Iran and IRAQ fell to the Mongols. In 1258, Hulagu captured Baghdad and killed the last Abbasid caliph, al-Musta'sim. The Mongols ruled Iran for more than 100 years. During that time, they adopted many of the manners, customs, and religious beliefs of the Iranian people. At the same time, however, they established the Mongol legal code as the law of the land and imposed a system of taxation.

After 1335, Mongol rule broke up into a number of minor dynasties, leaving Iran in a weakened state. Between 1381 and 1404, the military campaigns of TAMERLANE swept away these rival Mongol dynasties and devastated Iran in the process. For nearly a century after Tamerlane's death in 1405, his descendants fought for control of the region. Finally in 1501, a local Iranian dynasty, the Safavids, took control of Iran and formed a unified central government. The Safavids established Shi'ite Islam as the official state religion, and they provided the foundations for the modern nation of Iran. (*See also* **Islam, Conquests of; Islam, Religion of; Islamic Art and Architecture; Mongol Empire.**)

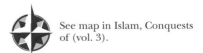

See map in Islam, Conquests of (vol. 3).

Iraq is situated around the Tigris and Euphrates Rivers in the ancient region known as Mesopotamia. The history of medieval Iraq was shaped largely by natural conditions and geographic location. The central part of Iraq was a rich agricultural region sustained by an extensive system of irrigation fed by canals from its major rivers. The fertility of this region enabled it to become densely populated, with a network of agricultural villages capable of supporting large cities. At the same time, Iraq was easily accessible, making it vulnerable to invasion. Over the centuries, Iraq experienced successive waves of invasion by Persians, Arabs, and Turks. Each of these foreign groups had an important influence on Iraqi culture and society.

Islamic Invasions. Before the Islamic conquests of the 600s, Iraq was a key province of the SASANIAN Empire. Under the Sasanians, Iraqi irrigation systems were expanded and improved, roads and bridges were built, and rural settlements reached a level never again equaled in medieval times.

Because of its location, Iraq was invaded by Persians, Arabs, Turks, and Mongols throughout the Middle Ages. In spite of constant political turmoil, Islamic scholars in Iraq achieved greatness in science, medicine, philosophy, history, law, and literature. This manuscript illumination, from Baghdad in the 1200s, shows two scientists making lead.

* **caliph** religious and political head of an Islamic state

* **bedouin** nomadic Arab(s) of the deserts, especially in Arabia

Wars between the Sasanians and Byzantines ended in 628 with a Sasanian defeat. This left Iraq weakened to the point that it was unable to repel the Islamic invasion of the Arabs a few years later.

The first Islamic invasions of Iraq came in 633, and by 637 the region was firmly under Arab control. The Muslim Arabs ruled Iraq from two new cities: Basra and al-Kufa. At first, these cities served as settlements for Arab troops, but they quickly evolved into the cultural and administrative centers of Iraq. The early Islamic period was a time of great instability in Iraq. The whole province became a hotbed of regional disagreement. This was largely a result of Iraqi resentment of leadership in Medina and political rivalries among Arab tribal clans.

When the UMAYYADS took control of the Islamic Empire, they established their seat of power in SYRIA, despite the fact that Iraq was more populous and economically important. The Iraqis soon came to regard Umayyad rule as foreign and burdensome, and they became increasingly rebellious. Iraq became an important center of Shi'ism, which provided one way of resisting Umayyad rule. In turn, the Umayyads tried to maintain order by imposing central authority more forcefully. Umayyad rule had a disruptive effect on rural settlement. Many peasants fled to Iraqi cities to escape heavy tax burdens, leaving agricultural lands vacant and unproductive.

In 749, the Umayyad dynasty was overthrown by the ABBASIDS. The Abbasids established their capital in Iraq and founded a new capital city, BAGHDAD. Under the Abbasids, Iraq became the focal point of Islamic civilization. By the 800s, Baghdad was a great intellectual center, a city of libraries and research centers. Islamic scholars in Iraq made outstanding achievements in literature, history, law, philosophy, medicine, and science. It was in Iraq that Islamic civilization incorporated the legacies of Greece, Persia, and India to create a level of brilliance unmatched in the medieval world.

The Abbasids were able rulers, but Iraq eventually declined. Religious controversies, social tensions, and political disputes periodically erupted in violence. Iraqi Muslims who followed the Shi'ite branch of Islam revolted against the Sunnite caliphs* several times. The death of the caliph HARUN AL-RASHID in 809 led to civil war that ended with a destructive siege of Baghdad. A rebellion among bedouin* and peasants in southern Iraq began in 890 and remained a destructive force for years. Such problems diverted attention and money from Iraq's long-term needs. As a result, the region suffered a gradual decline that also affected much of the Islamic Empire.

In the mid-800s, the Abbasid caliph al-MU'TASIM brought large numbers of Turkish slave soldiers to Baghdad. These troops soon assumed a great deal of power and influence in Iraq, and the caliphs were at their mercy. This led to the decline of central Islamic authority and to economic and agricultural decay. The city of Baghdad began to shrink as people fled to the countryside, and by the 900s large areas of that city were abandoned ruins.

Periods of Decline.   Iraq continued to decline after a Persian dynasty, the Buyids, seized control of the province in 945. The Buyids sold important government positions to people who were interested only in

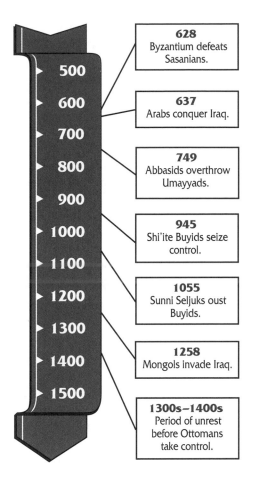

628 Byzantium defeats Sasanians.	
637 Arabs conquer Iraq.	
749 Abbasids overthrow Umayyads.	
945 Shi'ite Buyids seize control.	
1055 Sunni Seljuks oust Buyids.	
1258 Mongols invade Iraq.	
1300s–1400s Period of unrest before Ottomans take control.	

* **principality** region that is ruled by a prince

becoming wealthy themselves, and they gave land to military officers who did little to maintain it. These policies were disastrous for Iraq. Central authority almost disappeared, irrigation systems fell to ruin, and trade and agriculture declined. Yet the Buyids also promoted the Shi'ite faith, and this branch of Islam expanded greatly in Iraq during the period. The Buyid period also was marked by increasing Persian influence on Islamic culture, particularly in literature.

Buyid rule in Iraq ended in 1055 when a large group of Turkish nomads, the SELJUKS, seized Baghdad. The Seljuks were Sunnites, and they saw their mission as protecting and restoring the Sunnite faith and stopping the spread of Shi'ism. The Seljuks fostered the study of Islamic law, theology, and MYSTICISM, but they did little to improve the Iraqi economy or to restore agriculture to the rural countryside.

Beginning in 1118, Seljuk power in Iraq began to decline, and the Abbasids were able to reassert their authority gradually over the next hundred years. The Abbasids made attempts to improve conditions in the province, but these improvements did not last long. In 1258, the Mongols attacked Iraq in an invasion marked by terrible slaughter and destruction. Baghdad was besieged and sacked, and the last Abbasid caliph, al-Musta'sim, was killed. The Mongols remained in control until 1335.

During the later Middle Ages, the history of Iraq was characterized by short-lived empires and minor principalities*, social chaos, and little economic growth. The country was torn apart by frequent revolts. Bedouin ravaged the countryside, driving trade and commerce away and destroying agriculture completely. The BLACK DEATH swept through Iraq in 1347. This disaster was followed by the terrible invasions of TAMERLANE in the late 1300s and early 1400s. Tamerlane's attacks on Baghdad caused such destruction that the city did not recover until modern times. In 1534, the Ottoman Turks seized Baghdad, and Iraq became part of the Ottoman Empire. Iraq remained under Ottoman control until the early 20th century. (*See also* **Iran; Kufa; Mongol Empire; Ottomans and Ottoman Empire.**)

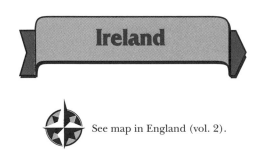

Ireland

See map in England (vol. 2).

* **secular** nonreligious; connected with everyday life

According to Irish tradition, the history of Ireland began in the 400s when St. PATRICK brought Christianity to the region. The new religion spread slowly and paved the way for other Latin influences on the original Celtic culture. A network of monasteries became the dominant feature of the early Irish church.

Many Irish monks went overseas as missionaries, traveling to Scotland, England, and even Italy and Germany. They brought Irish Christianity to these places and established religious foundations that became centers of learning. The monastery schools of Ireland were so famous that they attracted scholars from England. The quality of Irish art, especially the illuminated manuscripts such as the Book of KELLS, was unsurpassed. By the 700s, the monasteries had become wealthy and had come increasingly under secular* control. Some monasteries even went to war with each other over property rights or became involved in local political disputes.

* **Gaelic** word used to describe the Celts of Ireland and Scotland, and especially their language

* **Celtic** referring to the ancient inhabitants of Europe, known as Gauls in France and Britons in Britain

* **jurist** legal expert; learned writer of law

* **wattle** sticks interwoven with twigs or branches

Although Latin was the language of the church, most people in Ireland spoke Gaelic*, a Celtic* language. Irish people belonged to clans—large family groups—which were led by elected chieftains.

Ireland had no towns or formal lawmaking bodies during this early period. The legal system was a traditional one, supervised by jurists*. Individual nobles and free farmers lived in isolated homesteads. Often located on islands in lakes or bogs, the typical homestead was a stone or earthen fort surrounding wattle* and wood dwellings.

No strong political units appeared in Ireland until after the VIKING invasion in 795. The Irish reacted to the invasion by forming larger and more powerful political units. The idea of a kingdom of Ireland, ruled by one high king, gained acceptance and led to power struggles among the chieftains. Finally, out of an obscure kingdom west of the Shannon River came Brian Boru, who in 1005 felt strong enough to proclaim himself "king of the Irish." According to legend, he is remembered as the victor of the Battle of Clontarf (1014) against the Vikings. In reality, the battle was more a defeat for the Vikings' allies in Ireland, who had challenged Brian Boru's supremacy.

In 1155, Pope Adrian IV, in an attempt to reform the Irish church, granted HENRY II OF ENGLAND overlordship of Ireland, and a new chapter of violence opened in the history of Ireland. At about the same time, Richard Fitzgilbert de Clare, called Strongbow, entered Ireland from England at the request of Rory O'Connor, one of the Irish chieftains who was battling the Irish king. Strongbow eventually became so powerful that Henry became worried and sent a large army in 1171. Feudal lords, chieftains, and even Rory O'Connor surrendered to Henry. In 1175, O'Connor recognized the overlordship of Henry, and Ireland came under the control of the English crown.

English Settlement. Over the next century, English settlement of Ireland expanded to cover two-thirds of the island. A new government was imposed on Ireland, and a system of courts was established to administer English common law. The English also introduced taxation and obligatory military service. Reaction varied from fierce resistance to emigration. Most Irish lords, however, seemed willing to accept the new order, provided that they could keep at least part of their estates. Intermarriage was common, and it seemed that a new Anglo-Irish society would emerge. But this was not to be. The Gaelic lords revolted, and after successful military campaigns in 1257, 1261, and 1270, the Irish kingship was restored.

Invasions from Scotland, the worst FAMINE in the Middle Ages, and the resulting disease wreaked havoc on the English colonists. Some even rebelled against the English king, who tried unsuccessfully to impose new legal controls on the Irish and English rebels. In 1366, the English established the Statutes of Kilkenny, an attempt to outlaw Gaelic culture. England excluded Gaelic Ireland from the protection of common law and prohibited Irish advancement in the church. Both measures made peace between the two countries impossible.

English Domination. Although medieval lords, Irish and English, were left to govern their own estates, English culture was dominant. This was especially true in the Pale, a fortified area around DUBLIN. The

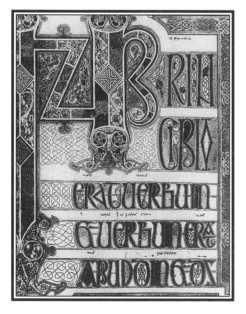

The rich Celtic illumination style is seen on this title page from the Lindisfarne Gospels. The Latin inscription across the top translates "Here begins the gospel according to John." The large, decorative text reads "In the beginning was the Word, and the Word was with God." The small notations above the words are called glosses. They were written in Old English to help readers who did not understand Latin. The high quality of illuminated manuscripts from Irish monasteries was widely imitated but never surpassed.

* **earl** governor of a region in Anglo-Saxon times. The term was later used for a noble title.

* **pretender** noble who claimed to be the rightful ruler when another held the power

Anglo-Irish earls* of the county Kildare controlled the Pale and its government. The Kildares supported the freedom of Ireland from English control, although they remained loyal to the English crown. However, when the British royal house of York fell and was replaced by the Tudor dynasty, the situation in Ireland changed. In 1487 and again in 1491, the Anglo-Irish leaders recognized two different pretenders* as the king of England in Dublin. King Henry VII intervened by sending an army, but this move proved too expensive and was soon abandoned. The earl of Kildare was restored to power in Ireland. In 1495, the Parliament at Drogheda (north of Dublin) decided that Ireland would be bound by English law. The Parliament also enacted Poynings' Law, which ended Irish parliamentary independence for more than 300 years by making that body subject to the supervision of the English privy council (the king's personal advisers). Within the next generation, the house of Kildare fell, and a new breed of civil servants who were fiercely loyal to the British crown arrived in Ireland. Henry VIII declared himself the "king of Ireland," and medieval lordship in that country ended. (*See also* **Celtic Languages and Literature; England; Kingship, Theories of; Monasticism.**)

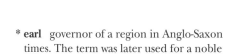

Islam, Conquests of

Following the death of the prophet MUHAMMAD in 632, his Muslim followers began a campaign of military conquest that continued for several centuries. The aim of these conquests was to extend the early Islamic state's political sovereignty. The conquered populations did not become Muslim right away, and the Islamic religion spread gradually. In time, a distinctive Islamic civilization developed that was noted for its art and architecture, its political and social institutions, and its literary and scientific accomplishments.

Initial Conquests. The Muslim leaders of the small Islamic state created by Muhammad saw their mission partly as one of spreading Islam and partly as one of establishing political control over the independent and warlike tribes of Arabia. The initial Islamic conquests resulted in the seizure of the Arabian peninsula, SYRIA, EGYPT, and IRAQ. By 645, these areas had become the heartland of an emerging Islamic Empire.

Upon Muhammad's death, his successor, ABU BAKR, faced widespread opposition from Arabian tribes that challenged continued Muslim control or followed rival prophets. Abu Bakr thus organized a group of armies to subdue the Arabian peninsula. After two years of conquest, the entire Arabian peninsula was brought under Muslim control. The young Muslim state—bolstered by additional soldiers, administrators, and resources from the conquered regions—was now ready for more far-reaching conquests.

The first major offensive to extend Muslim rule beyond Arabia was directed at Syria, a region with Arabic-speaking populations. In targeting Syria, the Muslims challenged the BYZANTINE EMPIRE, which controlled much of the region. In 633, Muslim armies in Syria met little

* **caliph** religious and political head of an Islamic state

Byzantine opposition. However, a second phase of conquest, lasting until 636, generated a strong response from the Byzantines, who amassed a large army to drive out the Muslims. In several major encounters, the Muslims decisively defeated the Byzantines, and by 648, Syria was firmly under Muslim control.

The conquest of Iraq from the empire of the SASANIANS occurred about the same time. In the initial phase of the conquest, Muslim armies took several Iraqi towns before leaving to fight in Syria. The main phase of the conquest began under the caliph* UMAR I IBN AL-KHATTAB. After an initial crushing defeat by the Sasanians, Umar organized massive new forces that marched into central Iraq and delivered a striking blow to the Sasanian army. Despite continued Sasanian resistance, the Muslims quickly won additional victories until all of Iraq was under their control by 642.

The final phase of the initial Islamic conquests involved Egypt, which was also under Byzantine control. However, by the time the Muslims turned their attention to Egypt, the Byzantines were discouraged and disorganized by their defeats in Syria, and the region fell quickly to the Muslim armies.

By the mid-600s, Muslim supremacy over the Middle East was complete. Several factors contributed to this swift victory. The Byzantine and Sasanian Empires were weakened at this time by recent conflicts with each other and by internal political turmoil. Their large armies were scattered thinly over their empires and lacked unity. In some areas, the Muslims gained support from the local populations because of dissatisfaction with imperial rule. The most important factor, however, was the good organization among the Muslim ruling elite. It had the ability to build a powerful,

Islam spread quickly after the death of Muhammad in 632. Within the next 100 years, Muslims had conquered the Middle East, North Africa, most of Spain, and the Indus River valley in Asia. Even though some of these areas did not remain under Muslim rule, the influence of Islamic culture remained strong in many of these once-conquered lands.

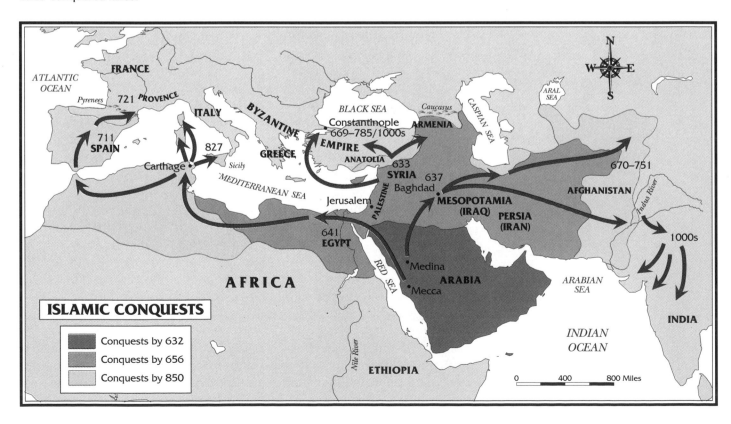

ISLAMIC CONQUESTS

- Conquests by 632
- Conquests by 656
- Conquests by 850

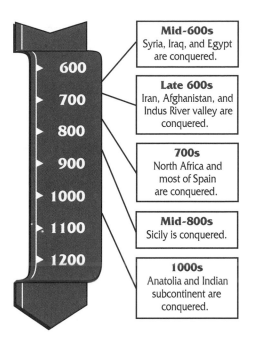

Mid-600s
Syria, Iraq, and Egypt are conquered.

Late 600s
Iran, Afghanistan, and Indus River valley are conquered.

700s
North Africa and most of Spain are conquered.

Mid-800s
Sicily is conquered.

1000s
Anatolia and Indian subcontinent are conquered.

600
700
800
900
1000
1100
1200

* **siege** long and persistent effort to force a surrender by surrounding a fortress with armed troops, cutting it off from aid

capable fighting force that was swifter and more skilled than the armies of its adversaries.

Later Conquests.   The Islamic conquests were interrupted briefly by civil war from 656 to 661. They then resumed at a slower pace, first under the UMAYYADS and then under the ABBASIDS. This phase of conquest was undertaken by a well-organized empire with large, well-equipped armies and many resources. Military campaigns took place wherever there was an opportunity for conquest, and many of these places were very distant from the Arabian heartland.

Between 670 and 751, the Muslims seized most of IRAN and parts of Afghanistan. From there, they marched to India and established Islamic communities in the Indus River valley. This area remained cut off from the rest of the Islamic world, however, until the 1000s, when military campaigns spread Islam throughout much of the Indian subcontinent.

During the 700s, the Muslims gradually gained control of ARMENIA and the Caucasus region, despite strong opposition from the Byzantines and from the Khazars, a nomadic people in the region. By the 900s, however, much of the region had reverted back to local control. In ANATOLIA, the Muslims faced even stronger resistance from the Byzantines, and frontier fighting became a continuing way of life. Although the Muslims made temporary advances, most campaigns brought no lasting success. Several sieges* of CONSTANTINOPLE between 669 and 785 brought the Byzantine capital to the brink of defeat, but these sieges failed to breach the city's superb defenses. It was not until the 1000s that Anatolia was finally conquered for Islam.

In North Africa, the Muslims encountered a strong enemy in the BERBERS, who nearly drove them out. However, the Muslims gained control of the region by the early 700s. From North Africa, the Muslims moved on to Spain in 711. After defeating Roderick, the king of the VISIGOTHS, they advanced north to the Pyrenees Mountains. The Muslims never conquered parts of northern Spain, however, and these areas became the nucleus of Christian kingdoms that eventually reconquered Spain from the Muslims beginning in the 1000s. In 717, a Muslim force crossed the Pyrenees into France, but it was defeated by CHARLES MARTEL in 732 and was unable to establish a foothold.

In the Mediterranean, the Muslims attempted to take control away from the strong Byzantine navy. They were unable to do so in the eastern Mediterranean, but they did come to dominate the western Mediterranean in the early Middle Ages. They controlled SICILY from 827 to 831 and also raided coastal towns in southern ITALY and in PROVENCE during the early medieval period.

Significance of the Conquests.   The Islamic conquests created a powerful new empire that dominated much of the medieval world. It weakened the power of the Byzantine Empire, created new patterns of international trade, and established a strong religion over a vast area. The conquests also gave rise to a rich new culture that combined elements of Islam with traditions of other older cultures. In many respects, Islamic civilization was the most advanced and cultured of the medieval world. (*See also* **Arabia; Islam, Political Organization of; Islam, Religion of.**)

Islam, Political Organization of

* **caliph**   religious and political head of an Islamic state

In Islam, there is no clear division between religion and politics. Medieval Muslims believed that the purpose of the state was to create the right conditions for living a proper Muslim life. The head of the *umma,* or community of believers, was the caliph*, who was both a political and a religious leader. The caliph's primary responsibility was "to command good and forbid evil," and Islamic law was the foundation of the state.

By 713, the Arabs controlled a vast Islamic Empire stretching from Morocco in the west to India in the east. As the empire expanded, a need arose for a political system that would allow the caliph to maintain control over the conquered lands. The result was the development of an administrative system of public officials to manage and enforce the policies of the Islamic state.

The needs of the early Islamic state were basically financial—to maintain the prosperity of the empire through taxes and rents flowing into the central treasury. The first financial department of the empire was established by caliph UMAR I IBN AL-KHATTAB in the 600s. Its officials were concerned with collecting revenues, converting payments in goods into money equivalents, and disbursing funds to tribal chieftains who would help maintain order. This department formed the basis for all subsequent ministries, or diwans.

* **jihad**   holy war undertaken as a sacred duty by Muslims

Under the UMAYYADS, Islamic administration became more sophisticated. The caliph had a wide range of duties—leading the jihad*, protecting his subjects from the tyranny of local officials, and interpreting the religious law (shari'a). Judicial functions were carried out by local judges (qadis), although the caliphs were also called on to help people with grievances. The central administrative department remained the one concerned with financial affairs. It organized the collection of taxes and distributed revenues as salaries and for public and charitable works, such as the building of mosques and irrigation projects. As government bureaucracy expanded, the increased paperwork led to the creation of a chancery* and a department of the seal, where documents were copied and sealed as a precaution against fraud.

* **chancery**   office of public records and documents

In the early years of Islam, decision making was centralized with the caliph, who was helped by a small staff of clerks. During the ABBASID dynasty, the office of vizier* was created. The vizier was a powerful right-hand man to the caliph. In later times, when many caliphs withdrew from the day-to-day conduct of affairs, the vizier became the sole power. Certain families gained a reputation for possessing special skills as viziers, and the office became almost hereditary.

* **vizier**   Muslim minister of state

After the 800s, the political authority of the caliphs declined, and control of the provinces passed to local governors and military commanders. Provincial governments tended to model their administrations on the central administration in BAGHDAD. The central administration, meanwhile, became more complex. The financial office was expanded to include various departments concerned with specialized areas such as palace administration. Especially important were departments concerned with the police and the army. By the 900s, when military groups became a dominant force in the empire, the army departments were the most important in the central administration and in the local governments. As military powers grew, a dual system of authority arose. The caliph remained the moral and religious leader of the empire, but military commanders and SULTANS held military and executive power.

The Mongol invasions of the 1200s brought far-reaching changes in Islamic administration, especially in the eastern parts of the Islamic world. The government of that part of the empire became increasingly decentralized, with local rulers wielding dictatorial powers in exchange for payments of tribute to the caliphs. In the western part of the empire, however, the MAMLUK DYNASTY maintained the tradition of a strong, highly complex central administration. The military bureaucracy established by the Mamluks enjoyed the same all-encompassing power as the early caliphs had. (*See also* **Caliphate; Imam; Iran; Iraq; Mongol Empire; Seljuks.**)

Islam, Religion of

I slam is one of the world's major religions. In Arabic, the word *Islam* means submission, and the term refers to an unwavering adherence to one god, Allah, and to the religious practices of the prophet MUHAMMAD. This submission to the faith, shared by all Muslims, instills in them a strong common bond and a sense of belonging to a single community of believers.

During the Middle Ages, the Islamic religion spread rapidly from its place of origin in ARABIA. It soon encompassed an area that extended from the Atlantic Ocean in the west to the Indus River in the east. During this period, Islam emerged as a dominant religion and culture.

Origins and Early History.   Islam arose among the nomadic* peoples of the Arabian peninsula. In pre-Islamic times, the Arab peoples accepted an unwritten code of conduct rooted in tribal traditions of blood kinship and common customs. Their worship was directed toward numerous spirits and deities; their rituals focused on animal sacrifice and pilgrimages to sacred places. Such beliefs and rituals did not satisfy everyone's religious urges, however. Certain individuals, known as hanifs, began searching for a god that was above all others.

Growing dissatisfaction with Arab polytheistic* beliefs and an acquaintance with certain Jewish and Christian ideas prepared the way for the teachings of Muhammad in the early 600s. Muhammad based his preaching on divine revelations in which he felt called by God to proclaim his word. Muhammad's teachings were a complete rejection of polytheism and the spiritual values he saw around him. His ideas attracted followers from diverse tribal groups, and soon a small but united Muslim community was established. By the time of his death, Muhammad had, for the first time, united Arab tribes under a single authority and in a single community no longer based on tribal bonds but on a common faith.

The Qur'an.   Muhammad's divine revelations were collected in the QUR'AN (Koran), the holy book of Islam. The word *Qur'an* means recitation. This title reflects the fact that the book is a collection of divine messages received and transmitted by Muhammad during the years of his ministry. Muslims believe that the Qur'an contains the very words of God, and that Muhammad was God's mouthpiece. For this reason, Muslims consider it the most authoritative book of divine guidance. Its 114 chapters, or

* **nomadic** wandering from place to place to find food and pasture

* **polytheistic** believing in several gods

suras, are written in Arabic in rhymed prose. The Arabic of the Qur'an is considered to be the most beautiful writing in the language. Muslims who speak many different languages memorize the Qur'an in Arabic. Only the Arabic text is acceptable for religious or legal use, though the Qur'an has now been translated into many different languages.

The Qur'an does not offer a systematic code of conduct or behavior, nor does it provide a detailed study of the nature of God or of religious beliefs. As the Islamic Empire grew and changed, Islamic leaders faced many situations that had not existed at the time the Qur'an was revealed. Other sources had to be found to supplement the Qur'an in order to satisfy the needs of a rapidly evolving community and to provide a broader basis for an Islamic way of life. Islam solved this problem through the development of its tradition, law, and theology.

Religious Tradition.   The early Islamic community based its code of behavior on the Qur'an and the traditions of Muhammad and his companions. Muhammad's customary practice, known as Sunna, was considered the ideal model of behavior, and it became the basis of early Islamic religious duty and conduct. In later years, if the Qur'an offered no specific solution to a problem, Muslims sought guidance in the Sunna tradition, searching for precedents for their views and practices in the words and actions of the Prophet. By the late 700s and the early 800s, Muhammad's Sunna had become as important as the Qur'an as a source of authority. It was handed down through oral accounts known as Hadith. Hadith consisted of an unbroken chain of people who reported a tradition over several generations, and a written text of these oral accounts. Since oral accounts handed down over generations might be questionable in terms of their authenticity, Hadith were carefully examined and confirmed to be accurate. By the 800s, great collections of Hadith had become widely recognized and respected as being authentic. These collections are important historically because they show that tradition had become widely accepted by the Muslim community as a source of Islamic conduct and belief. The study of Hadith became a major activity at Islamic religious schools.

Religious Law and Worship.   Islam is more than just a religion; it is also a way of life. At its core is shari'a, Islamic law. Muslims believe that shari'a reflects the will of God and that it includes all of God's rules relating to human activities. Islamic law is thus all-inclusive, encompassing all Muslim religious, political, social, and private life. The law is also unrestricted by national boundaries; all Muslims, no matter where they live, are subject to Islamic law.

The rules of shari'a are generally divided into two categories: religious duties that are owed to God, and practical duties toward individuals and society. In practice, these categories are equally important. Within them, Islamic law calls for the ritual of daily prayer and yearly pilgrimage*; it defines the conduct of business activities and criminal procedures; and it provides details on forbidden foods, ways of dress, and proper conduct in public. In these and other areas, Islamic law is concerned more with how a person actually behaves than with his or her intentions. Proper actions are important because they reflect obedience to God's will. Muslims believe that God has sent the law to guide humanity, and his intent is beyond

* **pilgrimage**   journey to a shrine or sacred place

human reason and understanding. As a result, Muslims must obey God's law whether they understand it or not.

The basic religious practices prescribed by Islamic law are known as the five "pillars" of Islam. These are the practices that all Muslims must follow. The first pillar is the statement of faith, or *shahada,* which says, "There is no god but Allah, and Muhammad is his messenger." The second pillar is ritual prayer, or salat. Salat is performed facing Mecca at five precise times of the day. Each prayer consists of recitations from the Qur'an and a series of bows and prostrations*. Islam does not have priests, so communal prayers are led by a competent, adult Muslim. The third pillar of Islam is zakat, the giving of alms* to the poor. The fourth pillar is fasting, or *sawm.* Fasting is observed during the month called Ramadan, when Muslims abstain from food and drink during daylight hours. After Ramadan ends, Muslims celebrate for several days at a festival. The last pillar of Islam is the hajj, a pilgrimage to the holy places of Mecca and its vicinity. No matter where they live, Muslims are expected to go on the hajj at least once during their lifetime if they have the financial means to do so.

The development of the science of law was one of the main concerns of the early Muslim community. The knowledge gained at that time was communicated to later generations through a system of jurisprudence* worked out by Islamic scholars. These scholars determined how the law should be applied by examining four "roots" from which the law is derived. The two most important roots were the Qur'an and the Sunna of Muhammad. If these were not sufficient, scholars looked to the consensus of the Muslim community *(ijma)* or to reasoning by analogy* (qiyas).

Islamic Theology.   Muslim theology* developed after Muhammad's death as a result of controversy about leadership of and membership in the Muslim community. At first, this controversy was more about political authority than religious issues, but the debates often were framed in religious terms, with opposing sides using theological arguments to justify their claim to rule.

The controversy reached its peak over the question of who should succeed Uthman, the third caliph*. The choice was between ALI IBN ABI TALIB, a cousin and son-in-law of Muhammad, and MU'AWIYA, a leader of the UMAYYADS. The political groups that supported each candidate soon developed into religious groups, and they debated the issue of predestination* versus free will. The Umayyads claimed leadership on the basis of predestination, while their opponents contended that Muslims were free to refuse obedience to unlawful rulers.

Islamic theology also emerged as a result of encounters with the theologies of other religions or cultural traditions. A theological group known as the Mu'tazila accepted Greek principles of reason and logic and used them to defend their religious views. Their basic religious doctrines stressed God's unity and his justice. They emphasized that God does what is best for his creation. He neither desires evil nor creates it. Although humans are created by God, he is not responsible for their evil; rather, they have free will and the power to do good or evil. The Mu'tazila never gained a large following. Some Muslims regarded them as heretics, and strong opposition to their views arose in the 900s. At that time, a more

* **prostration** lying face down in respect, submission, or worship

* **alms** money or gifts given to help the poor and suffering

* **jurisprudence** system of laws

* **analogy** explanation of a difficult, abstract idea by comparing it with a simpler and often concrete image

* **theology** study of the nature of God and of religious truth

* **caliph** religious and political head of an Islamic state

* **predestination** doctrine that God alone determines whether a Muslim goes to paradise or hell

This unusual Islamic depiction of Adam and Eve is from an Iranian manuscript of the 1200s. According to Islam, Adam is the first of 28 prophets, a group that also includes Abraham and Jesus Christ. The last prophet is Muhammad himself.

conservative view that stressed literal interpretation of the Qur'an and the limitations of the human intellect in understanding God's supreme power took hold. It also contended that God creates both good and evil, and humans have no free will to act on their own.

In its later history, Muslim theology increasingly became the concern of specialists. Meanwhile, a group of Islamic thinkers emerged who were greatly influenced by Hellenistic* philosophy. Their attempts to introduce Hellenistic ideas into Islam brought them into conflict with traditional groups in the Muslim community. Islamic philosophy had little direct influence on Islamic life, but it was important for two reasons. It influenced the development of Islamic MYSTICISM and asceticism* known as Sufism. Also, it provided a link by which the philosophy of the ancient world was transmitted to medieval Europe.

Sufism and Shi'ism.   Beginning in the 1000s, Sufism became an important feature of Islamic religious life. Like mystics* in other religions, Sufis practiced asceticism; they engaged in secret, mystical training; and they followed rituals designed to produce strongly emotional religious experiences. The early Sufis led lives of poverty and prayer away from society, and they did not expect conflict with the political authorities. Islamic scholars and orthodox Muslims attacked the Sufi way of life, however, accusing the Sufis of placing mental prayer above ritual prayer, which was one of the five pillars of the faith. The Sufis also claimed to be inspired by God, and this was seen as a challenge to Muhammad's role as the Prophet.

Over time, the Sufis developed a system of communal life with a variety of different orders, or societies. Each order was headed by a master, or sheikh, and had its own religious rituals. Sufi orders maintained monasteries, where members lived and prayed together. Some orders preferred silent meditation; others were famous for including dance, music, and poetry in their rituals.

In the later Middle Ages, Sufism influenced large segments of Muslim society. After the Mongol invasions in the 1200s, the Sufi orders became a unifying force in Islamic society. They carried out much of the Islamic missionary activity, and Sufi sheikhs became respected spiritual guides and educators. At times, the Sufis also played a powerful political role by providing the spiritual foundation for the rule of sultans*.

Unlike Sufism, which began as a religious group and slowly gained political importance, Shi'ism began as a political party and was gradually transformed into a powerful religious sect. The Shi'ites arose out of the conflict over the successor to the third caliph. They supported Muhammad's cousin and son-in-law Ali and his descendants as the rightful heirs to the CALIPHATE. In the political struggles that followed, many Shi'ite leaders, called IMAMS, were murdered by their opponents or killed in battle. Over time, the Shi'ites developed sophisticated religious theories focused on the imams and their role in the Muslim community. Shi'ism became the major opposition to Sunnism, the majority Muslim group. A branch of the sect, the Ismailis, controlled Egypt during the FATIMID DYNASTY, and Shi'ism became the dominant religious force in Iran after 1500. Like Sufism, Shi'ism has had an enormous influence on the development of Islam to the present day. (*See also* **Arabic Language and Literature; Islam, Political Organization of; Muhammad; Mysticism; Sunna.**)

* **Hellenistic** referring to Greek history, culture, or art after Alexander the Great

* **asceticism** way of life in which a person rejects worldly pleasure and follows a life of prayer and poverty

* **mystic** person who experiences divine truths through faith, spiritual insight, and intuition

* **sultan** political and military ruler of a Muslim dynasty or state

Islamic Art and Architecture

See
color plate 10,
vol. 2.

* **portico** roof supported by columns, forming a porch or covered walkway

* **minaret** tall, slender tower of a Muslim mosque from which the faithful are called to prayer

* **patronage** the support of an artist, writer, or scholar by a person of wealth and influence

* **mosaic** art form in which small pieces of stone or glass are set in cement; also refers to a picture made in this manner

During the Middle Ages, the Islamic world developed a unique and highly distinctive style of art and architecture. This style blended native Arabic design elements with those of other cultures that were absorbed into the Islamic Empire. Variations developed in different regions, but certain elements were common to all. These common elements included highly decorated surfaces, patterns of curving and often interlaced lines, and the use of brilliant colors. Like Islam itself, Islamic art and architecture were a reflection of the social, political, cultural, and religious ideas and traditions of the Islamic world.

The Formative Period

The period from 600 to 900 is considered the formative period of Islamic art and architecture. In the earliest part of this period, art and architecture reflected a variety of influences, including the cultural and artistic traditions of the BYZANTINE EMPIRE and the SASANIANS of Persia (present-day Iran). The artistic traditions of these and other cultures were transmitted throughout the Muslim world partly as a result of the Muslim pilgrimage to MECCA, the hajj, which facilitated communication between Muslims of different regions. Also at this time, religion strongly influenced artistic design, particularly with the use of religious phrases from the QUR'AN to decorate objects and structures and with the development of the mosque.

The mosque was the most important architectural creation in the early centuries of Islam. The mosque that MUHAMMAD founded in Medina in the early 600s became the model for mosques erected later throughout the Islamic world. This mosque began as a simple open enclosure with a mud-brick wall, a shaded portico*, and a pulpit where Muhammad addressed his followers. As the Islamic community in Medina grew, the mosque was enlarged with more costly materials. In the 700s, four corner towers were added to serve as minarets*, and a recessed space called a mihrab was installed on an inside wall. The mihrab, which marked the spot where Muhammad had stood while leading Muslims in prayer, became a standard feature in all later mosques.

The Umayyad Period.
Serious patronage* of architecture began when the UMAYYADS took power in the mid-600s and established their capital in DAMASCUS, Syria. During the Umayyad period (661–750), no single architectural style was used. Instead, the mosques and other religious structures built in Syria at that time were elaborately decorated as a way to proclaim the power and ideals of the new Islamic state.

One of the most important religious structures of the Umayyad period was the Dome of the Rock in JERUSALEM. Completed around 691, this magnificent building still stands today. Its central dome covers a large rock where, according to legend, Muhammad ascended into heaven. The interior of the building is colorfully decorated with marble panels and mosaics* of vines, trees, and inscriptions from the Qur'an. The Dome of the Rock is one of the holiest sites in the Islamic world.

Another notable feature of the Umayyad period was the construction of rural residences for members of the Umayyad dynasty and other wealthy Muslims. These range in size from modest dwellings to immense palaces. Among their most luxurious features were baths modeled on those of the Roman and Byzantine eras. One notable palace, Qusayr

Islamic manuscripts are well-known for their beautiful illuminations, which often feature fine and elegant writing known as calligraphy. This Persian miniature from the 1400s is from the *Miraj of the Prophet.*

Amra, was known for its wall paintings done in a style that highlighted the use of light and shade. Another Umayyad palace, Khirbat al-Mafjar, consisted of bath and residence areas separated by a courtyard and a small mosque. Inside were elaborately patterned geometric mosaics and dramatic decorations with figures of men, women, animals, and birds.

The Abbasid Period.   When the ABBASIDS took power in 750, IRAQ became the new center of the Islamic Empire. In order to administer their vast empire, the Abbasid caliphs* built large complexes that combined residential and administrative functions. The most notable of these were in BAGHDAD and SAMARRA. The circular palace complex at Baghdad—called the Round City—no longer exists. Its outer wall had four gates that led into the palace compound. Its central core consisted of the palace itself, a mosque, and security buildings. Surrounding this was a ring of government buildings and residences for government workers and members of the caliph's staff.

    The palace complex at Samarra was known for its lavishly decorated rooms and the abstract style of designs carved on the walls of its central halls and domed chamber. Wall paintings of bathers or courtesans* were a notable feature of the harem, or women's quarters. The mosque of Samarra had a distinctive feature not found in other parts of the empire— an unusual tower surrounded by a spiral ramp that served as a minaret.

    Samarra was the principal residence of the caliphs for only a short period, but its artistic and architectural impact extended long afterward.

* **caliph**   religious and political head of an Islamic state

* **courtesan**   female in attendance at a royal court

* **ceramics** referring to pottery, earthenware, or porcelain objects

* **stucco** fine plaster used for decoration and ornamentation

* *eyvan* large, vaulted hall that is walled on three sides and opens directly to the outside on the fourth side, usually onto a courtyard

Samarra's residents appreciated fine ceramics*, and this stimulated traders to bring ceramics from China and inspired local potters to create their own works blending local and Asian designs. The use of lavish textiles influenced scores of weavers and embroiderers, and a taste for fine glassware encouraged the development of glassmaking as well.

The Spread of Islamic Artistic Traditions.   During the 800s, the cultural influence of Syria and Iraq was felt as far west as SPAIN and as far east as central Asia. The spread of artistic traditions to these regions was no doubt the result of greater contacts within the Islamic world. The closer the political links were to Baghdad, the closer the artistic links were as well.

In eastern IRAN, Abbasid and Iranian influences blended to create a distinctive Persian Islamic artistic tradition, notable for its use of abstract decoration. In EGYPT, mosque architecture reflected such Iraqi features as square courtyards surrounded by arcades (arched covered passageways), the placement of mosques within walled enclosures, and Iraqi patterns in ornamental stucco*. In North Africa, a mix of Abbasid and local artistic traditions resulted in richly ornamented, melon-shaped domes on mosques and ornate designs in colored tile on their walls. In Spain, where an Umayyad dynasty ruled from 756 to 1031, Syrian influences created an architectural style that had a great influence in the western Mediterranean. The two principal monuments of this period in Spain are the Great Mosque of CÓRDOBA, and the palace city of Madinat al-Zahra. Both were notable for their simple rectangular design, their use of arched arcades, and their colorful architectural decoration.

The Development of Regional Styles

The artistic styles of Iraq and Syria dominated Islamic art and architecture in the early period of the empire. Between 900 and 1500, however, each section of the Islamic world developed its own regional artistic traditions. For the most part, these traditions evolved independently, although certain trends had a wider impact and affected many regions. This was especially true in the development of monumental tombs. Another trend that affected many regions was a renewed interest in realistic images of figures as a decorative element on ceramics, metalwork, and glass and in book illustrations.

Iran and Central Asia.   In the medieval period, Iran and central Asia formed a single cultural region. From the 900s to the 1100s, this region was very prosperous, and during that time, the basic traditions of Iranian Islamic architecture were established. Two of the most notable aspects of Iranian architecture were the diversity of tombs and the evolution of mosque design through the addition of domes and large vaulted halls called *eyvans*.

Popular enthusiasm for visiting the graves of saintly religious figures may have prompted some political leaders to construct their own tombs, and many such tombs were built in Iran. Some of these tombs are notable for the use of elaborate brickwork patterns, tiled domes, arcaded galleries, and elaborate stucco decoration. The tomb of Qabus ibn Washmgir in Gurgan, built in 1006/1007, is particularly striking because of its unusual height (167 feet), its placement on a hill, and its shape—a ten-pointed star. Iranian tombs were constructed in a variety of other shapes, including cylinders, octagons, domed squares, and towers.

During the 1000s, Iranian tombs commonly used decorative brick-work, often with inscriptions. Later, in the 1100s and the 1200s, glazed ceramic tiles often were used to highlight parts of the design. In the Blue Tomb of Maragha, built in 1196, glazed ceramic decoration appears on every exterior surface. By the late 1200s, glazed tiles had become a major component of Iranian architectural decoration. Sometimes small pieces of different colors were fitted together as a mosaic. In other instances, large panels of both glazed and unglazed tiles were fitted together and then attached to the exterior of the building.

The classic design of the Iranian mosque was established in the 1000s and the 1100s. Among its most prominent features were domes, *eyvans,* and supporting columns for roofs and ceilings. Classic Iranian style also featured large openings in the lower walls of the dome. Domes were especially important in the mosques of central Iran, where the SELJUKS had their center of power. The main mosque of the city of Isfahan, for example, had several domes as well as four large *eyvans. Eyvans* were a typical feature in various types of Iranian structures, including palaces and caravansaries*.

* **caravansary** lodging in the East where caravans stopped to rest, usually surrounding a spacious courtyard

From the 900s to the 1100s, the people of Iran made advances in various art forms, particularly metalwork and ceramics. Bronze containers, candlesticks, oil lamps, pitchers, and cups often were embellished with silver and copper inlays, while Arabic inscriptions and figures of birds, animals, and people adorned dishes, platters, and other ceramics. In the 1100s, Iran was a major center for ceramics production.

The Mongol invasion and conquest of Iran in the mid-1200s did not have a significant effect on the evolution of Iranian architecture. After their conquest, the Mongols chose to live apart from their Iranian subjects, and little evidence remains of anything they built during the first decades of their rule. After their conversion to Islam in the 1300s, the Mongol rulers sponsored the construction of many new tombs, mosques, and other religious structures. Yet, the architecture of this era continued to use domes, *eyvans,* and other typical Iranian forms. New features included the dramatic use of contrasting glazed and unglazed ceramics on building facades* and the use of paired minarets over entrance portals.

* **facade** front of a building; also, any side of a building that is given special architectural treatment

Mongol rule had only a minimal effect on architecture, but it had a much greater effect on Iranian art. Increased contacts with China stimulated the development of a style of landscape painting that combined Asian traditions with Near Eastern figure painting to produce a richer, more varied style. This new style was featured in many of the Iranian illustrated manuscripts produced in the 1300s and the 1400s.

After the collapse of the Iranian Mongol dynasty* in 1335, military leaders divided up the Mongol Empire. The most important of the states that emerged was the one founded by TAMERLANE, with its capital at SAMARKAND. Under Tamerlane's patronage, a new style of architecture developed that featured construction on a grandiose scale. Among the characteristics of this style are entrance portals and domes of extraordinary height, and bold geometric designs in marble and ceramic.

* **dynasty** succession of rulers from the same family or group

Iraq and Syria.   The ninth century was the period in which Iraqi artistic influence spread most widely throughout the Islamic world. From the mid-900s to the late 1100s, Iraq was essentially under the control of foreign dynasties from Iran. As a result, its architectural traditions increasingly

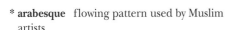

* **arabesque** flowing pattern used by Muslim artists

See color plate 11, vol. 2.

* **facades** front of a building; also, any side of a building that is given special architectural treatment

resembled those of Iran, although distinctive Iraqi features remained, such as the extensive use of molded stucco elements for decoration. During this period, tomb construction, manuscript illustration, metalwork, and CALLIGRAPHY all flourished. The tombs of the period often featured a distinctive pyramid-like structure and richly carved arabesque* designs. Iraqi manuscripts contained illustrations that concentrated on the human figure with little attention to settings.

Artistic life in Syria was at a low point from the mid-700s to the mid-1100s. Its main cities—Damascus, Aleppo, and Jerusalem—were controlled by foreign dynasties centered in Iraq or Egypt, and the beginning of the CRUSADES in the late 1000s only increased the stresses within the region. In the 1200s, however, a period of artistic and cultural activity began that continued under the AYYUBIDS and the early MAMLUK DYNASTY. Some elements of this revival show Iraqi influence, such as the use of molded stucco decorations. Syrian architects produced domes, vaults, and portals of carved stone—the preferred building material in Syria. They also used stones of different types and colors to decorate structures built of limestone and to highlight building facades. Typical features of Syrian madrasas (schools of religious learning) were richly decorated portals and inner courtyards onto which opened living areas, a small mosque, and large classrooms. Syria was also a center for the production of manuscripts, inlaid metalwork, ceramics, and enameled and gilded glass.

Egypt. After the FATIMID EMPIRE arose in Egypt in the mid-900s, an independent artistic tradition was created there that fused pre-Islamic Egyptian elements with newer Islamic themes. One of the most notable features of Egyptian Islamic architecture was the emphasis on ornamentation on the facades* of buildings. Some Egyptian mosques of the period had elaborately decorated facades with inscriptions, niches with carved figures, and other embellishments. Another artistic trend linked to the Fatimids was the creation of tombs, usually square chambers with domes, over the graves of both religious and secular figures. In the Ayyubid and Mamluk periods, tombs were commonly combined with madrasas.

During the Fatimid period, Egypt also evolved an independent artistic tradition in the decorative arts. The region was renowned for linen textiles, objects of rock crystal or gold inset with precious stones, and painted ceramics. Especially striking was the variety of decorative designs, which included Islamic, Egyptian, and Christian themes. In the later Ayyubid and Mamluk periods, these arts show more Syrian influence, and the decoration of metalwork, ceramics, textiles, and glass textiles was dominated by large-scale inscriptions and geometric patterns.

Spain and North Africa. From the 1000s to the 1400s, Spain and North Africa shared the same artistic heritage, which featured designs and decorative styles established during the first centuries of Islam. For much of this period, both regions were dominated by two North African Islamic dynasties—the Almoravids, who ruled from 1054 to 1147, and the Almohads, who ruled from 1130 to 1269.

The principal surviving structures from this period are mosques. The best preserved of these mosques feature numerous aisles, horseshoe-shaped arches, multiple domes, and elaborately decorated vaulted ceilings. Interior decoration was often minimal, reflecting the more somber and serious taste of the Almohad dynasty in particular. With the decline of the Almohads, new dynasties arose. Yet the artistic styles and traditions of these new dynasties remained relatively unchanged.

During the 1200s to the 1400s, the focus of architecture in the region changed from mosques to madrasas and hermitages* (called *zawiyyas*) for religious leaders and their followers. The madrasas of North Africa were similar to those in other parts of the Islamic world. They featured a central courtyard from which opened rooms for students and teachers, a small mosque, and classrooms. The courtyards often were decorated with geometric patterns and figures of flowers and plants carved in wood, glazed ceramic tiles, and carved stucco. The *zawiyyas* were built on a similar plan, although some were combined with the tomb of a saintly person.

The last Islamic dynasty in Spain—the Nasrids of GRANADA—served as an important link between the culture of Muslim Spain and that of later North African Islamic dynasties. The most notable architectural monument of the Nasrids was the richly decorated ALHAMBRA palace, built inside a fortified wall on a hill overlooking Granada. Lavish decoration was used throughout the Alhambra. Ceramic tile panels cover the lower wall surfaces, while carved and painted stucco cover the upper walls. Ceilings have elaborate geometric woodwork. The design and decoration of this building were the result of several centuries of artistic evolution in the western Mediterranean. This tradition lived on in North Africa after Granada fell to the Christians of Spain in 1492.

Turkey. Although Turkey did not adopt Islam until the 1000s, it developed a rich tradition of Islamic art. From the 1100s to the 1300s, the region was a popular refuge for Muslims fleeing disturbances in Iran, Iraq, and Syria, and these people brought their artistic traditions with them.

The most important Islamic rulers of Turkey in this period were the Seljuks of central ANATOLIA. The Seljuks and the high officials in their

* **hermitage**   solitary or secluded dwelling place

The Dome of the Rock was built in Jerusalem during the Umayyad period and completed around 691. The central dome covers a large rock, which, according to tradition, marks the place of Muhammad's ascension into heaven. The interior is colorfully decorated with mosaics that include inscriptions from the Qur'an. The structure is one of the holiest of Islamic sites.

administration financed the construction of madrasas, tombs, baths, palaces, and caravansaries. Mosques were of secondary importance. The most important structures were the madrasas, which were notable for their rich architectural decoration, especially on their portals. Two outstanding examples of Seljuk madrasas are the Karatay madrasa built in 1251/1252 and the Ince Minare madrasa built in 1260/1261. Both structures use a simple plan that has an elaborate portal leading to a central domed chamber. This chamber opens onto a large vaulted hall flanked by two domed chambers and several smaller rooms. The decoration of the portal shows Syrian influence, while the glazed ceramic decoration of the central domed chamber suggests Iranian influence.

By the end of the 1200s, the Seljuks were in decline. Soon, however, a new burst of artistic creativity emerged among the Ottomans in northwestern Anatolia. The Ottomans began the practice of building a series of structures centered on a mosque. Often included were madrasas, baths, schools for studying the Qur'an, and a tomb for the SULTAN. Such royal complexes allowed the Ottomans to perpetuate their glory while serving the needs of the Islamic community. Normally, only the mosques and tombs of these complexes had elaborate decoration. The Green Mosque in the early Ottoman capital city of Bursa was renowned for the exceptional richness of its decoration, as was the Green Tomb of Sultan Mehmed I located nearby. Both mosque and tomb are decorated with elaborate colored tile and marble.

Among the most important crafts in Turkey were rug making and ceramics. Rug making was one of the earliest Turkish crafts; some of the oldest rug fragments date from the 1200s and the 1300s. By the late 1300s and the early 1400s, Turkish carpets were being exported to Europe, where they were copied by Spanish weavers and depicted in European paintings. Most Turkish carpets were decorated with simple geometric patterns or with figures of flowers, vines, and other plants. In ceramics, Turkish designs of the 1200s and the 1300s often were based on Iranian styles. Ceramic production consisted primarily of colorful tiles used in architectural decoration and glazed containers for domestic use. Illustrated manuscripts, most prominent in the 1400s, also show the influence of Iranian style.

By the end of the Middle Ages, Islamic art and architecture were both remarkably distinctive and diverse. The Islamic style was a distinguishing feature of the Islamic world. At the same time, each region of the Islamic world integrated its own culture and traditions with the heritage of Islam, which it understood and interpreted in its own way. (*See also* **Books, Manuscript; Islam, Religion of; Mongol Empire; Ottomans and Ottoman Empire; Textiles.**)

> **Remember:** *Words in small capital letters have separate entries, and the index at the end of Volume 4 will guide you to more information on many topics.*

Italian Language and Literature

The Italian language spoken today evolved over many centuries from the Latin that was spoken and written during Roman times. The earliest texts that clearly document the existence of a distinctive vernacular* in the Italian peninsula are four brief legal documents (called the "Cassino Depositions") dating from 960–963. The writing in these papers is evidence of a language clearly different from the medieval Latin of the times.

* **vernacular** language or dialect native to a region; everyday, informal speech

Italian Language

Spoken Latin.   Scholars agree that the Latin spoken during the Middle Ages (often referred to as Vulgar Latin) had features that distinguished it from classical or literary Latin. These languages probably existed side by side. There is little written evidence to suggest the existence of a language that was mainly spoken but not used in literature or official documents. As a result, linguists* cannot easily determine when the variations in medieval Latin began or ended.

Several sources of information about the spoken language give clues to its development. These include the works of classical authors who intentionally reproduced everyday speech in their writings; the works of writers who inserted their own peculiar speech patterns into their writings; the *Appendix probi,* a list of both the correct and incorrect forms of words that was written in the third century by a schoolmaster for his students; word definitions found in the margins of medieval texts; and, finally, inscriptions such as the graffiti found in the volcanic ruins of Pompeii, dating back to A.D. 79.

Early Italo-Romance.   A major feature in the appearance of a written form of informal, everyday Italian is its relative lateness compared to the development of other vernacular Romance* languages. Scholars believe that this late development may have had two major causes. First, the Italian peninsula was politically divided during the Middle Ages, and this lack of political unity may have encouraged the splitting off of many different dialects. Second, Italy was the homeland of Classical Latin, which had such great importance in the ancient world that it may have discouraged people from adopting a different written form of the language. Even as late as the 1100s, there is only scattered evidence of a separate medieval Italian.

First Vernacular Literary Texts.   Literary texts in vernacular medieval Italian did not appear until after 1225. By that time, the speech of the region of Tuscany in Italy had achieved a kind of preeminence due to the works of DANTE, BOCCACCIO, and PETRARCH. Much of the writing from that period, including Sicilian poetry, is written in the Tuscan* dialect.

The Italian dialects of the 1200s borrowed from a number of other languages—Latin, especially in religious, philosophical, and law writings; northern French and Provençal* dialects; and Arabic. Arabic influences were particularly strong in Sicily.

Numerous dialects continued to exist at the beginning of the 1300s. Although Dante's *Divine Comedy* was written in a slightly modified Tuscan dialect, Dante himself was critical of all dialects and felt none was worthy of being the standard language of Italy. Ironically, Dante's work and the writings of his fellow Tuscans, Boccaccio and Petrarch, helped establish the importance of the Tuscan dialect and its eventual adaptation and adoption as the standard Italian language. Most modern knowledge of Italian from the late 1200s through the 1400s is really a knowledge of Tuscan in its written form.

The Italian language of today varies little from the Tuscan forms of the 1400s. The reader of modern Italian would have little difficulty reading Italian texts from the 1400s. One main reason that the language did not change after that period was that Latin retained a powerful hold on the

* **linguist** person who studies the structure of languages

* **Romance** referring to any of several languages that developed from Latin, such as Italian, French, and Spanish

* **Tuscan** dialect spoken in the region of Tuscany, which became the standard Italian language

* **Provençal** language spoken in southeastern France, in Provence; also, the literary tradition of that region

Italian imagination. Dante, Boccaccio, and Petrarch wrote in Latin as well as in the vernacular. Latin remained a "prestige" language for many kinds of writing, but the vernacular Tuscan-Italian was often considered inferior. Although many countries today, including the United States, have some dialects of their main spoken language, Italians continue to speak many more dialect versions of standard Italian—a fragmentation that can be traced to the developments of the Middle Ages.

Italian Literature

Italian literature during the Middle Ages was written in many different genres, or forms. These genres included poetry, drama, prose, and sermons.

Poetry. Medieval Italian poetry covered a vast terrain and produced some of the world's greatest literature. One of its most distinctive forms was the allegorical* or didactic* poem. These poems used religious subjects, myths, tales, proverbs, and often popular sentiments to teach lessons to the reader. For example, *Il libro,* written in the early 1200s by Uguccione da Lodi, is a 702-line poem that contains warnings against vice, reflections on human misery and death, and descriptions of the punishments of hell and the rewards of heaven.

Italian lyric poetry began at the court of Emperor FREDERICK II in Sicily from 1220 to 1250, but it eventually developed into a large and diverse body of literature. At Frederick's worldly court, poets composed lyrics in the Sicilian dialect, but they often imitated the widely admired forms of Provençal poetry. The subject of their poetry was love, which included descriptions of the lady, the role of the lover, and the effects of passion. The Sicilian poets are important in the history of Italian lyric poetry, for they were the first to use the Italian vernacular in an organized fashion as the medium for artistic expression. They also invented the sonnet*, which would eventually become the major poetic form in Italy and the rest of Europe.

In the mid-1200s, many poets were writing in central Italy under the guidance of Guittone d'Arezzo (ca. 1230–1294), the most important literary figure of his generation. In terms of the Italian lyric tradition, however, Guittone, unlike the Sicilians, expanded his subjects to include not only love but morals, religion, and politics.

Dante Alighieri (1265–1321) enjoys the reputation as Italy's greatest poet, a reputation based primarily on his *Divine Comedy,* although he composed numerous other poems. The *Divine Comedy,* a long vernacular poem of 14,000 lines, recounts the tale of the poet's journey through hell, purgatory, and heaven. Dante is guided through hell and purgatory by Virgil (the classical Roman poet) and through heaven by Beatrice (Dante's lover).

Dante influenced the work of another Italian poet, Giovanni Boccaccio (1313–1375). Boccaccio's allegorical *Amorosa visione* was modeled on the *Divine Comedy.* Boccaccio is remembered more for his great prose work, the *Decameron,* a collection of bawdy and witty tales set against the somber background of the Black Death.

The third great figure of medieval Italian poetry was Petrarch (Francesco Petrarca, 1304–1374), whose works mark the end of the Middle Ages and the beginning of the Italian Renaissance. Petrarch studied and admired classical Greek culture, and his poetry reflects a classically

* **allegorical** pertaining to allegory, a literary device in which characters represent ideas, morals, or philosphical or religious principles

* **didactic** designed or intended to teach

* **sonnet** fixed verse form of 14 lines; also, a poem in this pattern

Giovanni Boccaccio, one of medieval Italy's most famous writers, is best remembered for the *Decameron,* a collection of 100 stories told by 10 young aristocrats who have fled the city of Florence to escape the plague. Boccaccio, Dante, and Petrarch came to be known as the "three crowns of Florence."

* **liturgy** form of a religious service, particularly the words spoken or sung

* **friar** member of a religious brotherhood of the later Middle Ages who worked in the community and relied on the charity of others for his livelihood

Passion and Praise

Much of Dante's lyric poetry contains a flowing musical quality combined with the lofty theme of praise. The following stanzas, from the *Vita nuova*, are in praise of Beatrice:

"Such sweet decorum and such
    gentle grace
attend my lady's greeting as she
    moves
that lips can only tremble into
    silence,
and eyes dare not attempt to gaze
    at her.

"Moving, benignly clothed in
    humility,
untouched by all the praise along
    the way,
she seems to be a creature come
    from Heaven
to earth, to manifest a miracle."

inspired conception of art and beauty. The principal subject of his 366 poems is the poet's love for a woman named Laura.

Drama.   The first dramatic productions in medieval Italy were connected to the liturgy* of the church. Liturgical drama used multiple scenes to stage the entire life of characters, the history of a nation, or the history of humanity itself. Scenery and sets were adjacent to one another on the stage. This gave viewers a simultaneous picture of many places. The idea was to convey a dynamic universe.

Another medieval Italian dramatic form was the *lauda,* or song of praise. *Laude* were sung by friars* and accompanied by mime enactments of the subjects of the songs. By the early 1400s, the tradition of the *lauda* had evolved into sacred plays called *sacre rappresentazioni.*

Prose.   Medieval Italian prose developed into several different forms. Vernacular prose appeared in the late 1200s, much later than poetry. It arose in response to the needs of the newly dominant merchant classes in the cities. Many cities wanted records of their histories. This led to the creation of the chronicle. Chroniclers at first modeled their work on Roman histories, but later they expanded the form to include perspectives on morality and religion.

Italian prose during the Middle Ages included epic and chivalric writings about legendary kings and knights of the past. It was a tradition borrowed from the French and one that focused on non-Italian subjects such as Arthur, the legendary king of the Britons, and the CAROLINGIAN kings. The Arthurian and Carolingian legends entered northern Italy from France by the 1100s and were spread by both written and oral means. These prose romances were highly popular in Tuscany in the 1400s, especially in the works of Andrea da Barberino, who wrote four long works on the Carolingians. Italian epic and chivalric writing tends to be storytelling that is pure fantasy. As a result, it is almost impossible to detect in these works any comments about contemporary society.

A landmark in the development of vernacular narrative in Italy is the *Novellino,* published in the late 1200s. A collection of brief tales, the work records sayings, acts of courtesy, witty responses, valiant deeds, and noble loves. It does not moralize about anything in particular, and it may in fact be the work of more than one author.

Prose writing in the 1300s is more complex and varied and is dominated by the figure of Boccaccio. In his most famous work, the *Decameron,* seven young women and three young men meet in Florence and leave for a villa in the countryside to escape the Black Death. There they dedicate their afternoons to storytelling. The *Decameron* contains 100 tales, but they are structured and related in such a way that the overall effect is of a work consisting of messages about morals, society, and even literary theory.

Sermons.   Preaching has always been an essential activity of the Christian church. The earliest surviving vernacular sermons in Italy date from the late 1100s. These sermons do not elaborate on the meanings of the Scriptures but use scriptural quotations and examples from other sources to illustrate a point.

In the mid-1200s, a new religious order was created, the Order of Friars Preachers, or Dominicans, dedicated solely to preaching. The Dominicans had a keen awareness of the needs of their various congregations and trained their preachers accordingly. Their instruction manuals were printed in Latin, but their sermons were in the vernacular. Although the Dominicans at first discouraged publication of sermons in the vernacular, a large body (about 700) of the sermons of Giordano of Pisa survive from the early 1300s, probably because they were copied by one or more of his listeners.

Sermons were enormously popular and drew crowds of listeners. Toward the end of the Middle Ages, the stirring sermons of the Dominican Girolamo Savonarola (1452–1498) became part of the political conflict and upheaval in Florence. (*See also* **Allegory; Arthurian Literature; Chronicles; Dominicans; Drama; Latin Language; Sermons; Sicily.**)

See map in Papal States (vol. 3).

* **papacy** office of the pope and his administrators

Italy

Medieval Italy was a region rich in the heritage of the Roman Empire and the traditions of the Christian church, which was centered in the city of ROME. The area also was characterized by foreign invasion, local and regional warfare, and social tensions, as well as the development of extensive trade and a remarkable cultural creativity. By the 1300s and 1400s, Italy surpassed the rest of Europe with its literary, artistic, and intellectual achievements.

Germanic Invasions. In the 400s and 500s, Italy was invaded by a series of Germanic peoples. The first to invade were the VISIGOTHS, who entered Italy in 410 and sacked Rome. They continued their raids into southern Italy before retreating up the peninsula and moving farther west into France and Spain. In the mid-400s, the VANDALS raided coastal areas of Italy from their base in North Africa, and the HUNS invaded from the north. The most enduring Germanic invasion was by the OSTROGOTHS, who invaded in the late 400s. The Ostrogoths, under the leadership of THEODORIC, established a kingdom that included all of Italy, although their settlement in the south was slight. Theodoric's rule brought a period of peace and modest economic prosperity to the region.

Ostrogothic rule of Italy lasted until the mid-500s, when the region was conquered by the Byzantines and incorporated into the BYZANTINE EMPIRE. Byzantine control of northern Italy was short-lived, however. In 568, another Germanic people, the LOMBARDS, began invading and quickly took control of the north. By 570, they occupied much of the south as well, although the Byzantines maintained control of the island of SICILY and a few small strongholds on the southernmost part of the Italian peninsula.

In the late 700s, yet another Germanic people, the FRANKS, went to Italy to defend the papacy* from the Lombards. Led first by PEPIN III THE SHORT and then by his son CHARLEMAGNE, the Franks conquered the Lombards and governed northern and central Italy. When the empire of the Franks was divided in the 800s, Italy passed to a series of German emperors. At the same time, however, local power began to grow strong in northern Italy, and the rise of powerful, independent urban centers increasingly challenged the centralized power of the HOLY ROMAN EMPIRE and the papacy. These towns and cities were a vital element in the subsequent history of Italy.

The Rise of Towns. The Lombard invasion and occupation of northern Italy dramatically changed life in the region. The Lombards were warriors and farmers who had little use for urban centers. When they invaded, many of the leading inhabitants of old Roman towns fled for their lives, and the towns were left to decay. By the mid-600s, northern Italy was a wasteland of deserted cities with their Roman economic and political institutions destroyed and their inhabitants gone. Lombard attacks on the Byzantine areas of Italy contributed to the decline of towns in those regions as well.

Beginning in the late 700s and early 800s, Italian towns and cities came alive again. This was due in large part to increased trade relations with the Islamic world. Southern Italian ports such as NAPLES, Salerno, and Amalfi established important links with North Africa, EGYPT, and CONSTANTINOPLE, while new urban centers in the north, most notably VENICE, became important ports of entry for foreign goods. Venice, a favored trading partner of Constantinople, was on its way to becoming one of the most powerful commercial centers of the Mediterranean.

By the 1000s and the 1100s, the growth of trade and commerce had enabled certain Italian towns to develop into major commercial and

By the 14th century, Italy was divided into three different political regions. Northern Italy had many independent city-states, such as Milan and Genoa. Southern Italy remained a region of feudal kingdoms ruled by powerful dynasties. Central Italy comprised the area known as the Papal States, which were controlled by the pope.

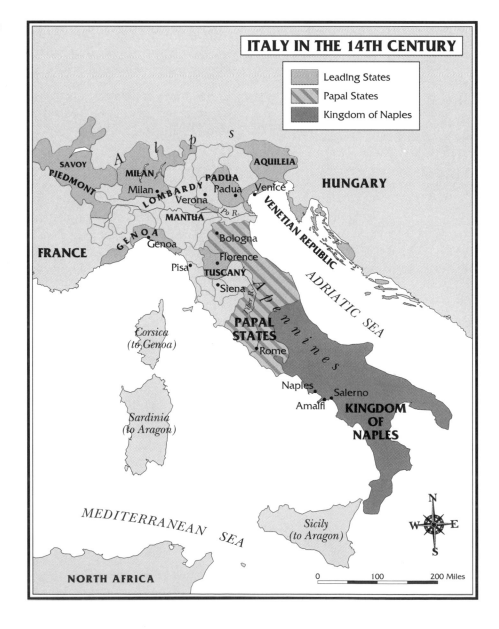

ITALY IN THE 14TH CENTURY

Leading States
Papal States
Kingdom of Naples

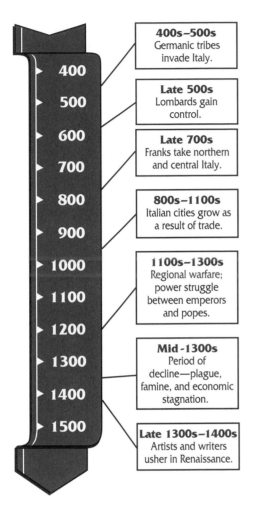

400	**400s–500s** Germanic tribes invade Italy.
500	**Late 500s** Lombards gain control.
600 700	**Late 700s** Franks take northern and central Italy.
800 900	**800s–1100s** Italian cities grow as a result of trade.
1000 1100	**1100s–1300s** Regional warfare; power struggle between emperors and popes.
1200 1300 1400	**Mid-1300s** Period of decline—plague, famine, and economic stagnation.
1500	**Late 1300s–1400s** Artists and writers usher in Renaissance.

* **despot** ruler with unlimited power or authority

* **city-state** independent state consisting of a city and the territories around it

* **duchy** territory ruled by a duke or a duchess

administrative centers. In north and central Italy, these towns now exercised their own political authority. They became powerful, independent cities ruled by citizen groups and were called COMMUNES. By the mid-1100s, communes controlled all the major cities of north and central Italy. Among the most important of these cities were GENOA, PISA, MILAN, FLORENCE, SIENA, Venice, and Bologna. In southern Italy, towns and cities remained under the control of nobles of powerful kingdoms, and they never gained the same degree of independence.

Regional Conflicts.   The period from the 1000s to the 1300s in Italy was one of almost constant regional warfare, as powerful cities and regions competed against one another for control of commerce and territory. The increasing power of cities in northern Italy also brought them into conflict with the Holy Roman Empire, as the German emperors tried to maintain their authority in that region. In 1167, many northern cities joined together in a defensive alliance against the empire called the Lombard League, but this alliance did little to end regional and intercity rivalries. In the 1200s, a struggle for power between the Holy Roman Emperors and the papacy divided Italians into two strong political groups, the GUELPHS AND GHIBELLINES. Warfare between these two groups continued until the early 1400s and increased the rivalries among Italian cities and provinces.

In many northern Italian cities, increased factional strife led to the rise of powerful despots* called *signori*, who made rule hereditary. At the same time, territorial gains by certain cities turned them into powerful city-states* whose authority extended well beyond the cities themselves. In the early 1300s, for example, Milan was ruled by the powerful Visconti family, and the duchy* of Milan became the most powerful city-state in northern Italy.

While regional warfare and the rise of independent city-states characterized northern Italy, southern Italy remained a region of feudal kingdoms ruled by powerful nobles. Since the 1000s, the kingdoms of Sicily and Naples were controlled by dynasties of the NORMANS, the ANGEVINS, and the kings of ARAGON. In central Italy, meanwhile, the PAPAL STATES were controlled by the popes. The politics and history of these regions were thus very different from those of the north.

In the mid-1300s, Italy began to experience a period of decline as a result of economic stagnation, growing unemployment, poverty, famine, and the BLACK DEATH. Bands of professional soldiers roamed the countryside killing, pillaging, and disrupting travel and trade. Local despots increased their control. More and more land was taken over by wealthy nobles or merchants, leading to a widening gap between rich and poor.

Despite the many tensions and problems of the late 1300s and the 1400s, Italy produced a vibrant urban culture of art, literature, and ideas. Writers such as DANTE ALIGHIERI, PETRARCH, and Giovanni BOCCACCIO produced remarkable literary works. GIOTTO DI BONDONE and other artists revolutionized painting. Italian intellectuals promoted humanism, or the study of classical literature and history combined with an emphasis on the effective use of language. The work of these and others paved the way for a remarkable explosion of artistic creativity at the end of the Middle Ages known as the Italian Renaissance. (*See also* **Banking; Cities and Towns; Exploration; Frederick I Barbarossa; Frederick II of the Holy Roman Empire; Papacy, Origins and Development; Ravenna; Trade; Tuscany.**)

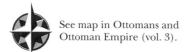

Ivan III of Muscovy

1440–1505
Russian prince

* **city-state** independent state consisting of a city and the territories around it

See map in Ottomans and Ottoman Empire (vol. 3).

* **autocratic** ruling with absolute power and authority

Ivan III of Muscovy was a Russian prince who, during his 43-year-reign (1462–1505), created a large state called Muscovy in the north of Russia. He became a grand prince at the age of 7 and sole ruler at the age of 22.

Historians have characterized Ivan as the "gatherer" of Russian lands. During his reign, his lands tripled in size, stretching deep into former Lithuanian territory in the southwest and beyond the middle Volga in the northeast. The independent territory of Ryazan and the city-state* of Pskov acknowledged and respected his rule. His only opposition came from the Kazan Tatars to the southeast, but even they came under his control for a time.

Ivan saw himself as the successor to the former Byzantine emperors, and for much of his reign he attempted to make his claim legal in the eyes of other rulers. In 1472, he married Sophia, the niece of Constantine XI, the last Byzantine emperor. He hoped that this marriage would strengthen his Byzantine claim. The rulers of Europe and the Ottoman Empire never recognized Ivan's vision, and he was forced to abandon his aspirations.

At home, Ivan had greater authority over more Russians than any other ruler in the Russian north prior to the 1400s. Ivan was regarded as the protector of the Russian faith—an important element in his hold on power. Even more important, as the system of nobility broke down, he enjoyed almost unlimited authority over his subjects. His ruling style and the extent of his authority set the stage for a new form of governance in Russia—rule by an autocratic* prince. (*See also* **Ottomans and Ottoman Empire.**)

Jacob ben Meir

ca. 1100–1171
Jewish scholar

* **Talmud** large body of collected writings on Jewish law and tradition

Jacob ben Meir was one of the greatest Jewish scholars of the medieval period. Called Rabbenu Tam, he was known for reviving interest in studies of the Talmud*. The school he established in France for Talmudic studies became a center of European Jewish learning.

Jacob ben Meir was the grandson of the famous biblical and Talmudic scholar RASHI and the younger brother of Rabbi Samuel ben Meir, another famous Talmudist. Little is known about his life except that he spent his childhood in Ramerupt, a town in northern France. When the Second Crusade passed through the town in 1146, Meir was seized by a Christian mob, who tried to crucify him. After narrowly escaping with his life, he moved to Troyes, where he remained until his death in 1171.

At his school, Meir revived the practice of logically analyzing the ancient Talmudic texts. His analyses, along with those of his nephew and pupil Rabbi Isaac ben Samud of Dampierre, were written down as a set of additions to the Talmud known as the tosafot. Printed alongside the text of the Talmud, the tosafot spread quickly throughout Jewish communities in Europe and became the basis for future Talmudic analysis. The tosafot were especially important because they helped to make the Talmud relevant in many different social and economic conditions.

A stormy and controversial personality, Meir often urged Jews to remain separate and aloof from their Christian neighbors. This attitude hardened the barriers that already existed between Jewish and non-Jewish communities. (*See also* **Jewish Communities; Judaism.**)

Jacopone da Todi

ca. 1236–1306
Poet and Franciscan friar

* **hair shirt** coarse garment worn next to the skin as a penalty for sin

* **penance** task set by the church for someone to earn God's forgiveness for a sin

* **theology** study of the nature of God and of religious truth

* **excommunicate** to exclude from the rites of the church

Born in Todi, Italy, Jacopone da Todi worked as a notary and legal official. When he was about 30, his wife died in a building collapse. According to legend, she was found to be wearing a hair shirt* under her clothing. This implied that she had been guilty of committing a sin. Shocked by this discovery, Jacopone abandoned his comfortable life. He gave his goods to the poor and began a life of penance*.

In 1278, he joined a convent of Franciscan friars. He studied philosophy and theology* and engaged in debates about the strictness of religious life in the order. He advocated absolute poverty and frequently criticized the negligent behavior of some of the friars. In 1298, he was imprisoned and excommunicated* for accusing the newly elected Pope Boniface VIII of corruption. At first, Jacopone was happy to suffer imprisonment for the sake of the Lord and poverty. Eventually, he appealed (unsuccessfully) to Boniface to release him from excommunication and prison. He remained in prison until 1303, when a new pope, Benedict XI, was elected.

Jacopone wrote poetry in the form of *laude,* rhythmic chants of praise. His themes were the insignificance of human life and the wisdom of sacrifice for the sake of divine love. Jacopone's best-known poem, "Donna del paradiso," is about the sorrow of Mary at the sight of Christ's Passion. It is possible that he also composed the *Stabat mater,* a famous hymn on the same subject. Jacopone's *laude* are among the greatest works of religious literature. (*See also* **Franciscans; Italian Language and Literature.**)

Jacques Coeur

ca. 1395–1456
Merchant, financier,
and royal adviser

Jacques Coeur was a wealthy merchant and an adviser, banker, and moneylender to King CHARLES VII OF FRANCE. He helped reform the currency of France and amassed enormous personal wealth in the pursuit of his extensive business ventures.

Jacques Coeur was born in Bourges, the son of a furrier. In 1438, he was appointed royal treasurer, with the responsibility for supplying clothing, furs, jewels, arms, spices, and art objects to the court. His commercial operations extended beyond the royal court, and his agents traded throughout Europe and the Near East.

Jacques Coeur's political and financial operations were based principally on his relationship with Charles. As a member of the King's Council, he made himself indispensable to the king. Coeur lent the money needed to regain Normandy from the English in 1450, a step toward driving the English off the continent and bringing an end to the Hundred Years War in 1453. He reformed and stabilized the currency (one much-used coin was called "le gros de Jacques Coeur"), and he assured the credit of the kingdom's financial system.

Diplomacy aided his business interests. He enjoyed friendly relations with the popes, and he secured loans from Italian bankers to make up for his lack of capital. Jacques Coeur acquired much land in his business ventures, and at Bourges he built the most beautiful French palace of the 1400s.

Jacques Coeur's success aroused jealousy among rivals, and their accusations eventually persuaded Charles VII to act against him. In 1453, he was banished from France and forced to pay a fine equivalent to the value of all his possessions. Jacques Coeur went into exile in Rome, where the pope gave him the protection of the church. While in Rome, he joined a fleet sent by Pope Calixtus III against the Turks. He died at Chios in 1456, perhaps in battle. (*See also* **Hundred Years War.**)

Jahiz, al-

ca. 776–868/869
Islamic prose writer

* **caliph** religious and political head of an Islamic state

* **theology** study of the nature of God and of religious truth

* **satire** use of ridicule to expose and denounce vice, folly, and other human failings

* **bestiary** collection of animal tales, popular in the Middle Ages, that often contained religious symbolism and moral lessons

Abu Uthman Amr ibn Bahr al-Jahiz was a writer whose works are considered among the great classics of Arabic literature and an important source for the history of medieval Islamic culture. He was born in Basra, then one of the greatest cultural centers of the Islamic world, and he may have been from an Abyssinian slave family. In Basra, al-Jahiz was exposed to all kinds of people and ideas, including the cultures of Persia and India. His first writings, arguments upholding the Abassid dynasty's right to rule, came to the attention of the caliph* al-Ma'mun, and al-Jahiz was summoned to Baghdad. He spent most of his career in Baghdad, where he became familiar with classical Greek translations, particularly those of Aristotle.

Al-Jahiz wrote more than 200 works, about a third of which survive either whole or in part. His topics included philosophy, theology*, satire*, history, literary criticism, the natural sciences, and human nature. Al-Jahiz's works are difficult to characterize because of his enormous diversity of style. His major work, *Kitab al-hayawan (Book of Animals),* is a bestiary* that deals with the nature and behavior of different animals. At the same time, it has a religious theme—that the world and everything in it is proof of God's wisdom and mercy. In this work, al-Jahiz covers topics that range from the lighthearted, witty, and even obscene to the serious. Although he accepted much from the Persian tradition, his roots lay in Arabic humanities. His works inspired and influenced most Islamic authors in the generations to follow and established a tradition that gained both popular and official support. Arabic traditions and lore remained the heart of medieval Islamic culture. (*See also* **Abbasids; Caliphate.**)

James I the Conqueror

1208–1276
King of Aragon and count of Barcelona

James I the Conqueror was the ruler of Aragon and Catalonia, which are regions of modern Spain. (He was called Jaime I in Catalonia.) His reign was marked by a significant expansion of his territories, the establishment of governmental institutions, and the growth of cities. No king in medieval history revealed himself better than did James I in his *Book of Deeds,* a celebration of his subjects at the height of their triumphs.

James became king at the age of five during a time in which the aristocracy was divided and discontent. As he grew older, he was forced to create a new nobility loyal to him. Much of the internal tensions during his reign arose from the rivalry between the two parts of his realm: Aragon and Catalonia. The barons of Aragon often sided with townspeople in debates about the king's tax policies. These assemblies of barons and townspeople created the practice and tradition of political debate.

When Catalan merchants complained about being harassed by Moorish pirates, James I and his army set out to conquer the Balearic Islands off the coast of Spain. In late 1128 and much of 1229, the army besieged Majorca, the largest of the Balearic Islands, until it finally fell in December 1229. This detail from an Arabian fresco shows James I surrounded by his knights as they prepare for the conquest of Majorca.

* **Catalan** a native or inhabitant of Catalonia

* **Moorish** relating to the Moors, Spanish Muslims descended from the Arab conquerors

See map in Aragon (vol. 1).

Throughout his reign, James actively sought to expand his kingdom. At the urging of Catalan* merchants, who were harassed by Moorish* pirates, he conquered the Balearic Islands between 1229 and 1235. The conquered islands were distributed mainly among the Catalans, who had done most of the fighting.

Meanwhile, the barons of Aragon pressured James to seize Valencia, which the king did in 1238. The nobility attempted to impose Aragonese customs in the conquered province, but James allowed Catalan settlers to migrate to Valencia and also permitted Muslim law and religion to remain in many communities.

In 1266, the king helped Castile in its conquest of Murcia after a Moorish rebellion in that region. James's conquests in Spain were offset by defeats in southern France. In 1258, James signed the Treaty of Corbeil with King Louis IX of France. By the terms of the treaty, James gave up several claims in southern France in return for the French king's renouncing his rights in Catalonia. In 1269, James attempted a crusade to Palestine, but the king got only as far as southern France before the venture was canceled.

James found it harder to govern in peace than in war. He designated his son Pedro (Peter) as his heir in Aragon, Catalonia, and Valencia, and he ceded portions of the Balearic Islands (to be called the kingdom of Majorca) to Pedro's younger brother Jaime (James). Although the king feuded often with Pedro, the two were reconciled in 1275, when they crushed a rebellion of Aragonese nobles. James died in Valencia in 1276 and was succeeded in Aragon by Pedro (Peter III) and in Majorca by Jaime.

James's writings are considered the first great Catalan national history. The first-person narrative has a personal and spontaneous quality and covers the events of his reign in great detail. It was translated into Latin as *Liber gestarum*. (*See also* **Aragon; Catalonia.**)

Jean de Joinville

**ca. 1224–1317
French nobleman
and biographer**

* **Levant** countries bordering the eastern Mediterranean Sea from Turkey to Egypt

Jean de Joinville was the SENESCHAL, or administrator, of Champagne and the biographer of the French king Louis IX (St. Louis). His *Histoire de saint Louis (History of St. Louis)* is regarded as a monument of French prose and the finest biography of the sainted king.

The Joinville family were hereditary holders of the title of seneschal in their county. Jean de Joinville met Louis IX for the first time at Saumur in 1241. He later accompanied the king on the Second Crusade to the Holy Land (1248–1254) and was captured with the king in Egypt in 1250. Released with the king after the payment of a ransom, Jean de Joinville remained with Louis in the Levant* for another four years. The crusade left him with a debilitating fever that plagued him for the remainder of his long life. On his return to France, he devoted his time to the management of his lands, which had suffered during his absence. His second marriage in 1261 brought additional wealth and properties, and much of the remainder of his life was spent administering and protecting his estates.

* **canonization** act of officially declaring (a dead person) a saint

Jean de Joinville was summoned to the royal court in 1267 as Louis IX prepared to go on another crusade. Afraid that his estates would again suffer from neglect, Jean de Joinville refused to accompany the king. He also opposed the entire plan, fearing that the king was too weak to survive the journey. Louis IX died in 1270 while on the crusade. Jean de Joinville later devoted his attention to Louis's canonization* and testified at the hearings that preceded the king's elevation to sainthood.

Jean de Joinville lived into his 90s and spent much of his old age working on his biography of Louis IX. The work had been commissioned by the royal family.

For the most part, Jean de Joinville enjoyed good relations with Louis's successors, most of whom he outlived. Because of his age and experience, he was regarded as an expert in court rituals and ceremonies. (*See also* **Champagne, County of; Crusades; Louis IX of France.**)

Jerusalem

* **crusades** holy wars declared by the pope against non-Christians. Most were against Muslims, but crusades were also declared against heretics and pagans.

During medieval times, Jerusalem was the most important city of Palestine. It was situated on three hills (Zion, Golgotha, and Moriah) overlooking the Tyropean valley. Jerusalem was, and is, a holy city having unique religious associations with Judaism, Christianity, and Islam. The medieval history of Jerusalem reflects the relationships between its land features and the religious history and culture of these religious faiths. Jerusalem's medieval history spanned four periods: the Byzantine Christian period, the Early Islamic period, the period of the crusades*, and the Ayyubid, Mamluk, and early Ottoman period.

The Byzantine Christian Period (324–638).   When Emperor CONSTANTINE I converted the Roman Empire to Christianity in 324, Jerusalem was a minor provincial city called Aelia Capitolina. The size of the city was about the same as the present Old City. The city probably was enclosed by a wall and had features of a typical Roman provincial town: streets, temples, statues of emperors, a military fortress, and possibly theaters. The city also had strong religious associations. Jewish pilgrims came to Jerusalem to see the ruins of the Second Temple. (The temple had been

See map in Crusades (vol. 2).

built by Herod the Great in about 35 B.C. and was destroyed by the Romans in A.D. 70.)

The city was also significant for Christians. It was the site of the Crucifixion, burial, and Resurrection of Jesus. When the capital of the Christian Roman Empire was moved east to Constantinople, Jerusalem became the holiest city of the Byzantine world. New religious monuments were constructed. One of the first and most important was the Church of the Holy Sepulcher, built in 335 on the supposed site of Christ's tomb. During the 250 years that followed, many other buildings and monuments were erected to commemorate the life of Jesus Christ. The city became the focus for Christian pilgrims, with many new inns, monasteries, hospices*, and other facilities built to accommodate travelers. The city's construction boom had an important effect on artists and architects in other parts of the empire, and a major industry—the manufacturing of holy objects—developed.

* **hospice** house, often kept by monks, where travelers could stop and rest

The Early Islamic Period (638–1099). Jerusalem was important to Muslims because the prophet Muhammad had visited there. Although the city came under Muslim control in 638, the caliph* Umar I ibn al-Khattab forbade Muslims from taking over Christian sanctuaries and allowed Jews to settle again in Jerusalem. (Jews had left the city in great numbers following the destruction of the Second Temple.) During the next four centuries, the city experienced many changes. One of the most important was the establishment of the Second Temple area as a Muslim sanctuary. The ruined temple was cleaned and renovated. Its gates were rebuilt, and new monuments were built. These included the spectacular Dome of the Rock, believed to mark the place of Muhammad's ascension. It was completed in 691/692. This and other structures transformed the site into the third holiest place of Islam known as the Noble Sanctuary—the Haram al-Sharif—commemorating the lives of Muhammad and biblical figures such as Joseph, Jacob, and Abraham. During this period, Jerusalem acquired

* **caliph** religious and political head of an Islamic state

Jerusalem was, and is, a holy city for Jews, Christians, and Muslims. By the beginning of the Middle Ages, it had already been a center of Jewish religious and political life for more than 3,000 years. For Christians, the city is associated with events in the life of Jesus Christ, including the Crucifixion. To Muslims, it is the holiest city after Mecca and Medina because of events associated with the life of Muhammad. This woodcut map of Jerusalem is from the early 1500s.

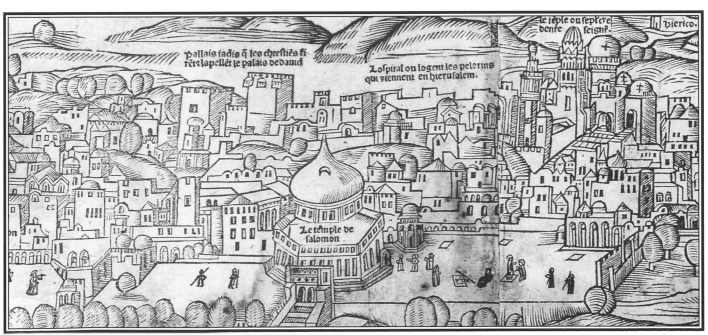

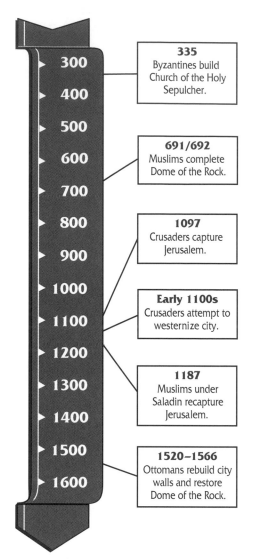

300

400

500

600

700

800

900

1000

1100

1200

1300

1400

1500

1600

335
Byzantines build
Church of the Holy
Sepulcher.

691/692
Muslims complete
Dome of the Rock.

1097
Crusaders capture
Jerusalem.

Early 1100s
Crusaders attempt to
westernize city.

1187
Muslims under
Saladin recapture
Jerusalem.

1520–1566
Ottomans rebuild city
walls and restore
Dome of the Rock.

* **minaret** tall, slender tower of a Muslim
mosque from which the faithful are called to
prayer

the Arabic name Bayt al-Maqdis or al-Quds, meaning the Holy House or
the Holy One. Muslims still call the city by these names.

The population of Jerusalem also changed. Christians still formed the
major portion of the population, but their culture became more Arabic.
Muslims lived in the southern part of the city. Jews settled in the area where
the present Jewish quarter is located.

The Period of the Crusades (1099–1187).   After the First Crusade, a
Christian king was installed in Jerusalem. This marked a turning point in
the city's history. For the first time since Herod the Great, Jerusalem was
once again a royal capital. Moreover, the conquering crusaders completely
transformed the city by their attempts to Christianize Jerusalem again in
the early 1100s. In doing so, the crusaders destroyed much of what was
there and built many new buildings.

The building boom of this period was spectacular. One controversy
about the building, involving both its construction and decoration, is the
degree to which artisans were local people or immigrants from Europe.
The mass building interrupted the historical growth of the city without
creating a new urban organization. The crusaders paid little attention to
the older structures of the city and killed or evicted many of its inhabitants. The impact of this period was very significant in that maps and
paintings for several centuries presented Jerusalem from a European
point of view.

The Ayyubid, Mamluk, and Early Ottoman Period (1187–1566).   In
1187, SALADIN recaptured the city. However, the Ayyubids' attention was
often turned elsewhere, since they did not regard Jerusalem as essential
to the security of their empire. There were even some brief periods when
Jerusalem was returned to Frankish rule. After the final defeat of the crusaders in the 1200s, Jerusalem was re-created as a Muslim city by the MAM-
LUK DYNASTY of Egypt. Once again, Jerusalem became a provincial capital,
now ruled from Cairo. Muslims became the majority in Jerusalem, settling in its northern quarter close to the Haram al-Sharif. Jews lived in
the south-central part of the city, but their population was small. The sec-
tor of the city near the Holy Sepulcher remained primarily Christian, but
the construction of two minarets* nearby emphasized the superior status
of Islam.

Since Jerusalem was more accessible than the holy places of Arabia, it
became the focus of another enormous construction program. More than
100 buildings were built or restored in the 300 years that followed the final
defeat of the crusaders. Among the greatest achievements were the re-
building of the city walls and the restoration of the Dome of the Rock,
both done by the Ottoman sultan Süleyman I in the 1500s.

The area around the Haram al-Sharif was filled with hospices, religious schools, convents, libraries, fountains, and the private tombs of
Muslim rulers. New streets and shopping areas were built, creating a
unique Islamic blend of social and religious institutions. The city created
by the Mamluks remained one of the most perfectly preserved late medieval Islamic cities in the Mediterranean region until the 1800s. (*See also*
Crusades.)

Jewish Art

* **synagogue** building of worship for Jews

* **illuminated manuscripts** medieval books that were beautifully lettered and illustrated by highly skilled artisans

* **codex** manuscript assembled in the form of a book instead of being rolled up like a scroll

* **Romanesque** referring to a style of architecture developed in Italy and western Europe between the Roman and Gothic periods and characterized by round arches, thick walls, and small windows

* **Gothic** referring to a style of architecture developed in northern France and spreading through western Europe from the 1100s to the 1500s, which was characterized by pointed arches, ribbed vaults, thin walls, large windows, and flying buttresses

* **Haggadah** book containing the ritual for the Seder service celebrated at Passover

The Oldest Synagogue

The oldest surviving medieval European synagogue (built around 1175) is in Worms, Germany. Destroyed by the Nazis in 1938, it has been rebuilt. The ground plan features a double nave consisting of two parallel spaces within the synagogue that are created by the two columns in the center. This design was adapted from monastic dining halls and the meeting halls of convents. The most prominent feature of this synagogue was a pulpit (called an almenor) situated in the center of the nave between columns. The double-nave style became standard for synagogue design in central and eastern Europe.

Artistic expression was an important part of medieval Jewish life. Despite the biblical prohibition in the Second Commandment against "graven (sculptured) images," other forms of Jewish art flourished, particularly in the design and decoration of synagogues* and in richly illuminated manuscripts*.

The earliest evidence of the Jewish artistic tradition is found in a synagogue in Dura Europos in Syria dating from the mid-200s. Surviving synagogues of the 500s in Byzantine lands contain beautiful mosaic floors that are richly decorated with geometric and astrological designs, symbols of the Jewish faith, and images of people or scenes from Jewish history and legend. Some of this decoration is similar to the Christian art of the period, probably due to the fact that the same artisans worked for both Jewish and Christian patrons. In medieval Europe, synagogues generally were simpler in design than churches and had a minimum of decoration. Those in Spain often showed a Christian influence in their architectural design and an Islamic influence in their decoration. Two surviving medieval Spanish synagogues (both now churches) are in Toledo, Spain. The older one dates back to the 1200s.

The major examples of medieval Jewish art are found in illuminated manuscripts from both Europe and the Islamic world. The earliest illuminated Jewish manuscripts are from the Islamic world. The oldest surviving one is an ancient codex* dating from around 894. The work, known as the Moshe ben Asher codex, contains the books of the Prophets. The text of the manuscript is prefaced by "carpet pages"—intricately designed ornamental pages with elaborate geometric patterns, floral designs, and symbols. The decorative elements in these early manuscripts are similar to those found in Islamic books, and the basic colors used—blue and gold—are also the same as in Islamic art. Most of the early illuminated Jewish manuscripts from the Islamic world are Bibles, although decorative elements are sometimes found in early children's textbooks, books of worship, and marriage contracts. An unusual feature of many Jewish manuscripts from the Islamic world is the use of micrography, the outlining of human and animal figures with tiny script.

The earliest illuminated Jewish manuscripts in western Europe come from Germany. The oldest surviving example, a two-volume commentary on the Bible, was created in Würzburg, Germany, in 1233. It has 17 miniature illustrated figures reflecting the Romanesque* style that was popular in southern Germany at that time. Among the most elaborate illuminated Jewish manuscripts is one created in Paris during the late 1200s or early 1300s. Painted in Gothic* style, it contains many miniature scenes related to the Bible, Jewish worship, and the afterlife. The most significant type of Jewish manuscript from Germany and France was the mahzor, a book of prayers and poetry for use in worship. The huge size of books of this type suggests that they were used in the synagogue rather than at home. The mahzor was similar to the Christian BREVIARY, a book of daily hymns and prayers. Another type of manuscript, with some of the most outstanding examples of medieval Jewish artwork, is the Passover Haggadah*. Examples of Haggadahs from 14th-century Spain feature full-page miniatures based on biblical stories. Other Passover Haggadahs from 15th-century Germany have illustrations and decorations that stress Jewish folklore and humor.

Some of the finest examples of early Jewish art are found in the synagogue of Dura Europos in Syria, dating from the mid-200s. All four walls are decorated with rows of frescoes depicting biblical scenes from the Old Testament. Jewish art flourished mainly in the decoration of synagogues and in richly painted illuminated manuscripts.

One of the most significant characteristics of medieval Jewish art was its adaptability. Jewish art took on the style of the culture in which it was produced: manuscripts produced in the Islamic world looked Islamic; those produced in Romanesque Spain looked Romanesque. This was also true of medieval Jewish architecture. (*See also* **Books, Manuscript; Byzantine Art; Gothic Painting; Hebrew Literature; Islamic Art and Architecture; Romanesque Art.**)

See
color plate 4,
vol. 1.

Communities of Jews were dispersed throughout Europe and the Islamic world during the Middle Ages. Exiled from their ancestral homeland in Palestine by the Romans in the second century, medieval Jews found themselves adrift and vulnerable to the power and authority of the rulers and populations of their host countries. In some areas, such as Iran and Iraq, Jewish communities thrived and became important centers of Jewish culture. In other areas, particularly in parts of Christian Europe, Jewish communities were smaller and less successful. The Jews fared well or poorly, depending on many political, economic, and cultural factors and their ability to manipulate or cope with these factors.

General Characteristics of Medieval Jewish Life

Despite the differences among Jewish communities throughout the medieval world, a number of generalities can be made about the quality of Jewish life during the Middle Ages. First, in almost any setting where there was a dominant religion—whether it was pagan, Christian, Muslim, or some other—the presence of the Jews was often regarded unfavorably.

Jews claimed a special relationship to God, the Bible, and the prophets, and they strongly adhered to their religious teachings and code of law. They resisted all efforts at conversion or intermarriage and were proud of their ancient ties to the Holy Land. Such attitudes antagonized the faithful of other religions. Christians felt that the very existence of the Jews was a challenge to the teachings of the New Testament and the mission of Jesus. Muslims felt that the Jews questioned the authenticity of the QUR'AN and the prophecies of MUHAMMAD. The Jews did little to counter these perceptions.

Second, in whatever country the Jews settled, their loyalty and reliability were always suspect, no matter how valiantly they fought in battle for the country or how patriotic and supportive they were of it. The fact that Jews always maintained a bond and kinship with Jews in other lands, even those at war with their own, fostered suspicion. In most cases, the Jews were no less reliable than any other segment of the population, but their conduct and their association with fellow Jews from other lands made them popular scapegoats for demagogues* trying to rally people to a particular cause.

A third general characteristic of medieval Jewish life was that the Jews insisted on conducting all their affairs, even in business and civil matters, according to the principles of Judaism and Jewish law as much as local authorities would allow. Since Jewish law dictated behavior in all matters of life, not just religious matters, the Jews established their own system of courts and justice. Jews who defied Jewish law felt the full pressure of their community, and those who informed on Jewish courts or fellow Jews to the local authorities were severely punished. This promoted the notion among the general population that the Jews believed themselves to be above the law.

Finally, the Jews had the ability to conduct vigorous international trade across borders that were closed to most people. This particular skill dated back to ancient times when Jews served as agents for traders transporting goods back and forth between Europe and Asia over caravan and sea routes. It was based on the fact that Jews could travel to foreign lands and establish secure financial connections with other Jews living there. The ability to travel great distances without having to carry large sums of money was invaluable for international trading, and it naturally led Jews into areas of business and banking. Limited in their ability to own land and discriminated against by society, Jews survived as best they could. This often led them into professions as merchants, moneylenders, and pawnbrokers—professions generally looked down on or actually despised by most people in society, despite the fact that economic activities depended on them.

Jewish Self–Government

Medieval Jewish communities in both Europe and the Islamic world enjoyed a substantial degree of autonomy, or self-government. The authorities of the countries in which Jews lived often granted them considerable rights to govern their own affairs, and these authorities interfered little unless their own power was threatened.

Jewish Self-Government in Europe.   In medieval Europe, local Jewish communities generally had two sources of authority: religious courts and community councils. The religious courts were presided over by

* **demagogue** leader who uses popular prejudices and false claims to gain power

* **rabbinical**   pertaining to rabbis, the spiritual leaders of the Jewish people

* **Sabbath**   day of the week used for rest and worship (Sunday for most Christians; Saturday for Jews)

* **Torah**   sacred wisdom of the Jewish faith, especially the first five books of the Bible

* **ostracism**   exclusion or banishment from one's community

rabbinical* judges, who were qualified to serve because of their knowledge of Jewish law. The jurisdiction of these courts encompassed such areas as contracts, marriage and divorce, dietary requirements, ritual purity, and Sabbath* and holiday observances. The community councils were presided over by Jewish elders whose authority was derived from their age, wealth, family lineage, or influence with Christian rulers. These councils dealt with issues affecting the community's public safety and social welfare. They were responsible to Christian authorities to see that taxes were paid and that law and order were maintained. They also were responsible for dealing with the authorities as spokespersons for the Jewish community.

The elders of the Jewish community administered a number of activities with funds collected by community members. Community funds were used to build synagogues and ritual bathhouses (mikvoth); purchase and repair Torah* scrolls; provide education for children of the poor; and meet the general needs of the ill, the aged, orphans, and widows. The councils also supervised voluntary societies that specialized in religious duties such as visiting the sick, preparing bodies for burial, providing loans, and studying religious texts.

Jewish communal authority rested on both Christian and Jewish traditions. The Theodosian Code, the Roman legal code issued in 438, recognized Jewish self-government in return for Jewish acceptance of Christian authority in political, economic, and social matters. By the late 1000s, the German emperors and the kings of England and Spain were issuing charters to Jewish communities that gave them judicial autonomy and local self-government. Jewish tradition also fostered local Jewish self-government. Isolated from the major Jewish centers in the Islamic world, European Jewish communities were forced to find their own solutions to problems facing the community.

People who violated Jewish communal laws were punished in several ways. One of the most effective punishments was the ban, the ancient Jewish penalty for breaking an oath. Applied to both violations of religious law and infringements of public ordinances, the ban resulted in the temporary or permanent social and religious ostracism* of an individual. A person banned could not eat, drink, study, pray, or do business with other Jews, nor could the individual or any family member be buried in a Jewish cemetery. In addition to the ban, community elders could require individuals to pay fines or endure penalties such as flogging or imprisonment. Jewish communal courts generally did not have the right to impose capital punishment.

The process of selecting local leaders in a Jewish community took various forms. In the small communities of northern Europe, the male members of the community gathered together and simply elected their heads, preferably by a unanimous vote. In the larger Jewish communities of Spain, leaders were chosen according to special rules designed to provide equal representation for all classes of the society. In the early medieval Jewish communities, a leader might serve as both a rabbinical judge and a member of the community board. Gradually, rabbinic authority became more professionalized, and rabbis were paid to assume particular responsibilities. In northern Europe, a rabbi's jurisdiction was essentially local until the late medieval period. In Spain, however, the

* **caliph** religious and political head of an Islamic state

* **Diaspora** the scattering of the Jews from the homeland to different countries

kings created a central rabbinic authority, the court rabbi, to represent Jews before the king.

Jewish Self-Government in the Islamic World. The privilege of Jewish self-government in the Islamic world was established in the mid-600s by the Pact of Umar, a document associated with the second caliph*, UMAR I IBN AL-KHATTAB. Later codified in the early 800s, this document confirmed the vital right to judicial autonomy.

Jewish self-government in the Islamic world functioned on three levels: imperial, regional, and local. On the imperial level, political power was held by two institutions. One was the office of the Diaspora*, whose head was known as the exilarch. The exilarchs claimed to be descended from King David, ancient Israel's greatest king, and their authority stemmed from this royal lineage. Their most important power was the right to appoint judges for provincial Jewish communities. They also represented the Jewish people before the caliph, and they became respected members of the royal court. The other, and more significant, imperial authority among the Jews was the head of the academy, or yeshiva. The head of the yeshiva, the gaon, exercised both spiritual and secular authority over the Jews of the Islamic Empire. The source of the gaon's authority was his knowledge of religion and Jewish law. In the early Islamic period, academies in Iraq enjoyed intellectual and political supremacy throughout the Islamic world, and Jews throughout the empire looked to the heads of these academies for guidance.

On the regional level, Jewish leadership emerged first in Muslim Spain in the 900s and then in North Africa and Egypt in the 1000s. Regional authority developed largely as a result of increasing Jewish population, greater economic self-sufficiency, and the rise of regional religious scholarship to compete with the scholarship of the imperial academies. Regional Jewish leaders usually had the title of nagid, or prince, and they exercised authority similar to that of the gaon and exilarch.

The local community was the most fundamental level of Jewish self-government. It had existed since ancient Greek and Roman times, when it was focused on the synagogue. The congregation of each synagogue was bound together through religious and social functions administered by a council of elders and various other officials. At the head of the community was the *muqaddam,* an appointed executive. His responsibilities depended on his qualifications and local needs. The *muqaddam* might serve as cantor*, judge, teacher, scribe, fund-raiser, or a combination of these. Local communities also had one or more professionally trained judges appointed by the imperial or regional Jewish authorities. The most important function of these judges was to settle disputes between members of the community. Another important local official was the supervisor of social services. Each community had several such officials, who were responsible for managing communal property and collecting rents, providing relief for the poor, and maintaining synagogues.

* **cantor** synagogue official who sings or chants the liturgical music and leads the congregation in prayer

Jews in Europe Before 900

Between the 400s and the 900s, the history of Jews and Jewish communities in Europe was characterized by two themes. The first was the gradual elimination of discriminatory laws against Jews. The second was the emerging recognition that Jews were a valuable part of medieval society. In this climate, Jews flourished and their communities grew.

Jewish communities were well established in Spain long before Christianity was introduced there, and the Jewish population there was larger and more important than in other parts of western Europe. Throughout the period of the VISIGOTHS, Jews were a powerful minority. They controlled large estates, served in government, and held influential positions throughout the Visigothic kingdom. After the conversion of the Visigoths to Christianity in the late 500s, several Christian kings initiated anti-Jewish policies aimed at depriving Jewish landholders of their estates, merchants of their markets, officials of their offices, and all Jews of their religion and freedom. In 711, however, Muslims overthrew the Visigothic kingdom. Some support for the Muslims came from the Jewish community.

In Italy, the OSTROGOTHS treated the Jews well, and Jews could be found in nearly all levels of society. The rights of Jews and Jewish communities were affirmed by the Ostrogothic king THEODORIC, in the early 500s. After the Byzantine reconquest of Italy and the invasions of the LOMBARDS in the 500s, Jews and their communities continued to flourish.

* **clergy** priests, deacons, and other church officials qualified to perform church ceremonies

* **papacy** office of the pope and his administrators

In the old Roman province of Gaul (present-day France), the MEROVINGIANS allowed Jews to become very influential in society. Jews served as judges, they operated mints, and they had important roles in commerce. Despite occasional opposition from the clergy* and the papacy*, the Jews generally had royal support for their activities. Monarchs recognized the Jews as a people with their own law, and the Jews were the only non-Christians in the CAROLINGIAN Empire permitted to practice their religion. Under the Carolingians, Jews served occasionally as royal agents and diplomatic envoys. Jewish settlements and commercial activity were encouraged, both within the Carolingian Empire and on its frontiers with Muslim Spain. Jewish intellectual and religious life flourished. Great rabbinical schools were established in various locations, and Jewish scholars were welcomed at the imperial court.

Jews in Europe After 900

After 900, attitudes toward Jews began to change, and the presence of Jews in medieval European society often provoked conflict and violence. This occurred largely as a result of increased antagonism on the part of Christians and the Christian church. Other factors included economic conditions and the Jewish role in medieval society. Increased tensions eventually led to the expulsion of Jews from a number of countries. England expelled the Jews in 1290. The Jews of France were expelled in 1182, 1306, 1322 (or 1327), and again in 1394. Many German Jews were expelled from towns in the 1400s, and perhaps the largest Jewish population, the Jews of Spain, were expelled from that country in 1492.

* **canon** a religious law

Jews and Christians. From the first, the canons*, councils, and leaders of the Christian church insisted that the Jews were inferior and must be excluded from all public rule over Christians. Before 900, this attitude had only minimal effect on Jews and Jewish communities. Later, however, it became official policy of the church. In 1063, Pope Alexander II made the right of Jews to live among Christians dependent on their willingness to surrender political power and serve the interests of Christian society. Failure to observe these limitations always provoked anger. The status of Jews

Jewish communities were held together by their religious teachings and code of law. In some areas of the medieval world, Jewish communities thrived and became important cultural centers. In other areas, Jews lived with antagonism and discrimination. This illumination showing Jewish builders comes from a medieval Passover Haggadah, a collection of writings, prayer texts, and hymns for the Passover ritual.

in Christian society was further clarified in the 1100s. In about 1120, Pope Calixtus II granted Jews full protection of the law, but only in return for their willingness to yield at all times to the demands of the church. As a result of such actions, Jewish life became characterized by a fine balance between rights and restrictions.

For the remainder of the Middle Ages, the attitude of the Christian church toward the Jews continued to darken, and this affected the attitude of Christian secular society as well. At various times, the Jews were regarded as outsiders, and even minimal contact with Jewish things was seen as a corrupting influence and a threat to Christian society. Sometimes Jews were falsely accused of horrible crimes, such as killing Christian children so that Christian blood could be used in Jewish rituals. Such attitudes led to terrible persecution and violence against Jews and their communities. This became particularly severe in the 1300s when the BLACK DEATH led to an overall breakdown in medieval society. Ravaged by death, famine, and economic problems, many Europeans vented their frustration and rage on the Jews, some believing that the Jews had caused the plague* by poisoning the wells.

* **plague** disease that swept across the medieval world several times, including the Black Death in the mid-1300s

Several factors contributed to the Christian image of the Jews. First, moneylending and pawnbroking were common Jewish occupations during much of the Middle Ages, and these professions were very unpopular among Christians. Jewish moneylenders generally granted loans in exchange for payments of interest from the borrower. Many Christians considered this form of lending usury*, and they believed it to be morally wrong and a threat to Christian society. Medieval Jews also were involved in international commerce as merchants and bankers. Although Jews did not monopolize commerce, their involvement and wealth were sources of resentment on the part of many non-Jews. In the 1300s and 1400s, economic failures often were blamed on the Jews because of their connections to business, and this was a factor in attacks on them and expulsions.

* **usury** in the Middle Ages, the practice of lending money in return for any payment of interest

Jews in the Islamic World

At the time of the Islamic conquests, starting in the 600s, the great majority of the world's Jews lived in lands that would soon become Muslim.

From the very beginning, there was a strong connection between Islam and the Jews, and Jewish communities in Islamic countries were among the most important centers of Jewish culture in the medieval period.

Jews in Arabia. By the 600s, there were two major centers of Jewish settlement in Arabia—the provinces of Hejaz in the north and Himyar (modern-day Yemen) in the south. Jews were also among the founders of the city of Yathrib (later Medina). When Muhammad established Islam in Medina, he turned the Muslim community against the Jews, had many killed, and seized their property in order to equip the Muslim army. Jewish communities that came under Muslim domination in later years were spared this type of treatment. The Jews were granted treaties that guaranteed the safety of their families, households, and belongings. They were permitted to keep their own religion and laws, but they had to hand over any weapons and show submissiveness to Islam. Under caliph Umar I ibn al-Khattab, the Jews were expelled from Hejaz but were allowed to remain in Himyar.

Jews in Palestine and Syria. From the mid-100s to the mid-600s, Jews were banned from the Palestinian city of JERUSALEM by the Romans and the Byzantines. During that time, the city of Tiberias became one of the major Jewish centers in Palestine. It was the seat of the Sanhedrin, the council of elders that presided over Jewish communities all over the world. When the Muslims conquered Jerusalem in 638, they permitted Jews to settle there again, and a Jewish quarter was established in coexistence with Christian and Muslim quarters of the city.

Under the Muslims, the Jewish communities of Palestine and Syria generally flourished, and Jews had considerable influence at the royal court when the region was part of the FATIMID EMPIRE. During the period of the CRUSADES, Jewish communities throughout Palestine were destroyed by Christian crusaders, and many Jews fled to Egypt and Syria.

Jews in Iraq and Persia. The Jews of Iraq and Persia began the Middle Ages as a powerful and highly cultured people. Jews had lived in these areas since ancient times, and some regions were almost completely Jewish. The Babylonian Jews were engaged in all branches of economic life, and their scholars and institutions of learning were second in importance to those in Palestine.

Despite the generally favorable relationship between Jews and non-Jews in this region, there were tensions that occasionally led to periods of persecution in the mid-400s, early 500s, and late 500s. When the Muslims invaded the region in the 600s, the Jews offered minimal resistance to their conquerors and soon adapted to the new circumstances. They learned the Arabic language, migrated from villages to Islamic urban centers, and played an important role in the Islamic CALIPHATE. During the rule of the ABBASIDS, for example, Jewish merchants and bankers held central positions in the international trade of the caliphate and controlled much of its finances.

The Babylonian Jews left a glorious legacy. They developed the Talmud* and successfully challenged the Karaites, a Jewish sect that questioned rabbinic authority and split the Jewish community. They also developed a great Jewish literature and made the first serious forays into Jewish philosophy. The rich cultural heritage established by the Babylonian Jews

* **Talmud** large body of collected writings on Jewish law and tradition

Ritual Murder

In the Middle Ages, sometimes a parent or a friend of a child who died claimed that the child had been abducted and killed by Jews for ritual purposes. Most such accusations were exposed to be untrue, but sometimes they resulted in riots and organized massacres, in which many innocent Jews were tortured and killed. These accusations have remained a blemish on Christian-Jewish relations into the 20th century.

* **dynasty** succession of rulers from the same family or group

was felt by Jews throughout the Islamic world for centuries. Eventually, however, Babylonian Jewry was not able to maintain its dominance, and the center of Jewish learning and culture shifted elsewhere.

Jews in North Africa.   Throughout the Middle Ages, North Africa, a region known as the Maghrib, was the home of large, culturally and economically significant Jewish communities. Jewish settlement in this region went back to ancient times, although little is known of North African Jews until the mid-800s. At that time, Jews lived in most of the major towns of the Maghrib. The most important Jewish center was in the city of al-Qayrawan, the capital of a province at the crossroads of Mediterranean trade routes. By the late 900s, al-Qayrawan had become the major spiritual and intellectual Jewish center outside of Iraq.

Jewish economic prosperity in North Africa reached its height in the 900s and early 1000s under the rule of the Fatimids, who showed more tolerance to their non-Muslim subjects than most other Muslim dynasties*. This tolerance fostered the growth and development of Jewish communities throughout the region, attracting many Jewish immigrants from Palestine, Iraq, and other areas in the east as well. By the late 1000s, however, Jewish communities in most of North Africa began to enter a period of decline.

The period of the Almohad dynasty, from about 1140 to 1230, was a disastrous time for North African Jews. The Almohads forced many Jewish populations to accept Islam. Those that did not were massacred and their homes and settlements were destroyed. The Almohads also initiated a series of harsh discriminatory measures that limited the political and economic rights of Jewish converts and forced them to wear distinguishing clothing. Faced with such threats, many of the Jewish intellectual leadership fled to more tolerant areas in the east. After 1230, Jewish cultural life in North Africa was enriched by refugees fleeing from anti-Jewish disturbances in Spain, and Algeria became the spiritual center of North African Jewry.

Jews in Spain.   From the 900s to 1100s, Jews in Muslim Spain enjoyed a brilliant period of political, economic, and cultural achievement. Although this golden age of Spanish Jewry came to an end in the mid-1100s, its legacy continued wherever Spanish Jews found refuge in the late Middle Ages.

When Muslim armies invaded Spain in 711, they were welcomed by the Jews, who had suffered persecution at the hands of the Visigoths. For the next 200 years, Spanish Jews kept a low profile, although they increased in number and power. The blossoming of Spanish Jewry in the 900s was linked to the rise of Hisdai ibn Shaprut, a Jewish physician, diplomat, and statesman who became a leading member of the Muslim royal court. Almost singlehandedly, Hisdai made Spain a leading center of world Jewry by encouraging the development of the arts and sciences. He corresponded extensively with foreign Jewish leaders, and he was largely responsible for making Spanish Jewry more independent of the Jewish academies of learning in the eastern Islamic world.

The 11th century was the high point of Spanish Jewish culture. At that time, Jews held prominent positions in Islamic government. Perhaps the most notable Jewish courtier* of the time was Samuel ha-Nagid, who served as minister of state to the caliph and military commander of forces in the

* **courtier** person in attendance at a royal court

province of GRANADA from 1030 to 1056. In addition to his political and military duties, he was head of the Jewish community, an outstanding religious scholar, a patron of the arts, and one of the four greatest masters of medieval Hebrew poetry.

When Spain was conquered about 1090 by the Almoravids, a Muslim dynasty from North Africa, Spanish Jewry declined. The Almoravids were more intense in their religious zeal, and relations between Muslims and Jews became strained. At the same time, the Christian reconquest of Spain was in full swing in the north, and this pressure added to the tensions between Jews and Muslims. As the Jews came under increasing pressure, many fled. Some made their way into Christian Europe, while others fled to North Africa.

Between 1146 and 1172, Muslim Spain was ruled by the Almohads, who were even less tolerant of the Jews than the Almoravids. As they had done in North Africa, the Almohads forced Jews to convert to Islam or face persecution and death. Faced with this threat, still more Jews fled Spain to find refuge in Christian Europe or in the eastern parts of the Islamic world. After the Almohad terror ended, some Spanish Jews resettled in the kingdom of Granada. A small Jewish community remained there until 1492, when Granada fell to the Christians and all Jews were expelled from Spain. The expulsion of the Jews from Spain ended more than one thousand years of continuous Jewish civilization in that country, and the Jews who left were dispersed throughout the medieval world. (*See also* **Anti-Semitism; Banking; Christianity; Conversos; Córdoba; Family; Hebrew Literature; Inquisition; Islam, Political Organization of; Islam, Religion of; Jews, Expulsion of; Judaism; Law; Maimonides, Moses; Spain, Muslim Kingdoms of; Usury.**)

Jews, Expulsion of

* **clergy** priests, deacons, and other church officials qualified to perform church ceremonies

* **banish** to force a person to leave the country

During the Middle Ages, Jews throughout Europe lived in danger of persecution or expulsion. They were generally despised by Christians because of their faith and envied by others because of their learning and prosperity. As an oppressed minority, they were convenient scapegoats for groups opposed to them for religious or other reasons, and they were prime targets for rulers looking for a handy source of funds. Monarchs discovered that, with help from the Christian clergy*, they could arouse hatred against the Jews and banish* them and then seize Jewish property.

The major expulsions of Jews took place in the late medieval period, when they were banished from cities, small principalities, and states. The first major expulsion took place in France in 1182 when King PHILIP II AUGUSTUS robbed the Jewish community to gain funds for defense. Philip (only 15 years old at the time) confiscated Jewish property and forgave all debts owed to Jews, provided that the debtors paid part of what they owed to him. The expulsion made Philip very popular and solved his financial problems, but it also deprived France of some of its ablest merchant leaders. In 1198, a more mature Philip II Augustus reversed his policy and allowed the Jews to return.

The next major expulsion of the Jews occurred in England. The Jews had entered England following the invasion of the NORMANS in 1066. For many years, they prospered as merchants and bankers, despite being heavily taxed and being unfairly taken advantage of by nobles. By the late 1200s, however, the economic health of the Jewish community had declined because of continued exploitation. In a last effort to gain profit from them, King EDWARD I expelled the Jews in 1290. The Jewish expulsion from England lasted until the 1600s.

In 1306, the Jews were expelled once again from France because the king needed money. King PHILIP IV arrested the Jews, confiscated their goods and business records, and then banished them from the country. The king added to his royal treasury by selling off Jewish property and collecting debts owed to the Jews. In 1315, King Louis X readmitted the Jews, in part to collect debts still owed to them. Expelled from France again in 1322, the Jews were readmitted in 1359, only to be expelled once more in 1394.

The most extensive, devastating, and unanticipated expulsions of Jews occurred in Spain and Portugal in the late 1400s. The Jews in these countries were more powerful, wealthier, and more integrated into society than Jews in other parts of Europe. This was due largely to a more tolerant attitude toward them by the Muslims, who occupied the region in the early Middle Ages. As Christians reconquered the region, however, the Jews began to suffer religious persecution and discrimination. Many converted to Christianity to escape persecution. By the late 1400s, it was increasingly difficult to assimilate these converts into Spanish society. The result was an increased demand for expulsion. In 1492, King Ferdinand and Queen Isabella of Spain expelled the Jews from their country, and King Emanuel I of Portugal did the same in 1497 as a result of his marriage settlement to the daughter of Ferdinand and Isabella. The expulsion from Spain was one of the harshest episodes of medieval religious persecution. The expulsion was combined with the Spanish Inquisition, which was aimed at discovering and punishing converted Jews who were thought to be insincere in their conversion to Christianity. (*See also* **Inquisition; Jewish Communities.**)

Jihad

* **martyr** person who suffers and dies rather than renounce a religious faith

Jihad refers to an armed struggle or "holy war" of Muslims against non-Muslims. Wars between Muslims generally are not considered jihad, although some Muslims believe that jihad also applies to wars against Muslims who have abandoned their religion. According to the Qur'an, jihad is an important duty of Muslims, and those killed in jihad are considered martyrs* who may enter paradise immediately.

According to Muslim belief, the earth is divided into an "abode of Islam" and an "abode of war." Peace can never exist between these two territories, and the abode of war must be brought under the rule of Islam by continuous jihad. The aim of jihad is the universal domination of Islam, rather than conversion. Other religious groups that had holy Scriptures, like Jews and Christians, could become protected peoples and continue to practice their religion as long as they accepted the political domination of Islam and paid a special tax. Only pagans had to convert.

Jihad is generally considered a communal duty rather than an individual one. If enough Muslims carry out the duty, others can be excused from it. However, when nonbelievers take the offensive and threaten Muslim territory, jihad then becomes the duty of all Muslims.

Some Muslims believe that a jihad can be led only by a caliph, the political and religious leader, except for defense against invaders. Valuables seized from the enemy in jihad are divided among participants and the caliph, who receives one-fifth. Land seized during jihad is considered communal property, to be administered by the caliph for the benefit of all Muslims. Enemies captured in jihad become slaves, who also are distributed among the participants. The caliph, however, may decide to exchange male prisoners for Muslim prisoners of war, hold prisoners for ransom, or execute them. Nonbelievers who convert to Islam before capture are allowed to go free and keep their property. Islamic law also provides rules concerning the conduct of jihad, including the use of certain weapons and equipment, the duties of leaders and warriors, the destruction of property, and negotiations of a truce. (*See also* **Law; Warfare.**)

Joan of Arc, St.

ca. 1412–1431
French national heroine

Joan of Arc was a poor, uneducated peasant girl who successfully led French troops during the later part of the Hundred Years War. She became a French national heroine and a saint. This earliest known rendering of Joan is sketched in the margin of the Paris Parlement's report on the relief of Orleans.

Joan of Arc (French *Jeanne d'Arc*) was born to a peasant family at Domrémy in northern France. She was deeply religious but had no formal schooling. She grew up during the HUNDRED YEARS WAR (1337–1453), when the English occupied part of France.

Henry VI of England had a claim to the French throne through the marriage of his parents, Henry V and Catherine of Valois. He also had an alliance with the House of Burgundy, a powerful political force in eastern France. The dauphin* Charles, son of the French king Charles VI who had died in 1422, also claimed the throne. By 1429, when Charles had still not been crowned, the French people began to question whether he should be king.

When Joan was about 13, she began hearing the voices of Sts. Michael, Catherine, and Margaret. She claimed that she had been given a divine mission to drive the English from France. In February 1429, she succeeded in obtaining an audience with the dauphin and convinced him that she could lead French troops in battle and secure his coronation. Charles ordered an official inquiry into Joan's claims. When she received the approval of the church, Charles appointed her to command a force at Orleans, a city under British siege*.

Dressed in armor, Joan led French reinforcement troops and supplies into the besieged city on April 29. The French attacked, and by May 8 the English abandoned the siege. Because it was a Sunday, the pious Joan forbade the army from pursuing the retreating English. A later campaign brought Charles to Rheims for his coronation on July 17. This was the high point in Joan's career.

When Charles arranged a truce with Burgundy and disbanded the army, Joan's personal influence began to diminish. During renewed fighting against the Burgundians at Compiègne in May 1430, she was captured. Charles, believing Joan had outlasted her usefulness, failed to ransom her. Joan's male dress and unconventional behavior, her claims to divine guidance, and her astounding success raised suspicions of heresy* and sorcery. In return for a large sum of money, her Burgundian captors turned her over to the Inquisition. A court of the Inquisition was assembled in Rouen in early 1431.

* **dauphin** eldest son of the king of France

* **siege** long and persistent effort to force a surrender by surrounding a fortress with armed troops, cutting it off from aid

* **heresy** belief that is contrary to church doctrine

* **annul** to cancel

At the trial, Joan conducted a heroic defense. She was eloquent under examination and steadfast when threatened with torture. Only when weakened by illness and faced with death did she submit to the pressure of the church's inquisitors. She received a sentence of life imprisonment. However, when she later resumed wearing male clothing, she was considered defiant and was condemned to be burned at the stake. Forceful and courageous even at her execution, Joan insisted on her innocence.

Joan remained a controversial figure in the years following her death. Charles ordered an investigation of her trial and, in 1456, Pope Calixtus III annulled* her sentence. The sheer force of her personality inspired people during her lifetime and centuries after her death. In 1920, Joan of Arc was made a saint, and she has remained a spiritual force in French history. (*See also* **Charles VII of France; France; Inquisition.**)

John, King of England

1167–1216
English king and signer of Magna Carta

King John of England was the fifth and youngest son of King HENRY II and his queen, ELEANOR OF AQUITAINE. He succeeded his brother RICHARD I THE LIONHEARTED in 1199. Although an intelligent and able administrator, John was highly eccentric and unstable. During his reign, he involved England in frequent wars with France and quarreled bitterly with Pope INNOCENT III. Shortly before his death, his barons revolted and forced him to approve Magna Carta, one of the great documents of English constitutional history.

During the 1100s and the 1200s, English kings claimed and ruled parts of France. With the support of his English and French barons and his

King John was the youngest of the five sons of Henry II and Eleanor of Aquitaine. His erratic rule was marked by bitter quarrels with the pope and with his barons. In 1215, the barons forced him to accept Magna Carta, which limited royal power and showed that the king was not above the law. This illumination from the 1200s shows King John accompanied by his hunting dogs.

 See map in England (vol. 2).

mother, John concluded a treaty with PHILIP II AUGUSTUS of France in 1200 in which he obtained recognition of all his French territories. However, his divorce from Isabella of Gloucester and his marriage to the French noblewoman Isabella of Angoulême—a move that increased his influence in southwestern France—caused a split with Philip and led eventually to war. After four years of conflict, John had lost most of his French possessions except for Aquitaine.

While he was involved in wars in France, John had a bitter dispute with Pope Innocent III. The pope had nominated Stephen LANGTON as a compromise candidate to be archbishop of Canterbury. John refused to accept Langton, but the pope installed him anyway and placed England under an interdict*. In retaliation, John confiscated the possessions of clergy who supported the interdict. Innocent III excommunicated* John in 1209, and in 1213 he gave his blessing to the French to invade England. Faced with this threat, John agreed to a humiliating settlement in which he surrendered England to the pope and received it back as a fief*.

In 1214, John attempted to recover his French possessions by invading southwestern France. He was soundly defeated by the French, who thereby gained political dominance in western Europe for the next century. By now, many of John's English barons had turned against him, and, in 1215, John was forced to approve Magna Carta, which established the principle that the king is not above the law. John had no intention of keeping the agreement, and civil war soon broke out. The king, however, was exhausted and ill, and he died in 1216. With his death and the succession of his nine-year-old son as HENRY III, the civil war ended. (*See also* **England; Magna Carta.**)

* **interdict** papal decree that forbids an entire district from participation in the sacraments and from Christian burial

* **excommunicate** to exclude from the rites of the church

* **fief** under feudalism, property of value (usually land) that a person held under obligations of loyalty to an overlord

John of Gaunt

1340–1399
English nobleman and son of King Edward III

John of Gaunt was the fourth son of King EDWARD III OF ENGLAND. During the 1370s, he played a major role in the affairs of England and, for a short time, effectively ruled the country.

In 1373, during the Hundred Years War, John led an expedition against the French from Calais to Bordeaux. It was a military failure. He returned to England in 1375 and assumed increasing control of the government from his aging father and his ailing brother EDWARD THE BLACK PRINCE. John supported the protests of religious reformer John WYCLIF against domination of the clergy and protected Wyclif from prosecution by the pope. In 1376, Parliament removed John's supporters from power, but he regained control by the time of Edward III's death in 1377.

Edward III was succeeded by his ten-year-old grandson, RICHARD II. In the early years of Richard's reign, John was suspected of sinister ambitions and was very unpopular. His residence in London, the Savoy, was the target of attacks during the Peasants' Revolt of 1381. Through his marriage to Constance, the heiress of Pedro I of Castile and León, John claimed a right to the Spanish throne. A two-year expedition against Castile (from 1386 to 1388) was a failure, and John eventually renounced his claim to that throne.

In 1396, he married his mistress, Katherine Swynford. The marriage made John the brother-in-law of the great English poet Geoffrey CHAUCER, whom he had long supported. John returned to England in 1389, where his son Henry Bolingbroke had joined an attack on Richard II's supporters. Richard II banished* Bolingbroke in 1398. Bolingbroke returned from exile the following year, shortly after John's death, to seize the crown from Richard II and to become Henry IV. (*See also* **Hundred Years War; Peasants' Rebellions and Uprisings.**)

* **banish** to force a person to leave the country

John Scottus Eriugena

died ca. 877
Scholar and teacher

* **ecclesiastical** pertaining to a church

John Scottus Eriugena was an Irishman who moved to France in the 800s to write and teach at the palace of Charles the Bald. (The word *scottus* was used before the 1300s to refer to anyone who came from Ireland.) John Scottus is considered one of the great philosophers of the western European tradition.

Many of John's works appear to have been written in the ecclesiastical* province of Rheims, in northern France. He commented on the arts, wrote poetry, and engaged in theological controversy. Among his earliest and most important writings were translations of significant works of Greek into Latin. John's major work, *On the Division of Nature,* was one of the most original works of the early Middle Ages. Arranged as a dialogue between a master and his student, *On the Division of Nature* addresses several themes central to Christian thought, including the Creation and the relation of God to the created world.

Judaism

* **rabbi** teacher of Jewish law and religion and spiritual leader of a Jewish congregation

* **Talmud** collection of Jewish law and tradition consisting of the Mishnah (laws and teachings) and the Gemara (analysis and interpretation of the Mishnah)

* **synagogue** building of worship for Jews

* **Torah** sacred wisdom of the Jewish faith, especially the first five books of the Bible

Judaism is the religion, thought, and way of life of the Jewish people. It includes beliefs about God, the universe, and the history and destiny of the Jewish people. It also includes a code of behavior, known as halakhah, that governs all aspects of Jewish life. During the Middle Ages, the practice, institutions, and beliefs of Judaism developed distinctive forms that have continued to influence it to the present day.

Medieval Judaism and Its Spread.   By about the year 500, the ancient religion of the Hebrews had developed into a faith known as Rabbinic Judaism. This faith, as taught by the rabbis*, had two fundamental beliefs: faith in one God and the belief that the Jews were a chosen people. The rabbis composed a large body of religious thought and law based on the Hebrew Bible and the teachings of the prophets. These laws and teachings were collected into a body of work known as the Talmud*. Rabbinic Judaism prescribed a way of life in which everything was designed to show the presence of God and to reflect belief in him. The synagogue*, a minor institution in earlier times, became the focus of Jewish life. The central activities of Jewish religious life came to be prayer and the study of the law, known as the Torah*.

From the 200s to the 1000s, Babylonia was the creative center of Judaism and the largest Jewish community in the world. The Talmud was taught and interpreted there in great academies called yeshivas. The head of an academy was known as a gaon. In the late 700s, the geonim (plural of *gaon*) of Babylonia emerged as the leading religious authorities of Judaism. Jews throughout the world sent them questions about Jewish law, and their answers were accepted by Jews everywhere.

Jewish communities enjoyed a high degree of literacy. It was considered a father's duty to instruct his children in the basic requirements of Judaism. This applied to Jewish children from all economic and social classes. The child in this illumination is being taught by a private tutor. Education also took place in community-sponsored schools.

See color plate 4, vol. 1.

* **Aristotelianism**   philosophy based on the work of the ancient Greek philosopher Aristotle

* **mystical**   referring to the belief that divine truths or direct knowledge of God can be experienced through meditation and contemplation as much as through logical thought

* **martyr**   person who suffers and dies rather than renounce a religious faith

* **cabalist**   follower of a system of religious belief based on mystical interpretations of the Bible

* **mystic**   person who experiences divine truths through faith, spiritual insight, and intuition

* **codification**   systematic arrangement of laws

The Babylonian rabbinic tradition was seriously challenged in the late 700s by a sect known as the Karaites. The Karaites preached that the only real source of Jewish law was the written law of the Bible, not the oral law of the Talmud as taught by the rabbis. The Karaite movement failed (even though Karaism survived), but the challenge it posed stimulated certain developments within Rabbinic Judaism. Rabbinic Jews began to pay closer attention to the language of the Bible, and they looked both to Muslim grammar and to the ancient Greek philosophers as a way to support religious and philosophical arguments.

Beginning in the 1000s, the Babylonian academies declined. This led to a decentralization of the Jewish world, as new yeshivas were established in North Africa, Spain, Italy, France, and Germany. One of the earliest centers outside of Babylonia was in the city of al-Qayrawan in Tunisia. A yeshiva was founded there in the late 900s. By the 1000s, France and Germany had established centers of Talmudic study, the most famous of which is associated with Rabbi Solomon ben Isaac (RASHI).

Medieval Jewish Philosophy.   The revival of Greek science and philosophy that swept the Islamic world between 850 and 1200 had a profound influence on Judaism. Greek science and philosophy were based on rationalism, the idea that reason is the foundation of all knowledge and the supreme authority in matters of belief and conduct. Many Jews were troubled by this concept, since it seemed to contradict the idea that guidelines for conduct and belief were revealed by God. Jewish thinkers attempted to harmonize reason and faith and to offer rational, philosophical explanations of Judaism. Saadiah Gaon (882–942) was the first rabbinic authority to use rational arguments to explain Jewish truths, including the existence of God. In doing so, he laid the foundations for a tradition of Jewish philosophy that persisted throughout the Middle Ages.

The greatest Jewish philosopher of the Middle Ages was Moses MAIMONIDES. An exponent of Aristotelianism*, Maimonides explained how many concepts in the Bible could be understood in rational terms. His ideas had a profound influence on medieval Jewish philosophy, but they also created a storm of controversy between the forces of rationalism and antirationalism within the Jewish community. Judah Halevi (ca. 1075–1141), a Spanish Hebrew poet, argued that philosophy was limited to the physical realm and could not be used to prove religious matters.

Medieval Jewish Mysticism.   Several different Jewish mystical* theories developed during the later Middle Ages. Each aimed at guiding people to a more intimate relationship with God.

One of the earliest and most important mystical schools flourished in Germany in the 1100s and the 1200s. Its followers were known as Hasidei Ashkenaz. The Hasidei Ashkenaz believed that God was everywhere all the time. They emphasized love of God rather than fear of God. The ultimate demonstration of this love was martyrdom. Many of the Jewish martyrs* who were massacred during the CRUSADES were from this group. Their piety, ethics, and religious practices had a lasting effect on the Jewish communities of Europe.

The school of Jewish mysticism known as CABALA emerged in southern France in the 1100s. Cabalists* recognized the words of the Bible as the

Origins of the Sabbath Candles

One of the disputes between the Karaites and the rabbis in the late 700s concerned the burning of a light in Jewish homes on the Sabbath. The Karaites interpreted the biblical verse "And a fire shall not burn in your home" literally and spent the Sabbath in darkness. The rabbis interpreted the verse to mean that it was forbidden to start a fire on the Sabbath, but it was permissible to allow one to continue burning from the day before. Thus, lighting candles at sunset on Friday and allowing them to burn into the Sabbath became a way of showing allegiance to the rabbis, a tradition that continues today.

key to divine truth, but they held that these words could not be understood through logical thinking. They regarded these words as symbols that only mystics* could completely understand. The most important cabalistic work was the *Sefer ha-Zohar (Book of Splendor).* Written in Spain between 1280 and 1286, it became a classic Jewish text. Cabala continued to develop and spread into modern times, and it has greatly influenced the prayer, customs, and ethics of later Judaism.

Medieval Jewish Law.   One of the most important developments in medieval Judaism was the codification* of Jewish law. The first attempt at codifying the law occurred in the 700s with a work known as the *Halakhot Pesukot (Judicially Determined Laws).* The process culminated in Moses Maimonides' systematic, comprehensive code called the *Mishneh Torah (Summary of the Torah).* This work classified Jewish law by subject matter and incorporated all Jewish legal literature that had been produced up to that time. Written in clear, concise Hebrew—a language available to all Jews, and not only to legal scholars—it influenced all later codes. A new code, the *Sefer ha-Turim (Book of Columns),* was produced in Spain in the 1300s. It arranged the law into four major categories. This arrangement was later adopted in the 1500s in a work known as the *Shulhan Arukh (Prepared Table),* which came to be recognized as the single most authoritative legal code of the Jewish world. (*See also* **Bible; Cabala; Hebrew Literature; Jewish Communities.**)

Julian of Norwich
1342–ca. 1416
Author and mystic

Julian of Norwich (England) was one of the greatest women of the Middle Ages. Although her book, *Revelations of Divine Love,* did not receive much attention at the time, it became famous in the 19th century. It is regarded today as one of the most important spiritual works of the medieval period.

The major turning point in Julian's life came on May 8, 1373, when at the age of 30 she lay dying, surrounded by her mother and several friends. As the local priest held a crucifix for her to look at during her final moments, she experienced visions of the crucified Christ. In all, she saw 16 visions, and she was miraculously cured.

Shortly afterwards, Julian dictated descriptions of her visions, but her work did not attract a large audience. However, 20 years later, she dictated another longer account, in which she included her reflections on the meaning of her experience. Julian claimed to be uneducated, but the second version of *Revelations* shows how well she understood church teachings and the Bible. In simple and moving language, she told of her sorrow for sin and her joyful gratitude for God's love.

Julian belonged to the tradition of anchorites, persons (most often women) who lived shut away from society. In England, they lived in small rooms attached to a parish church. On the Continent, they more frequently were found in clusters of cells under the protection of monasteries. They shunned both lay society and the religious life of the regular clergy. Anchorites were similar to HERMITS except that hermits could move from place to place. (*See also* **Birgitta, St.; Catherine of Siena, St.; Kempe, Margery; Mysticism; Women, Role of.**)

Jury

See *Trials*.

Justiciar

* **archbishop** head bishop in a region or
nation

Justiciar was the name given to each of the royal advisers who represented the NORMAN kings of England and ruled on their behalf when the kings were in Normandy. Following their conquest of England, the Norman kings spent most of their time in France managing the affairs of state there and fighting the kings of France.

Justiciars served as the kings' representatives in England for almost two centuries. Each one governed in a king's name during his absence. The first such representative was LANFRANC OF BEC, archbishop* of Canterbury from 1070 to 1089, who served WILLIAM I THE CONQUEROR. The first royal representative to be called a justiciar was ROGER OF SALISBURY, who represented King HENRY I in the early 1100s. Roger's bold, creative actions in the areas of finance, government reform, and law made him the most important man in England after the king.

The office of justiciar reached the peak of its prestige during the reigns of HENRY II and HENRY III, when a series of extremely able justiciars served the English crown. This period, beginning in the mid-1100s and lasting about a century, has been called "the age of the justiciars." The greatest justiciar was probably Hubert WALTER, an extremely talented administrator whom RICHARD I THE LIONHEARTED also made bishop of Salisbury.

The office of justiciar disappeared in the mid-1200s after the English kings lost control of Normandy. When they took up permanent residence in England, the justiciar was no longer needed. (*See also* **Angevins; England; France.**)

Justinian I

ca. 482–565
Roman emperor

* **imperial** pertaining to an empire or
emperor

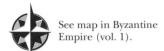 See map in Byzantine
Empire (vol. 1).

*J*ustinian I was born at Tauresium on the Balkan peninsula to a Latin-speaking peasant family. When Justinian was only a boy, his uncle Justin brought him to CONSTANTINOPLE. There he received a thorough education and served as an officer in the imperial* guard.

In 518, Justinian's uncle became Emperor Justin I. Justinian became the emperor's trusted assistant and, in the last years of Justin's reign, the power behind the throne. When Justin died in 527, Justinian became emperor.

Justinian felt strongly about the Roman traditions of imperial power and authority. He sought to restore Roman rule in Italy, Gaul, Spain, and Africa, where Germanic kingdoms had been established. He launched military campaigns in Africa, Italy, and Spain, and he engaged in conflicts with the Persians, Huns, and Goths. In many of these battles, Justinian's forces were led by his well-known and capable general, Belisarios.

During Justinian's reign, the Christian world was divided by disputes over religious doctrine. Justinian attempted to bring together the different groups. However, the Latin church of the West did not welcome the emperor's interference in religious affairs, and, in general, his efforts failed. Furthermore, the long years of war created economic difficulties. Opposition to the emperor grew and erupted in the Nika Revolt of 532, which nearly cost Justinian his throne.

This famous mosaic of Emperor Justinian I is in the church of San Vitale in Ravenna, Italy. The emperor and three of his courtiers are wearing the paludamentum, a long cape pinned at the neck or right shoulder. Originally worn by the upper ranks of the Roman army, usually generals, it was later adopted by rulers, aristocrats, and some government officials. Justinian is shown in a procession led by two deacons and the archbishop of Ravenna. He carries a golden bowl, which he has brought as an offering to San Vitale.

* **jurist** legal expert; learned writer of law

Justinian is perhaps best known for codifying, or systematizing, Roman law. Justinian's Code of Civil Law, a collection of imperial decrees, was completed in 529. This was followed by the *Digest* (a collection of opinions of Roman jurists*), the *Institutes* (a textbook for students), and the *Novels* (a series of new laws), all of which were prepared under the inspiration and direction of the lawyer Tribonian. These legal works had the effect of eliminating outdated laws and adapting remaining laws to the needs of Justinian's day. They became the basis for the legal systems that developed in western Europe.

Justinian sponsored many public works, including fortifications, water supply systems, and the restoration and construction of cities and churches. One of the most notable projects completed during his administration was the construction of the church of HAGIA SOPHIA at Constantinople. When Justinian died, his nephew, Justin II, became emperor. (*See also* **Byzantine Empire; Law; Theodora I, Empress; Warfare.**)

Kells, Book of

* **Gospels** accounts of the life and teachings of Jesus as told in the first four books of the New Testament

* **evangelists** writers of the Gospels—Matthew, Mark, Luke, and John

See color plate 8, vol. 2.

The Book of Kells is a beautifully illustrated book of the Gospels*, believed to be from the late eighth or early ninth century. Although the origin of the book is uncertain, it was kept in the monastery of Kells in IRELAND from about 1006 until the 1600s. Then it was sent to DUBLIN, where it is now housed in Trinity College.

Among the many decorations of human figures and fantastic animals scattered throughout the text and opening pages are four full-page miniatures of the Virgin and Child, the arrest of Christ, the temptation of Christ, and a figure (either Christ or one of the evangelists*) in the company of angels.

Striking in its precise detail and elaborate decoration, the Book of Kells is considered a masterpiece of medieval art. (*See also* **Books, Manuscript.**)

Kempe, Margery

ca. 1373–after 1438
English mystic

Margery Kempe was an English mystic whose remarkable memoir, discovered in 1934, is considered the first autobiography written in English.

After Kempe, the mother of 14 children, became seriously ill, she had a religious experience that convinced her to live a more spiritual life. When she persisted in grieving over the sufferings of Christ, she was ridiculed by her neighbors and her family, except by her husband. Local church authorities sent her to prison and investigated her for HERESY but found her innocent.

At first, *The Book of Margery Kempe* was considered simply a bizarre account of her pilgrimages to JERUSALEM, ROME, and SANTIAGO DE COMPOSTELA in Spain. However, today her story is appreciated as an intimate and revealing look at a misunderstood woman who was sincerely committed to the search for spiritual truth. (*See also* **Birgitta, St.; Julian of Norwich; Mysticism; Women, Role of.**)

Khwarizmi, al-

ca. 780–ca. 850
Mathematician
and astronomer

* **algebra** branch of mathematics in which letters representing unknown numbers are combined according to the rules of arithmetic

* **algorithm** set procedure for solving a mathematical problem

Muhammad ibn Musa al-Khwarizmi is an important figure in the history of mathematics. He provided a link between the early modern world and the mathematics of the ancient Babylonians and Hindus. Through the work of al-Khwarizmi, medieval Europe learned to perform written arithmetic and to use the zero.

Al-Khwarizmi lived in Baghdad during the first great flowering of Islamic science. He wrote two important books about mathematics. His treatise on *Calculation with the Hindu Numerals* describes how to do arithmetic using symbols for the numbers 1 through 9 and using a zero for creating the numbers 10, 20, and so forth.

A second book, the *Compendious Book on Calculation by Completion and Balancing*, tells how to solve problems that include an unknown element. In the Arabic title, the word for completion was *al-jabr*. The book's first part was translated into Latin about 300 years after al-Khwarizmi wrote it. The translator shortened the title to the *Book of Algebra*, thus introducing the term *algebra** that is still used for certain mathematical operations. The problems in the book reduce to linear and quadratic equations, but al-Khwarizmi did not use a special symbolism, as we do today. Rather, he set out his problems in words, using a special technical vocabulary. The mathematical term *algorithm** is derived from his name.

European scholars had little interest in mathematics when al-Khwarizmi wrote his books, and they did not learn of his methods for centuries. The decimal system reached European schools in the early 1200s, but algebra was not introduced to the classroom until the late 1400s, when German schools began to teach it. (*See also* **Mathematics.**)

Kievan Rus

Kievan Rus covered a vast territory from the Black Sea in the south to the Baltic Sea in the north and from the Polish and Hungarian borders in the west to the Volga River in the east. The area is now part of present-day Ukraine, Russia, and Belarus. The state, the first to emerge among the East Slavic tribes, was named for the city of Kiev, situated on the west bank of the Dnieper River. Here, grand princes lived from the late 800s to the early 1100s. Although the Kievan state was eventually

The Kievan state was multinational from its earliest years. In the late ninth century, East Slavic and Finnish tribes of northern Russia were ruled by Rurik, a Viking, and his descendants. After establishing themselves in Novgorod in northern Russia, Rurik's descendants moved southward, making Kiev their new capital. By the 11th century, the Kievan state had expanded to include Poles, Jews, Greeks, Turks, and Slavs.

* **principality** region that is ruled by a prince

divided into smaller competing principalities*, it continued to exist until the conquest of Russia by the MONGOLS in the late 1230s.

Origins and Early History.   Although the early history of the East SLAVS is uncertain, it is believed that about the year 500 some of them migrated from the lower Danube River area north and east into the region west of the Dnieper River. Later, groups of East Slavs migrated north into the forest regions and colonized parts of northern Russia. The Slavs who moved into northern Russia displaced, killed, or assimilated the native Baltic and Finnish tribes who lived there.

The Slavs probably farmed the land using some form of the slash-and-burn technique that required cutting trees, burning fields, and then moving on after the crops (mostly grains) were harvested. This method of agriculture gave the soil time to recover, but it prevented people from establishing permanent settlements.

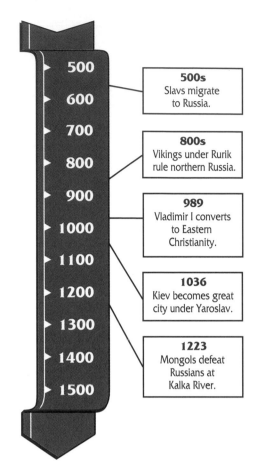

500	
600	**500s** Slavs migrate to Russia.
700	
800	**800s** Vikings under Rurik rule northern Russia.
900	
1000	**989** Vladimir I converts to Eastern Christianity.
1100	
1200	**1036** Kiev becomes great city under Yaroslav.
1300	
1400	**1223** Mongols defeat Russians at Kalka River.
1500	

* **tribute** payment made to a dominant foreign power to stop it from invading

Russian CHRONICLES from the 1000s record that in about 860 the East Slavic and Finnish tribes of northern Russia invited a VIKING leader named RURIK to rule them. Although the nature of this invitation is disputed, it appears true that Rurik and his followers established themselves as rulers of NOVGOROD and other Slavic areas of northern Russia in the late 800s. It is also true that Rurik's descendants became the grand princes of Kievan Rus.

The years following Rurik's death in 879 were a time of conquest and expansion. Rurik's successor, Oleg, left Novgorod and invaded Kiev, where he defeated the local rulers. After Oleg made Kiev his capital in 882, he conquered the local Slavs and forced them to pay tribute* to him. By 980, almost all the East Slavic tribes were under Kievan control.

Although East Slavs were the largest ethnic group in Kievan Rus, the Kievan state was multinational. Besides Slavs, Balts, and Finns, the continued expansion of Kievan Rus brought other peoples under its control, including Scandinavians, Poles, Jews, Greeks, Turks, Slavs from the south, and other people from the Near East. As the Kievan state expanded, the grand princes sought to establish trade ties with the BYZANTINE EMPIRE. To force Byzantium to grant them favorable trading conditions, they attacked Constantinople in 907 and again in 941–944. The Byzantine defeat of the grand prince Svyatoslav I in 971 put an end to the Kievan threat. On Svyatoslav's way back to Kiev, he was captured and killed, and his skull was made into a drinking cup.

Height of Power.   After Svyatoslav's death, a struggle over succession erupted among his sons. Vladimir I eventually emerged victorious in 980. Looking for a religion that would make Kievan Rus a player on the international scene, Vladimir considered Islam, Judaism, Roman Christianity, and Byzantine Christianity. He received representatives from each group in Kiev and sent his own representatives to further investigate these faiths.

In 988, Vladimir sent Rus soldiers to help the Byzantine emperor BASIL II in exchange for the hand of the emperor's sister, Anna, in marriage. When Basil did not keep his part of the bargain, Vladimir captured a Byzantine city. While there, he converted to Byzantine Christianity and married Anna. When he returned to Kiev, he set out to convert his subjects to his new religion, by force when necessary. In addition to the Christianization of the Russian people—one of the most enduring legacies of Kievan Rus—Byzantine ideas about politics, education, and the arts became part of the Kievan state.

Vladimir's death was followed by a fierce war of succession among his sons. The Kievan state was unified when YAROSLAV THE WISE became the undisputed grand prince in 1036. His 18-year reign was one of the greatest periods in Kievan Rus history. Learning and education flourished, Russian troops defeated their enemies, the famous cathedrals of St. Sophia were built in Kiev and Novgorod, and Russia's first law code, the *Russkaya Pravda,* was instituted. Under Yaroslav, Kiev became one of the great cities of Europe.

Political Decline.   The death of Yaroslav in 1054 marked the beginning of a long period of decline for the grand princes of Kievan Rus. Although Yaroslav had drawn up a plan for dividing power among his sons, another battle for succession erupted shortly after he died. Members of the princely family, as independent rulers in their own territories, fought against one another. Rus grand princes tried to restore order and reassert their authority at several peace conferences, but they were unsuccessful.

In the mid-1000s, invaders from the steppe* raided Kievan lands regularly and generally defeated the Rus troops sent to stop them. In the 1100s, the rise of the principalities of Suzdal and of Novgorod—which was developing strong trade with German merchants—accelerated the decline of Kiev.

Vladimir II Monomakh, called the last great grand prince of Kiev, and his son Mstislav were able to check the raids and the feuding for awhile. Yet the breakdown of Kievan Rus continued. By the 1200s, the once unified and powerful Kievan state was vulnerable and unprepared for the ferocious new group of horsemen who came riding across the steppe from Asia. The Mongol defeat of the Russian princes at the Battle of the Kalka River in 1223 was a warning of what was to come. The Russian principalities had been able to keep Hungarian, Polish, German, and other foreign forces from conquering Russian lands. However, they were no match for the mighty Mongol warriors when those warriors returned 13 years later in much greater force. The Mongol invasion (1236–1240) put a swift and dramatic end to Kievan Rus and ushered in a new chapter in Russian history. (*See also* **Christianity; Muscovy, Rise of; Scandinavia; Trade.**)

* **steppe** vast treeless plain of southeastern Europe and Asia

King's Evil

See *Royal Touch.*

Kingship, Theories of

Kingship, or monarchy, emerged as the most common form of government in medieval Europe, and with it came controversy and debate. Many of our modern ideas about government, natural law, political authority, and the nature and purpose of the state have their origins in medieval political theories about kingship.

"Mirrors of Princes."   Theories of kingship in the early Middle Ages emphasized the importance of a king's moral qualities. The principal writers of the day were monks, who were brought up on the writings of Pope GREGORY I. Their writings stated that a good king should possess wisdom, justice, and patience. In treatises known as "mirrors of princes," they proposed that the kings from the Old Testament, such as Solomon and David, were examples to be followed. ALCUIN OF YORK (ca. 730–804) advised the Frankish king CHARLEMAGNE that, besides being virtuous, his duties included establishing peace and harmony in his realm, Christianizing his subjects, and protecting the church.

Early theories of kingship highlighted the divine nature of a king's authority—that is, that the king was by virtue of his office an instrument of God. The crucial ceremony of divine kingship was anointing, the application of oil blessed by the church onto the head of the new king. In England and France, anointing of the shoulders or hands was sometimes performed as well, giving the new ruler the so-called ROYAL TOUCH. The royal touch was claimed to be the power of the king to cure disease just with the touch of his hand. Anointing secured the early reputation of the king as a person with responsibilities to the church and state and reinforced his Christlike image.

Investiture Controversy.   The stand that the king was the divinely ordained minister of God led to a conflict over the role of the pope* and the role of the king. This conflict erupted in 1075 in an event known as the Investiture Controversy. The conflict between Pope GREGORY VII and King HENRY IV of Germany began when Henry claimed the right to choose bishops and "invest" them with, or give them, the symbols of their office. Pope Gregory disagreed strongly. The pope's supporters maintained that all authority came from God and that spiritual authority was more important than earthly authority. Those who supported the king argued that God had established two authorities—spiritual and temporal (worldly), and the pope, as one of the king's subjects, had no right to interfere in state affairs. Although King Henry ended up giving in on the issue, the argument over the relative powers of pope and king shaped much of the medieval thinking about the nature of kingship.

John of Salisbury.   Following the Investiture Controversy, several leading political and religious thinkers took up the issue of kingship. The most important treatise on the subject in the 1100s was the *Polycraticus* of John of Salisbury (ca. 1110–1180). John saw the king as a wise and virtuous Christian who, by obeying both the law of the land and God's higher law, sets a moral example for his subjects. He protects his people, administers justice, punishes wrongdoers, and leads his army against the enemies of God. According to John, the church commands the king to perform his duties. In his view, the king is a servant of the church and has a responsibility to help the clergy with their spiritual work.

John felt that the king was an integral part of the realm. The king may be the lawmaker, but he is also under the law, just as is any other member of the realm. This relationship of a king to the law was the subject of many theorists in the 13th century.

New Conflict Between Pope and King.   In the late 1200s, another struggle between a king and a pope produced more writings on the nature of royal and papal power. This second controversy began in 1296 when Pope BONIFACE VIII forbade King PHILIP IV THE FAIR of France from taxing the clergy* without his approval. Philip's supporters contended that the king had the right and even the duty to tax church lands as part of his sacred duty to do what was best for the kingdom. In addition, they argued, the revenues from church taxes helped protect the clergy and their property. Using arguments based on history, Roman law, theology*, the BIBLE, and church documents, royal supporters emphasized that the king's authority came from his duty to his people and extended to everybody in his kingdom, including the clergy. Philip IV won in his conflict with Boniface VIII. The idea of power based on law strengthened the royalist argument, and it put kings in a stronger position in the late Middle Ages to defend themselves against the pope.

Theories of kingship in the late Middle Ages often centered on the relationship of a king to his kingdom. The king was thought to be the embodiment of the kingdom and its inhabitants, and to derive his powers

* **pope** bishop of Rome and head of the Western Christian Church

* **clergy** priests, deacons, and other church officials qualified to perform church ceremonies

* **theology** study of the nature of God and of religious truth

and duties from the realm. Some theories promoted the idea that a well-administered monarchy was inherently the best form of government. Marsilius of Padua, who died about 1342, stated in his work *Defensor pacis* that one of the most important roles of a king was to keep the peace and maintain social order.

In general, one assumption in particular survived beyond medieval kingship: government should possess a high moral purpose. Theories of kingship stubbornly kept the idea of a government that was subordinate to natural and divine laws. Not until the 1800s did Europe discard its medieval theories of kingship. (*See also* **Canossa; Church-State Relations; Germany; Holy Roman Empire.**)

Knighthood

See color plate 10, vol. 1.

The status of knights in European society grew during the Middle Ages. Before 1200, they were a separate social class, one that was above the peasantry but well below the nobility. After 1200, however, the gap between knights and nobles closed. By the end of the Middle Ages, knights and nobles were members of the same aristocracy.

Knights and Nobles.   Knights (called *milites* in Latin) emerged in the late 900s as a separate class of armed men whom the nobility employed to defend their castles. Knights and nobles were two distinct classes until about 1200. The nobles (*nobiles*) were wealthy hereditary landowners with almost unlimited authority over their territory, and the knights who served them were usually poor and of humble origin.

Gradually, the knights blended into the nobility, acquiring the privileges and rights of the old aristocracy and marrying into their families. As this social change occurred, knights were referred to as *domini* (lords). Some knights acted in lordly fashion, such as by placing fortifications around their lands.

The church contributed to the growing prestige of knights by emphasizing the role of warrior as a Christian vocation, similar to that of the priesthood. The dubbing* of a knight became a "sacrament of knighthood." In addition, the CRUSADES against the Muslim Turks in the Holy Land and the popularity of such military orders as the Hospitalers, Knights Templars, and Teutonic Knights helped to raise the prestige of the Christian warrior even further. Such works as the *Song of Roland, Tristan and Iseult,* and the ARTHURIAN romances celebrated the deeds of knights. As knights acquired land of their own, they ceased to remain a class apart from the nobility, and a new, enlarged aristocracy of nobility and knight-landowners was created.

Medieval sources use a variety of terms for knights and nobles, suggesting that there may have been intermediate levels between knights and nobles. In the early 1100s, writers distinguished between common knights, knights of moderate nobility, and knights of the highest nobility.

Later Changes.   Originally all *milites* in good health were expected to serve their lords in battle. As territories merged, quotas were set on the number of knights in the service of a lord. The earliest evidence of quotas came during the reign of the English king WILLIAM I THE CONQUEROR, who

* **dubbing** formal ceremony in which a person receives a title from his overlord

This illumination from the late 1200s shows a young man preparing for the ceremony of knighthood. Knights were originally a separate social class of armed men employed by the nobility to defend their castles. By the end of the Middle Ages, they had blended with the nobility and had become part of the same aristocracy.

* **abbot** male leader of a monastery or abbey. The female equivalent is an abbess.

imposed military quotas of up to 60 knights on virtually everybody under him. The abbot* of Abingdon, for example, had 30 knights for service in the royal army and 30 more for garrison duty at Windsor Castle. When King HENRY I called these knights to royal service in 1101 and one of the Abingdon Abbey's knights declined to serve, the abbot was obliged to find a substitute.

As the length of service the knights owed their lords decreased to 40 days a year, kings and lords accepted money (scutage) in place of service. They used the money to employ, instead, battle-ready knights who made their living by hiring themselves out as soldiers.

During the 1100s and 1200s, the practice by kings and lords of accepting payment instead of service from their knights spread from England and Normandy to France and other parts of Europe, including southern Italy, Sicily, and Greece.

The expense associated with knighthood was often very great. The clothing, armor, and arms were elaborate and costly. Many heirs to a family knighthood postponed the ceremony of knighthood until they could better afford it. Others remained unknighted throughout their lives. By the 1200s, knights were part of the hereditary nobility. They no longer had to fight to gain social status.

* **longbow** archer's weapon about five to six feet in length for the rapid shooting of arrows

In the late Middle Ages, the military role of the knight changed, as weapons and infantry tactics became more sophisticated. The use of the longbow*, pike, and cannon meant that knights on horseback were no longer the warrior elite. As their importance on the battlefield decreased, knights engaged in more pageantry. The late Middle Ages experienced a marked increase in spectacular tournaments and in the formation of new orders of knights, such as the Order of the Garter. The arms, armor, and banners of knights seen in museums today are likely to have come from the late medieval or early modern period. (*See also* **Armor; Chivalry; Feudalism; Knights, Orders of; Nobility and Nobles.**)

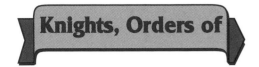

* **chivalry** rules and customs of medieval knighthood

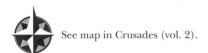 See map in Crusades (vol. 2).

The three greatest medieval orders of knights began in the 1100s when crusader knights formed military orders to protect Christian pilgrims in the Holy Land. Some European countries—Spain, Portugal, and Hungary—in conflict with Muslims formed their own national military orders. In the late Middle Ages, the kings of Europe created honorary orders of chivalry*.

Knights Hospitalers. The Knights of St. John of Jerusalem, or Knights Hospitalers, organized themselves to protect a pilgrims' hospital in Jerusalem. Pope Paschal II officially recognized the Hospitalers as a new religious order in 1113.

Hospitalers wore black cloaks with a white cross on the left shoulder. In battle, they dressed in red, but the crosses they wore on their front and back and on their shield and battle flag were always white. Their distinctive cross with eight points came to be known as the Maltese cross.

The order gained popularity, power, and influence by building hospitals in the Holy Land and Europe. The Krak des Chevaliers—the order's headquarters in the Holy Land—was one of the largest castles ever built. After the Turks recaptured the Holy Land, the Hospitalers withdrew to CYPRUS. In 1309, they conquered the island of Rhodes and used it to fight Turkish pirates. Later, after the island of Malta became their home base, they were known as the Knights of Malta.

Knights Templars. The Poor Knights of Christ, or Knights Templars, were formed in 1119 when five French knights banded together to defend the Holy Sepulcher (the place where Christ was believed to be buried), to protect pilgrims, and to fight the Turks. They became known as the Knights Templars after King Baldwin II of Jerusalem gave them a house on the site of the Temple of Solomon.

They wore white cloaks with a red cross and a white linen sword belt and carried a white shield with a red cross. The order grew so rapidly in the 1200s that it divided into three groups—knights, priests, and brothers. The order prospered from donations, banking, moneylending, and other business enterprises. However, its wealth and independence aroused envy and caused the order to be persecuted in France, England, and CASTILE. Many Templars were killed. Pope Clement V abolished the order in 1312.

Teutonic Knights. The third great order of knights was German. Like the Hospitalers and Templars, the Teutonic Knights began with a pilgrims' hospital in Jerusalem called St. Mary's of the Germans. Members of the order wore black crosses on white cloaks, shields, and banners.

Though few in number, the Teutonic Knights were respected for their zeal and dedication. In 1225/1226, the duke of Masovia invited the order to conquer the Prussians and the Lithuanians, Europe's last remaining non-Christian tribes. With iron discipline, the Teutonic Knights transformed the Prussian wilderness into a powerful and prosperous state. Marienburg, which became the headquarters of the Teutonic Knights in 1309, is the largest castle in Europe.

Other Orders. Spain, Portugal, and Hungary organized national military orders to fight against the infidels (non-Christians) who threatened their borders. The three Spanish orders (the Knights of Alcántara, Calatrava, and

* **heretic** person who disagrees with established church doctrine

* **secular** nonreligious; connected with everyday life

Santiago de Compostela) and the two Portuguese orders (the Knights of Aviz and the Portuguese Order of Christ) fought against the Muslim Moors. The king of Hungary formed the Order of the Dragon for knights who vowed to fight the Turks. The dukes of Austria organized the Order of the Eagle and the Order of St. George to fight against the Hussite heretics* in Bohemia.

Many medieval rulers established their own secular* orders of knights. After the loss of the Holy Land, the king of Cyprus bestowed knightly honors on Christians who made the pilgrimage to the tomb of Christ. He also dubbed Knights of the Sword of Cyprus. Several other European kings followed his example. In 1348, EDWARD III OF ENGLAND formed the English Order of the Garter, modeled after the legendary Knights of the Round Table. Other chivalric orders included the Order of the Annunziata (1360) of the dukes of Savoy and the Order of the Golden Fleece (1430) of the dukes of Burgundy.

The orders often had distinctive emblems that reflected their names, such as the English Order of the Bath (1399), the French Order of the Porcupine (1394), and the Danish Order of the White Elephant (1462). Most of these secular orders were dedicated to chivalric values, such as protection of the weak and courteous behavior toward women, but some orders had more specific goals. For example, the Burgundian Order of St. Anthony was dedicated to maintaining hospitals for the care of people afflicted with LEPROSY, while the Order of la Jara in ARAGON was a temperance organization devoted to curbing excessive drinking. (*See also* **Chivalry; Knighthood.**)

Komnena, Anna

1083–ca. 1155
Historian

* **Byzantium** ancient city that became Constantinople; also refers to Byzantine Empire

* *en masse* French expression meaning in a body or as a whole

Anna Komnena aspired to be empress of Byzantium*, but instead she became a historian. A woman of great intelligence and energy, she wrote a history of the Byzantine Empire covering the period of the late 1000s and the early 1100s. Her account is especially valuable because it presents Byzantium's view of the First Crusade, when, as Anna said, "all the barbarous peoples dwelling in the land between the Adriatic and the Pillars of Hercules migrated *en masse** to Asia."

Anna's father, Alexios I Komnenos, became emperor of Byzantium in 1081. Anna was born two years later. She was betrothed as an infant to Constantine Doukas—the son and grandson of earlier emperors—who was expected to become the next emperor. Anna grew up as a popular favorite, cheered by the city's crowds, and she expected to share the throne one day with Constantine. (In Byzantium, no woman could become empress except by marriage to an emperor.) However, with the birth of a younger brother, John, in 1087 or 1088, Anna's glory was threatened. When her brother was named her father's successor in 1092, and when Anna's husband, Constantine, died, her hopes of becoming empress were nil. Despite plotting and scheming to have her second husband, Nikephoros Bryennios, elevated to the throne, she failed. She never recovered from the shock of this disappointment.

When her brother became emperor, he forced Anna to retire to a convent, but she refused to disappear quietly. She spent 30 years writing the *Alexiad*, a history of her father's reign. Because Anna had access to court documents and knew many of the people in her story, her history contains information available nowhere else. She provided excellent character portraits, especially of the women of the time. Excessively loyal to her father, she presented him as a great man who fought valiantly to preserve Byzantium from rebels and foreign invaders. Nevertheless, the *Alexiad* betrays a mood of despair, possibly stemming from Anna's own bitterness. She believed herself cheated of the throne, but had she become empress she probably would not have written her history. (*See also* **Byzantine Empire; Crusades; Historical Writing; Komnenos Family.**)

Komnenos Family

* **dynasty** succession of rulers from the same family or group

The Komnenos family, called in Greek the Komnenoi, ruled the Byzantine Empire for more than a century. Although their policies made Byzantium internally stronger and more orderly, the empire was attacked by foreign powers that eventually destroyed the dynasty*.

The first Komnenos emperor was Isaac I, who ruled from 1057 to 1059. After his brief two-year reign, his brother John refused the throne, and it appeared that the dynasty had ended. But John's widow was determined to preserve the dynasty, and her third son declared himself emperor as Alexios I in 1081. He ruled for 37 years, until 1118. Alexios had planned to make his daughter, Anna, his heir, but the birth of a son, John, made this impossible. John became emperor on the death of his father and ruled as John II until 1143.

The next Komnenos emperor was Manuel I. He, too, enjoyed a long reign from 1143 to 1180. He was overly ambitious, however, and made too many enemies. Byzantium was weaker when he died than it had been when he came to the throne. Manuel's son, Alexios II, inherited the throne as a boy and held it for only three years before he was overthrown by a cousin, Andronikos I. Andronikos was both a tyrant and a military failure. He was overthrown in 1185, and the dynasty came to an end.

The long lives of the Komnenos emperors and their political skills provided a century of internal peace and relative stability. They restored the economy and oversaw great achievements in art, literature, and scholarship. One of the period's most remarkable books was written by Anna KOMNENA.

During the reign of the Komnenos dynasty, Byzantium came under attack from two directions. Turks were making a strong push from the southeast. (Three centuries later they would conquer Byzantium.) From the west, the European powers, especially the Normans, were also putting pressure on the empire. The attacks of these powers proved fatal to the Komnenos dynasty. The first great Komnenos emperor, Alexios I, made his reputation as a military leader by fighting the Turks. Yet the Turks kept coming. During the reigns of Alexios I and John II, the Turks seized the Byzantine portions of Asia Minor. Alexios and John recovered some of this territory, but the Turks continued their assault. They won a major battle against Manuel I at Myriokephalon in 1176.

European armies had also become a regular threat. Even before the crusades* began, Norman armies under Robert Guiscard attacked the region in the 1080s. The Normans attacked again in 1107 under Robert's son, BOHEMOND I, and again in 1147 under Roger of Sicily. These attacks ended in defeat for the Normans, but they were wearing on the Byzantines.

* **crusades** holy wars declared by the pope against non-Christians. Most were against Muslims, but crusades were also declared against heretics and pagans.

Manuel tried a counterattack against Norman Italy in 1155 and was defeated. A peace settlement followed, but in 1185 a successful Norman attack on Thessaloniki led to the downfall of Andronikos I and the end of the Komnenos dynasty. (*See also* **Byzantine Empire; Normans.**)

Koran

See *Qur'an.*

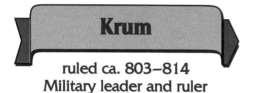

Krum

**ruled ca. 803–814
Military leader and ruler**

Krum was a military chieftain from Pannonia who became one of the greatest rulers of BULGARIA. During his reign, he unified the Bulgars and fought a successful war against the BYZANTINE EMPIRE.

Krum's defeat of the Avars early in his rule enabled him to unite the Bulgars who had lived under Avar rule. With the defeat of the Avars, Bulgars replaced them as overlords of the SLAVS and Rumanians living north of the Danube River.

After the Byzantines raided Bulgaria in 807, Krum's troops struck back. In 811, the Byzantine emperor, Nikephoros I, personally led a large army against the Bulgars. He succeeded in sacking Krum's capital of Pliska, but on his way home the Bulgars ambushed and destroyed his army and killed Nikephoros. The Bulgars made his skull into a gruesome drinking cup. Krum followed his victory by capturing two important Byzantine ports on the Black Sea.

In 813, after he had defeated the large army the Byzantines sent against him, Krum captured Thrace and invaded the area surrounding Constantinople. He sent many Byzantine subjects to Bulgaria to serve as soldiers in his army. In 814, as commander of a massive army, Krum marched on Constantinople. He never arrived, dying of a stroke on the way.

In his dealings with the Byzantine rulers, Krum resorted to military force only after diplomacy failed. For example, throughout his campaign against Nikephoros, he extended several peace offers, which the emperor ignored. Throughout 812 and 813, he attempted to negotiate with the Byzantines. Only after his gestures were rejected did he launch his attacks.

Krum was not only a great warrior but an effective administrator as well. He issued the first national law code in the history of the Bulgarian state, a fragment of which has survived. He tolerated other ethnic groups and employed a diverse group of people—Bulgars, Avars, Slavs, Greeks, and even an Arab—in his administration. In the Byzantine territories, he placed Greeks in high administrative positions.

Kufa

* **provincial**   referring to a province or an area controlled by an empire

* **garrison**   military post

The city of Kufa, located in present-day Iraq, was a provincial* capital of the Islamic Empire. It was a center of Islamic scholarship and also the birthplace of Shi'ism, one of the main divisions of the Islamic religion. Kufa's most glorious years were from 670 to 996.

The city was founded by Arabs around 638 as a permanent garrison* during the conquests of Islam. Arab settlers immediately gathered there to work the farmlands used by the region's former inhabitants. These settlers

* **caliph** religious and political head of an
Islamic state

* **nomadic** wandering from place to place to
find food and pasture

came from many tribes, with different customs and loyalties. As a result,
there was little social harmony.

Kufa also became a center of religious and political dissent. Kufa was
the capital of ALI IBN ABI TALIB, Muhammad's son-in-law and the fourth
caliph*. After Ali was murdered in 661, the people of Kufa remained
loyal to his memory. Shi'ism, the form of Islam founded by Ali's supporters, persisted in Kufa and then spread from there into Persia (present-
day Iran).

As a trading center, Kufa was famous for its covered market, dates,
silks, and perfumes. It was also an important center of learning. Arabic
writing was perfected in Kufa, and the city's historians produced works
that still serve as a major source of information about the early Islamic
conquests beyond Arabia.

Kufa declined as nearby cities prospered. BAGHDAD became wealthy
enough to attract Kufa's leading scholars, and a shrine to Ali in nearby
Najaf took away much of Kufa's religious importance. After 996, Kufa was
frequently raided by nomadic* tribespeople. A traveler in the late 1100s
described the town as a thinly populated ruin pestered by raiding desert
tribes. (*See also* **Abbasids; Caliphate; Iran; Iraq; Islam, Conquests of.**)

See
color plate 12,
vol. 1.

Travelers through the European countryside today see a landscape
that was the creation of the Middle Ages: mile after mile of open
fields, neat arrangements of trees, and frequent villages. This landscape seems natural, but it is a human invention. In the year 550, the landscape had a very different appearance. Open fields were rare. Trees grew
everywhere. Villages were few and far apart. The transformation from that
wild scene to today's landscape was the work of thousands of ordinary
rural people. Most of the work was done in the four centuries between 900
and 1300.

Land Use Before 900.   When the Middle Ages began, the countryside
of Europe could be divided into three general types. There were fields
where farmers regularly planted their crops. Beyond them was the wildwood, which consisted of areas that people used but did not develop.
Still further out were the free forests—vast unused wildernesses that
served as borders between territories. Most of Europe was wilderness or
wildwood.

Fields were the basic social form of land. A farmer commonly had two
fields that he worked with a scratch plow. One year he planted in one
field; the next year he planted in the other field. This method helped preserve the fields' fertility. Still, by 550, centuries of use had worn out the
land. The scratch plow, a prehistoric tool, could be used only on soft soils.
Much of the land, therefore, could not be farmed.

Wildwood contributed foods that the fields could not provide. The
wildwood had forest, marsh, lakes, and rivers. There people grazed animals, hunted and fished, and gathered berries, fruits, nuts, and honey.
Wildwood areas were sometimes farmed with a system called slash-and-
burn agriculture. Using this method, people cleared a field by hacking

Wildwood was an area that people used but did not develop. Here a swineherd takes his pigs to eat acorns near the edge of the forest.

down trees and bushes and then setting fire to the site. The cleared area would be farmed for 1 or 2 years and then left to recover for at least 25 years. The scratch plow was not very useful on these partially cleared plots; the farmers used hoes.

Beyond the wildwood lay the wilderness, uninhabited free forests and swamps. The wilderness had stood largely unchanged since prehistoric times. Before 900, most travelers avoided it. During the early Middle Ages, people turned some of the wildwood into permanent fields, but the wilderness areas remained untouched.

Expansion, 900 to 1300.   The Middle Ages were a time of great population growth. The population had dropped sharply after the fall of Rome in the fifth century but soon had begun to recover. By the year 1300, there were more than four times as many people in Europe as there had been in 650. In some places, such as France and Germany, the population increased by more than six times. This growth forced people to make greater use of the land. Around 900, farmers began using a three-field rotation system, planting crops in two fields while allowing one to rest. By the end of the century, much of the wildwood had been cleared and turned into open fields. A wheeled plow that could dig more deeply into the soil was introduced to medieval farms.

Still the population grew, and after 900 the people began clearing the wilderness. Groups of people moved away from settled areas into the forests and swamps. These pioneers entered mature forests and cut down the trees. They used the method of slash-and-burn farming to clear the land so that they could plant crops. Unlike the earlier slash-and-burn farmers, however, these newcomers stayed and continued to clear the land. Slowly they turned slash-and-burn areas into new fields.

Settlers in swamp areas had to turn wetlands into dry fields. They dug drainage ditches to dry out the land. From Flanders to Denmark, and especially in Holland, a system of ditches and barriers opened up swampy lowlands to settlement and farming. These pioneers worked without any master plan, and by 1300, the wildernesses of western, central, and eastern Europe had disappeared. The European countryside had taken on the domesticated look it still wears.

The clearing of the wilderness changed the social order. Because the empty lands were not the traditional property of any king or noble, the pioneering settlers, who owned the land they cleared, became a new kind of independent farmers without landlords. The old landlords then had to give their tenants more freedoms and lower their rents. If they failed to do so, their tenants would leave the old fields for the wilderness.

The new farms brought a rush of prosperity. The new fields were more fertile than the old, greatly increasing food production. Widespread famine, once common, became rare. Food surpluses allowed some people to quit farming altogether and to move to the cities, so that urban life and all of the arts and crafts associated with cities took a great leap forward. In 1348, the BLACK DEATH struck, devastating the population of Europe. Yet wilderness did not return; the landscape had been permanently tamed. (*See also* **Agriculture; Climate, Influence on History; Construction, Building; Famine; Forests; Hunting and Fowling; Taxation; Villages.**)

Lanfranc of Bec

died 1089
Archbishop of Canterbury

* **theology** study of the nature of God and of religious truth

* **diocese** church district under a bishop's authority

Lanfranc of Bec, also known as Lanfranc of Canterbury, was one of the outstanding church leaders of his day. In Normandy, he was a teacher, monk, and scholar, but after the Norman conquest he became head of the English church.

Lanfranc was born in the early 1000s in Pavia, Italy. He studied Roman law at Bologna and then went to France, where he became master of the cathedral school at Avranches. In 1042, he entered the monastery of Bec in Normandy. There he founded a school, became prior, and established himself as a leading authority in the fields of logic and theology*.

In 1070—four years after the conquest of England by the NORMANS—Lanfranc went to England, where he spent the last two decades of his life as archbishop of CANTERBURY. To reform the English church, he reorganized its dioceses*. As a trusted adviser to WILLIAM I THE CONQUEROR, Lanfranc was able to improve relations between the church and the crown. (*See also* **Angevins; England; Justiciar.**)

Langton, Stephen

died 1228
Theologian and archbishop

* **theologian** person who studies religious faith and practice
* **archbishop** head bishop in a region or nation

* **excommunicate** to exclude from the rites of the church

Stephen Langton was a respected theologian* who served as archbishop* of CANTERBURY during the troubled reign of King JOHN of England in the early 1200s. Langton played a leading role in the dispute between the king and the barons that led to the formulation of MAGNA CARTA, one of the most important political documents in English history.

Langton was raised in Lincolnshire in northern England. He then studied and lived in PARIS, where he remained for 25 years. There he wrote the highly respected theological work *Questiones*. Pope INNOCENT III invited Langton to Rome, where he became involved in the dispute between the pope and the king over the election of the archbishop of Canterbury. When Innocent arranged to have Langton elected the new archbishop in Rome, John announced his strong opposition to the plan. In response, Innocent excommunicated* the king in 1209.

When the French king PHILIP II AUGUSTUS threatened to invade England on behalf of the pope, John backed down and recognized Langton. When Langton returned to England in 1213, he supported the barons who opposed the king and played a leading role in their negotiations with John, which were difficult. By 1215, the barons had become so frustrated that they took up arms against the king. The document known as Magna Carta resulted from that struggle. Langton helped prepare the document that limited the power of the king by guaranteeing the rights of nobles, the church, and the city of London. By the time Langton died in 1228, he had established himself as one of the most able archbishops of Canterbury in English history.

Languedoc

Languedoc was a region of southern France that had its own special character. Its boundaries took shape in the late 1000s when the region was under the control of Count Raymond IV of St. Gilles. Later it became a royal province, and still later it became more integrated with northern France.

Early Middle Ages. At the beginning of the medieval period, Languedoc was part of the kingdom of a western Germanic tribe called the VISIGOTHS,

In the 1200s, King Louis IX had the fortified town of Aigues-Mortes built in Languedoc near the Mediterranean Sea. He used the town as the preparation and embarkation point for his two crusades. The name *Aigues-Mortes* comes from the Latin *aquae mortuae,* meaning dead waters. This refers to the salty delta marshland surrounding the city. This photograph shows the walls of Aigues-Mortes, which still stand today.

See map in Crusades (vol. 2).

* **heresy** belief that is contrary to church doctrine

and its capital was TOULOUSE. After the Frankish king CLOVIS defeated the Visigoths in 507, part of the area came under the control of another Germanic tribe, the FRANKS. However, most of the region remained under Visigothic rule and was known as the province of Septimania until the Arabs conquered it in 718.

For the next 60 years, the CAROLINGIANS, a dynasty of Frankish rulers, fought the Muslims for the area. Then, in 778, Languedoc became part of the Carolingian kingdom of AQUITAINE. However, during the 800s, Carolingian control declined. Attempts by various local lords to control the area in the 900s and early 1000s were unsuccessful. In the late 1000s, Raymond IV of St. Gilles, the count of Toulouse, tried to unify Languedoc, but he left on the First CRUSADE before unification was achieved. Raymond's heirs were unable to complete his work.

Although Languedoc remained politically fragmented, it prospered economically. Cities grew, foreign trade increased, and St. Gilles became the site of an important fair. Medieval fairs were important economic and social activities. Fairs provided opportunities for exchanging goods in regions that lacked established trading centers. Often held around the time of religious festivals, the fairs were also times for celebration with friends and family. Economic prosperity and population growth led to the creation of a new middle class and an interest in art and literature.

However, the area also became the site of religious persecution. The church, unable to respond to the reform spirit of the age, launched a campaign against what it believed to be heresy*. Groups who were attacked included the WALDENSIANS, who followed a strict interpretation of the Gospels, and the CATHARS, a group of Christian heretics in France, northern Italy, and parts of Germany. The Cathars were also known as the Albigensians because the center of their movement was the town of Albi in southern France.

When Count Raymond VI of Toulouse failed to suppress the Cathar heresy in his midst, Pope INNOCENT III called on northern France to mount a crusade against Languedoc. It was headed by the ruthless Simon de Montfort. Although Simon defeated the southern French army defending Languedoc, neither he nor his sons could establish political control or suppress the region's widespread heresy. In 1226, a second northern French army, sent by King Louis VIII, finally defeated the southern French forces once and for all.

Royal Province. By 1229, most of Languedoc was under direct royal control, and by 1271 the entire province had become part of the kingdom of France.

Despite the damage done to parts of western Languedoc by the Albigensian crusade, the 1200s were generally a time of economic progress. Languedoc's major cities—Toulouse, Montpellier, and Narbonne—grew rapidly. By 1300, the populations of each of the three cities had reached the 35,000 mark. The new port of Aigues-Mortes built by King LOUIS IX became an active commercial center. Industry thrived, especially textile production and weapons manufacturing.

In the 1300s, royal control of the province increased, and the move of the PAPACY to AVIGNON improved the region's economy. Soon Languedoc resembled Italy economically and socially more than any other part of western Europe.

Disaster and Recovery. In the mid-1300s, a series of disasters struck. The HUNDRED YEARS WAR began in 1337, and not long afterwards mercenaries* used by both the English and the French were wandering through Languedoc, looting and plundering the countryside. The BLACK DEATH, or plague, was a deadly infectious disease that struck in 1348 and killed as much as half the population in some parts of the region. In 1361, another plague struck with similarly devastating results. During the 1360s and 1370s, FAMINES struck the region regularly, depopulating towns and causing social unrest. By 1402, the city of Toulouse had lost two-thirds of its population. The collapse of the Avignon papacy around 1417 also hurt Languedoc economically.

During the 1400s, as Languedoc became more integrated into northern France, the situation improved. JACQUES COEUR, who controlled the king's finances, helped revive the region's economy by encouraging Mediterranean traders to use its ports. By the end of the century, the countryside was beginning to prosper again. A new international fair was organized at Beaucaire that rivaled the one at Lyons farther north. The university at Montpellier regained its earlier vigor, and Toulouse once again became an intellectual and cultural center.

After a century of disaster, the fortunes of Languedoc improved. By 1500, the region had regained much of its earlier vitality. However, now it was much more an integral part of the French nation. (*See also* **Fairs; France; Trade.**)

* **mercenary** soldier who fights for payment rather than out of loyalty to a lord or nation

Latin Language

As early as the first century in Rome, there was a distinction between literary, learned Latin and popular, spoken Latin. The extent to which these two languages differed may have been, at first, no more significant than the difference between informal and educated English today. Eventually, however, the two languages became quite distinct. Spoken Latin, called Vulgar Latin, was the ancestor of the Romance languages—Italian, Spanish, Portuguese, French, Catalan, Provençal, and Romanian.

Language of Learning.   In the Middle Ages, Latin was the language of scholarship and learning. People spoke Latin in schools and universities. Most educated people were actually bilingual in Latin. They used both literary Latin and their own vernacular, or everyday, language.

Literary Latin is a synthetic language, which means that it depends on inflections, or adding to a root word to indicate the relationship between words. For example, *ambulare* in Latin means to walk. The root *ambul* can be modified by adding *-at (ambulat),* which means he is walking, or by adding *-abat (ambulabat),* which means he was walking, or by adding *-avisset (ambulavisset),* which means he would have walked.

Because it was taught in school and based on an established heritage of authorities, literary Latin was not subject to the pressures of ordinary usage that contribute to changes in language. Latin was learned by instruction; the rules were taught first. The standard medieval Latin grammar books were the *Ars minor* of Aelius Donatus, written in the 300s, and the *Institutiones grammaticae* of Priscian, written in the 500s. Students increased their vocabulary from lists of words grouped according to subject matter (for example, plants, animals, agriculture, and warfare). Later in the Middle Ages, students had dictionaries to help them. The first Latin dictionary was the *Elementarium doctrinae rudimentum* of Papias, compiled in the mid-1000s. The Latin texts most studied in medieval schools were the Vulgate Bible, texts of church services, and educational texts from both the classical and medieval periods.

Vulgar Latin.   Before the Middle Ages, Latin-speaking Roman colonists, farmers, and soldiers spread throughout Italy and into the provinces of Gaul (now France) and Spain. The language of these people developed into distinctive regional forms with their own spelling, grammar, and pronunciation. By the 300s, Vulgar Latin, the speech of the common people and the informal speech among educated people, had become noticeably different from the Latin taught in the schools. Unlike literary Latin, which was based on fixed texts, Vulgar Latin was subject to the changes that shape living languages. By the 500s, separate dialects were spoken in different parts of Europe. These dialects later grew into the Romance languages—Italian, French, Spanish, Portuguese, Catalan, Provençal, and Romanian. (*See also* **French Language and Literature; Italian Language and Literature; Spanish Language and Literature.**)

Law

The rule of law was one of the most important concepts in the Middle Ages. It helped provide stability to the medieval world and a framework for the development of medieval society and government. There were two basic types of medieval law: civil law and canon law. Civil law was concerned with providing justice in criminal or political matters. Canon law was concerned with all matters related to religion.

European Law

The origins of medieval law in Europe are quite complex. The law was derived from both Roman and Germanic roots, the principles of which were very different. In northern Europe, civil law was based primarily on the customs and traditions of Germanic peoples. In southern Europe, the more formal traditions of ancient Roman law prevailed. Throughout all of western Europe, canon law reflected strong Roman influence since the Christian faith was based largely on the ideas and practices of the Roman Church.

The Influence of Roman Law.   In ancient times, the Roman Empire had a formal system of written laws that was applied equally throughout the empire. After the decline of the Roman Empire in the West in the late 400s, these laws remained in effect in many parts of the former imperial* realm, and especially in the East in the BYZANTINE EMPIRE. During the 500s, the Byzantine emperor JUSTINIAN I made an effort to restore the grandeur of the Roman Empire. As part of his plan, he arranged for legal experts to codify* the many different Roman laws that had developed over the previous thousand years. The resulting collection of laws was known as the *Corpus juris civilis* (Body of Civil Law), which included the *Justinian Code.* The *Justinian Code* was the basic legal framework throughout the Byzantine world. Beginning in the 1000s, it became one of the most important works in the intellectual centers of medieval western Europe.

The *Corpus* consisted altogether of four parts. The *Digest* stated basic legal principles and dealt mostly with private laws. The *Code* contained official decrees and replies from the emperors on controversial points of law. It also contained material connected with the judicial functions of public officers. The *Novels,* added to the *Corpus* over many years, contained various new legal decisions, many connected with church affairs. The *Institutes* consisted of a textbook of general legal principles.

The *Corpus* was relatively unknown in western Europe until the late 1000s. At that time, it was rediscovered by scholars, and it became the focus of study at LAW SCHOOLS in Italy, particularly at the law school at the University of Bologna. From then until the 1400s, it remained the most important book for academic legal studies throughout much of southern Europe. The *Corpus* helped shape legal theory and practice and served as an example for the codification of other laws.

The revival of Roman law had a great impact on canon law. Sometime in the 1120s or 1130s, a monk named Gratian taught canon law at Bologna, where he was influenced by the studies of civil law based on the *Corpus juris civilis.* Since Gratian had no comparable text for church law, he created his own collection of canon laws, which eventually became known as the *Corpus juris canonici (Body of Canon Law).* This work consisted of a great collection of canon laws organized according to topic. It gathered more material than any previous collection of canon laws and presented the material in a more comprehensive and coherent way. The *Corpus juris canonici* became a basic textbook for the study of canon law as well as an important legal reference work. All subsequent canon law during the Middle Ages was influenced by Gratian's work and the basic characteristics of Roman law.

Germanic Laws.   The Germanic tribes had no written codes of law before they invaded the Roman Empire. Their laws were based on customs and traditions passed down by word of mouth from generation to generation. The reaction of the barbarians* to Roman culture varied. Those

* **imperial**   pertaining to an empire or emperor

* **codify**   to arrange according to a system; set down in writing

* **barbarian**   referring to people from outside the cultures of Greece and Rome who were viewed as uncivilized

groups that settled in the more populated and advanced regions in southern Europe encountered a well-established Roman legal culture. As a result, they were influenced to a great extent by Roman law and legal practices, and they allowed the Roman part of the population to continue administering their own Roman-based laws. Those Germanic peoples who settled in the less romanized northern part of Europe were influenced very little by Roman law and saw no reason to allow the remnants of the Roman population to follow the ancient Roman laws. Instead, their legal codes reflected Germanic customs and ideas, such as the idea that the king is the source of most law and that victims of crimes must be compensated with some type of payment.

The oldest surviving barbarian laws, dating from between 476 and 483, are associated with the VISIGOTHS, who established a kingdom in the southern part of France and in Spain. Roman law had a great influence on the Visigoths. The earliest Visigothic rule of law had been the *Edictum Theodorici (Edict of Theodoric),* written about 458 during the reign of King Theodoric II. It had dealt primarily with the resolution of cases that had arisen between Goths and Romans. The terms of this order had come from Roman sources, particularly those parts of the law dealing with legal procedures.

One of the most important later Visigothic codes of law was the *Breviary of Alaric,* issued by King Alaric II in about 506. This work became the standard source of Roman law in western Europe until the rediscovery of the *Justinian Code* in the 1000s. The law of the *Breviary* applied only to persons of Roman origin. The Visigoths themselves were subject to the laws and customs of their own people. The *Breviary* represented an attempt on the part of the Visigothic kings to rule their state with a unified system of law.

Germanic law had several important characteristics. One characteristic was the distinction between social classes. Germanic society and law recognized three basic classes—slave, freed slave, and free (including ordinary freemen, counts, dukes, and kings). Another characteristic was the importance of kinship* and personal relationships; the ultimate basis of Germanic law was membership in a tribal group. These elements were reflected in FEUDALISM as it developed in western Europe.

Legal Traditions in France. Under the MEROVINGIANS and the CAROLINGIANS, attempts were made to codify the laws of the Frankish kingdom. The earliest written codification of Frankish law was accomplished during the reign of CLOVIS in the late 400s and the early 500s. This unified code of law contained elements of Roman law. However, preference in most legal areas was given to the customary Germanic laws of the FRANKS.

After the collapse of the Carolingian Empire, each region of northern France began to develop its own system of law. Eventually, there were separate bodies of law for every major principality* and many minor feudal* principalities. These various bodies of laws had common elements among them, especially concerning legal procedures. For example, many judicial decisions were made by the "good men" of the neighborhood rather than by a judge. These men would be called together and asked questions about a case, and a decision would be made, based on the answers. This principle gradually led to the development of the jury system. Courts

* **kinship** relationship based on family or tribal connections

* **principality** region that is ruled by a prince

* **feudal** referring to the social, economic, and political system that flourished in western Europe during the Middle Ages

Trial by Ordeal

Under Germanic law, the guilt or innocence of a defendant was determined largely by the oaths he and other witnesses gave in answer to the charges made against him. If the testimony conflicted widely, the judge would put the parties through a trial by ordeal. There were several types of ordeals. They included the ordeal of hot iron, in which a hot object was carried in the bare hand for a specified distance, and the ordeal of boiling water, in which a stone was grasped by hand from boiling water. The guilt or innocence of the person would be determined by how quickly the wound healed. The most common type of ordeal was the trial by battle, in which experienced fighters fought on behalf of the plaintiff and defendant. The victor of these ordeals was assumed to be innocent because victory was considered the judgment of God.

* **precedent** legal decision that serves as an example in deciding subsequent similar cases

* **common law** unwritten law based on custom and court decisions

* **vernacular** language or dialect native to a region; everyday, informal speech

* **notary** public official who drafts and certifies legal documents

throughout northern France were neighborhood courts made up of these "good men." Beginning in the 1200s, higher appeals courts staffed by legal experts were established to help resolve questions that could not be answered adequately by the lower courts. As time went on, the need for legal expertise and training increased and led to the development of a class of professional lawyers. Another characteristic of legal procedure in northern France was the use of precedent* to define new laws. Many of these legal principles were taken by the NORMANS to England after 1066 and formed a basis for English common law*.

The legal tradition of southern France was quite different from that of northern France. The north, with its strong Germanic tradition, was considered the region of customary law. The south, with its strong Roman tradition, was the region of written law. This difference became more pronounced after the decline of centralized power at the end of the Carolingian period. In the north, courts were based on private, personal ties and relationships between great lords and their dependents. In the south, however, courts retained their public character.

After 1100, the revival of the *Justinian Code* in the universities of Italy had a great influence on the law of southern France. By the late 1100s, a short manual of practical rules for administering Roman law appeared in the southern region of PROVENCE, and the first French vernacular* work on Roman law was written in 1160. The spread of Roman law in southern France involved several developments. One of these was the use of certain legal terms and concepts from the *Justinian Code*. Another development was the spread of the institution of the notary*. Throughout southern France, the customary law became a written law influenced by Roman models. This required trained professionals, and legal learning, therefore, became an important aspect of southern French law. As in Italy, universities in southern France offered the formal study of law. The most famous center for the study of Roman law in France was Montpellier, which had strong ties with the law school at the University of Bologna in Italy.

English Common Law. In England, Roman law had little practical influence. Instead, English law developed out of a mixture of the Germanic customs of the ANGLO-SAXONS and the legal traditions brought to England from northern France as a result of the Norman conquest of 1066. Canon law in England, however, like church law throughout medieval Europe, was based firmly on Roman tradition.

When the Germanic Anglo-Saxons settled in Britain between the mid-400s and mid-500s, they encountered a region long isolated from Roman contacts. Roman law was weaker there than anywhere else in western Europe. As a result, Roman legal ideas had little, if any, influence on Anglo-Saxon law, and Germanic customs were thus stronger than anywhere else in western Europe.

One of the most fundamental characteristics of Anglo-Saxon law in Britain was its system of different local courts. One of these courts was the private court administered by a local lord. The peasants who worked on the lord's manor sought justice in this manorial court. Two important public courts were the hundred court and the shire (county) court. The hundred court, which represented part of a shire, was where the free

The King's Bench was a central court in England that dates from the reign of Henry II. The King's Bench included a system of itinerant judges who circuited the countryside to hear cases. The King's Bench was an important development in English common law. This scene of the King's Bench in London is from the mid-1400s.

* **indictment** statement charging a person with the commission of a crime

* **grand jury** persons designated to inquire into alleged violations of the law to determine whether the evidence is sufficient to warrant a trial

* **theology** study of the nature of God and of religious truth

population came to receive and give justice. Held monthly, it heard most criminal and civil cases. Shire courts, the most important public courts, met only twice a year. Although open to all freemen, probably only the most important people of the shire attended. The presiding officer of a shire court was the SHERIFF. The Anglo-Saxon tradition of local courts was an important contribution to the development of English common law.

After the Norman conquest in 1066, the Norman kings and their successors built on combined Anglo-Saxon and Norman legal traditions. They established a distinct system of justice that eventually became known as English common law. For the first hundred years after the conquest, the primary means of providing justice in England was through the royal writ. This was a written communication in which the king could command judicial procedure to be applied to a given case and thus bring about justice. Although Anglo-Saxon kings issued writs as early as the 900s, writs did not become a significant legal procedure until the Norman period.

Perhaps the most important legal institution developed by the Normans was the inquest. This was a procedure in which individuals gave sworn testimony or evidence in a case to determine the answers to legal questions. Also known as the jury of recognition, the Norman inquest became the foundation for the English jury system.

Although the foundations of English common law were established under the early Norman monarchs, King HENRY II was perhaps most responsible for its development. One of Henry's important contributions was in the area of rights of possession. By his use of the royal writ and the jury, he made the legal system an effective tool for settling disputes over possession and ownership of property. In criminal law, Henry developed a special jury for the indictment* of criminals. This was the ancestor of the present-day grand jury*. He also established a system of circuit justice, in which traveling courts would go around the kingdom dispensing justice.

People in England and on the Continent were ordinarily tried for criminal offenses by oath and ordeal (judgment of God) until the 1200s. In the 1200s, England substituted trial by jury for the ordeal. On the continent, judicial torture and trial by professional judges replaced the ordeal.

During the remainder of the Middle Ages, English common law continued to develop. In time, it evolved into a well-defined system of courts with professional justices and lawyers. Professional societies, known as the Inns of Court, were established to train legal apprentices. The law itself was refined and expanded through decisions and innovations of judges. Indeed, this shaping of the law through legal decisions and precedents has remained a major characteristic of English common law.

Islamic Law

Islamic law is known as shari'a. It is a system of moral and legal principles ordained by God. An important aspect of the Islamic religion, shari'a is concerned with the practical issues that touch on everyday life rather than with theology*. Islamic law had its beginnings in the medieval urban societies of IRAQ, SYRIA, and the holy city of Medina in Arabia. As it evolved, this law spread throughout the Islamic world and became the universal law of all Muslims.

During the Middle Ages, Islamic law developed in accordance with Islamic religion. It was based on the idea that all social behavior should conform to the ideals set up by the religion. As a result, Islamic law and religion became inseparable. Because all Muslims were considered to be equal before God, the law applied equally to all Muslims regardless of social class. Moreover, since God, rather than the state, determined rights and duties, these were the same everywhere. There were no territorial distinctions with respect to the law. Islamic law thus was universal and applied to all Muslims throughout the world, no matter where they lived.

The effort to make all social behavior conform to religious norms gave Islamic law a vast scope that included all human conduct. This made Islamic law very different from law in Europe. In Europe, law applied primarily to such matters as contracts and obligations, civil wrongs, and criminal actions. Islamic law was concerned with those matters, but it also applied to all religious obligations, such as prayer and fasting—matters reserved for canon law in Europe.

An important idea of Islam was that Muslims were a universal community of believers. This meant that Islamic law would apply to all Muslims wherever they lived. This was very different from the situation in Europe, where civil law was territorial and effective only within certain political boundaries. At the same time, however, Islamic law did not apply to non-Muslims living in Muslim countries. It protected the rights of these nonbelievers to be governed by their own religion's laws except in matters affecting Muslims and criminal behavior.

The most important feature of Islamic law is its sacred character. The law comes directly from God through the QUR'AN and the teachings and traditions established by the prophet MUHAMMAD. As a result, the law is not subject to change. The task of judges is not to make law but to discover God's will from these sources and to comment on it. The courts could not rule on new situations and establish legal precedents; they could only apply the law as it is known from the commentaries of judges.

The evolution of Islamic law took many generations, and it was not complete until the early 800s. Several developments occurred in the 700s that had an important effect on the law. One of these was the development of local "schools" (in the sense of traditions of interpretation) that focused on the study of legal doctrines. This helped provide the law with authority and a strong institutional foundation. Another important development was the circulation, collection, and preservation of authoritative legal texts and traditions. This led to a new science concerned with the collection of legal traditions and the establishment of a body of law that was generally accepted throughout the Islamic world.

Jewish Law

Medieval Jewish law embraced all the rules and norms of Judaism, both those concerned with people's relationship to God and those concerned with human relationships among themselves and with society. All these norms, whether religious or legal, stem from the Torah—the first five books of the Bible—and from Jewish tradition.

Jewish law evolved over thousands of years. During the Middle Ages, there were two important periods in the development of the law. The first, which extended from the 600s to the mid-1000s, was known as the gaonic period. *Gaon* was the official title of the heads of Jewish academies in Babylonia in IRAQ. These academies wielded great power, and Jewish

> **Remember:** Consult the index at the end of Volume 4 to find more information on many topics.

communities throughout the world accepted their decisions concerning the law. By the end of this period, individual Jewish centers began to look to their own leadership for guidance. This led to the development of various local customs and laws, which differed from center to center and from community to community.

The other important period, which extended from the mid-1000s to the 1500s, was the rabbinic* period. This was a time in which great Jewish scholars helped refine the law and resolve contradictions in earlier Jewish writings. One of the great scholars of this time was Solomon ben Isaac, known as RASHI, who lived in northern France and Germany in the 1000s. Another great scholar was Moses MAIMONIDES, who helped codify Jewish law.

During the Middle Ages, Jewish law helped unify Jews scattered throughout Europe and the Islamic world. Jewish leaders imposed strict discipline to prevent Jews from seeking justice from non-Jewish courts, and efforts were made to persuade other authorities to give Jewish courts jurisdiction in various civil and criminal matters affecting Jews. These Jewish courts enforced decisions through fines and physical punishments. Some Jewish communities even maintained their own prisons. One of the most serious forms of punishment was a ban that excluded the offending person from the religious and civil life of the Jewish community.

While Jewish law was paramount in religious matters, in civil matters it was sometimes influenced by the secular laws of a particular country or region. Religious authorities were familiar with non-Jewish law and sometimes adopted elements of it. When a foreign principle was adopted, however, it was adapted to fit the principles and aims of Jewish law. If it did not fit with the basic Jewish principles of equality and justice, it was rejected. This process was a factor in the development of Jewish law during the Middle Ages. It also helped the Jewish community adapt itself as far as was necessary to its non-Jewish surroundings. (*See also* **Christianity; Islam, Political Organization of; Islam, Religion of; Law Schools; Parliament, English; Trials.**)

* **rabbinic**   pertaining to rabbis, the Jewish spiritual leaders and persons authorized to interpret Jewish law

Law Schools

Law schools flourished in the Byzantine Empire from the time of the emperor Justinian in the 500s. Under Justinian, Roman law was codified into a collection of civil law called the *Corpus juris civilis.* A major part of this work, the *Institutes,* was used as an introductory legal textbook. The impact of Roman law as transmitted by Justinian was profound. One of Byzantium's most famous law schools was in Beirut, but the law school in Constantinople also dates from the fifth century.

In western Europe, legal education was largely a practical concern before the 1100s. Judges and notaries* were trained for the tasks of drafting legal documents and conducting cases. However, as society became more complex, competing rights and legal jurisdictions created a need for individuals who could also analyze and interpret the law.

The earliest and most famous western European law school was established at the University of Bologna in Italy in the early 1100s. Scholars there were the first to begin using ancient Roman and Byzantine legal texts as the basis for a formal legal education. As other law schools were

* **notary**   public official who drafts and certifies legal documents

founded, most based their organization and methods of study on those of Bologna. In these schools, law was treated as a theoretical science rather than a practical skill. It was taught by professional teachers, who lectured on the rules of law contained in legal texts and analyzed legal contradictions or problems. Lectures were supplemented by repetitions, in which students would review what they had learned, and by disputations, in which they would debate questions and issues. To earn a degree, students first had to complete a course of instruction lasting four or five years in canon law* and five or six years in civil law*. A sequence of examinations completed a prospective lawyer's education. Those who passed their examinations were licensed to teach.

* **canon law** body of church law

* **civil law** body of law that regulates and protects the rights of individuals

The prestige of the law school at Bologna attracted students from all over Europe. Over time, the migration of students and teachers from Bologna contributed to the establishment of law schools elsewhere in Europe. Some law schools developed around famous teachers. Other law schools were founded by emperors, popes, or princes in order to fill their needs for individuals to take care of legal and administrative matters. The first law school established by an emperor was founded in 1224 by Holy Roman Emperor FREDERICK II, in Naples, Italy. In 1229, Pope Gregory IX founded the University of TOULOUSE in southern France to provide study in both theology* and church law. While other universities in Italy and France began to flourish at the beginning of the 1300s, legal education came much later to Germany. German students generally went to Italy or France to study, and the first German universities that offered civil law were not established until the mid-1300s and the 1400s.

* **theology** study of the nature of God and of religious truth

In the Islamic world, law schools represented traditions of interpretation of the Qur'an. Four such traditions, named after the founders, became dominant in various geographical regions: Hanafi in the Middle East, central Asia, and the Indian subcontinent; Shafi in east Africa, southern Arabia, and southeast Asia; Maliki in northern, western, and central Africa and Islamic Spain; and Hanbali in Saudi Arabia. Chains of tradition from teacher to teacher were maintained in institutions called madrasas, which were supported by state subsidies and by charitable giving. (*See also* **Law; Universities.**)

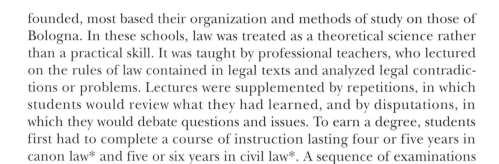

Leather and Leatherworking

Leather was an important material in the Middle Ages, and it was used in many different trades. Glovers, saddlers, shoemakers, pouch makers, bottle makers, and a number of other craftsmen all used leather in their trades. These skilled workers formed craft guilds to protect members from too much competition and also to ensure quality control for their products. The guilds established standards for all aspects of their trade. Guilds sometimes had great influence. One of the most powerful medieval guilds was the Worshipful Company of Saddlers, which began in LONDON at the end of the 1100s.

During the Middle Ages, leather was processed by three different methods. They were called tanning, dressing, and tawing. These processes remained relatively unchanged until the late 1800s.

Tanning involved three stages. First, a heavy hide was prepared by removing the outer layer of skin and fatty tissue. This was done by soaking the hide in a solution of lime and then scraping both sides with a knife. The lime helped separate the fibers of the hide, which allowed better penetration of a tanning solution that was added later. If a particularly soft leather was desired, the hide was immersed in a mixture of water and animal dung*.

* **dung** animal manure or excrement

The second stage was the tanning itself, which chemically changed the hide to prevent it from rotting or decomposing. To accomplish this, a prepared hide was soaked in solutions of water and oak bark for periods that varied from six months to two years, depending on the quality of the hide and the strength of the solutions. The oak bark contained tannin, a natural substance found in various plants, which helped preserve the hide. In the last stage, oils that were removed from the hide by the first two stages were replaced. This made the leather supple and water-resistant. The hide was also shaved to the desired thickness.

In the dressing method, a hide was treated with special oil from whale blubber, or fat. Oil-dressed leather was commonly known as chamois, after a breed of goat whose skin was often prepared this way. The hide was soaked in the whale oil and then beaten repeatedly to help the oil penetrate the hide. It was then exposed to the air, which caused a chemical reaction that prevented rotting.

* **alum** mineral salt that causes tissues and pores in the skin to contract; an astringent

The tawing method involved soaking a hide in a solution of alum* and salt. The leather produced by this method was stiff and white. It was softened by pulling the damp leather over a blunt-edged knife and working fats into the fibers. The crafts workers who produced this type of leather were called whittawers, or "white tawers." Cordovan, a fine leather produced in this way, was associated with the city of CÓRDOBA in Spain. Similar leather was produced in Britain and was called cordwain. Those who made the leather were called cordwainers, a term that came to mean a shoemaker.

The availability of the materials needed for the production of leather was an important factor in the location of leather-producing centers. England was a major leather-producing center in the Middle Ages because of its abundant supplies of oak bark, water, lime, and hides. France, Spain, Italy, and Germany also had important leather industries. (*See also* **Guilds.**)

Lenses and Eyeglasses

Magnifying lenses made of glass were used in various ancient cultures, including those of Greece and Rome. They were known as "burning glasses" because they could start fires by focusing the rays of the sun. These lenses probably also were used as magnifiers in various crafts, such as gem cutting.

During the Middle Ages, "burning glasses" and magnifiers remained in use, and medieval scholars discovered some of the principles behind these lenses. By the 1200s, for example, it was well-known that the phenomenon of refraction* explained how curved lenses could be used to magnify distant objects. The English scholars Robert GROSSETESTE and

* **refraction** phenomenon in which light rays change direction as they pass from one medium to another

Roger BACON both mentioned this phenomenon in their writings. Bacon also referred to the use of handheld magnifying lenses for reading and for examining small objects.

The discovery of such principles was an important step leading to the development of eyeglasses. The earliest known reference to eyeglasses dates from 1300 in Italy, and eyeglasses probably were invented in that country in the mid-1280s. It is not known who invented them, although evidence suggests that it was a craftsman from PISA or VENICE. The earliest depiction of eyeglasses was in a portrait painted in 1352.

These early eyeglasses were converging lenses, which are thicker in the center than at the edges. Such lenses can be used to correct presbyopia*, or farsightedness. Eyeglasses for correcting myopia*, or nearsightedness, were probably not developed until the 1400s, also in Italy. By that time, eyeglasses had become very fashionable among the wealthy, even for those whose vision was normal.

From the time eyeglasses were invented until the end of the medieval period, fitting a person with the proper lenses was largely a matter of trial and error. Little was known about optics* other than the law of reflection. Knowledge about the eye and about the principles that would help correct the problems of myopia and presbyopia did not come about until the 1600s. (*See also* **Glass.**)

* **presbyopia** condition associated with aging in which the eye loses its ability to focus on close objects

* **myopia** inability to focus on distant objects

* **optics** branch of physics that deals with the properties and phenomena of light

---

Lent

See *Christianity.*

Leo III, Pope

**died 816
Roman pope**

* **papacy** office of the pope and his administrators

Pope Leo III is best known for crowning CHARLEMAGNE emperor of the Romans on Christmas Day in 800, an act that laid the foundation for the later development of the HOLY ROMAN EMPIRE. He is also known for his efforts to reduce tensions between the Eastern and Western branches of Christianity.

After Leo became pope in 795, he faced opposition from the supporters of his predecessor, Adrian I, who had accused him of misconduct. In 799, Leo was seriously wounded by his enemies and left Rome to seek protection from Charlemagne. The following year, Leo returned to Rome and, with Charlemagne's help, cleared himself of all charges. He then crowned Charlemagne emperor. This coronation formalized the political separation of the West from the Byzantine Empire and confirmed the importance of the papacy.*

During his papacy, Leo resolved a controversy between the Eastern and Western Churches over the wording of the Nicene Creed, a statement of faith adopted in 325. The Byzantines objected to efforts by the Western Church to change a phrase concerning the relationship of the Father, the Son, and the Holy Ghost. Leo resolved the conflict by refusing to change the wording of the creed, yet acknowledging its importance to Western Christians.

Leo became a saint in 1673, largely because of his miraculous recovery from the wounds received from his enemies in 799. (*See also* **Charlemagne; Christianity; Papacy, Origins and Development.**)

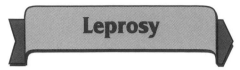

* **leper** person who has leprosy

See
color plate 5,
vol. 1.

* **vassal** person given land by a lord or monarch in return for loyalty and services

* **patron** person of wealth and influence who supports an artist, writer, or scholar

The medieval world ostracized lepers from society by imposing legal and religious sanctions on them. The leper at the center of this illumination is ringing a bell to warn others of his approach.

Leprosy, also known as Hansen's disease, is a bacterial infection. One form of the disease can lead to horrifying deformity and disfigurement if left untreated. Until modern times, no treatment for leprosy existed, and lepers* were shunned because of the repulsive nature of the disease.

During the Middle Ages, lepers were considered morally unclean. This attitude was already common as early as the 700s. It was derived partly from the horrifying nature of the disease and partly from Old Testament commands against the disease. Leprosy could strike anyone, although people from the upper classes seemed to be more prone to the disease. This may have had something to do with diet, since the disease seems to occur more frequently and more severely in well-fed persons.

Once a person was diagnosed with leprosy, a host of legal and religious sanctions were imposed. These sanctions were aimed at cutting off the leper from society. In 757, leprosy was accepted as grounds for divorce. In 1179, a church council ruled that lepers should not mix with other people nor be buried in a cemetery with healthy persons. In France, lepers were denied all or most rights of ownership, and if a vassal* was found to be a leper he might forfeit his property to his lord. Throughout most of medieval Europe, lepers were prohibited from entering churches and markets, washing and drinking directly from wells or streams, and touching merchandise and children. Lepers often were made to wear a reddish-colored robe with a hood to distinguish them from others, and they sometimes had to ring bells to warn others of their approach. Wealthy people with leprosy sometimes avoided such harsh rules by remaining secluded in their homes. Some lepers became wanderers, moving aimlessly from place to place.

The most common way of separating lepers from society in the Middle Ages was to place them in special leprosy hospitals. Many of these hospitals had a religious atmosphere, and the lepers led an almost monastic life. These hospitals, known as leprosariums, fed and clothed lepers and provided for their spiritual well-being. They did not provide therapy, since little was known about the disease. Leprosariums were established not only to benefit lepers and remove them from society but also to provide the patrons* of the hospitals with spiritual benefit. Caring for the

sick, like other charitable work, was seen as an opportunity for spiritual advancement.

Many leprosariums were founded in the 1100s and 1200s. Some of them were converted dwellings, although many were designed and built just for the purpose of caring for lepers. The leprosariums often had attached chapels for religious services. They might also have special cemeteries, since lepers were usually denied burials in regular cemeteries. Because the object was to remove lepers from society, leprosariums generally were built at the outer edges of cities. As cities expanded, the leprosariums often were moved farther out. Sometimes, leprosariums provided a home for healthy elderly persons as well as for lepers. These people usually paid a fee or a donation to stay there.

Leprosy seems to have reached a peak in the 1100s and 1200s and to have declined in the 1300s and 1400s. This decline is sometimes attributed to PLAGUES, which killed a huge percentage of the population in the 1300s. (*See also* **Hospitals and Poor Relief; Medicine.**)

Libraries

Although libraries originated in ancient times, the scope, organization, and purpose of library development changed dramatically during the Middle Ages. The size and range of library collections expanded, management techniques improved, specialized holdings and services developed, and the number of libraries increased rapidly. Greater access to books and information provided by the medieval libraries made them a powerful force behind the spread of knowledge and LITERACY.

Origins of Libraries. The word *library* comes from the Latin word *liber,* which means either a single book or a collection of books. To medieval scholars, the model for what a library should be was the famous ancient library in Alexandria, Egypt, which flourished from the third to the first century B.C. It had 700,000 manuscripts, and its librarians were the world's leading scholars. In ancient Rome, where books were plentiful, many prominent Romans, such as Cicero and Pliny, had their own libraries. However, these private collections did not survive in significant numbers after the fall of the Roman Empire in the West.

In the BYZANTINE EMPIRE, the origin of libraries was an altogether different matter. The palace library of the emperors thrived at CONSTANTINO-PLE, especially under the emperor JUSTINIAN I, who used its resources to support the great standardization and classification of law known as the *Justinian Code.* Like the ancient library at Alexandria, the library at Constantinople long served as a source of knowledge until the crusaders* sacked the imperial* capital in 1204. Following the attack, Byzantine book production declined.

Jewish and Islamic Libraries. Like Christianity, Judaism and Islam valued books and the written word. Medieval Jews inherited and continued the tradition of a temple library from ancient times. Jewish communities in Christian and Muslim lands supported their libraries in order to preserve their religious and cultural identity. Since Jewish libraries contained

* **crusader** person who participated in the holy wars against the Muslims during the Middle Ages

* **imperial** pertaining to an empire or emperor

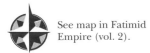

See map in Fatimid
Empire (vol. 2).

* **caliph** religious and political head of an
Islamic state

* **scribe** person who hand-copies manuscripts
to preserve them

See
color plate 8,
vol. 3.

Book Hunting

Librarians eager to improve their collections often traveled far and wide in search of much-desired new or rare volumes. They might visit a potential patron in hopes of convincing him to make a donation, or they might travel to a bookfair such as those held at London, Oxford, and Paris. In the 600s, the Englishman Benedict Biscop made five trips to Rome to obtain books for libraries at Wearmouth and Jarrow.

many translations from Hebrew and Arabic into Latin, these texts became important transmitters of learning to Christian Europe.

The Muslims not only inherited some of the world's richest libraries in the lands they conquered, they also developed their own tradition of academic and mosque libraries. UMAYYAD rulers built libraries in their capital of DAMASCUS, as did ABBASID rulers in BAGHDAD. At one time, Baghdad had 36 libraries. The most famous of these was the library of the caliphs*, known as the House of Learning, which had archives, laboratories, and a museum in addition to a library. Under the FATIMID rulers, the library in CAIRO grew to 1.1 million volumes. These library centers were supported by staffs of scribes* and grew to much larger collections than anything realized in the West.

The libraries the Muslims built in Spain attracted scholars from Christian Europe eager to study Arabic and Greek manuscripts. The caliphal library at CÓRDOBA was the largest, with 400,000 books. Access to the library was provided by a 44-volume catalog, and, at its peak in the 900s, it had a staff of 500 employees. Seville, TOLEDO, and GRANADA also had large libraries. Muslim libraries in Spain and North Africa served as bridges for the transmission of Arabic and Greek learning to medieval Europe.

Growth of Medieval Libraries in Europe.   St. Benedict of Nursia (ca. 480–543), founder of the BENEDICTINES, promoted the reading of books as an important part of monastic life. In Benedictine monasteries, where books were housed in the choir, in the dining hall, in the infirmary, and in monks' cells (rooms), monks took turns reading aloud at meals. Sometimes they memorized entire texts.

During the period of the CAROLINGIANS, there was increased interest in books and learning. CHARLEMAGNE, the Frankish king, established a palace school at AACHEN. Under the direction of ALCUIN OF YORK, the school quickly became an educational center that promoted reading, writing, and the standardization and spread of the LATIN LANGUAGE. It also served as a model and inspiration for the growth of monastic schools in other parts of Charlemagne's empire.

Religious orders also collected books and encouraged education for their monks and nuns. The Carthusians and the Cistercians, two religious orders founded in the late 1000s, required reading as part of their daily life. Cathedrals also established libraries, which were located in such places as York, Durham, and Canterbury in England; Toledo, Spain; Bamberg, Germany; and Paris, France. The support of wealthy patrons made libraries less dependent on the church. Robert de Sorbonne and Humphrey, duke of Gloucester, founded libraries at the UNIVERSITIES at Paris and Oxford, respectively. Private book collecting also became common among the nobility.

The invention of the printing press accelerated the growth of libraries. Before the appearance of printed books in the late 1400s, manuscripts were hand-copied by a team of scribes in a monastery scriptorium (writing room) or a palace workroom. When printing presses replaced scribes, book production moved out of the monasteries into separate printing facilities, where book printing and binding became a standardized process. Increased book production and lower book costs enabled libraries to build their collections as never before.

Islamic culture developed a rich tradition of academic and mosque libraries. Some of the largest and most famous libraries in the medieval world were found in Muslim cities. Muslims also inherited many well-stocked libraries in the lands they conquered. This illumination shows Islamic scholars at a public library.

* **liturgical** pertaining to formal religious rites and services

Improved Techniques.   Most of the features of a modern library, such as a reference section, were invented and refined in the Middle Ages. Innovations included alphabetization, placing CHRONICLES (historical records) in chronological order, and providing tables of contents, bibliographies, indexes, and short summaries called abstracts. After 1200, librarians created a body of reference works that included ancient Greek and Roman texts as well as medieval commentaries on these texts. These reference works were chained to workstations so that they could be read only in the library.

Modern procedures for the day-to-day operation of a library also were established during the Middle Ages. Rules required borrowers to handle the books with care. In fact, readers had to wear gloves to keep handprints from getting on the volumes. Borrowers had to promise that they would not lend a book to anybody else without permission from the librarian.

In monastic libraries, senior monks often read a book before it was put into circulation for the rest of the community. Exchanges among monastery libraries became common, and book-lending networks were established. In the 1200s, for example, it was already possible to arrange an interlibrary loan.

Most medieval libraries had a basic core of titles and authors. It usually included the BIBLE and commentaries; liturgical* texts; the works of the church fathers, especially AUGUSTINE, Ambrose, Jerome, and GREGORY THE GREAT; monastic rules, such as the Rule of St. Benedict; the *Summa theologica* of Thomas AQUINAS; the Roman classics of Virgil and Ovid; and assorted popular works such as those of BERNARD OF CLAIRVAUX.

Royal patronage helped some of the greatest libraries in Europe. For example, the famous Bibliothèque Nationale came into existence thanks to help from French kings Charles V, Louis XI, and Louis XII. (*See also* **Arabic Language and Literature; Books, Manuscript; Encyclopedias and Dictionaries; Gutenberg, Johannes; Hebrew Literature; Jewish Communities; Textbooks.**)

Lighting Devices

The main lighting devices in medieval churches, buildings, and homes were oil lamps, lanterns, torches, and candles. Large public gatherings, such as banquets or large funerals, were occasions for more lavish displays of light.

Byzantine Lighting Devices.   The most elaborate lighting devices in the Byzantine world were found in churches. One especially common type was the spouted lamp with a large bulblike container for the oil and a spout with a hole for the wick. Modeled on Greek and Roman lamps, these lamps were usually made of clay or bronze, and they were used in several ways. They could stand on end, hang from a hook or a ceiling beam, or be carried by hand. Bird shapes were popular, especially the Christian symbol of the dove.

The float-wick lamp, usually made of glass, was lit by oil floating on water, with an S-shaped bronze strip hung from the rim of the lamp acting as a wick holder. The Byzantines also invented a crown-shaped lighting

* **mosque** Muslim place of worship

fixture, called a *polycandelon*, that was widely used in churches. The device consisted of many small glass lamps attached to the crown with brackets. Lights were such an important part of Byzantine Church ritual that churches often spent as much as one-third of their money to buy and maintain lighting devices.

Islamic Lighting Devices. While Muslims adopted many Byzantine lighting devices they encountered during their conquests (including spouted lamps and the *polycandelon*), they developed several of their own types. An example was the Byzantine glass float-wick lamp, which became the oversized lamp decorated with multicolored enamel and gilding that was used in mosques*. Inscription bands around the mosque lamps often contained verses from the QUR'AN (Koran), especially the *Ayat-al-Nur (Verse of Light)*.

Western European Lighting Devices. European lighting devices that differed substantially from Byzantine models first appeared about 1000. Advances in German metalworking in the 1000s and 1100s contributed to the emergence of a new class of European lighting devices such as the Jerusalem chandelier, a giant metal chandelier 20 feet wide that held 72 candles. Its dazzling light was meant to suggest the glory of the heavenly city.

Seven-branched candlesticks were also popular. Cast in bronze and ranging in size from 8 to 20 feet tall, these candlesticks stood on a base that had the shape of animal claws. These massive candlesticks were commissioned by bishops for their cathedrals and by abbots and abbesses for their monasteries. The large candlesticks used on church altars were often decorated with enamel dragons or other elaborate artwork. After 1200, the artisans of VENICE made altar candlesticks of silver and crystal based on Byzantine models.

Most medieval people used simple lamps called *crusies* in their homes. These lamps had a pear-shaped or oval pan attached at the back to a flat, upright band with a hook-and-spike suspension device. Made of tin, brass, or iron, they sometimes had more than one spout. *Crusies* usually burned fish oil or tallow, a white animal fat used to make candles and soap. (*See also* **Byzantine Art; Cathedrals and Churches; Feasts and Festivals; Islamic Art and Architecture; Metals and Metalworking; Monasteries; Science.**)

This bronze lamp was made in the early Middle Ages. Lamps such as this one could hang from a hook or ceiling beam.

Literacy

Literacy, or the ability to read and write, was not commonplace in the Middle Ages. Until the late Middle Ages, very few people had the necessary skills to read a document or sign their name to it.

Byzantine Literacy. In the BYZANTINE EMPIRE, more people at all levels of society could read and write than in western Europe. Books were written in a form of Greek, which many people could at least partially understand without special study. Positions in the government requiring literacy in Greek were open to laymen. In addition, laymen were usually the teachers of reading and writing.

The Byzantine emperors themselves had a high level of literacy and learning. In fact, only two emperors in the thousand-year history of the empire were believed to be illiterate, and at least ten emperors were well-respected authors.

* **psalms** sacred songs from the Old Testament of the Bible

* **rhetoric** art of speaking or writing effectively

* **Torah** sacred wisdom of the Jewish faith, especially the first five books of the Bible

See color plate 13, vol. 1.

* **mosque** Muslim place of worship

* **clergy** priests, deacons, and other church officials qualified to perform church ceremonies

* **scribe** person who hand-copies manuscripts to preserve them

The wealthy often employed private tutors to educate their sons and, sometimes, their daughters. However, most literate Byzantines received their elementary education at school. After finishing their elementary education in their native city, some students moved to the capital of CONSTANTINOPLE or another large city for further study at a grammar school. There, a teacher called a *grammatikos* taught them literary Greek based on ancient poetry or the psalms*. The most accomplished students then went on to study and practice rhetoric* with a teacher called a *rhetor.*

Since many different ethnic groups lived within the empire, many languages were spoken—Syriac, Armenian, Coptic, Latin, Georgian, and Old Slavonic—each with its own literary traditions. People who lived in the empire were often literate in two languages—their own native tongue and Greek, the official language of the empire.

Hebrew Literacy.   A basic duty of every Jewish father was to instruct his children in the Torah* and in biblical interpretation. This religious duty resulted in widespread literacy among Jews, especially among sons. It applied to children of the poor as well as of the wealthy. Various forms of private and community-sponsored elementary education and advanced instruction developed in the self-governing Jewish communities of medieval Europe. In the late Middle Ages, some Jewish communities in Italy and in the Ottoman Empire expanded the areas of study to include scientific and philosophical subjects in works written by non-Jews, as well as traditional Jewish teachings.

Islamic Literacy.   As in the Jewish tradition, education designed to prepare young men for religious study was an important part of the Islamic tradition. In the Islamic world, introductory grammar schools taught handwriting and phonology (the translation of letters into sounds and vice versa). For some young men, grammar school was followed by intensive study of Scripture and religious law, sometimes at a college. The first colleges appeared in the 600s and 700s in mosques*. By the 10th and 11th centuries, the Muslim college, or madrasa, was a place that both taught and lodged students. Study also took place in private homes and libraries, in the homes of scholars, and in hospitals.

Although Arabic was the traditional language of the Islamic Empire, people were literate in other languages as well. The educated people of Persia (present-day Iran) enthusiastically adopted the Arabic language for the first few centuries of Islam. As time went by, however, Persian became the language of literature and everyday life, and only religious works continued to be written in Arabic. This was the case in many non-Arabic-speaking parts of the Islamic world, such as Turkey and India, where Arabic was cultivated as a learned language for religious purposes only.

Western European Literacy.   For much of the Middle Ages, LATIN—the language of the Roman Empire—was the language of all education, learning, and formal communication. Knowledge of Latin was largely confined to the clergy* and to members of noble families. Jobs and careers that required reading and writing were usually filled by the clergy.

Writing was mostly confined to formal manuscript production by scribes*. Little casual correspondence was done, and people relied heavily on oral communication. Script, or handwriting, had evolved into a form that was cumbersome and difficult to read. In the 800s, this script was replaced by a more legible style called the Caroline minuscule. Later, some monks used the angular Gothic script, which was swifter because it allowed continuous strokes without lifting the pen from the parchment.

Because Latin was not their native tongue, European monks composed glossaries, or alphabetized word lists, to help their students build their vocabulary. The first such glossary was completed in 1053. By the end of the Middle Ages, dictionaries were commonly used as companions to grammar textbooks in primary education.

By the 13th century, the student population of universities, estimated in the thousands, was far greater than had existed at monasteries and cathedral schools. The literate population was increasing. Universities trained clerics*, who were employed in growing numbers by the church and by kings. Literacy still meant reading and writing in Latin, however.

The emergence of the written vernacular* in the 1200s and 1300s boosted literacy. French became the written language of royal courts, even in England. In contrast to Latin, French could be learned not only from books but also by living among French people. Children were sent to France to serve in noble households, where they acquired the language easily. In the mid-1300s, university scholars began to standardize French spelling. Monarchs, such as CHARLES V OF FRANCE, established libraries that contained French translations of books previously available only in Latin. Other vernacular languages—including Italian, English, and Dutch—experienced a similar movement toward standardization.

The remaining obstacle to widespread literacy was the scarcity of books. Books were expensive, and small schools and members of the merchant class could scarcely afford them. Book production was slow and expensive—it could take a scribe more than a month to copy 100 pages of text. The invention of the printing press in 1448 made the manufacture of inexpensive books possible. As less expensive books became available to all segments of society, a new age of reading was born. (*See also* **Books, Manuscript; Clergy; Encyclopedias and Dictionaries; French Language and Literature; Gutenberg, Johannes; Latin Language; Libraries; Monasteries; Schools; Universities; Writing Materials and Techniques.**)

* **cleric** church official qualified to perform church ceremonies

* **vernacular** language or dialect native to a region; everyday, informal speech

Lithuania

Lithuania is a small nation located on the Baltic Sea, which separates northwestern Europe and Scandinavia. Lithuania's size has changed dramatically over the centuries as it has conquered surrounding territories or been added to the kingdoms of stronger neighbors. Lithuania was able to remain independent from European culture throughout most of the Middle Ages because it lay far from the major European cities and possessed no significant natural resources to attract the attention of the outside world.

The earliest Lithuanians were the Balts, a people from the east who had moved into the marshy area along the Baltic coast by the 400s. The Balts worshiped forces of nature such as thunder, the sun, the moon, and the stars. The name *Lithuania* first appears in historical records of the 1000s.

Medieval Lithuanians frequently fought Prussians, Poles, and Russians, their neighbors to the south and east. In the 1100s, Lithuanian forces expanded eastward into Slav territories in what is now Russia. In the late 1200s, Lithuania was attacked by the Teutonic Knights, a military order that had been founded in Palestine to fight the Muslims. A German ruler invited the knights to wage war on his Prussian neighbors, and this war spilled over into nearby Lithuania.

Pressure from foreign armies forced the Lithuanians to unite in their own defense. By the mid-1200s, the warlord Mindaugas had emerged as the strongest Lithuanian leader, and a state began to form around him. Mindaugas played his enemies against each other in a series of alliances. When the MONGOLS invaded eastern Europe in the late 1230s, the East Slavs asked Lithuania for protection, and as a result Lithuanian lords became rulers over much Slav territory. Although the Lithuanians had remained pagan*, their Slav subjects were Christian. The Lithuanians used their wealth from their trading networks, their armies, and their organizational skills to stay in power over subjects who followed a different religion.

In the mid-1300s, Lithuania became a power in northern Europe under Gediminas, a practical ruler who asked the pope to help end Lithuania's long war with the Teutonic Knights. At this time, Lithuania was organized into districts administered by governors. All lands were held on behalf of the Great Prince, as the ruler of Lithuania was called. The Great Prince could divide his realm among his sons.

When Gediminas died, Lithuania was divided among his sons. After a struggle, one of them, Algirdas, became ruler of Vilnius, Lithuania's main city. Under the leadership of Algirdas, Lithuania expanded into Slav lands as never before. By 1363, Lithuanian territory reached to the Black Sea. Still, the Teutonic Knights continued to harass Lithuania during the 1300s, ravaging the land and trying to lure discontented princes to their side. The war against the knights was carried on by Algirdas's son, Jagiello.

A practical ruler like his father, Jagiello sought an alliance through marriage. In 1385, he married Jadwiga, heiress to the Polish throne, and he became king of Poland and Lithuania. As part of the marriage terms, Jagiello and his relatives converted to Christianity. The rest of Lithuania soon became Christian as well.

Lithuania reached the height of its power under Vytautas, who ruled from 1392 to 1430. Vytautas finally ended the threat from the Teutonic Knights by defeating them at the Battle of Grunwald in 1410. For years afterward, Lithuania had strong ties to Poland. Through the late 1700s, the Great Prince of Lithuania was also the king of Poland. (*See also* **Baltic Countries; Knights, Orders of; Slavs.**)

* **pagan** word used by Christians to mean non-Christian and believing in several gods

Llywelyn ap Gruffydd

died 1282
Ruler of Wales

* **principality** region that is ruled by a prince

In the Middle Ages, the Celtic-speaking people of WALES were led by their native princes in wars against the English, who were bent on conquering Wales. One of the Welsh fighting princes—the last one to rule an independent Wales—was Llywelyn ap Gruffydd.

In 1246, Llywelyn rose to power in northern Wales. By 1258, he had become prince of north and south Wales. When an English noble named SIMON DE MONTFORT THE YOUNGER led a group of barons in a revolt against their king, HENRY III, Llywelyn joined forces with Simon de Montfort in return for his recognition of Llywelyn's rule. Simon de Montfort granted this recognition in the Treaty of Montgomery of 1267, which created a principality* of Wales ruled by Llywelyn and his successors.

When King EDWARD I came to the English throne in 1272, Llywelyn's fortunes changed for the worse. In 1276, Edward set out to conquer Wales. Llywelyn's refusal to pay homage* to Edward, along with several territorial disputes, led to war in 1282. Welsh forces met Edward's army, and Llywelyn was killed in the battle. Some accounts suggest that Llywelyn was betrayed, but no one knows for sure. His head was displayed on a pole in London—the customary treatment for those who were considered enemies of the English crown. Edward established England's rule over Wales and formally designated his son as Prince of Wales in 1303. Since that time, the eldest son of the English monarch has been called the Prince of Wales.

The Welsh mourned the death of their champion Llywelyn. Welsh poets wrote many fine poems in his honor. The most famous of these was written by Gruffydd ap yr Ynad Coch. (*See also* **Celtic Languages and Literature; England.**)

* **homage** formal public declaration of loyalty to the king or overlord

See color plate 7, vol. 3.

Lollards

* **transubstantiation** belief that bread and wine change into the body and blood of Jesus Christ during the Communion ceremony

* **sacrament** religious ceremony of the Christian church considered especially sacred, such as Communion and baptism

* **vernacular** language or dialect native to a region; everyday, informal speech

* **theology** study of the nature of God and of religious truth

* **heresy** belief that is contrary to church doctrine

* **secular** nonreligious; connected with everyday life

The Lollards were religious reformers in England during the 1300s and 1400s who followed the ideas and teachings of the English theologian John WYCLIF. Critical of the church's abuse of power and its vast wealth, the Lollards were persecuted for their beliefs. Among these beliefs were a denial of transubstantiation*, a rejection of the sacraments* and of priestly authority, and an emphasis on studying Scripture in the vernacular*.

The Lollards and their reform movement rose in the 1300s among the educated classes of England. Several early Lollard leaders had studied at Oxford University, where Wyclif taught theology* and philosophy. By the 1390s, several large and well-established groups of Lollards existed in many parts of England, and the movement began attracting people from the middle and lower classes. Among those who spread Lollard ideas were so-called poor priests, who traveled around the countryside preaching against the established religion.

After England introduced the death penalty for heresy* in 1401, the Lollards were denounced as heretics. Many were tried and convicted, and some were burned at the stake. Several Lollard uprisings were cruelly suppressed by church and secular* authorities, including a rebellion led by Sir John Oldcastle in 1414. After the Oldcastle rebellion, the Lollards were driven into hiding because of constant attacks by the authorities. Yet, the movement survived until the 16th century. Its calls for reform weakened the hold of the church on the English people and may have contributed to the English Reformation. (*See also* **Heresy and Heresies.**)

Lombards, Kingdom of

The Lombards were a Germanic people who occupied eastern Austria and northern Italy during the 500s. They were fierce fighters who served in the armies of the BYZANTINE EMPIRE. When the Byzantine emperor JUSTINIAN I died in 565, the Lombards ended their alliance with the empire and created their own kingdom in Italy. Lombardy, a present-day region in northern Italy, still bears their name.

Italy's Po River valley and the region called Tuscany came under Lombard control in the late 560s. Under King Agilulf of Turin, who ruled from

590 to 616, the Lombards seized the rest of the Italian peninsula. The Lombard kingdom reached the height of its power in the 700s under King Liutprand. From their royal center in the city of Pavia, Lombard kings ruled over a Christian people whose culture combined German and Roman traditions. The kings placed relatives and allies in neighboring cities and in rural fortresses to support their rule. They also appointed officials to run the armies and the courts.

By the time of Liutprand's death in 744, the Lombards controlled central and northern Italy except for the land held by the pope in Rome. Liutprand's successors wanted to add Rome to the Lombard kingdom. To prevent a Lombard conquest, Pope Zacharias formed an alliance with PEPIN III, the king of the FRANKS who twice had invaded Italy (in 755 and again in 756). The Lombards kept up the pressure on Rome. Pepin's successor, CHARLEMAGNE, invaded Italy in 773, defeated the Lombards, and captured Pavia in 774. Charlemagne took the Iron Crown of the Lombards and declared himself their king. Lombardy became part of Charlemagne's empire, and the independent Lombard kingdom ended. (*See also* **Italy; Rome.**)

London

See map in England (vol. 2).

* **barbarian** referring to people from outside the cultures of Greece and Rome who were viewed as uncivilized

L ondon, the capital of England, was one of the great cities of medieval Europe. The city owed much of its historical and economic significance to its location. Situated in southeast England on the Thames River, it was a major commercial port linked by shipping to the rest of Europe. Its status as an international port made it a center of economic activity and led to its emergence as the seat of political power.

London dates from ancient times when Celtic peoples inhabited the land along the banks of the Thames. During the Roman occupation of Britain, the Celtic village grew into a town called Londinium, and it became the hub of the Roman road system in Britain. The Romans built a wall around Londinium for defense, and the town's population grew to about 30,000 by the mid-100s.

Anglo-Saxon London. The Romans abandoned Britain in the early 400s, and Germanic barbarian* groups—the Angles, the Saxons, and the Jutes—swept into the country and pushed the Roman-Celtic people to its far western and northern reaches. Although London was largely abandoned, the city remained an important center of trade. When Christian missionaries began arriving in Britain in the late 500s, London became a base of missionary activity. It also served as a royal base of Anglo-Saxon kings, who taxed the shipment of goods in and out of the town.

In 871, London was occupied by yet another invading army. This time the VIKINGS took over the city, but they soon met resistance from Anglo-Saxons led by King ALFRED THE GREAT. Alfred recaptured the city in 886 and encouraged people to settle within the old Roman walls. In an effort to make London an urban center and a place from which to defend the rest of England, Alfred gave land to bishops and Anglo-Saxon leaders called elders, or aldermen, in return for their commitment to defend the city. The aldermen were allowed to collect tolls and dues that ordinarily went to the king.

Between the late 800s and mid-1000s, London grew into a major port, as merchant ships from FRANCE and FLANDERS unloaded their goods on London docks. As economic activity expanded, a rudimentary city government began to develop. It consisted of city bishops and reeves (high officers of the king) who banded together to keep the peace, to punish wrongdoers, and to support one another in difficult times. During this period, the English king, EDWARD THE CONFESSOR, rebuilt the Benedictine abbey church in London. This great church, known as WESTMINSTER ABBEY, came to serve as a royal palace as well as a center of English government. London thus became both the economic and political focal point of the kingdom.

The Normans' Transformation of London. After the NORMANS conquered England in 1066, London gained importance. Rather than resist the Norman invaders, Londoners surrendered. Because of their decision to submit, the city was granted a charter that allowed it to keep its own laws and customs. This was an important step toward self-rule. The city prospered while other parts of England suffered under the pressures of Norman rule. The coronation of WILLIAM I THE CONQUERER as king of England in London's Westminster Abbey confirmed the city's importance.

Under Norman rule, the population of London grew and trade continued to expand. Arabian gold, Chinese silks, Russian furs, Egyptian gems, and French wines were all imported into the city. Most of its export trade, however, was in wool, which was handled by Flemish merchants. The look of the city began to change under the Normans as well. They introduced the custom of building primarily in stone, and many new churches, monasteries, and hospitals were constructed between 1066 and 1200. Another formidable Norman building was the Tower of London, which was built by William I in the late 1000s to serve as a fortress. One of the most impressive construction projects of that time was a stone bridge across the Thames River. Completed in the early 1200s, it remained intact as the famed London Bridge until it was demolished in the 1800s.

The Emergence of Self-Rule. Beginning in the 1100s, London began to gain important concessions toward self-rule. During the reign of King HENRY I, Londoners were granted the right to choose their own SHERIFFS and run their own judicial courts. In 1215, Londoners joined the English barons in their feud with King JOHN and succeeded in having certain demands included in MAGNA CARTA. They secured protection for merchants, the right of free navigation on the Thames, and the establishment of London's system of weights and measures as the standard for the rest of the kingdom. By about 1220, the city was controlled by an elected mayor and his officials.

A more organized city government emerged in the 1200s. During that time, London was divided into districts called wards. Inhabitants of each ward elected their own aldermen and chose individuals to pave and clean the streets, to fight fires, and to keep the peace. Fines were handed out for such offenses as throwing garbage into the street or allowing geese or pigs to roam free. Taxes were collected in each ward and brought to a central administrative building called the Guildhall. The mayor and the aldermen heard cases and handed down justice in the Guildhall, and city records were stored there. Officials assigned to help the mayor run the city and carry out the laws became part of the city government.

Mayor Richard Whittington of London

Richard Whittington (1358–1423) is perhaps the most famous mayor in London's history. Whittington was the son of a squire in Gloucestershire, a county in southwest England. He married well and became a mercer, a seller of expensive fabrics. In city government, he served as a councilman, an alderman, and a sheriff before becoming mayor. He supported Henry IV's seizure of the throne from Richard II and also helped Henry V by giving him sizable loans. In return, the kings gave Whittington the right to sell goods to the King's Wardrobe, the name for the office of the monarch's chief purchasing officer. Whittington left no heirs, and his fortune was used to build almshouses and libraries and to pay for church repairs. Whittington's life was mythologized in the early 1600s in the popular English story of Dick Whittington and his cat. According to the story, Dick made his fortune when he sold his only possession, a cat, to the king of Morocco, whose land was plagued by mice and rats.

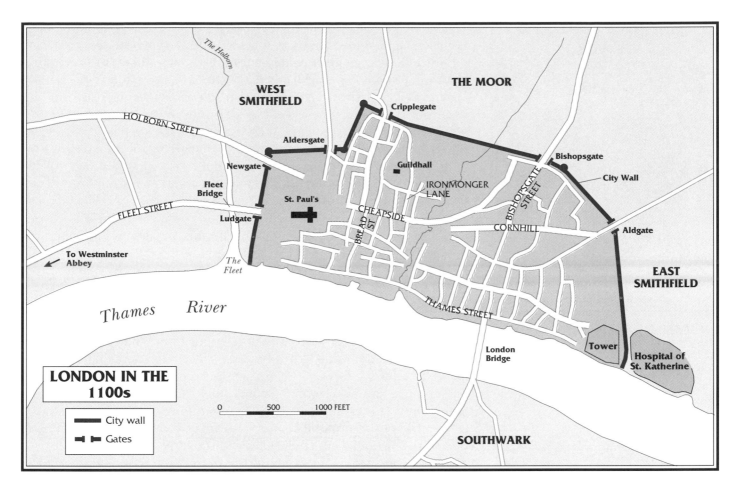

LONDON IN THE 1100s

— City wall
◄■ ► Gates

0   500   1000 FEET

By the 1100s, London had become a major port as well as the economic and political focal point of England. The city had already begun to spread outside its walls.

English kings were not at all happy with the growing independence of Londoners. The 1200s were marked by constant conflicts between monarchs and the town. At the root of these conflicts was money; Londoners struggled to resist the monarchs' demands for taxation and to prevent intervention in their internal affairs. In 1285, growing political turbulence and violence in the city led King EDWARD I to take away Londoners' right of self-government. Edward appointed his own official to preside over city courts and to maintain control over the citizens. Self-rule was restored 13 years later, however.

London in the Late Middle Ages.   Despite continuing conflicts with strong-willed monarchs, London continued to grow and prosper during the 1300s. New docks were built along the waterfront, and vacant spaces within the city were filled up with shops and houses. At this time, London became increasingly important as a commercial and financial center, and the palace at Westminster became the administrative and legal heart of England.

London was still a walled city in the 1300s, although suburbs had begun to spread outside the walls. Seven gates pierced the city wall. Their names—such as Ludgate, Newgate, Cripplegate, and Bishopsgate—survive today as reminders of the past. Within the walled area, which became known as The City, the main street was Cheapside (from the Anglo-Saxon word *cheap,* meaning barter). Cheapside bustled with activity, its broad space filled with people buying and selling goods. Workshops were located on side streets,

One of the most famous structures of medieval England was the Tower of London. Work on the first tower, the White Tower, was begun by William I in the late 1000s. This view of London in the early 1400s shows the White Tower prominent at the center. The scene is from a manuscript of poems of Charles of Orleans, who was captured during the Battle of Agincourt in 1415 and remained a prisoner in the Tower for 25 years.

* **journeymen** day laborers

* **fraternities** groups of people joined together for common purposes or interests

which took the names of the trades located there. For example, Ironmonger Lane was named for ironworkers who fashioned horseshoes, tools, and other iron objects; tailors could be found on Threadneedle Street. Most houses in London were small and dark, with little room for more than eating and sleeping. The city streets thus became a vast meeting place in which to negotiate business, greet friends, or just enjoy the city scene.

The history of London in the 1300s was characterized by a struggle for power between different social classes. All artisans or craftspersons belonged to powerful GUILDS. In 1319, King EDWARD II gave the guilds the right to control who could open a shop or carry on a business in the city. Only a "freeman," or official citizen, could open a shop or sell goods. The guilds had the power to bestow citizenship on people of their choice. Those who were not "free" had to work as journeymen* or else set up shops outside the city's jurisdiction. This class distinction led to political turmoil. Gradually, the city's leaders realized the need to govern in the interests of all the people rather than just a wealthy ruling class, and a degree of stability was achieved.

In 1348 and 1349, the BLACK DEATH had a devastating effect on London, killing as much as one-third of the population. While the city government survived, the social structure of the city changed dramatically. With labor scarce because of the decline in population, journeymen demanded higher wages and better working conditions. They tried to form their own guilds and to press for a greater voice in city government as well. During this period of social mobility, the opportunities available in London attracted people to the city from all over the country.

As people flocked to London, the newcomers banded together in small neighborhood guilds or fraternities* for security and help in times of trouble or sickness. The needs of these people led to the creation of hospitals and numerous churches. City life also improved with such projects as the construction of pipes for carrying fresh water. Londoners became increasingly responsible for charitable work and for improving the quality of life. In the 1400s, this concern led to the establishment of almshouses, groups of dwellings for the sick or aged. These differed from hospitals in that they provided more privacy and independence for their occupants.

During the late 1400s, prosperity drew increasing numbers of people to London. By the end of the 1500s, the city's population had swelled to about 200,000—making it the largest city in England. (*See also* **Cities and Towns; Construction, Building; England; Parliament, English.**)

Louis VI of France

1081–1137
King of France

* **abbey** monastery under the rule of an abbot or abbess

* **Capetians** the succession of rulers descended from Hugh Capet

Nicknamed "the Fat" because of his obesity (at age 46 he could no longer mount a horse without aid), Louis VI effectively imposed law and order on the Île-de-France, the royal territory of central France, which included the cities of Orleans and PARIS.

Louis was the son of Philip I and Berthe of Holland. He was educated at the abbey* school of St. Denis outside of Paris. Louis became king in 1108 and married Adelaide of Savoy seven years later. Sweet-natured and friendly, Louis was a capable ruler whose main accomplishment paved the way for the growth of royal power in France. Louis believed that if the Capetians* were to achieve mastery as kings of France, they had to take control of their own royal lands, which had long been dominated by strong-willed feudal lords over whom the king had little control.

In the 1100s, the Île-de-France contained the castles of many lords who used them as bases from which to raid the countryside. Violence was so widespread that even the king could not travel safely through the region. For much of his reign, Louis waged war on the lords of the Île-de-France. He attacked the castles, burning many of them, and he imprisoned the nobles. By 1130, most of the robber lords had been subdued. At the same time, Louis won the support of the church by protecting church lands. He also encouraged the growth of towns and granted some degree of self-government to them.

Within his own government, Louis sought to rid himself of the handful of families who controlled the high offices of the king's household. The most powerful of these officials were the SENESCHAL, the constable, the butler, the chamberlain, and the chancellor*. After dismissing some of them, Louis left the offices vacant and made Abbot SUGER OF ST. DENIS his chief counselor. Louis also recruited members of the lesser nobility to carry out the real work of government. Because these knights owed their wealth and position to the king, they formed the core of a growing body of families loyal to him.

Louis was less successful in his dealings with the great barons whose territories surrounded the Île-de-France. Among these territories were the great fiefs* of Champagne, Flanders, and Normandy. The duke of Normandy was also King HENRY I of England. Louis waged two wars against Henry, but both ended in disaster for France. Louis tried repeatedly to replace the strong barons with ones who would obey him, but his attempts failed. Shortly before his death, however, Louis strengthened the monarchy by arranging a marriage between his son, Louis VII, and Eleanor, heiress to the powerful duchy* of Aquitaine. (*See also* **Capet, Hugh; Eleanor of Aquitaine; France.**)

* **chancellor** official who handles the records and archives of a monarch

* **fief** under feudalism, property of value (usually land) that a person held under obligations of loyalty to an overlord

* **duchy** territory ruled by a duke or a duchess

Louis IX of France

1214–1270
King and saint

* **regent** person appointed to govern a kingdom when the rightful ruler is too young, absent, or disabled

See color plate 6, vol. 3.

Louis IX ruled France during a period of peace and prosperity. In the 1200s, France was a leading power in Europe. The administrative skills of the hardworking and serious Louis made his country even stronger. A deeply religious man, Louis became the symbol of the ideal Christian monarch.

Louis became king in 1226 on the death of his father, Louis VIII. Because the new king was too young to rule in his own name, his mother, BLANCHE OF CASTILE, became regent*, directing royal affairs, encouraging Louis's religious feelings, and advising him until he came of age. Early in his reign, Louis faced many challenges from rebellious nobles, but he overcame these challenges with his mother's help. One challenge came from King HENRY III OF ENGLAND, who wanted to recover the French province of Normandy, which had once belonged to the English kings. After several decades, Louis was able to persuade Henry to give up his claim to Normandy.

In 1234, Louis married Margaret of Provence, with whom he had 11 children. Margaret did not get along with the strong-willed Blanche, who continued to act as her grown son's adviser. The king led the Seventh

Louis IX was an able administrator and a deeply religious man who became the symbol of the ideal Christian monarch. He fought in two crusades, dying while on the second one. In 1297, only 27 years after his death, Louis was canonized and became St. Louis the Confessor. This sculptured bust of a young King Louis is from the Sainte Chapelle in Paris.

Crusade to the Holy Land in 1248. During his six-year absence, Blanche again acted as regent. Unsuccessful as a crusader, Louis was captured and had to surrender a town to win his release. He then spent four years improving the defenses of Christian strongholds in Palestine before returning to France.

Louis greatly improved the administration of France. He reformed the government of the city of Paris and established institutions to care for the poor, the sick, widows, and orphans. He acted as a judge in many disputes, including one between the English king and the barons of England. Louis also restored peace between France and Aragon, one of the Christian kingdoms of Spain, by giving up French claims to Aragonese territory on the French border. Louis was a patron of the arts, although he was interested in the arts purely in the service of religion. He commissioned the building of one of the finest examples of GOTHIC ARCHITECTURE, the Paris church called the Sainte Chapelle.

Despite poor health, Louis left France on another crusade in 1270. He died soon after landing in Tunisia in northern Africa. His son, Philip III, started a movement to have Louis declared a saint. In 1297, Louis was made St. Louis the Confessor. (*See also* **Crusades; France.**)

Lübeck

* **mercantile**   pertaining to merchants, trade, and commerce

* **principality**   region that is ruled by a prince

See map in Germany (vol. 2).

The city of Lübeck is located on the northern coast of Germany on the Baltic Sea. Throughout its long history, the city has served as a major seaport and a center of international trade. During the Middle Ages, Lübeck was the leading city of the HANSEATIC LEAGUE, a major trading alliance of northern European cities. It helped create a unique mercantile* culture that still influences northern German life and politics.

Early History.   The origins of Lübeck date back to the VIKING era, when trading centers sprang up along rivers and on the islands around the Baltic Sea. Old Lübeck was established as a trading post where products from the rich hunting and fishing areas to the north were exchanged for the finished goods of the HOLY ROMAN EMPIRE to the south. This original settlement was destroyed in 1138 during a series of wars among local principalities*.

In 1143, Count Adolf II of Holstein founded a new city on a river island that was more defensible than the old site. The new town was thought to be unconquerable, but in 1147 Lübeck was destroyed again by Niklot of Mecklenburg. After that, Count Adolf built a strong fort to prevent a recurrence of the disaster. Adolf's control of Lübeck was short-lived, however. In 1157, the city was taken by Henry the Lion of Saxony after a devastating fire. Lübeck was refounded again the next year and, under Henry's rule, it became the prosperous religious, political, and economic center of the region.

Henry's rule of Lübeck ended in 1181 when the city was taken by the Holy Roman Emperor, FREDERICK I BARBAROSSA. The emperor granted Lübeck a new charter in 1188. For the next decade, the city's merchants extended their trade, reaching even to Russia by 1199. Increasingly, however, they faced competition from Denmark, but they had little aid from the emperor. In 1201, while the Holy Roman Empire was embroiled in civil war, the Danish king, Waldemar II, seized Lübeck and made it part of his own domain.

Under Danish rule, Lübeck continued to prosper, and the city's laws served as a model for more than 100 cities near and around the Baltic Sea. In time, however, the citizens of Lübeck grew tired of Danish rule, and, in 1223, they rose in open revolt. By 1227, the Danish forces were defeated, and the new Holy Roman Emperor, FREDERICK II, granted Lübeck a new charter that made it a "free city" in terms of both trade and government.

Lübeck as a Free City. Without the protection of a monarch, Lübeck had to defend itself against robber barons, sea pirates, and local counts who controlled the overland trade routes. This was difficult to do alone, so Lübeck entered into a defensive pact with other cities in the region. By 1299, a number of cities had formed an alliance, with Lübeck as the acknowledged leader. As others cities joined this alliance, it became known as the Hanseatic League.

During the 1200s and 1300s, Lübeck underwent many changes. The city's role as leader of the Hanseatic League brought it tremendous wealth, and international trade became its main source of income. The city grew in size, and many new houses, churches, and other structures were built. It became the second largest city in Germany, after COLOGNE. Although the plague* killed up to a quarter of the population in the mid-1300s, the city quickly recovered and regained its superiority.

Toward the end of the 1300s and into the 1400s, Lübeck was faced with a number of challenges. A war between the Hanseatic League and Denmark resulted in a Hanseatic victory in 1370. Beginning in 1380, workers' GUILDS in Lübeck demanded greater political rights, and calls for armed violence threatened the city's stability. The conflict was resolved, and the guilds gained greater power. Pirates were a continuing threat until they were defeated decisively by the Teutonic KNIGHTS in 1398. In the 1400s, wars in the eastern Baltic region hurt commerce, and the conquest of the important commercial city of NOVGOROD by IVAN III OF MUSCOVY in 1478 disrupted trade for a generation. Despite such challenges, Lübeck continued to prosper. In the 1500s, however, the Hanseatic League became divided along religious lines, and many of its cities lost their independence to powerful monarchs. Lübeck's power and prosperity then declined. (*See also* **Baltic Countries; Germany; Muscovy, Rise of; Scandinavia; Trade.**)

See map in Trade (vol. 4).

* **plague** disease that swept across the medieval world several times, including the Black Death in the mid-1300s

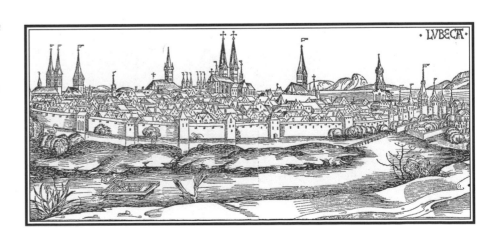

The city of Lübeck, Germany, became an important medieval seaport and international trade center. It was also the leading city of the Hanseatic League. This woodcut from the *Nuremberg Chronicle,* written in 1493, shows a panoramic view of the walled city.

Lull, Ramon

ca. 1232–1316
Christian mystic, poet, and philosopher

* **theologian** person who studies religious faith and practice

* **vernacular** language or dialect native to a region; everyday, informal speech

* **seneschal** person who manages property and financial affairs, such as for a royal court

* **mystic** person who experiences divine truths through faith, spiritual insight, and intuition

Ramon Lull (also known as Ramón Llull and Raymond Lully) was a poet, philosopher, and theologian* who devoted his life to converting Muslims and Jews to Christianity and to reunifying the Eastern and Western Christian Churches. Born on the Mediterranean island of Majorca off the coast of Spain, he pioneered the use of the vernacular* for theological and philosophical writings. He also contributed to the creation of Catalan, the everyday speech of Majorca and CATALONIA, as a literary language by using it in poetry, novels, and mystical works.

Born to a wealthy family, Lull was raised as a noble and served as the seneschal* of Prince James, the future king of ARAGON and Majorca. In about 1263, he had a mystical religious experience that convinced him to embark on a mission of converting the Muslims to Christianity. He abandoned his courtly life, sold his possessions, and spent several years studying Arabic, Latin, and Christian theology and philosophy. About 1274, Lull had another mystical experience. He had a vision of a universe that was unified by God and reflected the divine qualities of God. This vision became the basis for a series of works written over the remaining course of his life. These works, known collectively as the *Ars Magna (The Great Art)*, dealt with the means of establishing ultimate truth through faith. They inspired generations of Christian religious thinkers.

From 1287 onward, Lull made a number of journeys to the papal court at Rome and to various royal courts in western Europe to request aid for his missionary plans, for church reform, and for the CRUSADES. He also traveled extensively throughout North Africa and to CYPRUS and Asia Minor (present-day Turkey) doing missionary work. Legend has it that Lull was stoned to death in 1315 while attempting to convert Muslims at Bougie in North Africa (in present-day Algeria). However, it is more likely that he died a natural death in Majorca the following year.

The *Ars Magna* was Lull's greatest achievement as a philosopher and theologian. As a mystic* and a poet, his masterpiece was *The Book of the Lover and the Beloved*. Lull's poetry reflected the tradition of the TROUBADOURS and also the influence of Muslim poets. Most of his works were written originally in Catalan and then translated into Latin. The Catalan versions inspired others to write in that language and helped make it an important literary language. (*See also* **Mysticism; Spanish Language and Literature.**)

Lydgate, John

ca. 1370–1449
English poet

* **vernacular** language or dialect native to a region; everyday, informal speech

John Lydgate was one of the most well-known, prolific, and influential writers of his day. In time, however, he was overshadowed by the brilliance of Geoffrey CHAUCER, whose work had inspired both the style and content of Lydgate's poetry. Lydgate was important as a representative of the habits, thought processes, and ambitions of the medieval poet. His main contribution was to make the literary vernacular* of Chaucer better known and understood by readers of his and later ages.

An ordained priest, Lydgate was educated at a BENEDICTINE monastery and at Oxford University. By 1420, he had established his reputation as a poet, and his works were in great demand. Much of Lydgate's poetry was commissioned by wealthy patrons, such as King HENRY V. These works often were full of praise for the patrons and their accomplishments. Lydgate also wrote many highly moralistic and religious works, including short fables and poems about the lives of saints. One of his works, which was titled *Life of Our Lady* and which praised the Virgin Mary, was one of the best religious poems of the 1400s. Many of Lydgate's poems contain allegory* and satire*. There was also a series of entertaining works known as mummings* that were written for holidays and civic occasions.

In sheer output, Lydgate was without equal in his lifetime. He composed more than 140,000 lines of verse, including translations of many famous works. His most successful major poem, the *Troy Book*, was a translation of an earlier Italian work. Although popular in his own day, Lydgate's work did not seem equally interesting and important to later readers. (*See also* **English Language and Literature.**)

* **allegory** literary device in which characters represent an idea or a religious or moral principle

* **satire** use of ridicule to expose and denounce vice, folly, and other human failings

* **mumming** allegorical work consisting of animated comic scenes told by a narrator

---

Ma'arri, al-

973–1057
Arab poet

* **theologian** person who studies religious faith and practice

Abu'l-Ala Ahmad al–Ma'arri was the last major Arab poet of the Middle Ages. Due to his extraordinary intellect, amazing memory, and remarkable creativity, he was called "the poet of philosophers and the philosopher of poets."

Born into a distinguished family in the Syrian town of Ma'arrah, al-Ma'arri was stricken with smallpox at age three and left scarred and blind. Nevertheless, as a young man he traveled widely to pursue an education. In 1007, he went to BAGHDAD, where he joined a distinguished circle of writers, theologians*, poets, and philosophers and was exposed to wonderful new ideas. In time, his reputation generated envy, and he returned to Ma'arrah. The death of his mother soon after his arrival home drove him into seclusion for the remainder of his life. Many of his greatest works were written during this period.

As a poet, al-Ma'arri was centuries ahead of his time. His highly unconventional style, rich imagery, sophisticated use of language, and frankness were hallmarks of his poetic genius. The main theme throughout all of his work was life and the human tragedy. Al-Ma'arri's greatest poetic work, *al-Luzumiyyat (The Necessity of What Is Unnecessary)*, focuses on the world's shortcomings. Al-Ma'arri questions the value of formal religion, and he scorns human foolishness, hypocrisy, and injustice. The originality of his thought and his liberal yet pessimistic view of life made his works outstanding examples of medieval Arab literature. (*See also* **Arabic Language and Literature.**)

Macbeth

died 1057
King of Scotland

Macbeth was a medieval ruler of Scotland, a kingdom north of ENGLAND on the island of Britain. Immortalized by the English playwright William Shakespeare in his play *Macbeth*, the real Scottish king's life is reflected in the broad outline of the play. The real-life Macbeth belonged to a family of provincial Scottish rulers from Moray, a county in northeast Scotland. He came to the throne in 1040 after killing King Duncan I. In 1046, Scotland was invaded by Siward, earl of Northumbria, a region in northern England. Siward appointed another king, but Macbeth managed to recover his kingdom. By 1050, Macbeth was in full control of Scotland, perhaps because of an agreement between himself and the English king, Edward the Confessor. In 1054, Siward of Northumbria once again invaded Scotland, this time defeating Macbeth decisively. Malcolm, the son of King Duncan, was made king of southern Scotland. Three years later, in 1057, Malcolm killed Macbeth at the Battle of Lumphanan. (*See also* **Scotland.**)

Machaut, Guillaume de

ca. 1300–1377
French poet and composer

* **ballade** lyric poem of three stanzas in which the last line of each stanza is repeated as a refrain

* **rondeau** poem of 13 lines in 3 stanzas and in which the opening line serves as a refrain at the end of the second and third stanzas

* **virelay** lyric poem that consists of stanzas of varying length and number and with long and short lines

* **counterpoint** one or more independent melodies added to a given melody

Guillaume de Machaut was the most influential French poet and composer of the 1300s. Machaut was unsurpassed for the remarkable variety and intricacy of his poetic and musical forms and for his ability to celebrate ideal beauty. His poetry had a great influence on other French writers, such as Jehan FROISSART and CHRISTINE DE PIZAN, and on the English poet Geoffrey CHAUCER.

Little is known of Machaut's life other than the fact that he had several influential patrons. The first of these was John of Luxembourg, the king of Bohemia. Other patrons included John's daughter, Bonne, who was queen of France, and Philip the Bold of BURGUNDY. During his long career, Machaut dedicated a number of poems to his patrons.

Machaut used a variety of poetic styles, including ballades*, rondeaux*, and virelais*. Many of his works deal with the themes of love and courtly romance, but he also wrote about the ravages of war and the terrors of the BLACK DEATH. Machaut's poetry was meant to be read aloud, and it is written with great attention to sound and rhyme patterns.

Machaut also composed much music, some of which was intended to be accompaniment for his poems. Machaut's music was renowned for its sophisticated rhythm and counterpoint*. His principal contribution as a composer was his arrangement of vocal and instrumental parts in secular songs. (*See also* **Courtly Love; French Language and Literature; Music; Romance of the Rose; Troubadour, Trouvère.**)

Magic and Folklore

Magic and folklore had an important place in the thoughts and experience of medieval people. Magic distinguished between the natural world and the supernatural. Folklore was one way people passed down their understanding of the world to the next generation.

Western European Magic and Folklore

God was seen as the supreme power of the cosmos. Next powerful were angels, as well as demons. Demons had many powers not given to humans—they could fly and appear and disappear at will—but they were considered evil. After these supernatural powers came the heavenly bodies, which influenced all earthly things—seasons, tides, and the growth of plants and animals.

To medieval people, the term *natural* meant only those events which were usual, or which occurred most of the time, in nature. Anything out of the ordinary was considered unnatural. Unnatural phenomena included the marvelous—such as a heavy object being forced upward into the air instead of falling down to earth—as well as the unknown.

* **sorcery** magic performed with the supposed aid of evil spirits

* **divination** foretelling the future

See color plate 5, vol. 2.

* **Lent** Christian period of fasting that precedes Easter

* **amulet** small object or ornament worn as a magic charm to ward off evil

* **treatise** long, detailed essay

Magic aimed at producing such phenomena, either by the magician's own efforts or with the help of demons or demonic forces. There were two general types of magic—white magic and black magic. Medieval people saw important distinctions between the two, and only black magic, or sorcery*, dealt with the devil or with demons. ASTROLOGY, ALCHEMY, and divination* were also accepted ways of human interaction with the universe. Astrology and divination, however, aimed at foretelling what would occur, not at intervening in events or bringing them about.

Books of magic abounded in the later Middle Ages. These books included magical procedures, medical prescriptions, household formulas, and tricks and practical jokes, with recipes for such items as invisible ink and for ways of carrying fire without burning your hand.

Medieval people perceived objects in the natural world as having inner "natures," or essences. They also felt that certain objects had a likeness, or "sympathy," with one another. The use of these likenesses for special purposes was known as "sympathetic magic." For instance, the leaves of the hepatica plant had the shape and color of the liver, and so they were used as a remedy for liver ailments.

Great importance was attached to symbols as representations of the inner qualities of natural objects. Animals, plants, and minerals were assigned certain degrees of virtue or importance. The lion was considered to be the king of beasts, and it was used as a symbol for Christ. Numbers, colors, and shapes were also commonly used symbols. The number seven was considered especially significant because it represented the seven basic colors in nature as well as the seven known planets. Black was linked with the planet Saturn and was associated with sorrow, or with a person of strong will. Green was the color of Venus and symbolized hope. Red stood for Mars and signified charity and victory. Symbolism using colors and animals was used extensively in medieval HERALDRY.

Medieval folk superstitions varied from place to place, but they were all rooted in the countryside. As forests were cleared and swamps drained, certain places between communities were considered to have supernatural power, such as the village cemetery or crossroads.

With the growth of towns, the medieval tradition of the carnival was created. The carnival usually consisted of three days of festivities before Lent*. Such rituals allowed townspeople to assert their folk traditions. In Paris, people paraded through the streets with a wicker dragon to honor the legendary dragon subdued by St. Marcel. Other cities had similar festivities.

Byzantine Magic and Folklore

The Byzantine world's interest in magic, which it inherited from the Greeks and Romans, ranged from the use of charms, spells, amulets*, and magical HERBS to divination and astrology. The last two were more advanced forms of magic and were the subjects of scholarly treatises*.

Byzantine interest in astrology was especially strong. The ancient Greek astrological school in Alexandria remained open until 564, and the emperors Leo VI and Constantine VII included astrology in their ENCYCLOPEDIAS. In the 1000s and 1100s, Byzantine scholars compiled several collections of astrological writings from earlier periods. Although astronomers such as Theodoros Meliteniotes (ca. 1310–ca. 1388) condemned astrology, many astrologers continued to flourish to the end of the Byzantine period.

Other traditions of prophecy and divination from the ancient period were also popular. Byzantine copyists preserved treatises on divination that used mirrors, divining dishes, sand, water, and dream interpretation. The encyclopedic work of Constantine VII included a great body of information about magic and divination from the 600s and the 700s.

Folk magic—the use of spells, charms, herbal magic, and amulets—was widespread. Byzantine texts suggest that magicians who had the power to cast spells rivaled the saints in popularity. Although the church criticized magic, accusations against magicians were rare. In fact, the only known extended campaign against magic occurred in CONSTANTINOPLE during a time of civil unrest in the 1300s.

Many classical and Eastern folktales, myths, and legends came to Europe by way of the Byzantine world. Early Byzantine manuscripts of the *Physiologus,* a collection of fables from the late ancient period that became the basis for medieval bestiaries*, reached Europe in this way, as did Aesop's fables.

* **bestiary** collection of animal tales, popular in the Middle Ages, that often contained religious symbolism and moral lessons

Jewish Magic and Folklore

Medieval JUDAISM had a rich tradition of folklore and magic, beginning with the Talmud, which was completed about 500. The Talmud is a large collection of religious law, wisdom, and learning accumulated over many generations of Jewish history.

In addition to providing an extensive commentary on the BIBLE, the Talmud contains narrative sections. These sections involve myths, legends, FABLES, tales, magic, proverbs, riddles, jokes, astrology, magic, superstition, folk medicine, amulets, incantations*, and dream interpretation, as well as stories about ANGELS, demons, and holy people and folk customs associated with the ceremonial year and life cycle.

* **incantation** magical chant

The folkloric tradition of the Talmud continued in the medieval commentaries and explanations of the Bible called midrashim that were created from the 600s to the 1100s. Some midrashim reflect the influence of Islamic folklore. For example, *Pirkei de-Rabbi Eliezer,* written in the 700s, presents a collection of biblical legends modeled on Arabic collections of prophetic tales, which were themselves influenced by earlier Jewish legends. Islamic legends also influenced other midrashim, including the massive *Midrash ha-gadol,* written in the 1200s, which is of Yemenite origin.

Medieval Jewish translators not only inherited and passed on the culture of the Greek and Arab civilizations to medieval Europe. They also transmitted folklore from the East, such as the Indian *Panchatantra,* which was translated into Arabic in the 700s, into Hebrew in the 1100s, and finally into Latin in the 1200s. The Latin version, *Directorium vitae humanae,* became the basis for all later European versions of the Indian storybook.

Medieval Jewish literature was rich in supernatural tales. In the 800s, the traveler Eldad ha-Dani related remarkable legends about the Ten Lost Tribes of ancient Israel who lived in a wonderland beyond the magical river Sambatyon. Stories about extraordinary rabbis* and holy men were also full of folklore, legend, magic, and miracles.

* **rabbi** teacher of Jewish law and religion and spiritual leader of a Jewish congregation

* **Sabbath**   day of the week used for rest and worship

* **Torah**   sacred wisdom of the Jewish faith, especially the first five books of the Bible

* **nocturnal**   active during the night

* **satyr**   woodland deity that was part man and part goat or horse

The famous *Sefer Hasidim* from medieval Germany is not only about Sabbath* observance, Torah* study, ritual, law, and other religious matters. It is also full of all kinds of supernatural legends and folktales that show that medieval Jews in Germany shared most of the superstitions and magical practices of the world in which they lived. It dealt with nocturnal* demons and evil spirits, as well as sorcerers and witches who preyed on innocent victims. The *Sefer Hasidim* gave advice on how to defend oneself against these evil forces. This folk element helped make the work one of the most popular in Jewish history.

Islamic Magic and Folklore

Most Islamic folklore and magic was inherited from the Arab world. During the time of MUHAMMAD, Arabs believed in jinn, invisible spirits believed to inhabit rocks, trees, dunes, pools, caves, and even people. In the Arabic world, jinn were comparable to the fairies, nymphs, and satyrs* of European folklore.

Muhammad accepted the existence of jinn, and the QUR'AN (Koran) mentions numerous magical practices. However, according to Muslim tradition, magic can do only harm. Muslims believed that Muhammad fell ill when one of his enemies in Medina cast a magic spell on him. Despite the overwhelming negative picture of magic and spells in the Qur'an, Muhammad is reported to have allowed the use of spells to treat certain diseases, counteract poison, and ward off the evil eye. Although Muhammad did not employ amulets as such, his usage of religious formulas from the Qur'an led to their use as charms. Amulets later became so popular that they have become the most common class of jewelry in the Muslim world.

Although Islam officially condemned magic, Muslim leaders distinguished between true and false magic. In the chapter on magic in Ibn al-Nadim's encyclopedia, *Fihrist* (written in the 900s), the author explained magic as the harnessing of devils, jinn, and spirits to do what a person wants and made the distinction between authorized (praiseworthy) and unauthorized (blameworthy) magic. The great philosopher Ibn Khaldun (who died in 1406) also had a long chapter on magic in his *Muqaddima,* in which he made a similar distinction between true and false magic. In medieval Islam, the magical sciences of ALCHEMY and astrology were regarded as true magic. Of the two, alchemy was more highly respected as a science, and it was considered less in conflict with Muslim religious principles.

Magic and supernatural spirits occupied a prominent place in medieval Islamic folklore—clearly shown by the still-popular collection of tales, *Thousand and One Nights.* The stories are full of jinn and other spirits. One spirit appears as a giant ogre, while another vampirelike creature, called a *ghul* (*ghoul* in English), feeds on the dead. The tales feature many magical elements, such as rings with magical powers, lamps, stones, magic mirrors, and flying carpets.

Because of the highly traditional nature of Islamic society and its ability to isolate itself from Western ideas, Islamic magic and folklore survived intact until modern times. (*See also* **Agriculture; Bestiary; Byzantine Literature; Cabala; Death and Burial in Europe; Feasts and Festivals; Jewish Communities; Medicine; Mysticism; Science; Thousand and One Nights; Witchcraft, European.**)

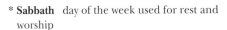

Armenian Folklore

In the medieval folktales of Armenia, demons called *dew* substitute their own offspring for human children, and immortal giants feast in their mountain halls. Nymphs bathe in the meadows, and dragons emerge from the rivers to devour animals and kidnap maidens. Medieval Armenians also believed that in time of war supernatural winged dogs flew to the battlefield to revive fallen heroes by licking their wounds.

Magna Carta

Magna Carta, or the Great Charter, is the most famous document in English history. Granted by King JOHN at Runnymede in 1215, it is considered a cornerstone of the English constitution and a source of English liberties. In granting this document, the king acknowledged that he, no less than his people, was subject to the rule of law and answerable for any violations of it.

King John did not grant Magna Carta freely. He was forced to grant it by English barons under the leadership of Stephen LANGTON. The barons, displeased with the king's heavy taxation and misgoverning, devised the document to guarantee certain feudal* rights. The charter contains 63 articles covering a wide range of topics. These can be grouped into five main areas: the rights and liberties of the church, financial concerns, royal courts and the treasury, the sharing of power between the king and his barons, and the king's relationship with his subjects. One of the most important articles states that no free man may be imprisoned, outlawed, or exiled except by the lawful judgment of his peers according to the law of the land.

Magna Carta is a feudal document in that it rested on the medieval idea that a lord had certain obligations to his vassals*, and the vassals had the right to force him to fulfill those obligations. It went beyond feudalism, however, in applying this idea to the broader relationship of ruler and subject. Although chiefly concerned with the noble classes, the charter's protections gradually were extended to all English subjects through acts of PARLIAMENT and decisions of the courts. (*See also* **England; Feudalism.**)

* **feudal**   referring to the social, economic, and political system that flourished in western Europe during the Middle Ages

* **vassal**   person given land by a lord or monarch in return for loyalty and services

 See map in England (vol. 2).

Maimonides, Moses

1135–1204
Jewish philosopher, jurist, and theologian

Rabbi Moses ben Maimon, known as Moses Maimonides, was born in CÓRDOBA, Spain, in 1135. The family was forced to flee when Córdoba was overrun by the Almohads, a fundamentalist Islamic group. After nearly two decades of wandering in Spain, North Africa, and Palestine, Maimonides eventually settled in Cairo, Egypt. There he became court physician to SALADIN and served as the unofficial head of the Jewish community.

Maimonides wrote many important works in both Hebrew and Arabic that were widely studied and translated. The subjects of his works included philosophy, logic, medicine, and astronomy. His greatest and most enduring works, however, were those on Jewish religious law and learning. His two most famous works were the *Mishneh Torah (Summary of the Law)*, completed around 1178, and the *Moreh Nevukhim (Guide of the Perplexed)*, completed between 1185 and 1190. The first is a 14-volume, comprehensive study of Jewish law that eventually became the standard for the interpretation of Judaism that is still used today.

The *Moreh Nevukhim* uses philosophical ideas to discuss theological* problems. Its use of philosophy and nonliteral (not word-for-word) interpretation of verses from the Bible disturbed many rabbis*, and some regarded the work as heretical.

Maimonides died in 1204, and, in accordance with his wishes, he was buried in Tiberias in present-day Israel. (*See also* **Aristotle in the Middle Ages; Jewish Communities; Ibn Rushd; Ibn Sina.**)

* **theological**   pertaining to the nature of God, the study of religion, and religious beliefs
* **rabbi**   teacher of Jewish law and religion and spiritual leader of a Jewish congregation

Mali

In the late Middle Ages, Mali was a wealthy and powerful empire in western sub-Saharan Africa. Located on the Sankarani tributary of the upper Niger River (the southwestern part of modern Mali), this Islamic empire was one of the main sources of the world's gold supply. In the 1300s, at the height of its power, Mali controlled most of the trans-Saharan trade of western Africa.

In the 1000s, the kings of Mali had adopted ISLAM. Under the leadership of Mari Jata (also known as King Sunjata), Mali expanded and became more powerful in the 1230s. Mari Jata conquered lands to the north and west of the Sankarani and gained control of the southern end of the trans-Saharan trade routes in western Africa. He established Niani on the Sankarani as the capital of his enlarged empire, and it remained the capital of Mali for the next four centuries.

Mari Jata was succeeded by his son, Mansa (King) Uli. Uli's two brothers succeeded him, followed by a nephew who was later deposed by a freed slave named Sakura. Sakura continued the expansion of the empire and increased trade by encouraging traders from Morocco and Tunisia to come to Mali. On his return from a PILGRIMAGE to Mecca, Sakura was murdered.

Mansa Musa, who ruled from 1312 to 1337, was the grandson of Mari Jata's brother. He was considered to be Mali's greatest king. His brother, Mansa Sulayman, ruled from 1341 to 1360. During their reigns, Mali carried on a thriving caravan trade across the Sahara with Morocco, Tunisia, and Egypt.

Mali's decline dates from Sulayman's death. His successor, Mari Jata II, was a corrupt tyrant who plundered the treasury and almost destroyed the government. Later kings proved weak and ineffectual. Although Mali lost control of much of its trans-Saharan trade in the 1400s and 1500s, it retained control of its southern gold-producing areas. Two-thirds of the world's gold once came from this region, and gold was traded for various commodities, such as salt, slaves, horses, copper, sugar, dates, and figs. (*See also* **Ethiopia (Abyssinia); Mining; Slavery; Timbuktu; Trade.**)

When Mansa Musa, ruler of Mali, made a pilgrimage to Mecca, he went with a caravan of camels carrying gold for the sacred city of Islam. This detail from a map of Africa, taken from a Spanish atlas of the 1400s, shows Mansa Musa, with orb and scepter, overseeing his kingdom.

Malory, Sir Thomas

ca. 1393–1471
English writer

* **romance** in medieval literature, a narrative (often in verse) telling of the adventures of a knight or a group of knights

* **Holy Grail** cup that Jesus drank from at the Last Supper

Thomas Malory was the author of *Le Morte Darthur (The Death of Arthur)*, the finest medieval romance* about the legendary King Arthur and his Knights of the Round Table. Few books in the English language have had a greater influence on later novelists, poets, and playwrights.

Little is known of Thomas Malory. Most scholars believe that he was an English knight and adventurer who once served in PARLIAMENT and was imprisoned, justly or unjustly, for a variety of crimes. Some of his time in prison may have stemmed from his involvement in the WAR OF THE ROSES. Malory probably wrote *Le Morte Darthur* while in jail.

Le Morte Darthur relates the Arthurian legend while celebrating the medieval idea of CHIVALRY in all its glory. It tells of Arthur's life, his marriage to Guenevere, and his creation of the Round Table. It introduces noble knights, including Sir Lancelot and Sir Tristram, and describes their heroic deeds. Accompanying tales of brave knights and fair damsels is the story of the quest for the Holy Grail*. The story concludes with a haunting description of the end of the Round Table, the destruction of Arthurian society, and the death of Arthur and his mystical voyage to Avalon, the land of the dead in Celtic mythology.

Malory's work is noted for its excellent dramatic narrative and its rhythmic and simple language. The most famous medieval edition of the book was published in 1485 by the English printer William CAXTON. (*See also* **Arthurian Literature; Chansons de Geste; English Language and Literature; Tristan, Legend of.**)

Mamluk Dynasty

* **sultan** political and military ruler of a Muslim dynasty or state

* **emir** officer in the Mamluk army

* **oligarchy** form of government in which a few people hold all the ruling power

Many Islamic dynasties had armies made up largely of Turkish slaves, called mamluks. These slave corps often became powerful political forces. In Egypt and Syria, a Mamluk dynasty ruled for nearly 300 years. The dynasty was not hereditary and leaders were drawn from the ranks of the military. This illustration of a medical consultation is from an Egyptian Mamluk manuscript of the 1300s.

The Mamluk (pronounced MAM-luke) dynasty consisted of a series of rulers, usually unrelated, who governed EGYPT and SYRIA from 1250 to 1517. The head of the Mamluk state was the sultan*, and the senior officials were known as emirs*. The Mamluk state was a military oligarchy*. The sultans and leading emirs generally came from the ranks of the military, and they achieved their position and power through skillful and ruthless maneuvering of political groups.

The term *mamluk* means slave and was used in the Muslim world to refer specifically to military slaves. Slaves from the vast Turkic lands beyond the Oxus River were first used in the Muslim armies of the ABBASIDS in the 800s, and their use quickly spread throughout the Muslim world. By the 1200s, many different Islamic dynasties had armies composed mostly of Turkish slaves, and these slave corps became very powerful political forces.

The Turkish Period. During the reign of the AYYUBID ruler al-Salih Ayyub (1240–1249), the nucleus of his military force was the Bahriya corps, an elite regiment of Mamluks of Kipchak Turkish origin. When al-Salih died, the Mamluks murdered his son. Soon after, in 1250, the Bahriya commander, Aybak, married al-Salih's widow and became sultan. This marked the beginning of the Mamluk dynasty.

In 1257, Aybak was murdered, and his young son took control. In 1259, however, a Bahriya commander named Qutuz seized the sultanate with the support of Mamluks under his command. This incident reflected a pattern that endured throughout the Mamluk period. The Mamluk troops seldom transferred their loyalties from a sultan to his son. Instead, they supported a powerful commander from among themselves and elected that person as sultan.

In 1260, Sultan Qutuz extended Mamluk rule by driving Mongol invaders out of Syria. This victory brought Syria into the Mamluk Empire and established the Mamluks as defenders of Islam. Soon after, Qutuz was murdered by a new Bahriya commander, Baybars al-Bunduqdari, who proclaimed himself sultan. Baybars ruled until 1277.

Between 1277 and 1382, the Mamluk Empire was ruled by a succession of ruthless sultans. The period was filled with bitter internal struggles, yet there were a number of great achievements. The Christian kingdoms of Syria were conquered in 1290, and drainage and irrigation projects were undertaken there. Extensive construction of all kinds took place throughout the empire. Under Sultan al-Nasir Muhammad, medieval CAIRO reached its peak of population and wealth, and his reign was regarded as a golden age. Such achievements, however, were accompanied by serious problems. The power of the sultans was weakened by military infighting, and this led to political instability. The BLACK DEATH claimed a heavy toll on the population between 1347 and 1349, striking especially hard among the young Mamluk troops.

The Circassian Period.   In 1382, a Mamluk of Circassian origin, al-Zahir Barquq, seized the sultanate. From this point on, succession to the throne and advancement in both the military and government generally was restricted to Mamluks of Circassian descent.

This period was marked by various crises and the gradual decline of the empire. One of the first of these crises was the threat of invasion by the Mongol conqueror TAMERLANE. In 1400, the Mamluks suffered a humiliating defeat at the hands of Tamerlane, who stormed the Syrian city of Aleppo and conquered DAMASCUS. Fortunately, Tamerlane decided not to attack Egypt. In 1403, drought along the Nile River reduced the region's agriculture production and led to a financial crisis that weakened the Mamluk economy. The economy also was hurt by the high costs of maintaining military readiness for foreign wars and the luxurious lifestyle of the Mamluk leaders.

The years from 1496 to 1517 were a time of constant crises combined with a decreased ability to deal with them. The last major sultan, Qansuh al-Ghawri, tried to preserve the Mamluk state, but he was an old man and his efforts were hampered by dwindling resources and a failure to recognize the real dangers that threatened the empire. One of these dangers came from Portugal. In the late 1400s, Portuguese navigators discovered a route to India by sailing around Africa. Using this route, the Portuguese then disrupted Muslim trade routes to India and dominated trading ports there. In doing this, they destroyed the Mamluk treasury, which was heavily dependent on the revenues from the spice trade in the region. The most serious danger was the OTTOMANS, who had gained increased power in the Middle East. In 1516, the Ottomans launched an attack on Syria, and their better-armed forces destroyed a Mamluk army there in August of that year. Five months later, the demoralized Mamluks were crushed by the Ottomans outside Cairo, and the Mamluk dynasty came to an end. (*See also* **Caliphate; Egypt; Islam, Conquests of; Islam, Political Organization of; Mongol Empire; Ottomans and Ottoman Empire.**)

The End of the Mamluks

Although the imperial power of the Mamluk state was destroyed in 1517, the Mamluks as a group survived for another 300 years. The Ottomans placed Mamluk governors in control of various provinces and even allowed them to keep private armies. When Napoleon Bonaparte invaded Egypt in 1798, his forces were met by a Mamluk army, which the French defeated. Mamluk power actually ended in 1811 when a new ruler of Egypt, Muhammad Ali Pasha, systematically massacred the Mamluk leaders. This action effectively destroyed a class of warriors that had existed for almost 1,000 years.

Ma'mun, al-

ruled 813–833
Abbasid caliph

Al-Ma'mun was the seventh caliph of the ABBASID dynasty. A patron of scholars and a man of many interests, he was a strong supporter of science and art, and his reign was noted for its great cultural achievements. Politically, however, his reign was marked by many rebellions and insurrections. One of al-Ma'mun's most enduring legacies was the introduction of Turkish slave soldiers, known as mamluks, into the Muslim armies. The practice of using slave soldiers became very popular and was adopted throughout the Islamic world.

Al-Ma'mun was the son of caliph HARUN AL-RASHID. In an effort to prevent a struggle for succession, Harun named three of his sons as heirs and gave each control of a different part of the empire. Unfortunately, Harun's plan failed. After his death, civil war erupted between al-Ma'mun and his older brother, Muhammad al-Amin, who had become caliph. Al-Amin sought to expand his control by adding his brother's eastern provinces to his lands, which included BAGHDAD, IRAQ, and several western provinces. After three years of fighting, al-Ma'mun defeated al-Amin and

* **viceroy** person appointed to rule a country or province as the official deputy, or representative, of the ruler

had him executed. The civil war ended, but the death of al-Amin left anger and resentment among his supporters in Baghdad and Iraq.

As the new caliph, al-Ma'mun met further resistance from Baghdad. The caliph's viceroy* was driven from the city as the people rioted. The people eventually grew weary of the unrest and accepted the viceroy's return. Shortly afterward, however, the people of Baghdad rebelled again. Strong military and political pressure enabled al-Ma'mun to regain control of the city, but he never felt comfortable there.

The unstable conditions brought about by the civil war also led to insurrections in other areas, and al-Ma'mun was plagued by these problems throughout his reign. Toward the end of his reign, al-Ma'mun led successful campaigns against the Byzantines and rebellious Muslims in Egypt. (*See also* **Mamluk Dynasty.**)

Mandeville's Travels

See map in Crusades (vol. 2).

The most popular book of the late Middle Ages was a work called *The Travels of Sir John Mandeville.* The book was written in French in the 1350s by an unknown author who represented himself as Sir John Mandeville, a widely traveled English knight. The book combines tales of the marvels of Asia with informative and practical advice for pilgrims to the Holy Land. More fiction than fact, the book was probably based on earlier travel books. The *Travels* appealed to a wide audience, and it was translated into almost every European language.

The appeal and originality of the *Travels* stemmed from the way the author merged two previously separate kinds of travel: religious pilgrimage and worldly exploration. During most of the Middle Ages, pilgrimages to religious shrines and holy places—such as JERUSALEM, ROME, CANTERBURY, and SANTIAGO DE COMPOSTELA—were the most highly regarded type of travel because these places had spiritual significance. By the 1300s, however, medieval Europeans were attracted by more worldly adventures. The *Travels* reflects both views of travel. The first half is a guidebook for pilgrims to the Holy Land, while the rest tells of the astounding mysteries and spectacular sights that Mandeville supposedly saw on his journeys to Asia. Woven into the tales is Mandeville's opinion about the shape of the earth (he believed it was round) and his belief that the earth was inhabited everywhere. These views, amazing for the time, inspired such future explorers as Christopher Columbus and English adventurers Sir Walter Raleigh and Martin Frobisher on their own voyages of discovery. (*See also* **Exploration; Pilgrimage.**)

Mansur, al-

ruled 754–775
Muslim caliph

* **caliph** religious and political head of an Islamic state

Al-Mansur was the second caliph* of the ABBASID dynasty. All succeeding Abbasid caliphs were descended from him. The founder of the city of BAGHDAD, al-Mansur changed Islamic rule from a system loosely based on family and tribal relationships to a more structured one based on ability and training. His rule helped create a strong Islamic state with a firm political foundation and a sound economic policy.

Al-Mansur was chosen caliph after the death of his brother, Abu'l-Abbas, despite many better qualified candidates in his family. Soon after, his claim to the CALIPHATE was challenged by his uncle Abd Allah ibn Ali, the powerful conqueror of SYRIA and destroyer of the UMAYYAD dynasty.

Despite this challenge and others, al-Mansur maintained his rule by military might, political intrigue, and the murder of a rival.

To dramatize his claims to power, al-Mansur built a magnificent administrative complex called the Round City. It became the focal point of Baghdad, which in turn became the most important city of the Abbasid Empire. During his rule, al-Mansur strengthened the Islamic state in various ways. He formalized Islamic government by appointing skilled allies, rather than relatives, as advisers. He remodeled the army by replacing old Arab tribal forces with professional soldiers. He promoted city development by expanding market areas, and he adopted economic policies that encouraged merchants and artisans* to work harder. The pattern of government he established was a characteristic of Abbasid rule for hundreds of years.

* **artisans** skilled craftspeople

Manuel, Don Juan

**1282–1348
Spanish prince, soldier, and author**

* **dialect** form of speech characteristic of a region that differs from the standard language in pronunciation, vocabulary, and grammar

* **vernacular** language or dialect native to a region; everyday, informal speech

* **prose** writing without meter or rhyme, as distinguished from poetry

* **Moors** Spanish Muslims descended from the Arab conquerors

* **hereditary** passed on from parent to child

* **anecdote** short narrative concerning interesting or amusing incidents or events

Don Juan Manuel was a wealthy and powerful Spanish prince and soldier. He was also a master writer in the vernacular*. As CHAUCER and DANTE turned English and Italian into poetic languages, Juan Manuel made the Castilian dialect* of Spanish a rich prose* language. In his writings, Manuel used a direct, forceful language that greatly influenced the Spanish writers who followed him.

Don Juan Manuel was the grandson of Ferdinand III and the nephew of ALFONSO X EL SABIO (the Learned), both of whom were kings of CASTILE and León. Juan Manuel's life of adventure began early. When he was only 12 years old, he led an army into battle against the Moors* who were attacking the province of Murcia, where he was hereditary* governor. During the next 50 years, he participated in political plots, as he sought to expand his own interests or to take revenge on his opponents. Although related by blood or marriage to the leading figures in both Castile and ARAGON, his taste for adventure often resulted in political isolation. At various times, he allied himself with the king of Castile, the king of Aragon, and even the Moorish king of GRANADA. Despite such shifting alliances and uneasy relations with various rulers, he managed to escape danger time and again.

Don Juan Manuel is remembered today for his writings rather than for his melodramatic life. His best-known work is *Libro del Conde Lucanor et de Patronio (Book of Count Lucanor and Patronio)*, written between 1331 and 1335. It is a collection of 51 stories that includes folk tales, animal fables, anecdotes*, and events from the lives of historical figures. The stories are told as the responses of a wise counselor, Patronio, to the questions of a young nobleman, Count Lucanor. The strong and direct language of the stories contrasts with the elaborate, delicate language typical of other Spanish writing of the period. Juan Manuel's use of language reflects a personal style that was new to Castilian prose. Another of Juan Manuel's works is *Libro de las Armas (Book on the Family Coat of Arms)*. It includes an account of his visit at age 12 to the deathbed of his cousin, Sancho IV the Fearless. In a vivid and striking scene, Juan Manual recounts his cousin's story of his violent life and his regrets.

What is most memorable about much of Juan Manuel's writing is the way he brought himself into the narrative. He did this through his personal recollections and judgments of people and events. Although Juan Manuel's writings concern problems that no longer greatly affect daily life, the clarity and immediacy of his writing are still greatly admired. (*See also* **Spanish Language and Literature.**)

Maps and Mapmaking

Maps during the Middle Ages reflected popular views of the shape and extent of the known world as well as religious beliefs about humans and their place in the universe. Medieval geography was, for the most part, not a separate field of study but a combination of science, literature, and imagination. By the end of the Middle Ages, Europe was ready to embark on an era of exploration and discovery that had never been experienced before, much of it made possible by the observations and ideas of geographers, explorers, and merchant-travelers.

Islamic Maps and Mapmaking

Medieval Islamic geography, which formed the basis for mapmaking, was not thought of as a specific science. Rather, it combined aspects of science and literature. Many works on geography were written, the majority in Arabic. People of other nationalities and non-Muslims made important contributions as well as Arabs.

Early Islamic Period. Geographical concepts were expressed in the QUR'AN, while specific geographical data were also found in pre-Islamic* poetry. As the Islamic culture absorbed the learning of the Greeks, Persians, and Indian cultures, Islamic science began to flourish. A more scientific geography began in the 700s in the city of BAGHDAD, during the CALIPHATE of al-MANSUR. It was further encouraged by caliph al-MA'MUN in the 800s. With their support, observatories were constructed, maps and scientific instruments were produced, and geographical and astronomical works were translated and adapted from works in Indian, Persian, and Greek. One of the most frequently translated works was *Geography*, written by the ancient Greek geographer Ptolemy.

General information on geography was often included in philosophical, astronomical, historical, and encyclopedic works. The earliest works dealing specifically with geography concentrated on such practical needs of government as topography*, administrative data, commercial and postal routes, and descriptions of boundaries. In the 800s and 900s, this type of work evolved into a special category of writings called "routes and kingdoms."

Schools of Geography and New Information. During the 900s and 1000s, two schools of Islamic geography emerged. The first was known as the Iraqi school because its main characteristic was the placement of Iraq at the center of the Islamic Empire. The second school was that of an Islamic scholar named al-Balkhi. He and his followers focused on the world of Islam and gave central importance to the holy city of MECCA. They introduced the concept of a country as a geographic unit and discussed such things as the languages and races of people, their occupations, and their

* **pre-Islamic** referring to the period before the founding of the religion of Islam in the early 600s

* **topography** graphic representation, usually on a map, of the surface features of the earth, such as mountains

Abraham Cresques was cartographer to Peter III of Aragon. In 1375, he produced his Catalan Atlas shown here. Although the atlas was largely illustrative in nature, the location of towns was based on a network of compass bearings. The compass, astrolabe, and quadrant made both navigation and mapmaking more accurate during the Middle Ages.

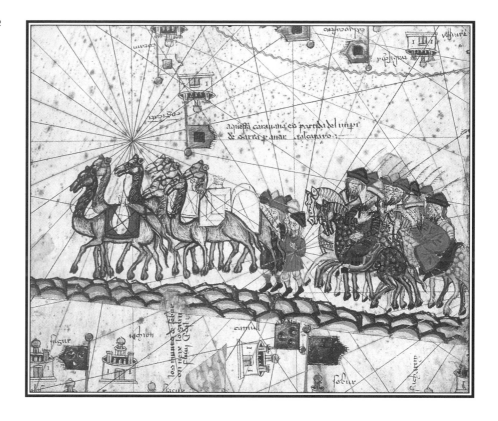

* **cartography**   mapmaking

customs and religions. Firsthand observation was an important source of information for these writers. A key feature of the al-Balkhi school was its attention to cartography*. Maps and descriptive texts usually appeared side by side. The maps were round or oval, and they showed the locations of roads and towns. Together, the maps created by the al-Balkhi school are known today as the "Atlas of Islam."

A spirit of exploration and inquiry in this period generated an interest in travel beyond the familiar areas of the Middle East, India, and Africa. It also created a great demand among the public for written accounts by travelers. Some of these accounts were reports of authentic journeys, while others were combinations of fact and legend. The anonymous series of stories known as the THOUSAND AND ONE NIGHTS incorporated some of these semilegendary accounts.

Unique among geographers of this period was al-Biruni. Apart from his important contribution to regional geography (he described India in detail), he compared and evaluated the contributions to geography of the Arabs, Greeks, Indians, and Iranians. He advanced bold theories of geography and astronomy, arguing that (contrary to the prevailing views) life was possible south of the equator. He alone among Muslim geographers suggested that the Indian Ocean connected with the Atlantic Ocean.

Later Medieval Period.   Between the 1100s and the 1500s, new geographic ideas were limited to the appearance of new categories of written works. Among the Islamic works written in this period were geographic dictionaries, cosmographies*, and seafaring literature. The largest and most famous geographic dictionary was written by a scholar named Yagut. This work contained many place names as well as a wealth of geographical and

* **cosmography**   description and map showing the main features of the heavens and the earth

historical information. Travel literature also continued to be popular. The most famous traveler of the period was IBN BATTUTA, whose travel accounts were some of the most reliable sources of geographical information. One of the most innovative and influential geographers of the period was al-Idrisi, who used data from Islamic and European geographers and travelers to create a book on world geography. This work, although outdated or inaccurate in places, remained unmatched in the medieval Islamic world. Among mapmakers, al-Idrisi's influence remained strong through the 1500s.

Throughout the medieval period, Islamic geography faithfully preserved ancient and foreign geographic concepts. It ultimately failed to produce its own distinct geographic concepts or to combine old concepts with new information. Instead, its chief importance was in accumulating facts and information. Still, for some parts of the world, or for certain periods of their history, medieval Islamic geographers provide major—if not the only—sources of information.

Western European Maps and Mapmaking

Throughout medieval Europe, most people accepted the notion that the earth was at the center of the universe. Scholar St. Isidore of Seville in the sixth century had interpreted the earth as being wheel-shaped and flat, with different climate zones like flat circles over the earth. In the 1200s, university scholars might have read geographic works like *De imagine mundi,* which was written at least 100 years earlier. They were introduced to ideas that the earth was egg-shaped, that it was at the center of the universe, or that hell was within the earth. They might also have read Sacrobosco's work *Sphere,* which stated that the earth was round.

Medieval Maps. The *mappa mundi** was the main type of circular world map used in western Europe in the Middle Ages. One type, the popular *O-T* map, took its name from the Latin term *orbis terrae* (orb, or circle, of the earth). The axis of the *O-T* maps was based on a letter *T* placed within an *O*-shaped area. East, which represented paradise or Jerusalem, the holy city, was at the top. The map was subdivided into Asia, Africa, and Europe, with the length of the *T* drawn between Africa and Europe. Most *O-T* maps assumed that the earth was flat, and they remained popular even when exploration began to reveal that the earth was a sphere. The *mappa mundi* often had illustrations of geographic myths, religious or moral stories, or representations of contemporary places.

New Geographic Tools. The development of the compass as a geographic tool, possibly in the 1100s, transformed medieval mapmaking. Earlier medieval maps had often placed east at the top because they were oriented toward Jerusalem. With the introduction of the compass, European cartographers took their cue from the compass needle and placed north at the top of maps. Other navigational instruments began to affect mapmaking as well. The astrolabe* and the quadrant* were both in use by the end of the 1200s, and they helped make mapmaking more precise by making navigation itself more accurate.

Challenge of New Information. Armed with such scientific instruments, medieval sailors discovered a wealth of new information about their world. The new knowledge they gained presented a major challenge to old notions

* *mappa mundi* type of circular map of the world

* **astrolabe** instrument used to observe and calculate the position of heavenly bodies, to navigate, and to tell time

* **quadrant** instrument used for measuring altitudes

Mappa Mundi: A Medieval View of the World

The *mappa mundi* had its origin in ancient Roman maps, which gradually were modified to reflect Christian religious beliefs. On a *mappa mundi,* Jerusalem often was placed at the center of a world that consisted only of Europe and the little that was known of Asia and Africa. The maps were highly decorative, often containing illustrations of geographic myths, short moral tales, and drawings of contemporary sites. Although inaccurate by modern standards, the *mappa mundi* provides an important insight into the medieval view of the world.

* **meridian** any of the imaginary circles around the earth, passing through the North and South Poles, which are used to mark degrees of longitude

* **parallel** any of the imaginary circles around the earth, parallel to the equator, which are used to mark degrees of latitude

* **projection** representation of the earth's surface on a flat surface, such as a grid

of the known world and to mapmaking in general. Scholars had to reconcile maps representing how people thought the earth should be with the new knowledge that sailors were uncovering.

Roger BACON was at the forefront of change. He recommended that an accurate and complete survey of the known world be made, and he designed a world map to accompany his recommendations. According to Bacon, the inhabited world stretched over more than half of the earth from east to west.

New discoveries during the Middle Ages kept challenging old geographic notions. Scandinavian writers and Norse sagas provided information about little-known northern regions. Explorers penetrating the Atlantic Ocean added knowledge of various island groups and parts of Africa's northwestern coast. Missionaries and merchant-travelers, such as Marco POLO, traveled eastward into Asia and reported their findings.

Portolano sailing charts, which later played a vital role in the age of discovery, came into prominence late in the 13th century. They were coastal maps depicting harbors and navigational hazards such as reefs. They used bright colors and sharp lines drawn on parchment, with names in Latin or sometimes Italian. Portolano charts emerged around the same time as the introduction of the magnetic compass in Europe. These charts used no meridians* or parallels*. Instead of degrees, directions were marked in terms of compass bearings. The early maps had 12 directional points, after the 12 primary winds known in ancient times. These were later reduced to 8—N, NE, E, SE, S, SW, W, NW.

The craft of the maritime chart makers evolved into the profession of the cartographer, or mapmaker. Because mapmaking required considerable skill at drawing, early cartographers were often artists. With the advent of the printing press in the 1400s, maps were produced with greater consistency and for wider distribution. However, navigators at first considered hand-drawn charts to be more accurate and often preferred them to printed ones.

Despite the use of new instruments and the gathering of new information, medieval maps continued to be inaccurate by today's standards, largely because there was at yet no means of measuring longitude precisely. Maps began to assume modern form when mapmakers used them to locate places by latitude and longitude on a calculated projection* of the earth's sphere onto a plane. The modern map evolved with further developments in mathematics and technology that occurred after the Middle Ages. (*See also* **Astrolabe; Exploration; Navigation; Science.**)

Marie de Champagne

**1145–1198
Countess of Champagne**

* **regent** person appointed to govern a kingdom when the rightful ruler is too young, absent, or disabled

Marie de Champagne was a patroness of the arts in medieval France. Born in 1145, she was the oldest child of King Louis VII of France and ELEANOR OF AQUITAINE. In 1164, Marie married Henry I of Champagne, which was one of France's wealthiest counties. Marie lived at a time of great prosperity for Champagne, when the counts of the region were among the king's most powerful vassals.

Marie was widowed in her mid-30s. From 1181 to 1187 and again from 1190 to 1197, she served as regent* for her young son Henry. During her reign as countess of Champagne, Marie made the court at the city of Troyes a center of arts and culture. She was patroness to several poets, including the poet CHRÉTIEN DE TROYES. He wrote several stories of COURTLY LOVE in her honor and claimed her as his inspiration. (*See also* **Champagne, County of; France; French Language and Literature.**)

Marie de France

late 1100s–early 1200s
Poet

* **vernacular** language or dialect native to a region; everyday, informal speech

* **romance** in medieval literature, a narrative (often in verse) telling of the adventures of a knight or a group of knights

Marie de France was one of the most remarkable writers of the Middle Ages. At a time when many written works were anonymous, Marie boldly asserted herself by signing her first name to her work. During her career, Marie wrote numerous fables and short stories in verse called lais. They are considered the finest achievement of their kind.

Almost nothing is known about Marie's life. Even her identity is a mystery. It is known that she was a native of France who probably lived in England and wrote during the late 1100s and early 1200s. She knew both Latin and English and was familiar with the vernacular* literature of her time.

Marie's fame rests on 12 lais. These short stories of adventure and COURTLY LOVE in aristocratic settings were probably based on Celtic myths and legends. Unlike the heroes of medieval romances*, the characters in Marie's stories do not seek out adventure. Instead, adventures happen to them. While the settings are true to life, the lais often contain elements of folklore or of the supernatural. One example is *Bisclavret*. While the setting is described in realistic detail, the subject is a werewolf, who is sympathetically portrayed. Marie moves back and forth between the real and the supernatural, expressing delicate shades of emotion with great skill. In addition to the lais, Marie wrote more than 100 fables, each providing a moral lesson. These fables were enormously popular. Marie also

Marie de France's *Lais* are stories of adventure and courtly love that often contain an element of the supernatural. She was the first medieval woman poet writing in French who signed her work. Marie is shown here writing at her desk.

* **purgatory** place of temporary suffering or punishment after death and before entering heaven

wrote a long verse poem called *Espurgatoire* about a character's descent to purgatory*. It is one of the oldest examples of a popular tradition of works, written in the vernacular, that presents visions of the afterlife. (*See also* **Celtic Languages and Literature; Dante Alighieri; Fables; French Language and Literature.**)

Markets

See color plate 3, vol. 1.

* **gallows** wooden structure consisting of a crossbeam on two upright poles, used for hanging criminals

Les Halles, Marketplace of Paris

In 1183, the city of Paris, France, established its first permanent market, called Les Halles. This marketplace consisted of two large sheds. Doors were cut into the walls, through which the merchants and craftspeople sold their products. The workshops of tailors, shoemakers, goldsmiths, leather tanners, and other tradespeople surrounded Les Halles. These workshops were actually small buildings so close together that their upper stories and roofs touched. The alleyways of Les Halles were twisting and winding, and they were filled with jostling city folk buying, selling, or browsing. Les Halles remained the main shopping area of the city until the late 1960s, when it was demolished and replaced by a huge shopping center.

The medieval market served the needs of a local area. It was more than just a place to buy and sell food and other goods. People came to the market to meet friends, to hear the latest news, and to be entertained. Most large European towns and cities had at least one marketplace that was open once, twice, or perhaps several times a week. Markets also existed in rural areas. Such markets, wherever they were located, were vital to the economy of medieval Europe.

The medieval market bustled with activity. Usually located in a large open space, the typical marketplace consisted of temporary wooden stalls and tables where sellers displayed their produce or wares. Other shops and stalls often lined side streets off the main marketplace. Some large towns and cities built special halls to house the market and thus protect goods, sellers, and buyers from bad weather. Although most of the merchandise at markets consisted of food items, other goods—such as pottery, spices, and fine cloth—were also sold. Specific areas often were set aside for certain merchandise: livestock was sold in one part of the marketplace, food in another, and cloth in another. As the main meeting place in most towns and villages, the marketplace served other functions besides buying and selling. GUILDS and other organizations performed various entertainments in the marketplace, public officials read proclamations there, and criminals were executed at gallows* located in the market square.

Medieval markets were owned by towns, institutions, or individuals, but these owners had to obtain permission to operate the market from a king or a feudal lord. Permission often was purchased since markets produced profits from rents, tolls, and fines. Market owners taxed the merchants who attended the market, collected tolls from both buyers and sellers, and fined people for breaking the rules of the marketplace. In exchange, the owners protected the traders by establishing regulations. Some regulations restricted when and where commercial transactions could take place. Other regulations guaranteed the use of proper weights and measures, or maintained fair prices and quality control. Still others protected consumers from unfair treatment. Officials were elected or appointed to monitor the marketplace, and regulations were enforced in local courts according to national laws, local codes, and special merchant laws.

Before the 800s, there were few markets in Europe because most families and estates were self-sufficient. Beginning in the 800s, however, increased urban population and economic activity led to the creation of many new markets around churches, monasteries, castles, and city gates, and at important crossroads. Sometimes markets provided the nucleus for towns by attracting merchants and artisans to centers of exchange. From

The clothing market in Bologna, Italy, in the 1400s was a busy place. This miniature is taken from the *Statutes* of the city's guild of tailors and clothing makers. Members of the guild had to follow regulations governing where they could show their merchandise. This enabled government and guild officials to ensure that established standards were followed.

* **barter**   exchange of goods and services without using money

the 1000s to the 1200s, population expansion hastened the development of markets. The growth of industry and the creation of guilds also contributed to the expansion of market activity. At the same time, markets became more complex, as the barter* system was replaced by a system of exchange based on money.

The number of markets decreased in the 1300s, largely because of population declines caused by FAMINE and PLAGUE. Those markets that survived continued to play a vital role in medieval life, and they began to grow again in size and significance in later centuries. (*See also* **Fairs; Food and Drink; Trade.**)

Marriage

See *Family.*

Mary, Cult of

* **veneration**   profound respect or reverence

Throughout the Middle Ages, Mary, the mother of Jesus, occupied an exalted position among the Christian saints. Her image dominated medieval painting and sculpture. Prayers and hymns were written in her honor. Churches and great cathedrals were dedicated to her, and she was credited with many miracles. By the 1100s, a cult of Mary was firmly established, and legions of Christian faithful prayed to her daily to intercede on their behalf.

The veneration* of Mary dates from early Christian times. From the fifth century, church councils used the title "Mother of God" when referring to Mary, and she soon became a symbol of the church and of the purity of

Christian faith. Special feast days were established in her honor, and these played an important role in the Christian calendar. By the 1100s, the cult of Mary had spread throughout Europe, and it was further popularized by the Franciscans and Dominicans in the 1200s. St. Bernard of Clairvaux, a Cistercian, advanced Mary's cult in his writings by calling her the intermediary between God and humans, while other scholars called her the "Queen of Heaven." The image of Mary as "Queen of Heaven" was common in medieval art, which often depicted her crowned and seated on a throne holding the baby Jesus in her arms.

The cult of Mary stressed her warmth and maternal character, qualities that helped endear the church to people and win converts. Beliefs in Mary's Immaculate Conception* and Assumption* had their roots in her revered position in the Middle Ages, but these beliefs did not become official church teachings until modern times. (*See also* **Christianity; Gothic Painting; Gothic Sculpture; Pilgrimage.**)

* **Immaculate Conception** belief that the Virgin Mary was conceived free of original sin

* **Assumption** belief that the body and soul of the Virgin Mary were taken from earth to heaven after her death

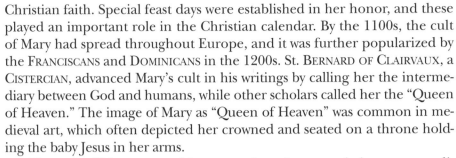

Mass, Liturgy of the

* **cleric** church official qualified to perform church ceremonies

* **theologian** person who studies religious faith and practice

* **sacrament** religious ceremony of the Christian church, considered especially sacred, such as Communion and baptism

* **psalm** sacred song or hymn, often referring to those contained in the Book of Psalms in the Old Testament

* **consecration** combined blessing and dedication

During the Middle Ages, clerics* and theologians* in western Europe debated which of the various sacraments* was the most important to the Christian faith. By the late Middle Ages, the issue was largely resolved. The Eucharist, or Holy Communion, was considered the most important sacrament. As a result, the liturgy of the Mass—the religious ritual, or ceremony, at which Communion was celebrated—became the central act of Christian worship.

The basic ritual of the Mass was established during the earliest days of the Christian church. By the Middle Ages, the Mass had become a formal and highly structured ceremony that began with prayers and psalms*, led to the consecration* of bread and wine, and ended with Communion—the taking of the bread and wine as the body and blood of Jesus Christ. Throughout the Middle Ages, the Mass underwent many changes, as prayers were added or dropped and various parts of the ceremony were changed to reflect changes in religious belief or practice. Different variations of the Mass also developed for use on different days of the week or on special occasions.

There were several basic forms of the Mass, known as rites. Ireland, Italy, France, and Spain all had their own distinct rites, and the eastern regions of the Mediterranean had theirs as well. One of the most widely recognized and used rites was the Roman rite. Originally the liturgy of the city of Rome, the Roman rite dated back to at least the 200s. This rite gradually spread throughout western Europe (the Carolingians adopted it as the "official" rite), and it became the dominant one. Areas under Byzantine control never accepted the Roman rite.

By the year 1000, the forms of the Mass were set within each rite. The Ordinary, or set portion of the Mass, included the Kyrie, the Gloria, the Credo, the Sanctus, and the Agnus Dei and was always the same, while the Proper portion of the Mass changed to reflect the saint or feast celebrated on a particular day. The precise forms varied from city to city, and even from church to church within a city. Different religious orders, such as the Franciscans and the Dominicans, also had their own special forms

* **vernacular** language or dialect native to a region; everyday, informal speech

* **creed** brief statement of the main points of religious belief

* **laity** those who are not members of the clergy

* **Lateran** referring to several councils of the Western Church, named for the Roman palace in which they originally took place

of the ritual. Most of the Mass was recited in Latin, although the sermon often was given in the vernacular*.

The medieval Mass was generally a very elaborate and complex ceremony involving colorful processions, chanting, the use of INCENSE, readings from the Bible, the recitation of prayers and creeds*, and homilies (sermons). The Mass was divided into two sections. The first part, known as the Mass of the Catechumens, was attended by all the faithful, including those who were not yet baptized. The second part, the Mass of the Faithful, was reserved for those who were baptized. It contained the most important part of the Mass—the consecration of the sacred bread and wine (considered the climax of the Mass), and the Holy Communion.

Until the 300s, it was common for people to take Communion at every Mass. After the fourth century, there was a decline in the taking of Communion by the laity*. By the Fourth Lateran* Council in 1215, Communion came to be obligatory for everyone only on Easter. The reasons for the decline in the taking of Communion by laypersons are unclear. However, in the 1200s, a separate celebration of the Eucharist was created to give people an opportunity to show their devotion to the sacrament. This celebration became known as the Feast of Corpus Christi (the body of Christ). It included a ceremonial procession by the clergy and the community through a town and sometimes out into the countryside. It was often accompanied by great displays of flowers and occasionally by reports of miracles. The text and hymns written for the service are often credited to Thomas AQUINAS, but there were probably other contributors as well. Late medieval society attached great importance to the Feast of Corpus Christi, and especially to its procession, and by 1350 the custom was widespread. (*See also* **Christianity; Gregorian Chant; Schism, Great.**)

Mathematics

Before the 1100s, Europe had been limited to the mathematical concepts of the ancient Romans, who used a system of ROMAN NUMERALS and basic mathematics to measure, survey, and conduct business. A few Roman philosophers studied the theoretical mathematics of the ancient Greeks, but those few Romans who were interested studied it in Greek, which all educated Romans knew. There was little written in Latin on the subject in the early Middle Ages. The Germanic peoples who took over Europe from the Romans in the 400s contributed even less.

About midway through the Middle Ages, Arab scholars presented a great body of mathematical learning to the world. The translation of many Arabic texts into Latin paved the way for the introduction of dramatic new forms of mathematics. It was the Muslims, as inheritors of the rich mathematical heritage of the Greeks, who passed on their advanced knowledge to medieval Europe.

Roman Heritage. Before the arrival of the new mathematical concepts of the Arabs in the 1100s, Europeans knew little about number theory and practical geometry. The two main sources for early medieval number theory were *De institutione arithmetica* of Boethius (who died in 524/525) and the seventh chapter of *De nuptiis philologiae et Mercurii* of Martianus Capella (who died in 440). Although both sources presented basic Pythagorean number theory, they hardly did more than define terms and explain basic theorems. Neither of these works, nor later works based on them, taught the reader how to add, subtract, multiply, or divide large numbers.

Finger reckoning was one of the two systems commonly employed in medieval Europe to make numerical calculations. By using their fingers, Europeans could in theory calculate with numbers up to 9,999, but in practice they rarely used finger reckoning for more than two digits.

The second system was an abacus, an ancient device that consisted of a board with counters on it that could be utilized to add, subtract, multiply, and divide. There were many different versions of the abacus in the ancient world; the Europeans employed the Roman form. The abacus was used for large numbers, and texts on its operation began appearing in the late 900s. One of the earliest of these texts was the popular *Regulae de numerorum abaci rationibus* of Gerbert of Aurillac, written about 980. The abacus was widely used into the late Middle Ages, even after the arrival in Europe of Greek and Arab mathematical knowledge. In some parts of the world, it is still utilized today.

New Learning. Arabic texts introduced three major new areas of mathematics to medieval Europe—written arithmetic using ARABIC NUMERALS, Euclidean geometry, and algebra*.

About 825, the great Muslim mathematician and astronomer Muhammad ibn Musa al-KHWARIZMI wrote the *Treatise on Calculation with Hindu Numerals,* a work that eventually changed European mathematics. In his treatise*, al-Khwarizmi described a decimal place-value system of numerals based on units of 10 and using the numbers 1–9 (plus 0 as a 10th symbol to represent the absence of a number). This became the numerical system that is utilized today. He also described rules for calculating with these symbols. Translated into Latin as *De numero indorum* sometime before 1143, this work introduced a new *written* arithmetic, as opposed to using an abacus.

A Latin version of Euclid's *Elements* that had been translated directly from the original Greek existed in the Middle Ages. However, the versions that transmitted Euclidean geometry to medieval Europe were the Arabic translations from Greek, which were then translated into Latin. In the 800s, al-Hajjaj made two Arabic translations of Euclid's work, one a complete translation and the other a shortened version. Most European scholars read one of the Latin versions of al-Hajjaj's shortened edition, which were translated by Adelard of Bath and Hermann of Carinthia in the mid-12th century. The basic text of Euclid's work remained remarkably accurate and uniform, considering that it was translated from Greek to Arabic to Latin and circulated in several versions.

Another Greek mathematical writer known to medieval Europeans through Arabic translations was Archimedes. Although the works of Euclid and Archimedes did not completely replace the earlier Roman geometric tradition, they established the important distinction between abstract and practical geometry.

Algebra was another form of mathematics that was introduced to Europe by the Arabs in the 1100s. As al-Khwarizmi's text on Hindu-Arabic arithmetic introduced Arabic numerals to Europe, his text on algebra became the basic medieval work for both Arabic and Latin treatments of that subject. The Arabic name of his algebra text was *Kitab al-mukhtasar fi-hisab*

* **algebra**   branch of mathematics in which letters representing unknown numbers are combined according to the rules of arithmetic

* **treatise** long, detailed essay

al-jabr wa'l-muqabala (Compendious book on calculation by completion and balancing). The term *algebra* comes from *Liber algebre,* the shortened Latin title of al-Khwarizmi's work that was read in Europe.

Algebra caught on more slowly than geometry. While merchants and surveyors found basic algebra practical and recreational, few European mathematicians seemed to have much knowledge of it before the 1400s. Algebra did not start making its appearance in university curriculums until it was taught in Leipzig in the late 1400s.

Contributions of the Late Middle Ages. A few Europeans went beyond merely adopting the Greek-Arabic mathematical heritage and made contributions of their own. One such mathematician was Leonardo Fibonacci. The son of a wealthy Italian merchant in the Italian city of PISA, Fibonacci traveled around the Mediterranean, working for his father and learning practical and theoretical mathematics from Greeks and Arabs. About 1200, he settled in Pisa, where he spent the last 40 years of his life teaching mathematics, advising the city government, and writing works that made him Europe's most accomplished mathematical thinker.

In Fibonacci's two major works, *Liber abbaci* and *Practica geometriae,* he wrote about Hindu-Arabic arithmetic and the geometrical theorems* of Euclid and Archimedes. But the two small treatises he wrote around 1225 on algebraic equations revealed more fully his original thinking as a mathematician.

The second innovative mathematician of the 13th century was Jordanus de Nemore (or Nemorarius), although details of his life and career are unknown. Jordanus's largest work, *De numeris datis (On Given Numbers),* dealt with traditional algebraic techniques. Jordanus also developed a partial system of alphabetic notation, which would be developed further by later mathematicians.

In the 14th century, mathematicians Thomas Bradwardine and NICOLE ORESME advanced the mathematical concepts of ratio and proportion. The work of Oresme in particular pointed to a trend in mathematics that would lead from the Middle Ages into the Renaissance. Medieval mathematics was largely a pursuit of university scholars, and its main focus was on teaching and philosophical applications. Later, in the Renaissance, various sectors of society would seek improved mathematical techniques for problem solving. Oresme's own work on ratios led him to question the scientific basis of ASTROLOGY. (*See also* **Arabic Language and Literature; Aristotle in the Middle Ages; Calendars; Clocks and Reckoning of Time; Universities.**)

* **theorem** statement or rule in mathematics that has been or is to be proved

Matilda of Tuscany

1046–1115
Italian countess

Matilda of Tuscany played an important role in one of the greatest disputes of the Middle Ages—the Investiture Controversy. This disagreement involved the popes and the German Holy Roman Emperors over the issue of who had the right to appoint local bishops and to give them the power and privileges of their office. Matilda was the primary supporter of the popes in this conflict.

Matilda had inherited extensive lands and titles from her parents. She ruled over the most powerful feudal state in Italy, which included the northern Italian regions of Lombardy, Emilia, and TUSCANY. These lands were long sought after by the Holy Roman Emperors, who hoped

People of the Middle Ages

Plate 1

Wenceslas II (also known as Václav II), was king of Bohemia from 1278 and king of Poland from 1300 until his death in 1305. He was an able ruler who spread Bohemian influence and brought economic prosperity to his people. This German manuscript illumination from the late 1300s shows the king seated on his throne, surrounded by his troubadours.

Plate 2

Constantine I the Great was the first Roman emperor to permit Roman citizens to become Christians. In this fresco, the emperor hands Pope Sylvester I the temporal crown and other symbols of the Donation of Constantine. The donation was a letter from the emperor, later proven to be a forgery, that granted the church temporal as well as spiritual authority.

Plate 3

Byzantine empress Theodora I (d. 548) was one of the most famous and powerful women of the Middle Ages. Wife of the emperor Justinian I, she took an active part in government administration. This mosaic from San Vitale in Ravenna, Italy, made in 547, shows the empress with her court.

Plate 4

Marco Polo was the most famous explorer of the Middle Ages. He spent many years at the court of Kublai Khan. He traveled throughout China on various diplomatic missions for the Mongol court and wrote of his extraordinary adventures. This miniature, from a 14th-century manuscript of his book, *Travels,* shows Polo visiting a nomad camp in central Asia.

Plate 5

St. Francis of Assisi remains one of the most popular and beloved of Christian saints. This fresco, painted by Giotto di Bondone, shows Pope Innocent III confirming the rule of the Franciscan Order, an event that occurred in 1210.

Plate 6

Louis IX was a popular and able king who ruled France in the 1200s. A deeply religious man, he became the symbol of the ideal Christian monarch. In this 15th-century illumination, the king is shown embarking on a crusade. Louis led the Seventh Crusade to the Holy Land in 1248, and he went on another crusade in 1270. Louis was made a saint in 1297.

Plate 7

In this illumination from the 1400s, Llywelyn ap Gruffydd, Prince of Wales, kneels to be beheaded, as England's King Edward I watches from the window above. Llywelyn, the last prince of an independent Wales, had refused to pay homage to the king. After Llywelyn's execution in 1282, Edward I was able to extend English rule into Wales.

Plate 8

Written about 1100, the *Song of Roland* is a French epic poem that relates the deeds of the emperor Charlemagne and his nephew, Roland. In this 14th-century French illumination, Charlemagne finds the body of Roland, who has died a hero's death fighting the enemy.

Plate 9

Pope Innocent III was one of the most influential popes of the medieval period. During his papacy in the early 13th century, he instituted many important reforms. He believed that the church should have political as well as spiritual power and that secular rulers were subject to that authority.

Plate 10

Frederick I, called Barbarossa or Redbeard, is considered the greatest king of medieval Germany. He established the feudal system in Germany and became a symbol of German unity. The king, who ruled in the 1100s, receives the Venetian ambassador in this Italian manuscript illumination from the 1300s.

Plate 11

Genghis Khan receives the homage of a vassal in this medieval Persian illumination. Genghis Khan was the unifier and ruler of the nomadic tribes of Mongolia. At the height of his power, the Mongol Empire stretched from eastern Europe to the Sea of Japan.

Plate 12

Gregory I the Great was pope from 590 until his death in 604. In this 12th-century French illumination, Gregory dictates his book, the *Morals on Job,* to his scribe, Peter. Gregory is famous for his many writings on the Christian faith and is considered one of the great medieval theologians.

Plate 13

Charles V of France grew up during the early period of the Hundred Years War, and he took over the government during troubled times. Called "the Wise," Charles is better known for his patronage of the arts and learning, which included the founding of a royal library. In this Flemish illumination from the late 1400s, Charles is shown receiving a book.

Plate 14

This illumination shows King David II of Scotland making peace with King Edward III of England in 1357. David, son of the legendary Robert Bruce, angered many Scottish nobles who had struggled to gain Scotland's independence from England.

Plate 15

This relief sculpture is in the Royal Chapel in Granada, Spain. King Ferdinand V and Queen Isabella are joined by their courtiers at the surrender of Muslim Granada to Castile in 1492. In the 1200s, the Christian states of northern Spain had begun to drive the Muslims from Spain. Granada was the last Muslim kingdom to be reconquered.

to extend their influence into northern Italy. Matilda's marriage to a papal relative in 1069 placed her firmly on the side of the popes in their feud with the emperors. After her husband's death in 1076, the childless Matilda bequeathed her lands to the papacy. As punishment for her support of the papacy, the emperor removed her imperial* titles in 1081.

Following the death of Emperor Henry IV in 1106, Matilda defended her own territories against the empire but ceased her aid to the papal allies in other parts of Italy. In 1111, she made peace with the new emperor, Henry V, and she decided to leave her lands to the emperor instead of the pope, as previously promised. These lands remained a source of conflict between the popes and emperors until the mid-1200s. (*See also* **Church-State Relations; Concordats; Italy.**)

* **imperial**   pertaining to an empire or emperor

Maximilian I, Emperor

1459–1519
German king and emperor-elect

Maximilian I, king of Germany, was elected Holy Roman Emperor in 1493. By advantageous marriages—his own and those of his son and grandson—and by military campaigns, he extended his influence across Europe.

Maximilian was the son and successor of the Holy Roman Emperor Frederick III. In 1477, he married Mary of BURGUNDY. Several deaths among the male members of her family made her and Maximilian heirs to the throne of CASTILE. Maximilian's main problem was at home with the Austrian and German princes, led by Berthold von Henneberg, archbishop of Mainz. Maximilian tried to persuade them to fund his military campaigns, but they resisted.

Maximilian went to war many times. From 1495 until his death, he engaged in conflicts in Italy against the forces of Charles VIII of France. His claims to Burgundy, both before and after Mary's death, brought him into conflict with the French king and the townspeople of GHENT and BRUGES. In eastern Europe, he defended his lands against the Turks, and in 1490 he tried unsuccessfully to capture HUNGARY.

Ambitious, intelligent, and a supporter of the arts, Maximilian became one of the great patrons* of learning, painting, and music. Maximilian engaged some of the finest composers of his time to write music for the imperial chapel in Vienna. He helped to write two biographical epics about himself—one about his courtship of Mary, and the other about his life and military adventures. (*See also* **Habsburg Dynasty.**)

* **patron**   person of wealth and influence who supports an artist, writer, or scholar

Mecca

The city of Mecca was the birthplace of MUHAMMAD, the prophet of Islam. It is thus one of the most revered places in Islam—an important site of pilgrimage and a focal point of prayer for Muslims. Since the 600s, Muslim pilgrims from all over the world have flocked to the city to visit its holy sites and shrines as part of a religious obligation known as the hajj*. Muslims everywhere also face toward Mecca when they pray.

Located in a dry, desolate valley in western central ARABIA (present-day Saudi Arabia), Mecca was a pagan* Arab religious center for centuries before the rise of Islam. In these pre-Islamic times, the place of worship in

* **hajj**   pilgrimage to Mecca that Muslims are required to make once in their lifetime
* **pagan**   word used by Christians to mean non-Christian and believing in several gods

Mecca is revered as the birthplace of the prophet Muhammad. It has been an important pilgrimage site for Muslims since the 600s. These Muslims are visiting the Kaaba, the cube-shaped shrine that is the focal point of Islamic worship. The Kaaba contains the Black Stone, one of Islam's holiest relics.

* **caliph** religious and political head of an Islamic state

the city was the Kaaba, a cube-shaped shrine containing idols that represented various pagan gods. The Kaaba remains the focal point of Islamic worship today. One of its holiest relics is the Black Stone, which is thought to be part of an ancient meteorite. The city in pre-Islamic times was also important as a crossroads of trade and as a cultural center.

During the first half of the 600s, Islamic conquests helped make Mecca increasingly international. Muslim pilgrims from all over the Islamic Empire came to the city and had opportunities to exchange ideas, develop commerce, and study with noted Islamic scholars. Between the 600s and the 900s, the caliphs* of the UMAYYAD and the ABBASID dynasties developed the city's cultural and religious life, and they appointed princes or governors to oversee the administration of the holy city.

By the late 900s, the caliphs had lost control of Mecca, and the city was governed by local princes of the Alids, a group claiming descent from ALI IBN ABI TALIB. These rulers, known as sharifs, were effectively independent of the CALIPHATE that ruled the Islamic Empire. Between 969 and 1117, the caliphs of the FATIMID EMPIRE sometimes were able to exert influence over the sharifs, largely by threatening economic boycotts. They threatened, for example, to disrupt the pilgrimage routes to Mecca and to cut off imports, both of which were essential to the Meccan economy.

After the fall of the Fatimids in 1171 and the fall of the caliphate of BAGHDAD to the Mongols in 1258, Mecca came under the influence of the MAMLUK DYNASTY of Egypt and then under that of the Ottomans, who overthrew the Mamluks in 1517. Despite a turbulent and unstable history of political control, Mecca remained an international center of Islam throughout the Middle Ages. Its symbolic role as the hub of the Muslim universe and its association with Muhammad and the origins of Islam made it the holiest city in the Islamic world. (*See also* **Mongol Empire; Ottomans and Ottoman Empire; Pilgrimage.**)

Mechthild von Magdeburg

1212–1281/1301
German mystic

* **mystic** person who experiences divine truths through faith, spiritual insight, and intuition

* **vernacular** language or dialect native to a region; everyday, informal speech

* **Beguines** pious laywomen in northwestern Europe, who lived in communities and cared for the poor and the sick

* **purgatory** place of temporary suffering or punishment after death and before entering heaven

The Benedictine nun Mechthild von Magdeburg was the greatest German woman mystic* of the Middle Ages. She was the first German mystic who wrote of her visions and dialogues with God in the vernacular*. Her work is thus regarded as a milestone in the development of popular literature, and Mechthild is considered at the forefront of German mysticism.

Little is known of Mechthild's life. Scholars think that she was of noble birth. She lived the life of a Beguine* in the German city of Magdeburg before taking refuge in the Benedictine convent of Helfta in 1268. Her visionary experiences about heaven, hell, purgatory*, and the Last Judgment were collected and written down by her spiritual adviser, Heinrich von Halle. These collected writings, titled *Das fliessende Licht der Gottheit (The Flowing Light of the Godhead),* became famous throughout medieval Europe.

The language of Mechthild's work is filled with the metaphors and allegories that were familiar to the courtly society of the 1200s. As with other medieval mystics, Mechthild said that she had experienced the mystical union of the human soul with God, and this became the primary theme of her writings. Her experience with this mystical union was a highly emotional one that took place in the heart rather than through the intellect. Mechthild was greatly admired throughout Europe. Her work inspired Dante, and she is prominently portrayed in his *Purgatorio*. (*See also* **Beguines and Beghards; Benedictines; Eckhart, Meister; Hadewijch of Antwerp; Mysticism.**)

Medici Family

 See map in Italy (vol. 3).

* **patron**   person of wealth and influence who supports an artist, writer, or scholar

The Medici family was a famous and powerful family in Florence in the late Middle Ages. The family's wealth, political power, and support of the arts had a great influence on the history of the city.

The family came to Florence in the early 1200s from the nearby Mugello River valley and quickly became wealthy and influential. In the late 1280s and the 1300s, a total of 53 members of the Medici family served on the city's highest council. Despite some family quarrels and some other problems (several family members were convicted of murder and other violent crimes), by the 1400s, the Medicis had established themselves as the leading Florentine family and one of the most powerful in all of Italy.

In 1397, Giovanni di Bicci de' Medici (1360–1429) founded the bank that established the family financially. The bank specialized in money changing (exchanging one kind of currency for another), deposits, bills of exchange, and international transactions. It had branches in Rome, Milan, Venice, Avignon, Bruges, and London. However, the main source of the bank's profits came from transactions with the papacy. The family also invested in textiles, jewelry, silver plate, and spices. Over the years, Giovanni acquired a great fortune, which he left to his sons.

Giovanni's son Cosimo, also a competent banker, actually ruled the city, although from behind the scenes. His financial and political power enabled him to influence decisions of government. By not flaunting his great wealth and by his skill at diplomacy, Cosimo earned the respect of Florentine citizens. As a patron* of the arts, Cosimo supported the work of scholars and artists, such as the sculptor Donatello and the architect Brunelleschi.

Cosimo's grandson Lorenzo, the unofficial governor of Florence at the remarkably young age of 20, made the Medicis even more important by marrying the daughter of a powerful family of the Roman nobility. Pope Innocent VIII made Lorenzo's son a cardinal of the church at the age of 13. (He eventually became Pope Leo X at age 38.) In 1523, Lorenzo's nephew, Giuliano, became the second Medici pope, Pope Clement VII.

Near the end of the Middle Ages, the Medici family fortunes began to decline. The Medici bank failed, and the invasion of Italy by King Charles VIII of France in 1494 forced Lorenzo's son Piero into exile. (*See also* **Banking; Gothic Architecture; Gothic Art.**)

Medicine

Medieval medicine owed a great debt to the ancient world. Throughout much of the medieval period, medical knowledge was based largely on the works of ancient Greek and Roman philosophers and thinkers. Only gradually did Europe develop its own traditions in medicine. By the end of the Middle Ages, medical principles and practices had greatly expanded, laying the groundwork for the development of modern medicine.

History of Medicine in Europe

In both the Byzantine world and Western Europe, the study and practice of medicine began as an extension of the medical theories and practices of ancient Greek philosophers and physicians, such as Hippocrates (460–377 B.C.), Aristotle (384–322 B.C.), and Galen (A.D. 130–200). Many of the works of these ancient writers were rediscovered first by Arabic scholars and then came to Europe as translations from Arabic texts. The works of the Greek physician Hippocrates were especially important in the early medieval period. His works on surgical techniques were studied extensively, and his emphasis on the healing power of nature made his work a source of reference for many centuries. Galen's works on the diagnosis and prognosis* of disease and on anatomy* were also extremely influential. Aristotle's scientific observations on anatomy were widely studied, but his influence on medicine extended beyond scientific observations. Although Aristotle's theories on medicine were shaped by his philosophical beliefs, they played an important role in medieval theories of medicine.

*** prognosis** forecast of the probable course that a disease will take

*** anatomy** structure of a living organism or its parts

Medicine in the Byzantine World. In the scientific fields, the greatest contribution of the Byzantine world was in medicine. The two most important periods in the history of Byzantine medicine were from 330 to 650 and from 1050 to 1453. The first period relied heavily on ancient texts. Several important Byzantine physicians lived during this time. Oreibasios of Pergamum (born ca. 325) compiled an encyclopedia of medicine that preserved the works of many ancient physicians, including Galen. Aetios of Amida (born ca. 502) was the first important Christian physician in the Byzantine world. His writings reflected the rational, scientific approach of the ancient Greeks as well as Christian mysticism* and faith. Aetios provided detailed descriptions of epidemics*, poisons, and various types of infections and illnesses. Perhaps the most influential Byzantine physician in this period was Alexander of Tralles. His work, *Twelve Books on Medicine,* became a well-known textbook throughout much of the Middle Ages.

*** mysticism** belief that divine truths or direct knowledge of God can be experienced through faith, spiritual insight, and intuition

*** epidemic** disease that affects a large number of people or animals

The other important period in the history of Byzantine medicine—from 1050 to 1453—marked the beginning of a new phase. During this time, a number of physicians willing to try new ways made significant contributions to medical knowledge. Michael PSELLOS wrote a comprehensive dictionary of diseases. Symeon Seth provided detailed descriptions of many types of drugs and discussed the healing powers of various foods. Medical teaching also took a step forward in the 1100s. John II KOMNENOS and his wife Irene built a hospital, situated near a monastery, that served as a center for medical education. Medical studies were pursued with far greater vigor and innovation than ever before.

Throughout the Byzantine era, the medical profession included not only laypersons but clergy* as well, many of whom made important contributions to medicine. Some clergy used their medical knowledge to establish hospitals and charitable institutions. Women were also allowed to study and practice medicine in the Byzantine world.

*** clergy** priests, deacons, and other church officials qualified to perform church ceremonies

After the mid-1400s, Byzantine medicine declined. Before this time, however, the knowledge of Byzantine physicians spread to other parts of Europe, where additional medical advances were occurring.

French surgeon Guy de Chauliac is shown in this manuscript illumination from the 1300s giving a surgery lesson. Textbooks, experience, and observation were the main elements of a medical education in the Middle Ages. Surgery did not become a formal part of medical training until the later Middle Ages.

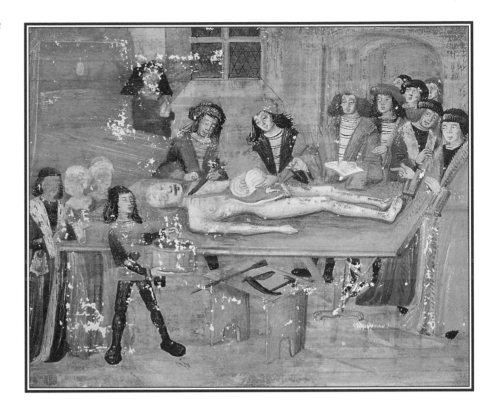

See color plate 5, vol. 1.

* **abbey** monastery under the rule of an abbot or abbess

Medicine in Western Europe.   During the early medieval period, medicine in western Europe was associated primarily with the clergy. As early as the 600s, monks were reading ancient texts on medicine, and monastery libraries had a fair number of texts on both the principles and practices of medicine. Monasteries not only housed these texts; they also put them to practical use. Someone had to take care of the sick, and that job often fell to monks.

By the 900s, the study of medicine spread beyond the monasteries, and it became possible to pursue medical studies at cathedral schools (schools located within the cathedral complex that existed to train priests). Such studies preserved the knowledge of ancient works on medical theory, even though medieval medicine was based more on practical observation and experience than on abstract ideas.

In the late 1000s, a new and different medical tradition began in Italy at the city of Salerno and the nearby abbey* of Monte Cassino. Salerno physicians, who had a reputation as skilled medical practitioners, produced their own medical literature, much of which focused on principles and philosophy rather than on practical medical knowledge and experience. This new focus was due largely to a man known as Constantine the African.

Constantine had come to Salerno from North Africa sometime in the mid-1000s. He entered the monastery at Monte Cassino and began translating Arabic medical works into Latin. Many of these works dealt with general principles and philosophies, which were new to medieval Europe. This approach, which was adopted at Salerno, affected the study of medicine throughout western Europe.

The trend that started at Salerno became a general characteristic of European medicine in the 1200s. This was due largely to the influence

Medicine and the Black Death

The Black Death, or bubonic plague, arrived in Italy from Asia in 1347. By 1360, it had killed perhaps one in three Europeans. In 1348, King Philip VI of France ordered the medical faculty at the University of Paris to explain the plague and its treatment. The report that was produced maintained that an alignment of three planets had generated poisonous fumes, and this foul air was the cause of the plague. The recommended treatment was to eat and drink moderately, purge harmful substances from the body, and flee from areas infected by the plague. Such treatment was ineffective. Today, we know that the plague was caused by bacteria spread to humans by fleas from infected rats.

* **pharmacology** science of drugs, their properties, uses, and effects

* **thesis** original idea stated, usually in a paper, and supported by argument

of additional ancient medical works translated into Latin. After about 1150, many medical writings were translated into Latin from both Greek and Arabic. Included among these were works by Galen and by outstanding figures in Islamic medicine. One medical text, *The Canon of Medicine,* by IBN SINA (known as Avicenna in the West) was used in the West almost up to the modern period.

These newly translated works were very significant for Western medicine. Arabic medical encyclopedias confirmed the belief held by many European physicians that medicine should be studied using reason and logic, closely linked to philosophy and methodical observation. Specialized Arabic texts also introduced to Europe such medical fields as surgery and pharmacology*, in which Islamic physicians had made great advances.

While many of the medical writings in this period focused on theory, a major exception was the field of surgery. Surgery in the 1200s was marked by the importance of direct experience rather than theory. A number of medical advances were made through observation. It was discovered, for example, that wounds healed best if left alone or if cleansed with wine. This more practical approach was often at odds with the theoretical approach to medicine at the universities. In fact, some universities in France excluded the study of surgery. This was not the case in Italy, however, where surgery remained part of the medical curriculum and a respected branch of medicine.

Medical Education in Western Europe

During the early Middle Ages, most medical instruction was individualized and accomplished through basic medical studies and by apprenticeship (training under an established physician). Medicine was taught in schools that were located in cities, in monasteries, and even in public lectures at which physicians spoke about basic medical knowledge.

With the rise of centers of medicine—such as Salerno and Monte Cassino—in the 1000s, medical education began to follow more established rules. In the following century, medicine became less connected with the church as well. This trend was reinforced by several church councils that forbade monks and clergy from practicing or teaching medicine for the sake of monetary gain.

When medical education shifted to the universities in the 1200s, a sharp break occurred between the study of medicine and the study of liberal arts. In many universities, separate medical faculties were employed, and medicine often ranked below such fields of study as theology and law. In addition, surgery was often not a part of formal medical training, and surgeons had a lower status than physicians.

The years of medical education fell into two phases. During the first phase, students worked toward a preliminary degree by attending classes for a period of two to four years. The students also had to pass a number of examinations and defend a thesis* on a particular topic. During the second phase of study, students faced a more varied and hectic program, including additional classes, required periods of teaching a variety of medical subjects, and more examinations. In receiving a university degree, the students promised to lecture on medicine as part of the university faculty for two more years.

Books were an important part of medical education, and there was an ever-growing need for them. This need stimulated the establishment of the first medical libraries at university medical colleges. In addition to book learning, experience and observation were important parts of medical education. Even beginning students were required to interrupt their class sessions with practical medical work. Students might, for example, spend time in a town under the supervision of a practicing physician. This type of work helped enrich the student's knowledge of medical diagnosis and therapy.

Eventually the classroom lecture format gave way to observation in the areas of anatomy and surgery. Around 1300, this approach led to the introduction of dissection* for teaching purposes at some universities. The best-known centers for the study of anatomy were in the Italian cities of Bologna and Padua. Education at these centers focused on the training of practicing surgeons. In many northern European universities, on the other hand, medical education focused more on training academic physicians who were primarily scholars rather than medical practitioners.

Medical Practice in Western Europe

The medieval physician could observe such things as a patient's pulse, blood, and various symptoms to diagnose an illness. Physicians could then provide a prognosis, but they could do little in terms of treatment other than bloodletting*, changing the patient's diet, or using different medications. A number of these drugs were known to European physicians through Arabic writers.

By the beginning of the 1300s, medicine was primarily a secular* occupation, although some clergy still provided medical services. Medicine became a more secular profession largely because of the emergence of medical schools. Another factor, however, was the limitations placed on the clergy by church law. During the mid-1100s and in the 1200s, several church laws were enacted that forbade monks and clergy from leaving their monasteries or churches to study medicine. Instead, they were encouraged to study religion.

Despite less clerical involvement, medical care continued to be influenced by Christian tradition. Monks and clergy still performed such medical tasks as setting fractures and applying medications to external wounds, and they often were required to hear their patients' confessions before treating them. Secular society also organized and administered medical care according to Christian principles. Many communities, for example, established hospitals to provide medical services for the poor and needy.

Throughout most of the Middle Ages, university-trained physicians were in the minority of those providing medical advice or care. University-trained physicians usually became teachers or served as medical advisers to kings, nobles, popes, clergy, and wealthy townspeople. The majority of medical practitioners continued to be trained by apprenticeship, and their connection to university-based medicine was limited. Among these were folk healers, apothecaries*, and barbers, who often provided medical care in addition to services in their own fields. (The barber's pole advertised his services as a surgeon—a bloody bandage wrapped around a white pole.) Full-time medical practitioners tended to concentrate in cities, while medical care in small towns or rural areas was often supplied by unlicensed healers. (*See also* **Barber-Surgeons; Herbs and Herbals; Hospitals and Poor Relief; Plagues.**)

* **dissection** act of cutting apart a plant or animal in order to carefully examine or study its structure

* **bloodletting** opening a vein to take blood; believed to aid the healing process

* **secular** nonreligious; connected with everyday life

* **apothecary** person who is trained or licensed to dispense medicine; a pharmacist

Mehmed II the Conqueror

1429–1481
Ottoman sultan

* **principality**   region that is ruled by a prince

* **vassal**   person or state in the service of a more powerful lord or state

* **devalue**   to reduce in value or worth

M ehmed II is considered the founder of the Ottoman Empire. During his rule as SULTAN, the Ottoman Turks conquered CONSTANTINOPLE and much of southeastern Europe and established their power on the ruins of the BYZANTINE EMPIRE.

In 1444, Mehmed was given the throne by his father, Murad II, who hoped to avoid a struggle for succession after his death. In 1446, however, Murad was forced to retake the throne to avert internal conflict. Mehmed returned to the throne in 1451 and set out to consolidate his power. He undermined the power of the grand VIZIER and gained control of the Janissaries, an elite corps of troops. Then he set out to conquer Constantinople, the Byzantine capital. The fall of the city on May 29, 1453, transformed the Ottoman state from a Turkish principality* into a world empire, with Mehmed as its ruler.

Mehmed next turned his attention to the neighboring states. By the end of his reign, he had conquered SERBIA, Albania, Hercegovina, and parts of BOSNIA and Greece. The Crimea (a region in present-day Russia) became a vassal* state and a base of operations for attacks on POLAND and MUSCOVY. By the time of Mehmed's death in 1481, the Ottomans were assaulting parts of Italy and preparing for further advances into eastern Europe.

The cost of the continual warfare undermined Mehmed's attempts to improve the economy of the empire. By the time of his death, Ottoman currency was devalued*, and social problems were erupting throughout the empire. (*See also* **Ottomans and Ottoman Empire.**)

Merovingians

* **dynasty**   succession of rulers from the same family or group

The Merovingian king Clovis converted from his pagan religion to Christianity between 496 and 498. His baptism is shown here in this illumination from the *Grandes chroniques de France,* a history of France compiled in the 1300s.

T he Merovingians were a dynasty* of kings descended from a group of romanized* Germanic people known as the FRANKS. From the late 400s until the mid-700s, the Merovingians ruled over much of the former Roman province of Gaul, which included the areas of modern-day France and parts of western Germany.

The Merovingians began as chieftains of the Salians, one of the early Frankish tribes. The early Merovingian chieftains, particularly Merovich and Childeric I, were loyal allies of the Romans and helped them in battle against the Saxons and the VISIGOTHS. By the middle of the 400s, the Salians were well established in and around the city of Tournai (in present-day Belgium). In 486, Childeric's son CLOVIS defeated a rival king. This date is considered the beginning of the Frankish monarchy.

Clovis and his successors continued many of the Roman traditions they inherited. They preserved the Roman fiscal* system and cultivated an image of themselves as defenders of Roman institutions and customs. Clovis enhanced this image by converting from paganism* to Christianity sometime between 496 and 498. As a result of his conversion, Clovis was made an honorary Roman consul* by the Roman emperor in 507. In return, Clovis defended and preserved the interests of the Roman Church in his realm. Such policies led to the eventual merger of Frankish and Roman traditions.

Once his authority was recognized, Clovis began to expand his kingdom to the south and north. In the south, he conquered the kingdom of Toulouse from the Visigoths. In the north, he eliminated the kings of other Frankish tribes around the cities of COLOGNE, Cambrai, and Le

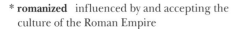

* **romanized** influenced by and accepting the culture of the Roman Empire

* **fiscal** pertaining to financial matters and revenues

* **paganism** word used by Christians to mean non-Christian religions that believe in several gods

* **consul** high public official

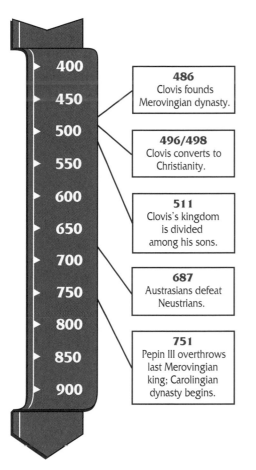

400

450

500

550

600

650

700

750

800

850

900

486
Clovis founds Merovingian dynasty.

496/498
Clovis converts to Christianity.

511
Clovis's kingdom is divided among his sons.

687
Austrasians defeat Neustrians.

751
Pepin III overthrows last Merovingian king; Carolingian dynasty begins.

Mans. After Clovis's death in 511, his sons continued his policies and gained control of the regions of Thuringia, Burgundy, Provence, and Bavaria.

When Clovis died, his kingdom was divided among his four sons. This division of the kingdom followed old Frankish inheritance customs, but it created a major problem. It led to continual civil war within the Merovingian family. Every male heir claimed kingship and sought to secure his place at the expense of his brothers. These conflicts eventually led to the creation of three major Merovingian kingdoms—Neustria, Austrasia, and Burgundy—each with its own king and court.

By the late 500s, the fighting among members of the royal family was further aggravated by conflicts between the kings of the three Merovingian kingdoms and their nobility. In Austrasia, for example, Queen Brunhilde tried to reinstate Roman taxation and fiscal and administrative policies to benefit her sons. In 613, Burgundian and Austrasian nobles overthrew her and handed her over to King Chothar II of Neustria for execution. Chothar, with the help of these same nobles, reunited the three kingdoms and passed them on to his son Dagobert I. In return for their help, Chothar gave the nobles the power to control their local countries. To counter the power of the nobles, both Chothar and Dagobert appointed local bishops and abbots who were loyal to them rather than to the nobles. The kings also encouraged noble families to send their children to the royal court for their education, hoping that this would create strong personal loyalties to the king.

The Merovingian kingdom reached its peak under Dagobert I. Following his death in 638, the balance of power between king and nobles was destroyed, and the Merovingian rulers fell under the control of the nobility. Increasingly, the kingdom found itself in a struggle between rival factions within the nobility for control of the king. The conflict was greatest between the nobles of Austrasia and Neustria. In 687, the Austrasian nobles defeated the Neustrians and strengthened their control over the kingdom. Finally, in 751, an Austrasian noble named Pepin III (also known as Pepin the Short) declared himself king of the Franks. He sent the last Merovingian king, Childeric III, into exile in a monastery. Pepin, the son of Charles Martel, is considered the first king of the Carolingian dynasty. (*See also* **France.**)

Metals and Metalworking

Throughout history, humans have extracted metals from the earth and then used them to make tools, weapons, sculptures, jewelry, and other objects. During the Middle Ages, metalworking gained importance because of the great demand for metal objects. Medieval metalworkers used techniques that were similar to those that had been used for thousands of years. But as the Middle Ages progressed, and metals were used for different purposes, metalworking became a more specialized occupation.

Metals, Metalworking Tools, and Techniques.   Most of the metals used in the Middle Ages were the same as those of earlier periods. Bronze, copper, brass, pewter, and tin were used to make a variety of practical and

Among medieval metalworkers, goldsmiths had a high social status. They sometimes rose to positions of power and wealth. Goldsmiths relied on the patronage of kings and nobles, for whom they made jewelry, weapons, and other items. They also made gold plates, cups, crosses, and other religious items for the clergy.

* **crucible** container used for heating substances to high temperatures

* **casting** process in which hot metal is poured into molds and allowed to cool, forming metal objects or pieces of various shapes

* **inlaying** setting metal, stones, or gems into the surface of ground material

* **etching** engraving pictures or designs on metal or glass by using the chemical action of an acid

* **gilding** covering with a thin layer of gold

* **embossing** decorating a surface with raised figures or designs

* **nonferrous** referring to metals that contain little or no iron

* **forge** special furnace or fireplace in which metal is heated before it is shaped

* **patronage** the support of an artist, writer, or scholar by a person of wealth and influence

decorative objects. Lead was essential in architecture to cover roofs and steeples and to channel water. Among the most important medieval metals were iron and steel. These were used extensively for weapons, armor, tools, and other practical items. The precious metals gold and silver were used primarily for jewelry and decorative objects as well as for coins.

Metalworking tools have remained relatively unchanged for centuries. Many modern hand tools bear a strong resemblance to those used in the Middle Ages. Medieval metalworkers used a variety of hammers, tongs, and punches. As technology developed, some of these tools were adapted for particular jobs. For example, hammers of different sizes and shapes were employed. An essential tool for most metalworkers was the bellows, a device used to keep furnace fires hot. Many metalworkers also needed a supply of crucibles* and molds for casting* metal.

The techniques of medieval metalworking differed somewhat, depending on the metals that were used. Blacksmiths, those who worked with iron and steel, had only a few techniques and a small range of tools. Their work consisted primarily of heating pieces of metal in a furnace and then bending, flattening, and shaping them using hammers, tongs, anvils, and chisels. During the later Middle Ages, blacksmiths learned more decorative techniques, such as inlaying*, etching*, gilding*, and embossing*. These techniques, as well as casting and enameling, were part of the craft of metalworkers who fashioned items of gold, silver, and other nonferrous* metals.

Only a few written records of metalworking tools and techniques survive from the period between the 700s and 1100s. The most important is a book titled *De diversis artibus,* written by the monk Theophilus between 1110 and 1140. The work describes the construction of a forge* and bellows, the manufacture of various tools, and several metalworking techniques. It also gives detailed lists of the tools found in medieval workshops. This book is the single most valuable source for the history of medieval metalworking.

Medieval Metalworkers.   From the earliest times, metalworkers (or smiths) were among the most important members of the community. One reason for this was that they were at the forefront of new technology. They were also important because they made the weapons, tools, and household implements that were essential to daily life.

In the early Middle Ages, most smiths worked with a variety of metals using various techniques. There was little specialization. The first major division in metalworking developed between ironworkers and those who made things of gold, silver, copper, bronze, and other metals. Although the basic difference between the two groups was in technique, it gradually developed into a difference in social status as well. Blacksmiths generally were regarded as inferior to goldsmiths, who worked with precious metals. Goldsmiths sometimes rose to positions of power and great wealth.

During the early medieval period, goldsmiths usually depended on the patronage* of the nobility. Kings and nobles commissioned goldsmiths to make elegant jewelry, richly ornamented weapons, and other precious objects. As the medieval church became more powerful, goldsmiths gained another source of patronage. Churches required gold and silver plates, gold altars, and other items for their services. Church dignitaries desired rings, crosses, and other jewelry made of gold, silver, and precious stones.

By the end of the Middle Ages, the majority of metalworkers were highly skilled craftsworkers whose activities were regulated and supported by craft GUILDS. Through these guilds*, blacksmiths and goldsmiths exercised their social power as an important segment of society. Population growth and economic development resulted in increased demand for their products. (*See also* **Armor; Gems and Jewelry; Mining.**)

* **guild** association of craft and trade workers that set standards and represented the interests of its members

Migrations, Germanic

etween the 200s and 600s, a number of different Germanic peoples from northern and eastern Europe began moving into the lands controlled by the Roman Empire. These barbarian invasions hastened the fall of the Roman Empire in western Europe and paved the way for the creation of the various kingdoms and states of medieval Europe.

Early Migrations.   Before the 200s, small numbers of Germanic peoples had migrated across the frontiers of the Roman Empire. Whenever they had come into contact with the Romans, Roman armies had checked their advance and pushed them back. Even so, extensive contacts had been established between the Germans and the Romans, largely as a result of trade. Roman influence had caused changes in Germanic society. The Germans, who previously had had little political organization, had begun to form tribes under individual leadership. This organization gradually had evolved into the concept of hereditary* kingship. The Germans also had abandoned their tradition of communal ownership of property and had recognized private property. This change had led to the development of a wealthy aristocracy, as some individuals or families had accumulated more property than others.

During the 200s, Germanic peoples made large-scale raiding expeditions across Roman frontiers. These frontiers had been left undefended because Roman troops had been occupied in civil unrest, including rebellion by troops against their own leaders. The FRANKS ravaged the Roman province of Gaul. The ALAMANNI raided northern Italy and threatened the city of ROME before retreating. The Goths terrorized the Balkan region in the eastern part of the Roman Empire. These invasions were a severe blow to Rome, but no territory was lost except for the province of Dacia in eastern Europe, which fell to the Goths.

Major Migrations.   Full-scale migrations of Germanic peoples began in the late 300s and the 400s. The primary reason for this movement was the appearance of the fierce HUNS from Asia. As the Huns moved westward into Europe, the Germanic peoples were pushed into Roman territory. The first Germanic peoples to encounter the Huns were the OSTROGOTHS (East Goths), who were defeated by the Huns in 375. Continued advances by the Huns drove the VISIGOTHS (West Goths) into the eastern provinces of the Roman Empire. In 378, the Visigoths defeated a Roman

* **hereditary** passed on from parent to child

See map in Germany (vol. 2).

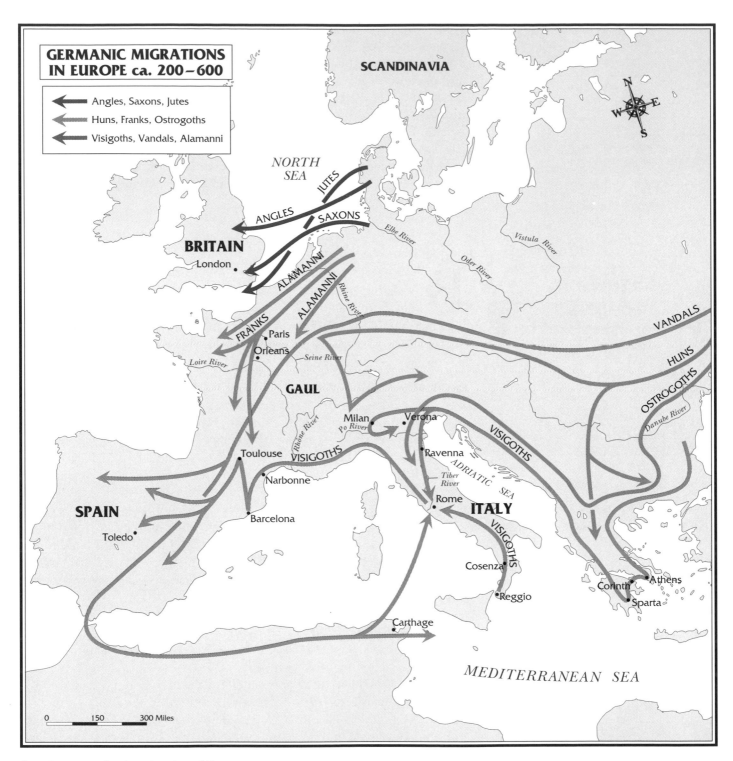

GERMANIC MIGRATIONS IN EUROPE ca. 200–600

- Angles, Saxons, Jutes
- Huns, Franks, Ostrogoths
- Visigoths, Vandals, Alamanni

A major reason for the migration of Germanic tribes in the early Middle Ages was the westward movement from Asia by the Huns, who pushed the Germanic people into Roman territory. The Germanic invasions hastened the fall of an already weakened Western Roman Empire.

army in Asia Minor (modern-day Turkey) and then wandered through the Balkans before entering Italy. Under the leadership of King Alaric I, the Visigoths sacked Rome in 410. From there, they moved into southern Gaul and then into Spain, where they established a kingdom that lasted until it was overthrown by the Muslims in 711.

The VANDALS were driven westward by the Huns in the early 400s. After crossing Gaul, they settled for a short time in Spain, before being forced farther south by the Visigoths when that tribe moved into that region. The Vandals crossed into North Africa and established a kingdom that lasted until it was overthrown by the BYZANTINE EMPIRE in 533.

The power of the Huns declined in the 450s due to defeats at the hands of combined Roman-Visigothic forces in Gaul and the death of the Hun leader, Attila. Freed from Hunnish control, the Ostrogoths established kingdoms in the eastern Roman provinces. They then went to Italy, where they established a kingdom that lasted until the 540s, when the emperor JUSTINIAN I brought the region under the control of the Byzantines. In the late 500s, Italy was invaded and taken over by another Germanic people, the LOMBARDS.

Various groups of Franks settled in Gaul in the 400s. By the early 500s, these groups were united under the leadership of CLOVIS, who then expanded Frankish control over Gaul and areas east of the Rhine River. Of all the Germanic kingdoms established in Europe, the kingdom of the Franks was the strongest and the longest lasting. Under the CAROLINGIANS, this kingdom became a powerful empire.

Germanic Britain.   By the time the Angles, Saxons, and Jutes invaded Britain in the mid-400s, the Romans had already abandoned the island because Roman troops were needed elsewhere. The invasions started in the southeastern part of the island and pushed north and west, driving the Celtic inhabitants to the fringe areas. By the mid-500s, a distinct boundary existed between Germanic Britain and the unconquered Celtic areas, which became IRELAND, SCOTLAND, and WALES. The invaders eventually established seven kingdoms—Kent, Sussex, Wessex, Essex, East Anglia, Mercia, and Northumberland. Under pressure from invasions by the VIKINGS beginning in the late 700s, these kingdoms achieved unity.

Anglo-Saxon England became the most Germanic of the kingdoms created out of the former Western Roman Empire. Roman law vanished and was replaced by laws based on Germanic customs. Christianity disappeared until it was reintroduced by missionaries from the church in Rome in the 600s. The Anglo-Saxon language was a Germanic language, unlike the languages that developed in the other former Roman areas, which were based on LATIN. (*See also* **Anglo-Saxons; Burgundy; Danegeld; England; France; Germany; Italy; Spain, Muslim Kingdoms of.**)

Milan

* **barbarian** referring to people from outside the cultures of Greece and Rome who were viewed as uncivilized

The city of Milan is in the region of Lombardy in northwest Italy. Throughout its history, Milan's location at the intersection of major trade routes in the fertile Po River basin has made it an important commercial center. During the Middle Ages, the city experienced much political upheaval. Invasion, revolution, civil war, and anarchy were serious and recurring problems. Nevertheless, by the end of the Middle Ages, Milan had become one of the richest cities in Italy—a center of trade, art, and government.

The medieval history of Milan began with the barbarian* invasions that swept through Europe after the fall of the Roman Empire. In 452, the HUNS invaded and looted the city. Next came the OSTROGOTHS, who

Construction on the Gothic cathedral of Milan began in 1386 under the patronage of the city's first duke. It is the world's second largest medieval cathedral after the Seville cathedral in Spain. More than 2,000 carved figures adorn the cathedral, which was not completed until the 19th century.

 See map in Italy (vol. 3).

* **archbishop**   head bishop in a region or nation

* **artisans**   skilled craftspeople

invaded in 489. By the early 500s, the city had recovered somewhat—only to find itself the target of a war between the Goths and Burgundians and the Byzantines. Poverty, disease, and famine marked Byzantine rule in the mid-500s. These problems made control of the resources of the Po valley extremely attractive.

In 569, a Germanic group known as the LOMBARDS seized Milan. The Lombards established a kingdom in the region and chose the city of Pavia, rather than Milan, as the seat of its royal court. Although Pavia was the center of government, Milan also gained in stature. Then in 774, the FRANKS, led by CHARLEMAGNE, took control of the region and ended the Lombard reign. Milan regained its political importance and experienced an economic, cultural, and religious renaissance, or rebirth.

Beginning in the late 700s, Milan fell increasingly under the power of its archbishops*. They were the principal landowners and overlords of the city. The nobility and the upper classes gained a great deal of political power as well. During this period, Milan became very strong economically, and neighboring cities became more and more dependent on it.

In 1042, Milan's merchants and artisans* rebelled against the increasing authority of the archbishops and the nobility. A period of civil war followed, during which the lower classes struggled for greater political power. This internal strife helped weaken the influence of the archbishops and the upper classes and led to the formation of a commune (an elected city government) in 1097. This commune was one of the first of many that were formed in northern Italian cities. During the period of peace that followed, Milan experienced tremendous economic growth, and the city expanded and prospered.

As Milan's power grew, it gained supremacy over other cities in Lombardy. Increasingly, those cities looked to the HOLY ROMAN EMPIRE for support against Milan, and Emperor FREDERICK I BARBAROSSA sent troops to subdue the city in 1158 and 1162. In 1167, Milan joined other northern

Italian cities in an alliance called the Lombard League. This league was opposed to the emperor and his attempts to gain control of all northern Italy and to break the power of the communes. The league won a great victory over imperial* forces in 1176, and the emperor was forced to recognize the liberty of the cities and their communes.

During the late 1100s and the early 1200s, Milan once again experienced civil unrest between the rich and the poor. A decisive victory for the nobles in 1277 ended the commune and ushered in a long period in which Milan was ruled by noble lords or despots* known as *signori*. During this period, which lasted until the end of the Middle Ages, Milan became a rich and powerful city. Its industry and trade increased, and it became a great center of the arts. (*See also* **Commune; Guelphs and Ghibellines; Italy.**)

* **imperial**   pertaining to an empire or emperor

* **despot**   ruler with unlimited power or authority

See map in Crusades (vol. 2).

* **theological**   pertaining to the nature of God, the study of religion, and religious beliefs

* **crusader**   person who participated in the holy wars against the Muslims during the Middle Ages

* **pagan**   word used by Christians to mean non-Christian and believing in several gods

* **mystic**   person who experiences divine truths through faith, spiritual insight, and intuition

Millennialism

Millennialism refers to the idea that, at some future time, the earth will experience a period of great peace and glory lasting 1,000 years. The idea has both specific and general meanings. In its specific sense, it is the belief that Jesus Christ one day will return to earth, conquer the forces of evil, and reign with the saints on earth for 1,000 years before the Last Judgment. In its more general sense, millennialism is the belief in the coming of sweeping changes for the better, brought about by supernatural forces.

The belief that Christ will return to earth for a 1,000-year reign is based on the Book of Revelation in the BIBLE. This belief was very popular among early Christians. But in the 300s and 400s, it was condemned by church fathers, such as St. AUGUSTINE, who argued that the Book of Revelation was not to be taken literally. From then until after the Middle Ages, this particular aspect of millennialism was never again widely believed. The more general meaning of a coming change for the better was rarely expressed in the early Middle Ages. However, the idea emerged again in the 1100s, and then it remained an important theme of medieval thought about the future.

Beginning in the 1100s, two traditions arose that reflected the general millennial view: political millennialism and theological* millennialism. Political millennialism was the idea that a "conquering hero" would establish a peaceful, Christian kingdom over the whole world. The idea grew out of Roman and Byzantine thought, and it may have spread through western Europe as a result of the CRUSADES. The idea of a conquering hero fit well with the expectations of the crusaders*, and prophecies often linked the hero with specific European monarchs.

Theological millennialism was the idea that there would be a spiritual renewal sometime in the future, when Jews and pagans* would be converted to Christianity and the church itself would be reformed and purified. This idea was based on the writings of St. Jerome, one of the early church fathers. Millennialism was developed further in the 1100s by a number of medieval mystics*, including HILDEGARD OF BINGEN, OTTO OF FREISING, and Joachim of Fiore and the Franciscan spirituals who expanded on his work.

Between 1200 and 1500, millennial prophecies were common throughout Europe. Some focused on a conquering hero and others on an era of spirituality and religious reform. During much of the Middle Ages, millennial ideas helped to instill hope and courage during times of disaster. Often inspired by calamities, such as the spread of the BLACK DEATH, millennial ideas gave people comfort by offering hope for a better future.

Millennialism also existed in medieval Islam. It was expressed in the idea of the coming of the Mahdi, a savior who would bring justice to the earth and eliminate oppression. The idea first arose in the late 600s, when the Shi'ite* and Sunnite* Muslim sects struggled for dominance. The Shi'ites anticipated a person who would return Islamic rule to the descendants of MUHAMMAD and free Islam from unlawful rulers. This belief became a vital aspect of Shi'ite faith. The Sunnites hoped for a restoration of the early CALIPHATE of the city of Medina. According to the Sunnites, the Mahdi would defeat his opponents, conquer the cities of CONSTANTINOPLE and ROME, reign over the whole world, and bring about an era of great prosperity. (*See also* **Christianity; Islam, Religion of.**)

* **Shi'ites**   Muslims who believed that Muhammad chose Ali and his descendants as the rulers and spiritual leaders of the Islamic community

* **Sunnites**   Muslim majority who believed that the caliphs should rule the Islamic community

Mining

* **ore**   mineral or rock containing a high concentration of one or more metals

* **Meseta**   large, mostly treeless plateau in central Spain

Mining in the Dark

The life of a medieval miner was not easy. The engineering of mine shafts was not well developed, so cave-ins were a persistent danger. The oil lamps worn by miners in the dark could ignite dust and cause fire or explosions. An exposed pocket of natural gas could choke a miner before he realized what was happening. The most feared and common danger, however, was drowning. Underground wells or streams often were exposed during mining activities, and if miners were not quick enough, water could fill the shaft and drown them.

The mining of metals dates back to ancient times, and mining was an important industry throughout the Roman Empire. During the early Middle Ages, the Germanic invasions brought an end to the mining industry in parts of Europe. Yet the mining of certain metals, most notably iron and tin, survived in Britain, France, Italy, and Spain. During that time, other metals generally were reworked and reused from metal objects already in use. This was particularly true of precious metals, such as silver and gold, and also of lead. Mining activity increased again beginning in the 900s, and all branches of mining were revived and expanded in the 1000s and 1100s.

Nine regions of medieval Europe were especially important for mining because of the abundance of ores*. Western Britain was rich in tin and copper. The Spanish Meseta* was richly endowed with copper, silver, and lead. France had large deposits of iron and zinc, and the Harz Mountains in Germany were an important source of silver, lead, and copper. In the late Middle Ages, the German region of Saxony became the most important mining region of Europe, and its silver and lead mines were a training ground for miners working in other parts of Europe. Other important mining regions were BOHEMIA, Slovakia, the eastern Alps and the Balkans, and SCANDINAVIA.

The tools and methods used in medieval mining were similar to those used by the Romans. Fires were set against rock, and the heat cracked the rock so that metals could be removed. Picks, hammers, and chisels were used to tunnel through rock and earth and to crush ores. Pure metals were extracted from ores by smelting*. Gold was found by panning* riverbeds. Because of the difficulty of transporting heavy ores, smelting and other extraction processes were done as close to the mines as possible. A supply of wood for fuel was very important. Many regions were well forested, but a lack of forests in Spain and Italy hindered mining and smelting activities.

* **smelting** process that uses heat to melt an ore and extract the pure metal

* **panning** method for separating gold dust or nuggets from gravel or sand

The question of ownership of the earth's mineral wealth led to a system of mining laws, which varied from metal to metal and from place to place. During the early Middle Ages, no mining laws existed, and communities exploited mineral resources as they saw fit. As FEUDALISM developed, mining rights were given exclusively to feudal lords and kings. At first, these rights were restricted to gold and silver, but other metals eventually were covered as well. In time, mining codes were established to resolve disputes and to encourage cooperation in mining activities. Courts, including special mining courts, became responsible for interpreting and enforcing these codes. (*See also* **Technology.**)

Minstrels

* **secular** nonreligious; connected with everyday life

* **vielle** stringed instrument that resembled a violin

* **lute** stringed instrument similar to a guitar, with a pear-shaped body and a curved back

Royal and noble families often had minstrels permanently employed in their households. They provided continuous entertainment throughout the day and into the evening. They also played at special occasions such as weddings, banquets, and tournaments. This illumination of an instrumental concert is from the Psalter of Rene II of Lorraine, dating from the 1400s.

Medieval minstrels were professional, secular* musicians. In addition to providing private entertainment at royal or noble courts, they provided most of the musical entertainment at public markets, festivals, processions, and celebrations.

During the early Middle Ages, feudal courts hired local or wandering performers known as *mynstralles* and *jeestours* for amusement during the long evenings. These entertainers played instruments or sang, told stories, performed magic tricks, juggled, and presented trained animal acts. As musicians, they were very versatile, often performing on a variety of instruments.

As feudal courts gradually became wealthier and more splendid, the pattern of daily court life changed. Nobles built large castles and spent great sums of money on personal luxury, festivities, and frequent entertainment. This, in turn, brought about an increased demand for musicians who were hired on a permanent or semipermanent basis. By the late 1100s, professional musicians, now known as minstrels, became a permanent part of court life, providing the nobility with various types of entertainment throughout the day and into the evening.

One of the earliest noble courts to hire permanent minstrels was that of Duke William X of Aquitaine, the father of ELEANOR OF AQUITAINE. Through Eleanor's marriages to King Louis VII of France and King HENRY II of England, resident minstrels became an important feature of the royal courts of both France and England.

Unlike entertainers who wandered from place to place (those entertainers became known as jongleurs), minstrels were permanent members of a particular noble household or town. Minstrels were also unique performers in that they specialized in playing musical instruments, and often a specific instrument.

The instruments that minstrels played included trumpets, drums, wind instruments (flutes and pipes), and stringed instruments such as vielles* and lutes*. The status of minstrels varied according to the instruments they played. Trumpet players and drummers ranked above, and were paid more than, minstrels who played wind instruments. Minstrels who played wind instruments ranked above those who played stringed instruments. In time, minstrels were divided into two groups, according to whether the sound of their instruments was loud or soft.

By the 1300s, minstrels had become a regular part of court life as well as an important part of the middle-class culture of towns. At royal courts, minstrels played not only for daily and evening entertainment, but also at special occasions such as weddings, banquets, tournaments, and dances. As towns grew and a merchant middle class developed, townspeople also sought regular entertainment. Minstrels were hired by city governments, organizations, and guilds* to provide music on regular occasions such as market days, festivals, religious processions, carnivals, and other public ceremonies. (*See also* **Music; Musical Instruments; Troubadour, Trouvère.**)

* **guild** association of craft and trade workers that set standards and represented the interests of its members

---

Mishrad

See *Judaism.*

Missions and Missionaries, Christian

* **pagan** word used by Christians to mean non-Christian and believing in several gods

* **abbey** monastery under the rule of an abbot or abbess

* **archbishopric** church district headed by an archbishop

Since the earliest days of Christianity, Christians have heeded the words of Jesus to "Go into all the world and preach the Gospel to every creature." As a result, the history of Christianity is closely tied to missionary activity. During the Middle Ages, Christian missionaries founded missions—centers of Christian teaching and learning—throughout Europe and used them as bases from which to spread Christianity among pagan* peoples. Because of missionary activity, most of the peoples of Europe had accepted Christianity by the year 1200.

Between the 300s and the 600s, Christian missionaries were very active in the westernmost parts of Europe. Martin of Tours, a Roman soldier who entered religious life, founded the first monastery in Gaul (present-day France) in the mid-300s. Christianity was brought to Scotland in the late 300s and the early 400s by St. Ninian, a Welsh bishop who built the first Christian church there. During the 400s, much of Ireland was converted to Christianity through the missionary efforts of St. PATRICK, who established many churches and monasteries. In the 500s, an Irish monk, St. Columba, founded several monasteries in Ireland and Scotland. In the 600s, a Celtic monk, St. Aidan, established an abbey* at Lindisfarne in northern England and played a crucial role in converting the people of that region. From Lindisfarne, missionaries such as St. COLUMBANUS later went back to the Continent and reestablished Christianity in Switzerland and northern Italy.

Starting in about 600, missionary activities were vigorously supported and directed by the popes in Rome. At the same time, missionary efforts often focused on kings or tribal chieftains, because once these individuals accepted Christianity, their subjects automatically followed. The first pope to direct missionary efforts was GREGORY I. In 596, he sent a Roman monk named Augustine and 40 companions to convert the ANGLO-SAXONS of Britain. Within a year, Augustine had converted the Anglo-Saxon king, Ethelbert, and 10,000 of his followers, and he had established an archbishopric* at CANTERBURY.

Serious attempts to convert the Germans were begun in the 700s by St. BONIFACE, perhaps the greatest missionary of the early Middle Ages. Through his efforts, papal influence was greatly expanded in Germany. From there, Christian missionaries entered Scandinavia. Conversion occurred slowly in Scandinavia, and Christianity suffered repeated reverses because of the strong pagan beliefs of the Scandinavian peoples. Parts of the region did not become Christian until the 1200s.

As in western Europe, the spread of Christianity in eastern Europe owed much of its success to the support of kings and princes. In the 800s, the Byzantine emperor Michael III sent two Greek brothers, CYRIL AND METHODIOS, to launch missionary activity among the SLAVS. Over the next few centuries, a series of Slavic monarchs supported the efforts of missionaries, and, by 1200, Christianity was generally accepted throughout much of the region.

One major challenge to missionary activity was the rise of Islam in the Middle East and North Africa. Some Christians sought to convert the Muslims to Christianity. Others saw Islam as a scourge to be destroyed and Muslim lands as territories to be conquered. During the CRUSADES, missionaries went to the Islamic world to win converts while the crusaders* killed Muslims. For the most part, the missionaries were unsuccessful, although some, including St. FRANCIS OF ASSISI, won the respect of Muslims as holy persons.

* **crusader** person who participated in the holy wars against the Muslims during the Middle Ages

Beginning in the late 1400s, missionary activity shifted dramatically. With Europe largely Christian, missionaries looked to other parts of the world for potential converts. At the same time, missionary goals provided European rulers with a reason to expand overseas and conquer new lands. (*See also* **Clovis; Germany; Ireland; Peter the Venerable.**)

Monasteries

A monastery is a place of residence for a religious community. It may consist of either a single building or, more commonly, a group of buildings. Some of the greatest medieval structures were monasteries, and their designs often served as models for other types of architecture. During the Middle Ages, thousands of monasteries were built throughout Europe in order to serve the needs of a growing monastic movement.

Medieval monasteries were built in cities, in the rural countryside, and even in very remote settings. For example, the great monastery at Monte Cassino, founded by St. BENEDICT OF NURSIA in 529, was built on a rugged mountaintop in central Italy. Other remote sites for medieval monasteries included the desert slopes of Mount Sinai in Egypt, the small island of Mont-Saint-Michel off the coast of Normandy in northwestern France, and rugged Mount Athos in northern Greece. The building of monasteries in difficult-to-reach locations ensured that their inhabitants would have solitude in which to devote their lives to prayer, work, and dedication to God.

Monasteries serve as religious communities for either men or women. Monasteries may also be known as abbeys or priories, depending on their organization. An abbey is led by a chief monk called an abbot or a head nun called an abbess. A priory is headed by a monk called a prior or a nun called a prioress. As monasticism grew in the Middle Ages, abbeys often became overcrowded, and some of their members would leave to establish a new monastery. At first, the new monastery would retain connections to the old abbey, and its leader would be called the prior or prioress. Priories, therefore, tended to have slightly lower status than abbeys. When the priory developed and became more established, it gained independence from the original abbey. It thus became an abbey, and its leader took the title of abbot or abbess.

For the most part, the medieval monasteries of western Europe were rural residences where monks or nuns grew their own food, prayed, and focused their lives on God. These monasteries generally consisted of a core of buildings—a church, a dormitory for the monks or nuns, a dining hall, and work areas—as well as additional buildings to house the kitchens, stables, infirmary, and guest houses. The main buildings of the monastery usually were centered on a cloister, or enclosed garden courtyard. This cloister was closed to visitors and served as a place for quiet meditation for the monks or nuns.

Monastic architecture in western Europe took shape in the 500s under monastic rules established by St. Benedict of Nursia. His detailed ideas about how a monastery should be organized became the standard on which future monasteries were based. Medieval European monasteries were built on an orderly rectangular, gridlike plan. This type of design was used throughout the West, and monasteries provided inspiration for European secular* architecture. For example, the design of the great monastery of Cluny, the largest in medieval Europe, played a major role in the spread of ROMANESQUE ARCHITECTURE in western Europe. Similarly, monasteries built by the CISTERCIANS introduced a style that contributed to the development of GOTHIC ARCHITECTURE.

In western Europe, the 1200s saw the rise of the mendicant* orders, most notably the DOMINICANS and the FRANCISCANS. The followers of these orders, known as friars, devoted themselves to preaching rather than to contemplation. Since they were not concerned about withdrawing from society, their residences were usually in towns or cities rather than in rural areas. The monasteries of these orders were distinguished by the grand scale of their churches, which were designed to accommodate the large crowds who came to hear them preach.

From the earliest days of monasticism, many monasteries in the Byzantine Empire were located in cities. In fact, almost every Byzantine town had several monasteries. By the mid-300s, the city of CONSTANTINOPLE was a major monastic center, with perhaps hundreds of monasteries and tens of thousands of monks and nuns. Byzantine monasteries tended to grow without planning, giving them a haphazard quality. In addition to serving as a place for meditation and devotion, they were places where peasants could receive blessings and medical attention. Some of these Byzantine monasteries developed rather advanced medical facilities.

Medieval monasteries were the scene of many important developments. Mechanical clocks were developed in monasteries so that the faithful could be alerted to the hours of prayer. Monks developed musical chanting as a form of community praying. Monks also developed techniques for distilling alcohol and turning wine into brandy. Most importantly, however, monasteries served as centers of learning, helping to preserve and transmit knowledge through the creation of manuscripts and the training of leading scholars and thinkers. (*See also* **Christianity; Missions and Missionaries, Christian; Monasticism.**)

* **secular**   nonreligious; connected with everyday life

* **mendicant**   person who depends on begging for a living

Remember: Words in small capital letters have separate entries, and the index at the end of Volume 4 will guide you to more information on many topics.

Monasticism

* **ascetic** person who rejects worldly pleasure and follows a life of prayer and poverty

* **chastity** purity in conduct and intention; abstention from sexual intercourse

* **penance** an act of repentance for sin

Early in the history of Christianity, some men and women felt a need to lead lives of greater perfection and holiness than their neighbors. To achieve this, they separated themselves from ordinary society and lived alone or with other ascetics*. This desire for isolation from everyday life was the basis for monasticism. During the Middle Ages, monasticism became firmly established in both western Europe and the BYZANTINE EMPIRE as a major feature of Christian civilization.

Medieval monasticism had its origins in EGYPT in the early 300s. Two distinct forms of monastic life emerged at that time. One was the hermit, or anchorite, way of life, in which a single individual lived alone, isolated from society. The other form of monastic life was cenobitic monasticism, in which a community of monks or nuns (cenobites) lived together. From Egypt, monasticism spread to both the Byzantine world and western Europe. While both forms of monasticism became widespread in the Byzantine world, the cenobitic type became predominant in western Europe.

In the Byzantine Empire, monasteries appeared in PALESTINE, SYRIA, and Asia Minor (present-day Turkey) during the 300s, and, by the 500s, cenobitic monasticism was well established throughout the empire. Byzantine monasteries based their way of life on rules established by St. Basil of Caesarea in the mid-300s. Basil's rules emphasized prayer and long worship services, and they provided a code of conduct based on charity, obedience, chastity*, and good works. These rules remained the basis of Byzantine monasticism throughout the Middle Ages. The hermit form of monasticism also spread throughout the Byzantine Empire. Some hermits were known for their unusual forms of penance*. For example, the Stylites spent years living on the tops of columns, while the Dendrites lived in hollow trees or on branches. Beginning in the 600s, Arab invasions of the Byzantine Empire destroyed many monastic centers. At the same time, however, the monastic centers that remained were strengthened by an influx of monks who had fled from the Arabs. In the 700s, some Byzantine emperors attempted to abolish monasticism, but these attempts failed and monasticism continued to flourish.

In western Europe, monasticism appeared about the mid-300s. The real expansion did not begin, however, until the late 300s, when monasteries sprang up throughout Italy and Gaul (present-day France). In the 400s, Gaul was a favored place for monasticism, and monasteries were established near a number of cities, often near the tombs of bishops. Although western Europe had some hermits or anchorites, monastic communities of monks or nuns comprised the major form of monastic life. Western monasticism differed from that of the Byzantine world. In the Byzantine world, monastic life remained organized around individual monasteries, while in western Europe distinct monastic orders gradually developed.

In the 500s, two crucial events took place that had a great impact on European monasticism. One of these events was the founding of monasteries in Italy at Subiaco and Monte Cassino by St. BENEDICT OF NURSIA. The other was the rule that Benedict established, which described in detail how these monasteries were to be run. The Benedictine rule envisioned each monastery as a self-sufficient community of monks or nuns living together in one house. The head of the monastery was the abbot or abbess, who was chosen by the monks or nuns. Each monk or nun was supposed to renounce all possessions, and everything was to be the common property of the monastery. The rule also gave details on how the monastery was to be organized, and it provided an orderly routine for the monks or nuns, which included specific times for prayer, reading, and manual work. After the 800s, the Benedictine rule was adopted almost everywhere in western Europe as the basis for monastic life and conduct.

From the 600s on, the number of monasteries in Europe grew enormously. As monasticism expanded, the wealth and power of monasteries increased as well. Abuses also grew, and attempts were made by church councils, popes, and kings to reform monastic life. These reforms gave new vigor to monastic institutions and led to the development of new religious orders. Among these were the CISTERCIANS, who sought to regain the monastic ideals of St. Benedict, and the DOMINICANS and the FRANCISCANS, who played an important role in the educational life of the later Middle Ages. (*See also* **Beguines and Beghards; Brethren of the Common Life; Christianity; Hermits; Monasteries.**)

Mondino dei Luzzi

ca. 1270–1326
Professor of anatomy

* **anatomy**   structure of a living organism or its parts

* **dissection**   act of cutting apart a plant or animal in order to carefully examine or study its structure

* **cadaver**   corpse; dead human body

Mondino dei Luzzi (also known as Raimondo de' Liuzzi) was a professor of anatomy* at the University of Bologna in Italy. He is best known for his book on anatomy, which contained practical guidance on dissection* techniques and explanations of the structure and purpose of various body parts.

Mondino was born into a medical family. His grandfather owned a pharmacy, which Mondino later inherited, and his uncle was a doctor and university lecturer. Mondino studied at the University of Bologna and then spent his entire career there as a professor. Although he wrote several works, his most famous is *Anatomia Mundini*. This work drew on Mondino's own knowledge of the human body and experiences with dissections and also on the observations and writings of the ancient Greek physicians Hippocrates and Galen and the Arab physician IBN SINA.

Mondino intended the *Anatomia* as an instruction guide to accompany the dissection of a human cadaver*. Its text and techniques remained in use for more than 200 years. The book's success was due less to its content than to historical circumstance. When it appeared in 1316 or 1317, medieval doctors were just beginning to dissect humans for medical purposes. The book became a practical guide for them as they performed these dissections—one person read the text while another performed the dissection. (*See also* **Medicine.**)

Money

* **currency**   medium of exchange; money

* **mint**   to make coins by shaping and stamping metal; the place where coins are made

Throughout the Middle Ages, money consisted of metal coins. Paper money was unknown. The value of coins depended on the metal from which they were made. Gold was more valuable than silver, and silver was more valuable than copper. This widely recognized standard made it possible for coins from any region or country to be used as currency* throughout the medieval world. Many different coins were used during the Middle Ages. Their design and weight, the inscriptions on them, and the purity of the metal in them varied greatly.

In the Byzantine world, gold, silver, and copper coins were minted* and used throughout the medieval period. One of the most important Byzantine coins was the gold nomisma. From about 500 to 1000, the nomisma was an important standard of exchange in Mediterranean trade. During most of the medieval period, the principal mint of the Byzantine world was in CONSTANTINOPLE. The coins made at other provincial* mints often differed greatly in manufacture and design.

The early Islamic world of the late 600s was familiar with Byzantine coins, but it had no coins of its own. As the Muslims conquered Byzantine territories, however, they adopted the minting practices already established there. Soon, the Muslims were also minting their own coins with distinctive Islamic designs and inscriptions. One of the most important early Islamic coins was the gold dinar. The dinar, with its Arabic inscriptions from the QUR'AN, reflected Islamic religious ideals. Islamic coins were minted throughout the Islamic world, from DAMASCUS and BAGHDAD in the East to CÓRDOBA in Muslim Spain in the West. In the Islamic world, the relationship between the value of different types of coins was not fixed. Instead, the value of coins was determined in the marketplace according to the value of their metals and the principles of supply and demand.

The coins of medieval western Europe were very diverse. They were issued by many different authorities, and they varied greatly in weight, design, and denomination*. Gradually, however, increased trade led to the development of coins with certain standard combinations of metal, weight, and appearance. This allowed coins of one region to be exchanged for those of another. One of the earliest standard coins in western Europe was the gold triens. The triens, which was derived from an early Roman coin, was the standard European coin in the 500s and 600s. In the late 700s, CHARLEMAGNE standardized the coinage of his realm. The basic coin was a silver coin called the denarius, or penny. The silver penny became the basis for almost all European coinage for the next 400 years. Charlemagne also introduced an accounting system that grouped 12 pennies into a unit called a shilling, and 20 shillings into a unit called a pound. This system was adopted throughout Europe as the basis for recording payments. It remained in use in England until the 1960s.

In the centuries after Charlemagne, the minting of coins in western Europe became increasingly localized, and the value of coins became less standardized. The designs of coins also varied greatly from one country or region to another. During this time, most coins were made of silver, and gold coins were rare. It was not until the 1200s that gold coins once again became common. The two most important gold coins at that time were from Italy: the florin of FLORENCE and the ducat of VENICE. These coins were widely circulated, and they became symbols of reliability and wealth for several hundred years. (*See also* **Banking; Trade.**)

* **provincial**   referring to a province or an area controlled by an empire

* **denomination**   specific value or measure

Mongol Empire

During the 1200s, the Mongols created a huge land empire that stretched from central Asia as far west as Hungary and to the shores of China in the east. The legendary Mongol ruler GENGHIS KHAN was both cruel and just, slaughtering those who resisted him, but allowing those who obeyed him to flourish under Mongol administration and to practice their own religion.

Origin of the Empire.   The Mongol peoples were a group of nomadic* tribes from the central Asian steppe* who lived by herding sheep and

* **nomadic**   wandering from place to place to find food and pasture

* **steppe**   vast treeless plain of southeastern Europe and Asia

The Mongols were among the most skilled and fiercest conquerors in history. They began their conquests under Genghis Khan in the early 1200s. In half a century, they amassed the largest empire in history, with conquests that extended from the Pacific Ocean to the Black Sea. This manuscript illumination shows a battle between Persian and Mongol armies. Persia was one of the many countries that fell to the Mongols.

See color plate 11, vol. 3.

* **vassal** person given land by a lord or monarch in return for loyalty and services

* **annex** to add a territory to an existing state

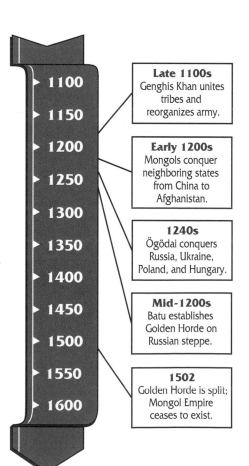

1100	**Late 1100s** Genghis Khan unites tribes and reorganizes army.
1150	
1200	**Early 1200s** Mongols conquer neighboring states from China to Afghanistan.
1250	
1300	**1240s** Ögödai conquers Russia, Ukraine, Poland, and Hungary.
1350	
1400	**Mid-1200s** Batu establishes Golden Horde on Russian steppe.
1450	
1500	**1502** Golden Horde is split; Mongol Empire ceases to exist.
1550	
1600	

horses and by raiding weaker tribes. Temüjin, who became Genghis Khan, was born around 1167 and was the son of the chief of a subclan of the Börjigin (one of the Mongol peoples). After his father was poisoned by rivals, the family hid on the slopes of the Kentai Mountains. Temüjin was a very clever diplomat, and he gradually emerged as leader of the Börjigin clan. Later, he used his diplomatic and military skills to unite the other Mongol tribes. In 1206, he was proclaimed Genghis Khan (Lord of the Steppe) at a grand assembly.

One of Genghis Khan's first tasks was to reorganize his army. He broke up the old tribal armies and reassigned them into larger units based on a decimal system. Mongol society was organized around the army, and all male Mongols between the ages of 14 and 60 were enlisted in it. The skills required for the nomadic life of the Mongols were similar to those needed for cavalry warfare. Even the annual winter hunt was organized to provide military training as well as food. This organization, which made it easy to mobilize the army quickly, caused a Persian historian in the 1200s to call the Mongols "a peasantry in the dress of an army."

Expansion of the Empire. After uniting the tribes in the Mongolian homeland, Genghis Khan set out to conquer three neighboring states: the Chin and the Hsi-hsia in China and the Qara Qitai in Transoxania. Although the Hsi-hsia were not conquered, the king married one of his daughters to Genghis Khan and became the Mongol ruler's vassal*. Although the Chin were not completely conquered until after Genghis Khan's death, the Mongol leader was very successful against the Qara Qitai. By 1218, he had annexed* their land. His state bordered on the lands of the most powerful Muslim ruler of the time, the Khwarizmshah, whose territory lay in what is now northern Iran and parts of Tajikistan and Uzbekistan.

In 1218, Genghis Khan sent a great caravan of 1,500 camels to the Khwarizmshah as a peace offering. On the way, one of the Khwarizmshah's local governors seized the caravan and its goods and executed everyone except one messenger, who returned to Genghis Khan with the news of the massacre. Furious over the massacre, Genghis Khan attacked the lands of the Khwarizmshah in 1219.

The Mongols attacked cities one by one. If a city offered no resistance, they just plundered it. But if a city resisted at all, they punished its population by enslaving the women and children and massacring the men. The only exception were skilled workers, whom they took to Mongolia. The Mongols believed that city dwellers were more likely to surrender than to face this punishment, and they were right. The inhabitants of many cities surrendered to the Mongols.

A Thousand Years' Ruin

The effect of the Mongols' conquest on the regions they overpowered was mixed. In some places, they rebuilt what they had destroyed. In other places, however, the devastation was complete. According to a Persian historian writing in the 1340s, "there can be no doubt that even if for a thousand years to come no evil befalls the country, yet it will not be possible completely to repair the damage, and bring back the land to the state in which it was formerly."

Throughout the 1220s, Mongol armies conquered Khorasan, Afghanistan, western Iran, northern Iraq, Georgia, Crimea, and southern Russia. In 1225, Genghis Khan returned to Mongolia. He was making plans for his final campaign into China when he died in 1227.

Division of the Empire. When Genghis Khan died, his empire was divided among his three surviving sons and his grandson. His son Ögödai led campaigns into Persia (where the Muslims had returned to power). His main achievements, however, were the invasions of Russia and eastern Europe. When Ögödai died in 1241, the Mongols had conquered much of Russia, Ukraine, Poland, and Hungary. By July 1241, they had reached the outskirts of Vienna.

Following Ögödai's death, dissension erupted among Genghis Khan's children and grandchildren, and no one had enough support to be elected Great Khan for several years. Various branches of the dynasty established rival states. Genghis's grandson Batu established the GOLDEN HORDE in the Russian steppe. Other Mongol rulers, including the Ilkhanids, converted to Islam in the late 1200s and 1300s, causing still more tensions. Mongol rulers gradually became local rulers who faced many challenges within their territories. By 1502, for example, the Golden Horde had split into numerous states, and the vast region it once governed ceased to exist as a Mongol state. In the end, the Mongol Empire proved to be too large and diverse to hold itself together. (*See also* **Iran; Iraq; Samarkand.**)

Mosaics

* **mortar**   mixture of sand, lime, cement, and water

See color plate 7, vol. 2.

Mosaics are an art form that utilizes small stones or colored bits of glass or precious metals set in mortar* or some plasterlike material. During the Middle Ages, the making of mosaic mural decoration was linked primarily with BYZANTINE ART. Finely detailed mosaics were created on the vaults and domes of Byzantine churches. Between the 1000s and the 1200s, floor mosaics were also used to decorate churches and other important buildings.

Medieval mosaics were expensive substitutes for painting. Mosaic artists first drew each figure on a layer of plaster before pressing the mosaic tiles, called tesserae, into it. The effect was quite spectacular. The colored glass sparkled and glittered, while the stones, often used for flesh tones, provided a dramatic contrast. Many mosaics had shimmering gold backgrounds created from a specially made gold glass. Despite the hard edges of the materials used in mosaics, the effects could be just as subtle as in paintings, and much brighter in color.

Many medieval mosaics were large, monumental works that required the labor of many artists. These artists usually trained and worked together in special workshops. The techniques of mosaic, which originally were developed in ancient Greece and Rome, were perfected in the Byzantine world. The Byzantine workshops were well-known and admired throughout Europe and in the Islamic world, and Byzantine artists often traveled to different countries to create mosaics for wealthy patrons. In time, mosaic workshops were established in a few centers in western Europe and in KIEVAN RUS in eastern Europe.

Producing a large mosaic required many workers to create the tesserae, to design the images, to prepare the surfaces for the mosaic, and to attach the tiles. A specially skilled artist usually worked on the heads and faces of people in a scene, since this required the greatest refinement. Over the centuries, the tesserae grew progressively smaller, allowing ever-increasing refinement in contours and coloring. By the 13th and 14th centuries, miniature mosaic icons* were being made with tesserae so small that they could barely be seen.

Some of the finest works of medieval mosaic were created in the Byzantine world. The mosaics in the church of HAGIA SOPHIA in CONSTANTINOPLE were especially important. Mosaic art also was important in various cities in Italy, including VENICE and RAVENNA, in the kingdoms of the CAROLINGIANS, and in parts of the Islamic world. (*See also* **Islamic Art and Architecture.**)

* **icon**   Christian religious image of a saint, often painted and placed on a screen in the church, most common in the Eastern Church

Mu'awiya

ca. 602–680
Caliph and founder of the Umayyad dynasty

* **caliph**   religious and political head of an Islamic state

* **plague**   disease that swept across the medieval world several times, including the Black Death in the mid-1300s

Mu'awiya, the fifth caliph* and founder of the UMAYYAD dynasty, was famous for his diplomatic skill, generosity, and combination of self-control and opportunism. As caliph, he made the city of DAMASCUS in SYRIA the capital of the Islamic Empire, unified and strengthened the empire and expanded its borders, and introduced strong monarchic and bureaucratic institutions into Islamic government.

The son of a leading merchant of MECCA, Mu'awiya joined with the Meccans in opposition to the rising power of MUHAMMAD. When Mecca fell to the Prophet in 630, Mu'awiya converted to Islam and served as Muhammad's secretary. In the 630s, Mu'awiya fought with the Muslim army when it invaded Syria and JERUSALEM. He became governor of Syria in 639 after plague* killed most of the Muslim leaders there. As governor, he expanded Muslim control in Syria, fortified the region against the armies of the BYZANTINE EMPIRE, and established Damascus as his capital. He also settled Arab tribesmen along the northern frontiers of the region and built a strong base of support among them and other segments of the population.

In 656, the assassination of Uthman, the third caliph and Mu'awiya's cousin, led to civil war between Mu'awiya's forces and those of ALI IBN ABI TALIB, Uthman's successor. The civil war ended in January 661, when Ali was murdered and his son, Hasan, renounced all claim to the CALIPHATE and acknowledged Mu'awiya as caliph. (*See also* **Umar I ibn al-Khattab; Yazid I ibn Mu'awiya.**)

Muhammad

ca. 570–632
Founder of Islam

* **Kaaba**   large stone shrine covered with black cloth. It was a place of worship for pagan Arabs and became the main Islamic place of refuge and protection in Mecca.

Muhammad, the Prophet and founder of Islam, was born in the western Arabian city of MECCA about 570. Mecca at that time was a very wealthy city, situated at the crossroads of important caravan routes. The city was also the site of a sacred shrine, the Kaaba*, to which pagan Arab pilgrims had come for centuries. The city's prosperity created social tensions between different classes, and its religious environment made it ripe for social reform.

Early Life and Preaching.   Muhammad's family belonged to Arabic clans within the powerful Quraysh tribe. His father died before he was born, and his mother died when he was only six years old. Thereafter,

In this Persian miniature, Muhammad, seated in a cave, is visited by his followers. Around the year 610, while meditating in a cave, Muhammad had his first revelation, in which an angel proclaimed him "messenger of God." During his lifetime, he received many other divine messages and shared them with his followers. These revelations, collected in the Qur'an, formed the basis of the Islamic religion.

* **pilgrimage** journey to a shrine or sacred place

Muhammad was raised first by his grandfather and later by an uncle. By Arab custom, an orphan could inherit nothing from his father or his grandfather. Thus, although Muhammad came from a prosperous family, he had no money of his own. This no doubt made him especially sensitive to the social problems and corruption of Mecca.

About 595, a wealthy widow named Khadija hired Muhammad as her agent on a journey to SYRIA. She was so pleased with the way Muhammad conducted her affairs that she offered to marry him. They married, and Khadija bore Muhammad one or more sons, who died in infancy, and four daughters. His daughter Fatima later married his cousin, ALI IBN ABI TALIB.

Around 610, while meditating in a cave near Mecca, Muhammad had a vision in which an angel proclaimed him "messenger of God" and gave him a message to convey to the people of Mecca. Muhammad continued to receive such messages, or revelations, for the rest of his life. From these revelations came the concepts that there was only one God and that on the Last Day all people would be raised from the dead to be judged by God and assigned to heaven or hell. Muhammad's revelations were collected in the QUR'AN.

After receiving his first revelations, Muhammad gathered a band of followers, who joined with him in worship and prayer. Within a few years, he began preaching in public to the people of Mecca. Most of the wealthy Meccans reacted to Muhammad's message with hostility because it criticized their attitudes and policies. They also feared that Muhammad might gain political power in the city. Despite active opposition, Muhammad was able to continue preaching because he had the protection of the leaders of his clan, who were prepared to avenge any injury to him. Many of Muhammad's clan did not accept his religion, but to disown him would have brought disgrace to the clan.

The Birth of the Islamic State. About 619, the chief of Muhammad's clan died, and the new chief was unwilling to guarantee Muhammad's safety. In 622, Muhammad found a solution to his problems. He met secretly with pilgrims from the city of Yathrib (later Medina), who accepted him as prophet and swore to protect him and his followers. He then told his followers to go to Medina and wait for him there. Muhammad arrived at that city on September 24, 622. This hegira, or emigration, marks the beginning of the Islamic calendar.

For the next few years, Muhammad's followers (known as Muslims) and the Meccans engaged in armed conflicts. In 624, the Muslims won an important victory at the Battle of BADR, but the struggle continued. Finally, in January 630, Muhammad marched on Mecca with 10,000 men, and the city surrendered without resistance. Most Meccans accepted Islam, and their skill at administration became an important asset to the Islamic state both during and after Muhammad's lifetime. By 632, many of the tribes throughout Arabia had accepted Islam, and the religion spread rapidly in the years to come.

Muhammad led a "farewell pilgrimage*" to Mecca in March 632. He fell ill three months later and died on June 8 in the presence of his chief lieutenant, ABU BAKR, and his favorite wife, A'ISHA, who was Abu Bakr's daughter. Even after his death, Muhammad continued to be regarded as the best model for human behavior. It became the goal of every Muslim to follow both the teachings of the Qur'an and the SUNNA, or customs, observed by Muhammad during his lifetime. (*See also* **Arabia; Caliphate; Islam, Religion of.**)

Muhtasib

* **caliph** religious and political head of an Islamic state

The *muhtasib* was an Islamic official who served as a representative of the caliph* in "encouraging good and forbidding evil." As such, he was a guardian of public conduct. The position of *muhtasib* was found throughout the Islamic world, but it was most important in Spain and North Africa. The power attached to the position varied greatly from place to place.

The primary area controlled by the *muhtasib* was the market. He supervised all trades and crafts; he ensured that goods were properly made, foods well prepared, and services performed correctly; and he guarded against fraud, misrepresentation, and deceptions of all kinds. Working conditions, sanitation, and public safety also came under his authority. Although the *muhtasib* was responsible primarily for the marketplace, his responsibilities also extended beyond it. He supervised mosques, schools, baths, and workshops and made sure that the city walls were in good repair and the streets clear of obstacles. As a defender of public morals, he helped break up public brawls, ensured that women were not harassed, and prevented drinking, gambling, and other improper activities. Through such responsibilities, the *muhtasib* played an important role in promoting order in Islamic towns and cities and in upholding Islamic ideals. (*See also* **Law.**)

Muqaddasi, al-

died ca. 1000
Islamic geographer

Al-Muqaddasi was the author of one of the most important and original Arabic works on geography of the Middle Ages. The book, *Ahsan al-Taqasim fi Ma'rifat al-Aqalim (The Best Divisions for Knowledge of the Regions),* was noted for its personal observations, its richly descriptive information about different cultures, and its attention to the customs and religious beliefs of other peoples.

Little is known about al-Muqaddasi except that he was born in JERUSALEM, grew up in PALESTINE, and began traveling when he was about 20 years old. He traveled widely throughout the Muslim world, missing only Pakistan and Spain. Al-Muqaddasi's book focused exclusively on Muslim lands, which he divided into six Arab and eight non-Arab regions. For each region, he gave general observations about the area followed by detailed descriptions of its districts and towns. He also described the physical features of each region and the customs of local populations, paying particular attention to language, food, dress, and religious beliefs. Al-Muqaddasi's concern with these various aspects of culture added a new, human dimension to the field of Islamic geography, and it set his work apart from that of earlier Muslim geographers.

Al-Muqaddasi used personal observations, discussions with experts, and literary and scientific works as sources for his book. Although not the first Muslim geographer to use personal observation, he was the first to give it such prominence in his work. (*See also* **Books, Manuscript; Maps and Mapmaking.**)

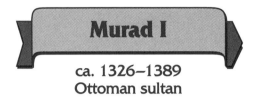

Murad I

ca. 1326–1389
Ottoman sultan

The Ottoman ruler Murad I was largely responsible for extending the OTTOMAN EMPIRE into southeastern Europe, an area that was formerly part of the BYZANTINE EMPIRE. Murad's conquests in Europe began in 1361 when he captured the Byzantine city of Adrianople, which became the European capital of his empire. He followed this success with the conquest of Thrace, a region in northeastern Greece, in 1364. Beginning in 1366, Murad led vigorous campaigns against BULGARIA and SERBIA, capturing the Bulgarian city of Sofia in 1385 and the Serbian city of Nish in 1386. To strengthen the Turkish presence in conquered regions, Murad transplanted colonies of Turks from ANATOLIA. Murad's victory at the Battle of Kosovo in Serbia on June 15, 1389, opened the entire Balkan region to Ottoman domination. Murad was not able to enjoy his victory, however. Just as the battle was ending, he was killed by a Serbian warrior.

In addition to his conquests in Europe, Murad was known for his creation of the Janissary corps. This elite group of soldiers consisted of captured Christian youths who were converted to Islam and trained under its strict discipline. The Janissaries became a powerful force in the empire, sometimes controlling the succession of sultans*. (*See also* **Byzantine Empire; Ottomans and Ottoman Empire.**)

* **sultan**   political and military ruler of a Muslim dynasty or state

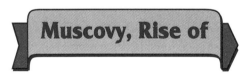

Muscovy, Rise of

* **principality**   region that is ruled by a prince

In three and a half eventful centuries—from 1147 to 1505—Moscow grew from a small fort to the capital of a powerful principality* called Muscovy, which was the heartland of the Russian people. The rise of Muscovy to a position of leadership in northern Russia paved the way for the later emergence of the Russian Empire.

Principality of Vladimir.   The forerunner of Muscovy was Vladimir, a principality centered on the town of Vladimir, a little more than 100 miles northeast of Moscow. In the 900s, KIEVAN RUS acquired possession of a well-forested, fertile territory in the northeast, between the Volga and Oka Rivers. Rostov was the main city of this northeastern region, which was thinly populated by tribes related to the people of Finland. In the first half of the 1100s, Prince Vladimir II Monomakh of Kiev gave the Rostov territory to his son Yurii Dolgorukii. Yurii and his sons, Andrei Bogoliubskii (died 1174) and Vsevolod III (died 1212), made the Rostov territory into the principality of Vladimir. As Kievan Rus fell apart, torn by princely wars and outside attacks, Slavic people from Kiev fled to Vladimir, mixing with the Finnic people to form a Russian population.

Towns and cities grew in the principality of Vladimir. Moscow was little more than a fortress until 1263, when Alexander Nevsky, grand prince of Vladimir, gave it to his son, Prince Daniel, making Moscow a princely seat.

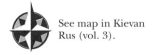

See map in Kievan Rus (vol. 3).

High Cost of Cousinly Conflict

Members of the Muscovite royal family sometimes fought bitter battles over the title of grand prince. Vasilii I, who died in 1425, named his ten-year-old son Vasilii as his successor, but the grand prince's brother Yurii thought that he should inherit the title instead. Yurii fought to become grand prince, but he died just one month after seizing the throne. The brothers' sons carried on the dynastic conflict. Vasilii II captured and blinded Yurii's oldest son. A decade later, Yurii's youngest son did the same to Vasilii II, who regained his throne to rule as Vasilii the Blind.

* **city-state**   independent state consisting of a city and the territories around it

* **metropolitan**   in the Eastern Church, a high-ranking bishop of a large city

By the early 1300s, the northern towns of Rostov, Tver, Ryazan, Vladimir, and Moscow had become more powerful than Kiev. Princes ruled each of these towns, but all were subject to the grand prince of Vladimir.

Mongol Overlordship.   In the early 1200s, Mongol warriors from east-central Asia, called Tatars, began expanding the MONGOL EMPIRE westward. In 1252, they established themselves as overlords of Russia. The Russian princes, including the grand princes of Vladimir, became lieutenants of the khans, or Mongol rulers. This meant that the khans had the power to determine which prince would be named grand prince of Vladimir. In 1318, Prince Yurii of Moscow married the sister of the khan and used his influence with the khan to have himself named grand prince of Vladimir. After Yurii was murdered by a Tverian who claimed the title of grand prince, his brother Ivan Kalita helped the khan defeat the rebellious Tverians. In 1328, Ivan Kalita became grand prince. After that time, the grand prince of Vladimir was always a senior prince of Moscow. As Moscow became more and more clearly the leading city of the region, the grand principality of Vladimir eventually came to be called Muscovy.

For a while, good relations existed between the Muscovite princes and the GOLDEN HORDE, as the Mongol army in Russia was called. In the mid-1300s, the Mongol Empire went through a period of internal strife, as members of the royal clan struggled for power. Some of Moscow's neighbors, such as Tver, tried to win the support of rival Mongol khans. Several times in the 1360s and 1370s, Moscow defeated other Russian city-states* in battle, proving that the Muscovite princes were not afraid to defy the orders of the Mongols, who claimed the right to settle all disputes among their subjects. By 1380, however, the Mongols had had enough of Muscovite independence. They sent an army to punish Grand Prince Dmitrii Donskoi. But Donskoi defeated the Mongol army in the Battle of Kulikovo, near Ryazan—the first time a Russian force had ever beaten the Mongols in battle. The end of Mongol overlordship came in 1447 or 1448, when Grand Prince Vasilii II named his son, Ivan, to rule with him as co-grand prince without asking the khan's approval. Although the Mongols made several attempts to restore their former power, their empire was in decline, and their hold on Russia was broken forever.

The Role of the Church.   Religion played an important part in the emergence of Muscovy as the leading force in northern Russia. In the early 1300s, when the cities of Tver and Moscow were competing for importance, a Slavic bishop named Peter was made metropolitan* of the Russian Orthodox Church. The Tverian prince tried to have Peter removed from office, but the Muscovite prince supported Peter and eventually began a campaign to have him made a saint. As a result, the church favored Moscow. All metropolitans after Peter settled in Moscow and supported the political ambitions of the Muscovite princes. By the mid-1400s, the Russian church had become less powerful than the grand prince. No bishop could be named to the post of metropolitan without the grand prince's approval, and a metropolitan who displeased the grand prince could be removed from office.

Growth of Muscovy.   A number of factors helped Moscow take the lead among the territorial lordships of northern Russia. One factor was the loyalty of the 35 or 40 military families who gave their allegiance to the

The onion-shaped dome that became characteristic of Russian architecture originated in Moscow in the late Middle Ages. This photograph shows the Bell Tower of Ivan the Great with its onion-shaped domes. It was built in the Kremlin in Moscow between 1505 and 1600.

* **dynasty** succession of rulers from the same family or group

* **annex** to add a territory to an existing state

Muscovite dynasty* during the 1300s. They fought to support their own positions at court as well as Moscow's interests. Another factor was Moscow's location, surrounded by the principalities of Novgorod and Tver on the northwest, Nizhnii Novgorod on the east, and Ryazan on the south. These territories provided a buffer between Muscovy and outside attackers. In addition, conflicts within the ruling families of these territories kept them from becoming a serious threat to Moscow's supremacy.

Of all the territories ruled by lords in northern Russia, Moscow was the only one that grew in both size and strength during the 1300s, as the Muscovite grand princes acquired new lands through purchase or treaty. Muscovy expanded still further during the 1400s, adding new territories through conquest. Grand Prince Ivan III annexed* Rostov, Tver, and the huge northern territory of Novgorod in 1448. He then launched a series of border raids against Lithuania, which controlled a large territory west of Muscovy. Ivan's aggression led to a war in which Lithuania lost a third of its territory to Muscovy.

Ivan III also devoted much attention to Moscow, his capital. He hired Italian architects and foreign craftsmen to build grand churches and palaces. During his reign, the Kremlin—the ancient walled fortress on the Moskva River in central Moscow—was given imposing new walls. Moscow was beginning to be seen as the heart not only of Muscovy but of Russia.

Over time, the people of Muscovy and the territories it annexed lost many of their traditional freedoms. As the power of the grand princes

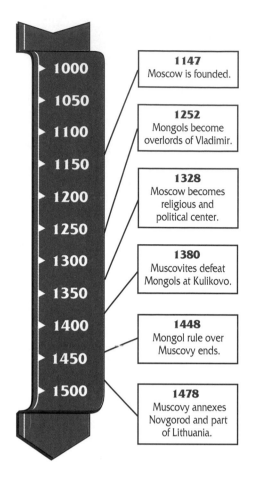

1147	Moscow is founded.
1252	Mongols become overlords of Vladimir.
1328	Moscow becomes religious and political center.
1380	Muscovites defeat Mongols at Kulikovo.
1448	Mongol rule over Muscovy ends.
1478	Muscovy annexes Novgorod and part of Lithuania.

* **tsar**   Slavic term for emperor

grew, the rights of their subjects shrank. No longer could soldiers follow the prince of their choice, for example, and all aristocrats, landlords, and soldiers were subjects of the grand prince. Princes and members of the nobility could be removed from their lands to Moscow to keep them from developing local followings, and an aristocrat's land could be confiscated by the grand prince and given to a more loyal subject. A person's standing in society was determined by service to the grand prince rather than by noble birth, wealth, or military might.

The elite of Russia was concentrated in Moscow, where the members of the duma, or princely council, became the most powerful figures at court. As the aristocracy became increasingly dependent on the favor of the grand prince, authority within the realm grew more and more centralized in the figure of the prince. Even the duma had little power to act in opposition to the grand prince's wishes. Because the economy was mainly agricultural, there was no rising middle class of independent merchants or tradespeople to oppose the grand prince's growing power. Furthermore, the peasant farmers, heavily taxed to support the costs of government, grew poorer and poorer. Beginning in the late 1400s, they were transformed into serfs, bound by law to the land on which they worked and to the landlord who owned it.

Ivan III died in 1505, leaving a domain of about 600,000 square miles—three times the size of modern France and more than 2,000 times as large as Muscovy had been in the early 1300s. Muscovy had emerged as the undisputed leader among the Russian city-states, had developed a strongly centralized government headed by an all-powerful grand prince, and had succeeded in absorbing or conquering its neighbors. The Middle Ages had seen the transformation of a rough frontier settlement into a powerful state. The stage was set for the appearance of the Russian Empire under Ivan IV, the next grand prince of Muscovy, who crowned himself tsar* in 1547. (*See also* **Dmitrii Ivanovich Donskoi.**)

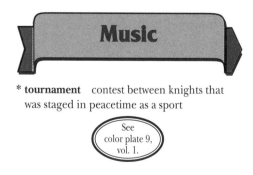

Music

* **tournament**   contest between knights that was staged in peacetime as a sport

See color plate 9, vol. 1.

During the Middle Ages, music was an important part of court life. It was featured in processions, banquets, dances, tournaments*, hunts, and general festivities. Music also reflected the division of rank and function in medieval society. Large noble households usually had their own bands of musicians, who followed their masters wherever they went, playing or singing for all private and public occasions. Smaller households might hire one or two minstrels or rely on traveling performers. Little is known about the music of the peasants, who had little time for relaxation and entertainment.

Islamic Music

Middle Eastern music flourished during the medieval period, when the region came under the influence of the Islamic religion. The attitude of Islam toward music was mixed. Some Islamic religious teachers disapproved of music because the prophet MUHAMMAD, founder of Islam, had criticized poetry, and songs were a form of poetry. Others disapproved of music because they associated it with wickedness and wrongdoing. Musicians, they

* **pilgrimage**   journey to a shrine or sacred place

* **secular**   nonreligious; connected with everyday life

The Minstrels' Schools

New songs and new instruments spread through Europe by means of minstrels' schools. These were actually meetings for musicians and singers that were held in many cities, usually in the spring, when the Christian holiday of Lent banned musical performances at court. The meetings attracted performers from all over Europe. They bought and traded musical instruments and taught one another new melodies. Few, if any, court minstrels or wandering musicians could read music, but the minstrels' schools allowed them to share their compositions with one another.

claimed, often drank wine and were ill-mannered, and they sometimes led young people into bad behavior. Still other scholars may have resented the wealth and success at court of popular musicians. Some princes and other members of the Islamic aristocracy were so afraid of criticism from the religious scholars that they listened to music only in secret, and those who wrote songs claimed that their slaves had written them.

Although scholars and teachers argued about its merits, music played an important part in Islamic life. Religious music included the call to prayer (chanted five times a day), the chanting of the QUR'AN (the holy book of Islam), songs for Muslims setting out on religious pilgrimages*, prayers chanted on religious holidays, hymns of praise sung on Muhammad's birthday, and epic songs recounting the events of Muhammad's life. The Mevlevi, a Muslim order founded in the 1200s, used music combined with a spinning dance to reach a state of mystical union with God. In Europe, they were called Whirling Dervishes.

Secular Music.   A few types of secular* music were accepted by the religious teachers and scholars. War songs, for example, were allowed because they were useful in rallying the troops, and songs that celebrated the rituals of birth and marriage were also permitted. Other types of secular music survived despite the scorn of religious teachers. Among these were caravan songs and love songs. Singers won favor—and sometimes immense fortunes—by performing at royal courts. These singers sometimes knew 5,000 or more songs and could accompany themselves on stringed instruments. They wore colorful clothing and long hair, a style that was borrowed by Spanish MINSTRELS during the Islamic occupation of medieval Spain.

Islamic music was carried on through oral tradition—that is, it was unwritten but passed from performer to performer and from generation to generation by memory. Beginning in the 1100s, some examples of written music appeared in Arabic writings, but they are illustrations of musical theory, not records of specific songs.

Influence of Islamic Music.   The center of Islam was Arabia and the Middle East, but the Islamic world stretched from Spain and North Africa to the border of China and southeast Asia. Traveling Muslim pilgrims and officials carried songs, instruments, and musical influences back and forth among these far-flung regions. The call to prayer and other forms of Islamic religious music became part of the fabric of life in places as far apart as Indonesia and Nigeria, and, in turn, Arab and Persian musicians absorbed influences from traditional Indian, Chinese, and African music. Islamic music also influenced European music. European performers adopted types of songs, such as the caravan song; certain dances, such as Morris dancing (originally Moorish dancing, from the Moors of North Africa); and many instruments, such as the trumpet and the lute.

European Music

At the beginning of the Middle Ages, Europeans defined music in two completely different ways. One group, consisting of scholars and philosophers, thought of music as an intellectual discipline. To them, the mathematical relationships between tones and the patterns of rhythmic intervals reflected the underlying order and harmony of the universe. Music was concerned with numbers and proportions; it had little to do with actual

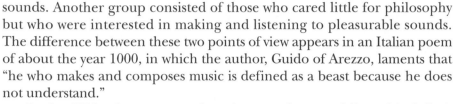

sounds. Another group consisted of those who cared little for philosophy but who were interested in making and listening to pleasurable sounds. The difference between these two points of view appears in an Italian poem of about the year 1000, in which the author, Guido of Arezzo, laments that "he who makes and composes music is defined as a beast because he does not understand."

By the 1200s, the concept of music as an abstract philosophical discipline had lost much of its force, and the term *music* generally referred to sounds that were sung or played. But much medieval music, even as late as the 1400s, was shaped by the earlier focus on mathematics and philosophy. For example, a French piece from the 1200s contains notes arranged in patterns of three and four. To the philosopher of music, four represented the elements of earth, air, fire, and water, and three represented God's triple nature as Father, Son, and Holy Spirit. Together they added up to seven, a mystical number that represented the union of the earthly with the divine.

From Oral Tradition to Written Music.   Almost nothing is known about the folk tunes or secular music of Europe in the early Middle Ages. The earliest known medieval music is religious music—holy texts that were chanted without instruments. The European music of the early Middle Ages belonged to the oral tradition, being performed spontaneously or by memory rather than kept in written form. By the 800s, however, systems of musical notation* had been developed, and liturgical* chants were being written down. The body of sacred music continued to grow throughout the Middle Ages. Thousands of liturgical chants and hymns have been preserved in medieval manuscripts from such distant places as Ireland and Armenia (a Christian kingdom east of Turkey and south of Russia). These pieces of music were traditional in origin, not brand-new compositions. Many of them were hundreds of years old and existed in countless variations. The form in which they were written down was sometimes not very precise, and, as a result, each performance might differ from every other performance in small but noticeable ways.

Written Music.   In the 1100s and the 1200s, composers working at the cathedral of Notre Dame in Paris started a new trend in musical composition, using an improved system of notation. Their music was identified with specific composers, and it was passed on to other musicians in a permanent, unchanging form so that it could always be performed exactly as it had been written. This was the start of musical literacy in the modern sense, but it took some time for the practice to gain widespread acceptance. It was applied first to liturgical songs and later to music that included both voices and instruments. Only in the 1400s did the writing of purely instrumental music become common. Around the same time, composers first indicated which instruments should be used to play specific pieces of music. By this time, it was also more common for the composer of a piece of music to be identified. At the end of the Middle Ages, European music was growing more varied, with national styles of composition developing in Italy, France, and England.

Music in Medieval Society

Music was probably part of everyday life in most places throughout the Middle Ages. Yet the everyday songs of the common people were not

* **notation**   system for recording music using written notes or symbols

* **liturgical**   pertaining to formal religious rites and services

written down and have not survived. Writing was in the hands of the church, especially during the early Middle Ages, and therefore religious music was preserved. This is true not just of western Europe but of other regions as well.

Most surviving Jewish medieval music consists of rules for chanting the biblical text, as well as prayers and hymns. Armenian medieval music was concerned with elaborate notation systems for sacred music. Although Armenian records contain thousands of liturgical chants, secular or folk music was discouraged by the church, and priests were forbidden to listen to the traveling minstrels who entertained villagers in medieval Armenia.

The music of the medieval BYZANTINE EMPIRE that survived consists of about 1,500 manuscripts, almost all of sacred music. Medieval Russian music, too, is known almost entirely through hymns and chants, and nothing is known of the songs sung by the musicians who provided popular entertainment on the streets of Russian cities.

Historical sources reveal that singing poets called BARDS flourished in the Celtic courts of medieval Ireland, Wales, and Scotland. They sang epics of national history and celebrated the praises of kings and princes. However, few of their poems survive, and the music to which these epics were sung has vanished.

Sacred Music.   The medieval church used music in a number of ways. Liturgical chants and other sacred songs, based on the BIBLE and especially the psalms*, were part of church services. The basic form of the early chants was plainsong, in which all participants sing the same notes at the same time. Later, a more complex type of music called part-song was introduced. In part-song, different singers produce different notes at the same time. Sopranos, for example, may sing the melody, while altos or baritones sing other notes that blend with the melody. As time went on, the music of choirs and organs played an increasingly important role in church services. Eventually, some services were almost entirely musical.

Hymns were a bridge between sacred and secular music. They dealt with religious subjects but sometimes adopted the melodies and language of popular songs. They were used by missionaries and religious teachers. In an age when few people could read or write, the rhyming words and memorable tunes of hymns made them excellent teaching tools.

Secular Music.   Outside the church, music was everywhere. A central figure of medieval life, especially in rural districts, was the jongleur, a wandering entertainer who juggled, performed acrobatic stunts, recited poems and stories, sang, and played simple instruments such as tambourines or pipes. Jongleurs were like traveling newscasters. As they traveled along the main trade and pilgrimage routes and gathered at the big seasonal fairs, they not only learned songs from one another but also picked up much news and gossip about local events and people. They made up songs about these current events, as well as verses praising or criticizing local rulers. The performances they gave for peasants and townsfolk were often the people's best source of information.

MINSTRELS were higher-ranking entertainers who only sang and played instruments. Their songs tended to deal with poetic subjects rather than current events. Some minstrels wandered from place to place; others were hired by wealthy or noble families as live-in musicians. The most favored

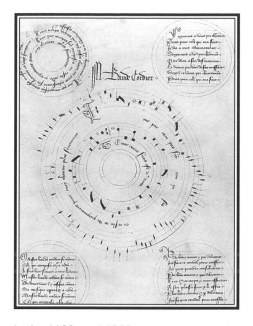

In the 1100s and 1200s, composers used an improved system of musical notation. Composers were identified by name, and notations were written in a permanent form that could be passed on to other musicians and performed exactly as written by the composer. This piece of secular music was composed by Baude Cordier in the 1300s.

* **psalms** sacred songs from the Old Testament of the Bible

* **chivalry** rules and customs of medieval knighthood

musicians obtained positions in royal courts. The TROUBADOUR was a special class of minstrel, often of knightly rank, whose poems dealt with love and chivalry*.

Jongleurs, minstrels, and troubadours were singers, but players of instrumental music filled other needs. Royal courts and noble households had instrumentalists to perform trumpet flourishes and drum flourishes on state occasions and to provide music for dancing. Music was a key feature of ceremonies, such as processions, banquets, and tournaments. Members of the nobility competed with one another to hire the best musicians. Many aristocrats played the harp or the lute to accompany themselves as they sang.

Music also had more practical uses. Ships' crews included musicians, especially trumpeters, whose job was probably to send signals rather than to entertain the sailors. The growth of the cities by the 1200s provided new opportunities for musicians. Towns and cities hired horn players called "tower musicians" to sound the alarm from watchtowers. Later, the duties of musicians expanded. Ceremonial fanfares were played from the clock tower or from the balcony of city hall at certain times of the day so that people throughout the city would know the time. Gradually, these performances grew into public concerts by town bands. The growing GUILDS of merchants and craftspeople sponsored their own bands, which entertained people on public holidays. By the 1200s, music had become an honored part of civic life. (*See also* **Celtic Languages and Literature; Gregorian Chant; Islam, Conquests of; Islam, Religion of; Musical Instruments.**)

Musical Instruments

* **pagan** word used by Christians to mean non-Christian and believing in several gods

* **crusader** person who participated in the holy wars against the Muslims during the Middle Ages

Music flourished in the ancient Mediterranean civilizations of Greece and Rome, but the music and instruments of the ancient world were lost in the turmoil of wars, migrations, and invasions that followed the fall of the Roman Empire. We do not know much about early medieval instruments because few people were interested in recording this information. Nearly all intellectual and artistic activities during the early Middle Ages took place in MONASTERIES, where interest in musical instruments was discouraged because the church associated instruments with pagan* rituals. Several sources from the 800s, however, do mention drums, harps, horns, and various stringed instruments.

For centuries, Middle Eastern musicians had been developing many kinds of instruments. After 1000, these instruments appeared in Europe, carried home by merchants, pilgrims, and crusaders* who had visited the Middle East. European musicians also acquired new instruments by way of Spain, much of which was under the control of Arab and North African Muslims from 711 until 1492. The Spanish Muslims used instruments that originated in the Middle East and the Islamic world. These instruments were carried north into the rest of Europe by traveling musicians and singers called jongleurs.

One important early Middle Eastern instrument was the lute, which consisted of strings stretched over a hollow skin and plucked to produce notes. Later, a wooden sound box replaced the hollow skin. Many versions

Medieval musical instruments were classified by the loudness of the sound they made. *Alta* (loud or high) instruments included the bagpipes, shawm, horn, and trumpet. These instruments were used mainly outdoors, at festivals or military ceremonies. *Bas* (soft or low) instruments—such as the lute, flute, harp, and psaltery—were generally played indoors and were used to accompany voices.

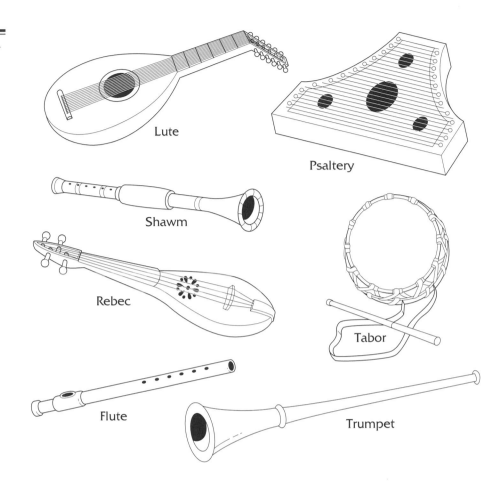

Lute

Psaltery

Shawm

Rebec

Tabor

Flute

Trumpet

of the lute existed, some brought by traveling Muslims from China and India. The number of strings ranged from 1 to 15. Islamic musicians also used stringed instruments played with bows, like modern violins; an early form of the bagpipe; and many types of drums and cymbals. Early Arabs and Persians made horns out of shells or animal horns, but, by the 1000s, Middle Eastern musicians were using large metal horns. European crusaders were impressed by Muslim military bands with their loud trumpet blasts, driving kettledrum rhythms, and the shrill music of shawms (long, double-reeded instruments with finger holes that produced loud, piercing sounds).

European musicians adopted the Middle Eastern instruments and created new versions of them. They grouped their instruments into two categories, *alta* (loud or high) and *bas* (soft or low). *Alta* instruments were used for military music, festivals, and ceremonies, especially outdoors. Indoor music was generally played on *bas* instruments.

Animal horns had long been used as signaling instruments by watchmen, hunters, and war leaders. Medieval knights carried the oliphant, a horn made from an elephant's ivory tusk, sometimes ornamented with gems or gold. The metal trumpet, imported from Muslim lands, became a symbol of power and rank. Also adopted from the Islamic world was the shawm, which produced sounds similar to the bagpipe but had no bag. Known throughout the Middle East and Europe, the bagpipe was at first used for court music but later was associated with popular tunes of the lower classes.

Flutes and recorders were widely used by medieval musicians, as were pipes (sets of hollow reeds or wooden tubes played by blowing across their tops). Small whistle-type pipes paired with tiny drums called tabors appeared in Spain and southern France in the 1100s and soon were in use throughout Europe. The pipe and tabor, used for dance music, were the standard instruments of wandering musicians.

One instrument favored by the church was the organ, which was used as early as the 900s to accompany religious singing. Many large organs were built in monasteries and cathedrals. These organs had knobs or levers that opened valves, letting air into large pipes to produce sound. The levers were later replaced by keyboards. Beginning in the 1400s, keyboards also appeared on new types of instruments made by clockmakers. Among these new instruments were the harpsichord and the clavichord, ancestors of the modern piano. They replaced an earlier stringed instrument called the psaltery, which was similar to a harp. Other stringed instruments, especially the guitar and the lute, were popular in Spain. After about 1200, they spread through Europe.

The music of the early Middle Ages used mostly voices, not instruments, and was mainly religious. The later Middle Ages, however, saw a flowering of instrumental music and music for nonreligious purposes, such as dancing. By that time, musicians had a wide variety of instruments with which to create new, more complex sounds. The development of music went hand in hand with the development of musical instruments. (*See also* **Music.**)

Mu'tasim, al-

795–842
Caliph

* **caliph** religious and political head of an Islamic state

* **aristocrats** people of the highest social class, often nobility

Al-Mu'tasim, the eighth ABBASID caliph*, had a special interest in military matters. He conducted the last major expedition against Byzantium by a Muslim caliph and introduced the use of Turkish slave soldiers in the Abbasid army.

Al-Mu'tasim was the son of the fifth caliph, HARUN AL-RASHID, and a woman of central Asian origin. Following the death of caliph AL-MA'MUN in 833, al-Mu'tasim took power after he beat back a brief challenge from al-Ma'mun's son. He then adopted the title *al-Mu'tasim Billah,* which means "he who looks to God for protection."

During his reign, al-Mu'tasim added many Turkish soldiers to the army and raised some of them to high positions. However, when the people of BAGHDAD complained about the rowdy behavior of the new troops, al-Mu'tasim ordered the building of a new city, SAMARRA, about 60 miles up the Tigris River from Baghdad. Samarra became the capital of the CALIPHATE from 835 to 892.

Although al-Mu'tasim used Turkish soldiers, most of his chief officers were Iranian aristocrats* who had aided various military campaigns, such as the defeat of the Byzantines in 838. In 840, however, a powerful Iranian commander was accused of plotting with other Iranian aristocrats against al-Mu'tasim. The commander was tried, convicted, and executed by starvation. After that, the power of Turkish officers greatly increased. (*See also* **Byzantine Empire; Islam, Conquests of; Islamic Art and Architecture.**)

Mysticism

* **theology** study of the nature of God and of religious truth

* **ascetic** referring to a person who rejects worldly pleasure and follows a life of prayer and poverty

* **cloister** part of a monastery or convent reserved for the monks and nuns

Mysticism is a highly personal religious experience that is a way of understanding and achieving unity with God. The mystical experience involves an individual spiritual journey that generally includes a renunciation of the material world, a cleansing of the soul through repentance, a devotion to prayer and contemplation, and a spiritual union with God attained through God's love and grace. The emphasis on emotion and feeling rather than on rational thought is what separates mysticism from most theology*.

Mysticism flourished during the Middle Ages, and medieval mystics (Christian, Jewish, and Islamic) had a powerful effect on their society and culture. Their writings are among the most profoundly beautiful expressions of religious faith ever composed.

Byzantine Mysticism.   Mysticism was an important feature of medieval Byzantine Christianity. Byzantines believed that faith and mystical experience were identical and that God is unattainable through reason. From the earliest times, prayer was very important. Those who detached themselves from everyday life to devote themselves to prayer were held in very high esteem. Because of their ascetic* life and devotion to prayer, Byzantine monks generally were considered the greatest spiritual leaders, and monastic spirituality and mysticism became a model for all Byzantine Christians.

Throughout the medieval period, the writings of monks were an important element of Byzantine theology. In the 300s, the Egyptian monk Evagrius Ponticus was well known for his doctrine of "permanent prayer" as the "proper activity of the mind." This doctrine became the foundation of spirituality in Eastern Christianity. Macarius of Egypt, another monk from the same period, gained recognition because of his belief that communion with God was a conscious experience available to all Christians and a necessary part of faith. This idea was reaffirmed in the late 900s and early 1000s by Symeon, abbot of a monastery in CONSTANTINOPLE, who became one of the most influential Byzantine mystics of the Middle Ages.

Western European Mysticism.   Mysticism flourished in western Europe in the later Middle Ages, particularly in the 1200s and the 1300s. This mystical rebirth drew on the spiritual traditions of Western monasticism and the teachings of St. AUGUSTINE, St. BERNARD OF CLAIRVAUX, and other theologians and mystics.

Many of the leading western European mystics were women seeking spiritual fulfillment. These women came from a wide variety of social classes and ways of life. Some were nuns living in cloisters*; others were laywomen devoted to leading an exemplary Christian life. All attributed their experiences to special senses of the soul—seeing and hearing with intense inner understanding. They wrote about their mystical experiences in highly colorful, descriptive, and imaginative language. Their spirituality often focused on the adoration of the infant Jesus or the crucified Christ. Some medieval women mystics condemned corruption and abuses within the church; others dedicated their lives to caring for the poor and the sick. Above all, they proclaimed themselves to be messengers of God and described their writings as God's Word filtered through them.

Germany gave rise to many famous mystics, including Meister ECK-HART, a Dominican writer and thinker; HILDEGARD OF BINGEN and her

* **Beguines** pious laywomen in northwestern Europe, who lived in communities and cared for the poor and the sick

* **Scholasticism** late medieval philosophy based on analytic thinking and the ideas of Aristotle

* **vernacular** language or dialect native to a region; everyday, informal speech

* **crusades** holy wars declared by the pope against non-Christians. Most were against Muslims, but crusades were also declared against heretics and pagans.

* **Qur'an** book of the holy scriptures of Islam

* **covenant** solemn and binding agreement

Sufi Ritual Exercises

Most Sufis participate in various ritual exercises, such as dhikr and *sama*. Dhikr is an individual or group exercise in which the name of God is repeated over and over, often involving rhythmic body movement, breathing techniques, and chants. *Sama* is a musical recital of religious poetry, often accompanied by recitations from the Qur'an, involving ritual dance. The type of poetry, music, and dance varies dramatically from group to group, ranging from carefully choreographed works to wildly free-spirited and emotionally charged works. The most famous example of *sama* is the wild music and dancing of the Whirling Dervishes.

contemporary, Elizabeth of Schönau; and MECHTHILD VON MAGDEBURG. In the Low Countries (present-day Belgium and the Netherlands), women mystics often were connected to religious orders such as the CISTERCIANS and the DOMINICANS or, like HADEWIJCH OF ANTWERP, were associated with the Beguines*. In Italy, two women mystics achieved special recognition. CATHERINE OF SIENA and Swedish-born St. BIRGITTA.

English mystics differed somewhat from their contemporaries on the Continent. They generally preferred a solitary life rather than an organized religious life in monastic orders. Distrustful of the movement known as Scholasticism*, they trusted even more than other mystics in the power to feel and to will rather than in the power to know through reasoning. The writings of English mystics were in the vernacular* rather than in Latin. Richard Rolle was a pioneer among English mystics in the 1300s. His intense spirituality and his commitment to guiding the spiritual lives of others made him very popular and influential. The leading women mystics in England were the visionary JULIAN OF NORWICH and the controversial Margery KEMPE, whose work, *The Book of Margery Kempe*, is considered the first autobiography in the English language.

Jewish Mysticism. Jewish mysticism had its foundations in early Judaism. A considerable amount of mystical literature was passed on to medieval times, including the highly regarded *Sefer Yezirah (Book of Creation)*. Mystical movements developed all over the Jewish world in the Middle Ages. These movements sought a more intimate relationship with God through observing a pious way of life. The people who practiced this way of life were known as Hasidim.

One of the earliest and most important of these mystical movements was that of the Hasidei Ashkenaz. This movement began in Germany in the 1000s, and it spread into northern France and England in the 1100s and the 1200s. The Hasidei Ashkenaz believed that the ultimate demonstration of love for God was martyrdom, and many of them were massacred during the crusades*. Their piety, their ethics, and many of their religious practices left a lasting impression on European Jews.

Another movement, known as Cabalism, started in southern France in the 1100s. The CABALA was a system of mystical thought in which words, letters, and numbers in the Scriptures were believed to contain mysteries that could be understood only by those who knew the secrets. Although the cabalists were few in number, they produced an enormous quantity of literature. Their most important work, the *Sefar ha-Zohar (Book of Splendor)*, was written (mainly in Spain) between 1280 and 1286. This book later became a classic Jewish text in Europe, and the cabala had great influence on later Jewish prayer, custom, and ethics.

Islamic Mysticism. Islamic mysticism is also known as Sufism. The Islamic mystical tradition springs from the Qur'an*, which describes a special covenant* between God and human souls that was established before the Creation of the world. The goal of Muslim mystics is to reestablish this loving intimacy between God and the human soul. For many Sufis, this is achieved through the mystical path, called tariqa, which involves searching the words of the Qur'an for God's hidden meaning. Sufism also arose from social and political forces at work in the early Islamic state. As the spartan tribal life of Arabia gave way to the sophisticated,

* **cosmopolitan** having an international outlook, a broad world view

* **pilgrimage** journey to a shrine or sacred place

cosmopolitan* atmosphere of the Islamic Empire, religious mystics began to renounce worldly goods and power as a necessity for attaining spiritual experience.

From the 800s to the 1400s, Sufism experienced a period of intense creativity that gave rise to communities of believers, pilgrimages*, poetry, and devotional literature. Sufi groups, each led by a Sufi master, appeared throughout the Islamic world. Among the most important centers of Sufism were Iraq, Egypt, and the Iranian province of Khorasan. Among the leading Sufis of the medieval period were the Iranian-born theologian al-GHAZALI and the Persian mystic Jalal al-Din RUMI, who was perhaps the greatest medieval Sufi poet. Sufi mystics also wrote manuals of the mystical path and compiled histories of the lives of the great Sufis. (*See also* **Beguines and Beghards; Brethren of the Common Life; Byzantine Church; Christianity; Islam, Religion of; Scholasticism; Visions; Women's Religious Orders.**)

Nagid

* **provincial** referring to a province or an area controlled by an empire

* **secular** nonreligious; connected with everyday life

In the medieval Islamic world, the Jewish leader of a provincial* community was known as the nagid. Nagids were found in North Africa, Spain, Egypt, Syria, Palestine, and Yemen. The main duty of the nagid was to serve as the chief judicial and administrative official of the local Jewish community. The nagid appointed judges, helped provide charity and assistance for needy Jews, and interceded with the Muslim government on behalf of the community. In religious matters, the nagid was responsible for supervising family law.

The office of the nagid appears to have originated in Egypt in the mid-900s or the 1000s and to have spread from there to other parts of the Fatimid Empire. As the position of the nagid grew in importance, the authority of the gaons of Palestine declined. (A gaon was the head of a Jewish academy who served as both spiritual and secular* leader within a Jewish community.) By the year 1100, the Egyptian nagid had replaced the Jerusalem gaon as the authority over Fatimid Jewish affairs. When the OTTOMANS conquered Egypt in 1517, however, the office of the nagid was dissolved. (*See also* **Jewish Communities.**)

Nahmanides, Moses

ca. 1195–ca. 1270
Spanish rabbi

* **Talmud** large body of collected writings on Jewish law and tradition

Moses Nahmanides, also known as Moshe ben Nachman or Ramban, was a renowned Jewish scholar, an enthusiastic defender of the Jewish faith, and a pioneer in reestablishing the Jewish community in JERUSALEM.

Born in CATALONIA in northeastern Spain, Nahmanides became a great Talmud* scholar whose writings included a strong element of Jewish MYSTICISM, or cabala. In his analysis of the Talmud, he challenged many points in the works of RASHI, the 11th-century Jewish scholar. Nahmanides also challenged the rational approach of the ancient Greek philosopher Aristotle, although he defended many of the ideas of Moses MAIMONIDES, whose work reflected Aristotelian philosophy and logic.

The turning point in Nahmanides' life came in 1263, when he was forced to participate in a public debate with a monk in the presence of Christian church officials. His forthright defense of JUDAISM led to threats against his life, which resulted in his voluntary exile several years later. In 1267, Nahmanides arrived in the city of Jerusalem in PALESTINE, where he reestablished the Jewish community that had all but disappeared during the period of the early CRUSADES. The synagogue he founded in the city still exists. (*See also* **Cabala; Hebrew Literature; Jewish Communities; Jews, Expulsion of.**)

Naples

* **papacy** office of the pope and his administrators

* **archbishop** head bishop in a region or nation

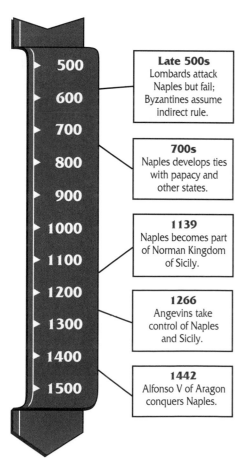

500	**Late 500s** Lombards attack Naples but fail; Byzantines assume indirect rule.
600	
700	**700s** Naples develops ties with papacy and other states.
800	
900	
1000	**1139** Naples becomes part of Norman Kingdom of Sicily.
1100	
1200	**1266** Angevins take control of Naples and Sicily.
1300	
1400	**1442** Alfonso V of Aragon conquers Naples.
1500	

The Italian port city of Naples has had a long and vivid past. Founded by the ancient Greeks as Neapolis (New Town), it became a popular resort for wealthy Romans in the last days of the Roman Empire. In the Middle Ages, Naples was dominated by the Byzantines, conquered by the NORMANS, fought over by Holy Roman Emperors and popes, and ruled by French ANGEVINS and Spaniards from ARAGON. Each of these groups contributed to the city's rich history and culture.

In the late 500s, the LOMBARDS tried to add Naples to their kingdom. They failed, and the city and the surrounding region, known as Campania, came under the indirect rule of the Byzantine emperors. During the 700s, the dukes of Naples became more independent of the Byzantines, and they developed close ties to the papacy*. In the same period, Naples was forced into a number of unstable partnerships with other states in order to preserve its independence.

Independence came to an end in 1139, when Naples was conquered by the Normans and made a part of their kingdom of SICILY. The Normans introduced FEUDALISM into Naples by claiming ownership of all the land and distributing portions of it to nobles in return for military service and loyalty. Local officials were allowed to continue in office, but they were answerable to royal officials and Norman dukes. The Normans strengthened their position in southern Italy by fortifying castles and improving the port of Naples. In time, merchants were attracted to the city and trade increased. As was their custom with conquered peoples, the Normans taxed Naples heavily to pay for wars and for the royal court. This burdensome taxation soon became a source of resentment among the people of Naples.

In the late 1100s, control of southern Italy was transferred through marriage from the Normans to the German Holy Roman Emperors. This was seen as a serious threat by the papacy, which hoped to someday add southern Italy to its PAPAL STATES. The German emperors maintained Norman policies and dealt firmly with any efforts by southern cities to establish self-governing COMMUNES like those in northern Italy. Revolts erupted in 1246 in response to Emperor FREDERICK II's policies. When the archbishop* of Naples supported an uprising of the upper class, the emperor ruthlessly crushed it. After Frederick II died in 1250, Naples became involved in the struggle between the GUELPHS AND GHIBELLINES, in which the popes and the Holy Roman Emperors competed for power. Naples generally supported the papal cause in hopes of gaining self-rule.

In 1266, Manfred, the German claimant to the kingdom of Naples and Sicily, was defeated in battle by Charles of Anjou, and control of Naples passed to the French ANGEVINS. Naples prospered under the Angevins, despite years of political turmoil and many unsuccessful revolts against Angevin rule. In the 1300s, the city became an important cosmopolitan* center, with strong ties to the city of FLORENCE and the region of TUSCANY.

Angevin rule ended in 1442, when the Spanish ruler Alfonso V of Aragon conquered the kingdom of Naples. (Aragon had conquered Sicily in 1282.) Alfonso improved the city's streets and aqueducts*, and he supported culture and learning. Under the Spanish rulers who followed, Naples enjoyed a rich cultural life, as artists were attracted to the city and scholars to its respected university. By the end of the 1400s, Naples had transformed itself from a southern Italian coastal city to the capital of the Aragonese kingdom in the south. It remained under Spanish control until the late 1700s. (*See also* **Byzantine Empire; Cities and Towns; Holy Roman Empire; Italy; Sicily.**)

See map in Italy (vol. 3).

* **cosmopolitan** having an international outlook, a broad world view

* **aqueduct** channel, often including bridges and tunnels, that brings water from a distant source to where it is needed

Navarre, Kingdom of

The kingdom of Navarre, located in northwestern Spain and southwestern France near the Pyrenees Mountains, played an important role in the early history of medieval Spain. Its native people, the Basques, successfully defended the region against Muslim invaders and struggled to maintain their independence from other Spanish kingdoms.

The kingdom of Navarre first took shape in the early 800s when Basques drove out Muslim troops from the region and established an independent principality* around the town of Pamplona. Although Navarre was threatened by surrounding principalities, it managed to maintain its independence through truces and through marriages between Navarrese families and rulers of the surrounding states. By the late 900s, the kingdom's frontier regions were dotted with fortresses.

Navarre was important in the 1000s because of its location on the pilgrimage* route to SANTIAGO DE COMPOSTELA. Pilgrims from all over Europe came through the kingdom, bringing a mix of cultures and languages. During this period, under the reign of Sancho III, Navarre became the dominant Christian state in Spain. Sancho greatly expanded his realm and its influence and helped Europeanize Christian Spain by supporting monastic reform. After Sancho's death in 1035, Navarrese dynasties held the thrones of Navarre, ARAGON, and CASTILE. In the future, these kingdoms vied for power, and Navarre was never again as powerful.

In the mid-1000s, Navarre lost its status as an independent kingdom when it was joined with Aragon and Aragon's king, Sancho V, became a vassal* of the king of Castile. Thereafter, Navarre stood in the shadow of Aragon, which had become the major power in Spain largely because of its defeat of the Muslims in 1118. The growth of Aragon completely enclosed Navarre's southeastern frontier, and the increasing livelihood of León and

* **principality** region that is ruled by a prince

* **pilgrimage** journey to a shrine or sacred place

* **vassal** person given land by a lord or monarch in return for loyalty and services

Navarre and the *Song of Roland*

In 778, Charlemagne led an expedition to Spain in an attempt to confront the Muslims. When he failed to capture the Muslim stronghold of Saragossa, Charlemagne marched back to France, but not before destroying the fortifications of the Navarrese town of Pamplona. The Basques of Navarre took revenge for this deed by ambushing the rear guard of Charlemagne's army in the Roncesvalles Pass in the Pyrenees Mountains. This event was glorified in the medieval epic, the *Song of Roland*. However, in that famous work of literature, the Muslims, or Saracens, were substituted for the Basques as the ambushers.

Castile closed off Navarre's southwestern frontiers. Navarre was thus blocked from any further expansion.

The 1200s saw further decline in Navarre's power. Under the Treaty of Guadalajara in 1207, Navarre lost northern territories to Castile, blocking its access to the Atlantic Ocean. In 1234, the king of Navarre died childless, and the crown passed to the French count of CHAMPAGNE, who was the king's nephew. In the late 1200s, Navarre became a direct possession of the French crown through inheritance. It remained a possession of French kings until 1328, when the king's daughter, Joanna II, was given control of the kingdom. For the next 184 years, Navarre was embroiled in political struggles among Castile, Aragon, and France. Attempts by Navarre to regain territory and power were unsuccessful, but the kingdom managed to maintain its independence during this period of unrest.

By the mid-1400s, Navarre was completely surrounded by its more populous and powerful neighbors, Castile, Aragon, and France. Used as a bargaining tool by its powerful neighbors, Navarre clung desperately to its last decades of independence. By the late 1400s, growing hostility between France and the recently united kingdom of Aragon-Castile made Navarre far too important because of its location to remain free. In 1512, King Ferdinand II of Aragon-Castile invaded Navarre and annexed its southern provinces to his kingdom. The northern provinces remained an independent kingdom of Navarre in France, but they were later united with France in 1589. (*See also* **Aragon; Asturias-León; Castile; Pilgrimage; Spain, Muslim Kingdoms of.**)

Navigation

See color plate 7, vol. 1.

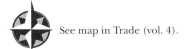

See map in Trade (vol. 4).

Navigation was an important skill in the Middle Ages. Western Europe, the Islamic world, and Asia were linked by numerous overseas trade routes. Adventuresome captains and their crews sailed these water highways, using their knowledge of the sea and of ship handling and a variety of scientific instruments. In the process, they opened new areas to trade and prepared the way for the age of exploration and conquest that began in the late 1400s.

European navigation began where narrow coastal strips were bordered by mountains. Lacking fertile land and cut off from access to the interior, the people of these regions—Greeks, Norwegians, Basques, and Genoese—took to the seas to fish and to travel from one settlement to another. At first, navigation remained limited to these coastal regions because there was no way for sailors to determine accurate routes when they were out of sight of land. Gradually, however, sailors learned enough about weather and climate, winds, and ocean currents to make voyages on the open seas possible. By the 800s, Norwegian sailors knew enough about the stormy North Atlantic to reach Iceland, and by the 1000s they had reached North America. In the 1300s, Italian navigators from GENOA were able to use their knowledge of winds to reach the Canary Islands, the Madeiras, and the Azores in the Atlantic off the coast of Africa.

Navigation in the Indian Ocean is known to have connected China with the Near East and Africa from before the Christian era. Navigation in

This illumination from an Arabian manuscript of the 1200s shows a ship crossing the Persian Gulf. Instruments such as the compass and astrolabe, along with navigational charts, maps, and manuals, were available to navigators to help them determine their position. The knowledge gathered by medieval navigators prepared the way for the age of exploration that began in the late 1400s.

---

* **nautical**   referring to sailors, ships, or navigation by sea

the Red Sea is equally old. It differed from navigation on the ocean in that boats traveled only by day and stayed close to the shoreline. The Red Sea was tricky and demanded exceptional navigational skill because of its winds, currents, and hidden reefs. The southern tip of the Sinai peninsula was particularly feared because of the meeting of winds from the Gulfs of Suez and Aqaba.

Medieval navigators possessed various nautical* devices that helped them reach their destinations and avoid obstacles. Nautical science included the use of the compass, which the Arabs acquired from China in the 1100s and then introduced to Europe. The compass began as a magnetized needle that floated on a thin reed placed in water. About 1200, the needle was mounted on a pivot, and soon afterwards it was attached to a card that indicated direction. By about 1275, the compass was commonly placed in a box mounted along the axis of the ship's keel, and, therefore, it could indicate the course that was being followed. From that time on, sailors could mark the course of a ship on a chart and so determine its position.

Nautical science also included the ASTROLABE, a device for measuring latitude with a large degree of accuracy. (Estimates of longitude, however, were very inexact until the invention of the chronometer in the 1700s.) For latitude, there were also tables showing changes in the altitude of the sun above the horizon at noon, for every degree and every day of the year. Both the astrolabe and latitude tables were of Arabic origin.

Numerous maps and manuals were also available to help navigators determine their positions. In Europe, navigational charts of the Mediterranean called portolanos used compass bearings and made it possible to fix a course in relation to a point of departure. However, since no allowance was made for the curvature of the earth, these charts were not very accurate. Even worse, early portolano charts showed different regions drawn to different scales. However, as navigators discovered new lands, additional information about bodies of water and landforms was added to these maps. The knowledge gathered by medieval navigators was of considerable importance to later explorers. (*See also* **Maps and Mapmaking; Ships and Shipbuilding; Trade.**)

Nevsky, Alexander

ca. 1120–1263
Prince of Novgorod

---

*city-state   independent state consisting of a city and the territories around it

Alexander Nevsky became a Russian national hero by defending NOVGOROD, a city-state* in northwest Russia, from its enemies. He turned back an attack by Swedish forces in 1240. In 1242, Novgorod was attacked by German knights, and Nevsky led the city's defenders to victory in a battle that took place on a frozen lake. At the same time, the MONGOL EMPIRE was invading Russia from the east. Nevsky, however, believed that Mongol rule offered protection against Russia's European enemies. He advised his fellow princes to accept temporary Mongol rule, and after Russia became part of the Mongol Empire in 1252, Nevsky ruled Novgorod for the Mongol overlords. He used his considerable influence to help his Russian subjects. He was later made a saint of the Orthodox Church, the Russian form of Christianity. (*See also* **Muscovy, Rise of.**)

Nicaea, Empire of

The conquest of CONSTANTINOPLE by crusaders* in 1204 temporarily destroyed the BYZANTINE EMPIRE. In its place, the crusaders set up the Latin Empire of Constantinople, though not without resistance from Byzantine Greeks in various parts of the old empire. One of the most important centers of resistance was the Empire of Nicaea, located in northwestern ANATOLIA.

The Empire of Nicaea was founded by exiled Byzantine leaders shortly after the fall of Constantinople. Its first emperor was Theodore I Laskaris, a son-in-law of a previous Byzantine emperor. During its brief existence from 1204 to 1261, the Nicene Empire helped preserve the culture and institutions of the Byzantine Empire and helped maintain the continuity of its emperors and patriarchs*. In some ways, the Nicene Empire was healthier than the Byzantine Empire. Agriculture prospered, and many new towns and fortresses were built. Government was simpler and more efficient, and court life was less expensive.

In addition to preserving Byzantine institutions, the Empire of Nicaea played an important role in the eventual restoration and reunification of the Byzantine Empire. Over the course of 57 years, the emperors of Nicaea expanded their domains to include parts of Greece and the Balkan region. They defended their empire against the Turkish SELJUKS and successfully held off invasion attempts by the Latin Empire. Gradually, the Empire of Nicaea became powerful enough to retake Constantinople. The city's conquest on July 25, 1261, resulted in the restoration of the Byzantine Empire. (*See also* **Byzantine Architecture; Byzantine Art; Byzantine Literature; Crusades.**)

Nicholas I, Pope

ca. 820–867
Pope

One of the most important of the medieval popes, Nicholas I was the first to insist that secular* rulers as well as church officials honor all of the pope's claims and powers. In Nicholas's time, the role of the papacy* was still being defined, and he greatly increased the pope's power in both religious and political affairs.

Nicholas was born in Rome, the son of a senior church official. At the age of 24, he himself entered church government and rose to the position of deacon*. He served as a principal adviser to Pope Benedict III, and when Benedict died in 858, Nicholas was elected pope. Although Nicholas was head of the church for less than a decade, his belief that the pope was meant to act as prince "over all the world" reshaped the papacy. Nicholas used his popularity to impose his will on archbishops, who had been accustomed to acting independently. He also insisted on the pope's right to control matters that were political as well as religious.

For example, in 862, the king of Lorraine (a duchy* in France) obtained a divorce by bribing church officials, even though Nicholas had forbidden the divorce. Nicholas canceled the divorce, dismissed the two archbishops who had granted it, and—despite the threat of an armed attack on papal headquarters in Rome by the king's supporters—finally forced the king to take back his wife. This and other incidents gave substance to Nicholas's claim that the pope was the supreme monarch within the church and a figure of superior authority in secular matters as well.

* **canonize** to officially declare (a dead person) a saint

Three months after Nicholas's death, his successor, Pope Adrian II, had him canonized*. Nicholas's concept of the papacy as a monarchy influenced church law and the actions of later popes. (*See also* **Papacy, Origins and Development.**)

Nobility and Nobles

During the Middle Ages, certain European families attained positions of great leadership within their societies. These "noble" families were often thought to have superior physical and moral qualities that set them above others. High birth (being born into or descending from one of these families) became a sign of nobility in itself. For the most part, however, birth and service to the state were only two aspects of nobility. Large landholdings and enormous wealth were the crucial elements that assured nobles of their power and prestige.

Origins of Nobility. Nobility in medieval Europe originated during the time of the Germanic invasions of the Roman Empire. The leading Germanic families seized many of the estates of the Roman aristocrats. In many cases, these Germanic families intermarried with the Roman families, forming a single network of nobles who provided kings with their governors and the church with its bishops and abbots. Those who served the king directly were given additional lands and privileges, and they became a special elite within the nobility.

The service of a class of loyal nobles became vital to the administration of many European kingdoms. In Britain, for example, Anglo-Saxon nobles shared in governing the kingdom, represented the kingdom in the absence of the monarch, and chose the monarch's successor from the royal family. Under the CAROLINGIANS, nobles in France played an important role in territorial expansion and in uniting people from various regions. The most important of these nobles became extremely powerful and established noble lineages* that extended for centuries. Their descendants emerged as the most powerful dukes, counts, and other royal nobles of the later Middle Ages.

* **lineage** direct descent from a particular ancestor considered to be the founder of a family line

Problems of Nobility. From the 1100s on, noble families throughout Europe faced serious problems of survival, and in each century many families died out. One factor in the decline of a family was the high rate of death among infants. In the Middle Ages, very few infants survived to carry on the name of the family and to inherit its lands and titles. Another factor was a low birthrate. Many noble families disappeared when the last remaining son or daughter failed to produce an heir. War was another peril. The noble families of CHAMPAGNE were virtually wiped out during the CRUSADES, and the HUNDRED YEARS WAR was a disaster for many others. For some families, such misfortunes were an opportunity. Lesser nobles were able to acquire land, titles, and offices from families that had declined.

Inheritance laws and customs posed the most serious threat to the nobility. The eldest son generally inherited his father's title and the largest share of his lands and wealth, while younger children shared the remainder. As each generation claimed its inheritance, the original estate became

Noble birth, service to the state, landholdings, and wealth were elements that assured the nobility of its power and prestige. Some noble families prospered and lasted for many generations; others declined. This illumination from the *Chronicles* of Jehan Froissart shows Louis of Anjou and his nobles entering Paris in 1335.

smaller. After several generations, often little remained to provide a sufficient income to support the family. Ultimately, those unable to support a noble lifestyle were no longer regarded as nobles, regardless of their high birth and family origins.

The highest nobility often had enormous wealth that lasted many generations. Other noble families managed to continue their noble status by enlarging their fortunes through marriage or inheritance from related family lineages. They might also gain a monarch's favor in order to receive additional lands, and they often sought to prevent the problems of dividing their estates by finding positions in the church for their younger children. Some noble families, planning for their future, increased their wealth and maintained their status by founding new villages, clearing new lands, levying new taxes on people who lived on their lands, and selling off distant holdings to invest in closer ones.

New Noble Class.   During the 1100s, a new class of lower nobility appeared—the knights. Originally low-born warriors, knights experienced a tremendous increase in prestige during the crusades and were amply rewarded for their participation. By the late 1100s, they enjoyed many of the titles and privileges once reserved for the old, established noble families. Endowed with land, titles, and privileges, the knights became a new noble class, and they soon began to copy the customs of the old nobility. They participated in formal ceremonies such as dubbing*, in which they received the title of "Sir." They acquired SEALS to authorize their documents and coats of arms to identify themselves and their offspring.

* **dubbing** formal ceremony in which a person receives a title from his overlord

Despite gaining noble status, most knights enjoyed only modest resources, often barely enough to support a family. Their lineages tended to be short, since there was little to leave the heirs. Moreover, the act of becoming a knight, which was widely restricted to the sons of knights, became less appealing because of the high costs associated with knighthood. By the late 1200s, few sons of knights became knights themselves.

Since knights commonly married women of low birth rather than other nobles, the ranks of the nobility steadily increased. In some places, this led to confusion over who was a noble and who was not. In some parts of France, only those born of two noble parents were considered noble, and in other parts of the country a single noble parent was sufficient to produce noble offspring. In Germany, the nobility was ranked on several different levels, with the knights occupying the fifth level from the top. In England, the distinction between barons and knights was established by law.

Nobility in the Late Middle Ages. In the later Middle Ages, the nobles of England, France, and western Germany no longer controlled the major economic resources of their societies. Instead, wealth had passed from large rural estates to the urban marketplace. No longer being necessarily from among the wealthiest families, the landed nobility lost much of their power and became increasingly dependent on forces beyond their control. Many turned to royal service in an attempt to add to their incomes and to maintain their social standing. Faced with such change, the nobility of the late Middle Ages was much less stable and influential than it had been centuries before. (*See also* **Feudalism; Inheritance Laws and Practices; Knighthood; Social Classes.**)

Normans

See map in Vikings (vol. 4).

* **aristocrats** people of the highest social class, often nobility

The Normans started as VIKING raiders from Scandinavia and ended up as the rulers of Normandy, a province in western France. From 1066 to the early 1200s, their descendants also ruled England. In addition, they founded small states in Sicily and the Middle East during the 1200s.

Around 820, Vikings sailed up the Seine River to raid the French countryside. The raids continued until 911, when King Charles the Simple of France made a treaty with Rollo, the Viking leader. In exchange for becoming Christians and protecting France from other raiders, Rollo and his followers received a large tract of land between the English Channel on the west and Paris on the east. Because the Vikings were called Northmen or Normans, their region came to be known as Normandy. Rollo and his descendants ruled as dukes of Normandy. Some Vikings became Norman aristocrats*, but nearly all of their subjects were French. The early dukes were extremely wealthy, partly from Viking plunder, partly from trade, and partly because they received rents from the church for their territory.

Anglo-Norman Kingdom. The Normans were a restless, active people who traveled to many parts of the Mediterranean world, but their greatest adventure was the conquest of England. A royal marriage—the English king Ethelred II the Unready married Emma, the daughter of Duke Richard I of Normandy in 1002—paved the way for the Norman conquest. Their son

* **dynastic union** two or more territories with separate administrations but under the same ruler

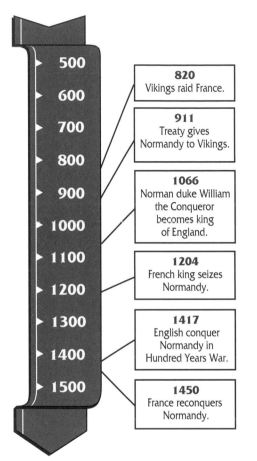

500	
600	**820** Vikings raid France.
700	**911** Treaty gives Normandy to Vikings.
800	
900	**1066** Norman duke William the Conqueror becomes king of England.
1000	
1100	
1200	**1204** French king seizes Normandy.
1300	**1417** English conquer Normandy in Hundred Years War.
1400	
1500	**1450** France reconquers Normandy.

Edward the Confessor became king of England in 1042. The reign of this half-Norman king brought many Norman traders, settlers, and churchmen to England. It also provided Normans with a claim to the throne of England.

In 1066, Duke William of Normandy—known as WILLIAM I THE CONQUEROR—invaded England in 1066 and destroyed the English royal claimant and aristocracy at the Battle of Hastings. He then took London and had himself crowned king of England. For a century and a half, England and Normandy formed a dynastic union*. After 1154, the ruler who was the king of England and the duke of Normandy was also the count of the French province of Anjou. These kings were called the ANGEVINS, and they strengthened the ties between England and Normandy.

Changing Hands. Although the Angevin kings recognized the kings of France as their overlords, they ruled their lands with a high degree of independence. In 1204, however, King Philip II Augustus of France invaded and conquered Normandy, turning the dukedom into a province of France. The Angevin king, John, continued to rule in England, and the political connection between England and Normandy was broken.

Because of its location on the English Channel and its historic ties with England, Normandy was involved in the Hundred Years War between France and England (1337–1453). In the early years of the war, the Angevins drew up a plan for a new Norman conquest of England, but the plan came to nothing. During the 1350s, parts of Normandy were occupied by English troops, and, in 1417–1419, King Henry V of England conquered Normandy. The English ruled Normandy for three decades, reviving the former connection with England and founding the University of Caen. In 1450, however, France reconquered Normandy, abolished the title "duke of Normandy," and made the province once more a secure part of the French kingdom. The early, independent dukedom survives only in a body of laws dealing with land ownership and inheritance. Shaped by the early Norman dukes and the Angevin kings, these Norman laws for centuries differed slightly from those of France's other provinces. (*See also* **England; France; Hastings, Battle of.**)

Norse Sagas

See *Scandinavia, Culture of.*

Norway

See *Scandinavia.*

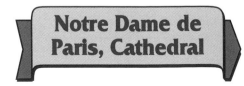

Notre Dame de Paris, Cathedral

The Cathedral of Notre Dame in PARIS is one of the most famous churches in the world. Situated on the Île de la Cité, an island in the Seine River, Notre Dame is a striking example of French GOTHIC ARCHITECTURE of the 1100s.

The construction of Notre Dame began under the direction of the bishop of Paris, Maurice of Sully. It is not known when construction actually started, but the official founding of the building is recorded as 1163,

* **choir**   part of a church near the altar that is reserved for the singers

* **nave**   main part of a church or cathedral between the side aisles

* **facade**   front of a building; also, any side of a building that is given special architectural treatment

* **flying buttress**   stone structure connected to the outer wall of a building by an arch; used to support the vaults

when Pope Alexander III laid a cornerstone for the choir*. The church was built in stages over a period of about 100 years. The nave* was probably completed by 1196, and the west facade* with its famous rose-shaped windows of stained glass was finished 30 to 35 years later. The towers, whose spires were never built, were completed about 1250. Over the years, the design of the cathedral was modified gradually in various ways, a practice typical of Gothic church architecture. One of its distinguishing features is the earliest use of flying buttresses*.

Notre Dame is an enduring symbol of France. It has stood through some of the major events of the nation's history and has inspired artists and writers over the centuries. In the 1800s, the French novelist Victor Hugo wrote a famous tale, *The Hunchback of Notre Dame,* whose plot involves the cathedral and the people of medieval Paris. (*See also* **Cathedrals and Churches; Construction, Building; Glass, Stained; Gothic Architecture; Gothic Sculpture; Paris.**)

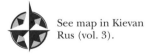

Novgorod

* **chronicles**   record of events in the order in which they occurred

See map in Kievan Rus (vol. 3).

* **principality**   region that is ruled by a prince

* **tribute**   payment made to a dominant foreign power to stop it from invading

* **retainer**   person attached or owing service to a household; a servant

Novgorod was one of the oldest and most important business and cultural centers in medieval Russia. Located on the northwestern plain of European Russia south of the present-day city of St. Petersburg, Novgorod was a major trading city of the HANSEATIC LEAGUE. Its nearness to the Baltic Sea and to river networks linking it to the Black Sea and Caspian Sea made far-ranging trade possible and contributed greatly to the city's prosperity. Medieval chronicles* often referred to the city as "Lord Novgorod the Great."

Origins and Early History.   Historians believe that Novgorod (a contraction for the Russian *novyi gorod,* meaning new town) was settled by merchants from SCANDINAVIA in the 800s or earlier. This early settlement was situated along the banks of the Volkhov River, which was linked to the nearby Volga and Dnieper Rivers and the Gulf of Finland. Thus situated, Novgorod had access to southern Europe, the Middle East, the Baltic region, and the North Sea.

Novgorod's earliest ruler is thought to have been RURIK, the king of the first Russian state. From the 900s, Novgorod was ruled by princes of KIEVAN RUS, a leading Russian principality* to the south. These princes appointed all officials, made laws, dispensed justice, collected fines for themselves, guarded the frontiers, protected trade routes, and maintained peace. Yet, domination by a rival city was a source of continual irritation to the Novgorodians, particularly since they had to pay tribute* to Kiev. When internal struggles and threats from Asian invaders weakened the power of Kiev in the late 1000s, the Novgorodians took advantage of the situation and demanded the right to select their own rulers.

Evolution of a Republic.   The new princes of Novgorod, who were descendants of the original founders of the city, were actually hired agents who held office for only a short time. The prince was required to protect the city's freedoms and to respect its laws. To prevent any one prince from becoming too powerful, each Novgorod prince was limited to 50 military retainers*. The princes also were forbidden to take action without the

This Russian icon depicts events in Novgorod's defense against one of its rival cities, Vladimir-Suzdal, in 1169. According to tradition, the outnumbered defenders of Novgorod showed their icon of the Virgin of the Sign, who invoked the aid of God to save them.

* **republican** pertaining to a republic, or government in which citizens elect representatives who are responsible to them for governing according to law

* **boyar** Slavic term for powerful lord, similar to medieval baron

* **indentured** under contract or obligation to work for another for a certain period of time

* **barter** exchange of goods and services without using money

* **city-state** independent state consisting of a city and the territories around it

approval of the elected senior official of the city, and they could make no laws without the consent of the people. In addition, a prince's income was an annual salary paid through a combination of taxes, tolls, and fines. Such policies eroded the power of the princes. By the late 1200s, the prince's office was little more than a symbol, with most of the real power lying in the hands of Novgorod's elected assembly and leading commercial families.

With princely power reduced, medieval Novgorod developed a republican* form of government and institutions. An ancient tribal assembly of freemen, the *veche,* became the ruling political power. The *veche* voted on all issues that involved the general welfare of the city. This included such things as declaring war, endorsing treaties, selecting new princes, electing senior officeholders, and choosing the head bishop of the church. Wealth and status determined eligibility for high office. The major officials elected by the *veche* usually came from the boyars*, a group of great wealthy landholders who formed the upper class of society. Directly beneath the boyars were the leading merchants and smaller landholders, while the remaining merchants (the majority) formed a third level. The lowest class of freemen were the laborers, artisans, peasants, and sharecroppers. Beneath them were slaves and indentured* persons. Although all groups had access to government, the politics of Novgorod were dominated by an elite that was actively supported by the upper classes and generally accepted by the lower classes. Nevertheless, compromises had to be made to satisfy the needs and concerns of all groups.

Economic Activities. Novgorod's importance as a trading center grew out of need. The city was situated in a marshy area that was unsuited for growing grain. As a result, the Novgorodians were forced to import much of their food from rural areas surrounding the city. In return, the Novgorodians exchanged manufactured items, such as household utensils and farm tools. This situation stimulated trade and also promoted the development of specialized crafts such as metalworking, leatherworking, cloth making, and carpentry.

In the 1000s, Scandinavian merchants set up a trading base in Novgorod. The Scandinavians were replaced in the 1200s by German traders who belonged to the Hanseatic League. The Hanseatic traders journeyed to the city primarily for the furs, wax, and flax that came to Novgorod from the forested areas of the interior. Silks, spices, and luxury goods were also important trade items, and they came to the city from Asia and the Middle East via the Volga River. The Hanseatic traders then bartered* for woolen cloth from FLANDERS and England, as well as for wines, linens, and weapons from other regions.

As trade grew, Novgorod prospered and evolved into a city-state* encompassing a huge area, which stretched to the Ural Mountains in the east and to the principality of MUSCOVY in the south. By the late 1400s, the population of the city-state of Novgorod was more than 500,000. The city itself contained over 30,000 residents, making it the second largest city in Russia.

The Decline of Novgorod. Novgorod's dependence on grain from southern Russia weakened its position in dealing with rival states. Whenever differences arose between Novgorod and Muscovy, the grand princes of Moscow cut off supplies of grain, thus threatening Novgorod's independence. Concerned with this potential danger, the Novgorodians tried to weaken the power of Moscow's grand princes by becoming involved in struggles between ruling families for the crown. This interference increased the hostility between Novgorod and Muscovy and led to retaliation. In 1456, Moscow's grand prince, Vasilii II, defeated the Novgorodians in battle and brought the city under his control.

The succession of Vasilii's son, IVAN III, encouraged the Novgorodians to test the power of Moscow. They formed an alliance with LITHUANIA, a rival of Muscovy. Ivan responded with force, and once again Novgorod was defeated. Although defeat sapped Novgorod of much of its strength, its leaders remained defiant. Faced with continued resistance, Ivan worked to undermine the power of Novgorod's ruling classes by gaining the support of its lower classes. He succeeded, and Novgorod became a part of Muscovy in 1478. The *veche* disappeared, as did all elected officials. By the end of the century, Ivan had forcibly moved the Novgorodian upper classes to the interior of Muscovy and had given their lands to his own loyal supporters. (*See also* **Metals and Metalworking; Trade; Wool.**)

Nubia

* **Coptic**   referring to early Egyptian Christians

* **artisans**   skilled craftspeople

* **bedouin**   nomadic Arab(s) of the deserts, especially in Arabia

Nubia was the name given in medieval times to a region along the Nile River valley south of EGYPT. The region was less fertile than Egypt, and waterfalls along the Nile made travel difficult. As a result, Nubia never attracted Egyptian settlers. Its native inhabitants were African in racial origin and speech. The Nubian culture, however, was strongly influenced by that of Egypt. By the late 600s, most Nubians had adopted the Egyptian Coptic* faith (a branch of Christianity), and the region remained Christian throughout the Middle Ages.

Medieval Nubia consisted of several kingdoms, which were composed primarily of small villages. Most people were peasant farmers, although there were artisans* in the region's few towns. Islamic conquests in Africa had little effect on Nubia. In the mid-600s, Muslim armies made two unsuccessful attempts to invade the region. After the second attempt, the Nubians signed a peace treaty with the Muslims that guaranteed their political and religious independence. This treaty, which remained in effect for more than 600 years, laid the foundation for a flourishing trade between Nubia and Egypt that brought the region great prosperity.

After the MAMLUK DYNASTY took power in Egypt in 1250, many Arab bedouins* were driven south into Nubia. They gradually overran the region, causing the medieval Nubian kingdoms to disintegrate into warring principalities. (*See also* **Christianity; Egypt.**)

Nuremberg

* **imperial**   pertaining to an empire or emperor

Nuremberg, in south-central Germany, was one of the great historic cities of Germany and an important imperial* city during the Middle Ages. Although the city was a center of trade and government in the HOLY ROMAN EMPIRE, it never rivaled the great cities of ITALY in size and wealth. Nuremberg, however, did enjoy great prestige and prosperity as a residence of German kings and emperors.

The city began around 1040, when King HENRY III OF GERMANY built a castle atop a hill known as the Nuremberg and granted the right to establish a market to the settlement that formed at the base of the fortress. In the

* **magistrate** ruling official of a town

* **charter** written grant from a ruler conferring certain rights and privileges

* **principality** region that is ruled by a prince

* **dynasty** succession of rulers from the same family or group

* **ghetto** section of a European city to which Jews were restricted

* **diet** government meeting, similar to a parliament

See map in Germany (vol. 2).

mid-1100s, the Holy Roman Emperor, Conrad III, established imperial territories around Nuremberg, which stimulated the city's growth. A magistrate*, first appointed by Emperor FREDERICK I BARBAROSSA in the late 1100s, administered justice for the community. In 1219, the city was granted an imperial charter* by Emperor FREDERICK II.

From 1250 to 1273, the merchants of Nuremberg assumed control of the city government. At the same time, citizens successfully resisted attempts by the nobles of BAVARIA to incorporate the city into their own principalities*. The authority of the imperial magistrate declined as well, and Nuremberg became a free city. The construction of Nuremberg's first city hall, between 1332 and 1340, symbolized its freedom from direct imperial control.

Several significant events marked the history of Nuremberg in the 1300s. In 1348 and 1349, the city's GUILDS and its governing council took opposite sides in a struggle between dynasties* for the throne of the Holy Roman Empire. This "guild revolution" was quickly suppressed, and the guilds never exercised any real political influence in the city thereafter. At about the same time, the city received permission from the emperor to expel the Jews and to construct a market on the site of the Jewish ghetto*. Finally, in 1356, Emperor Charles IV passed an edict known as the Golden Bull, which required each newly elected German king to hold his first diet* in Nuremberg.

Nuremberg's association with German emperors and kings brought the city great prestige. Moreover, its role as a royal residence stimulated economic development and was an important factor in its prosperity. During the late Middle Ages, Nuremberg was a center of trade and international banking as well as an important industrial center. It became the foremost producer of metalware in Europe, including weapons, household utensils, and technical instruments. After 1470, the city became a major center for the printing of books, and it nurtured great artists, poets, and historians. (*See also* **Anti-Semitism; Germany; Jews, Expulsion of; Metals and Metalworking; Printing, Origins of.**)

Oaths and Compurgations

* **allegiance** loyalty to a noble or king, who granted property and protection in return for military service or taxes

* **dub** to tap lightly on the shoulder with the flat side of a sword by way of conferring knighthood

An oath is an act of calling on God to bear witness to the truth. In medieval times, oaths helped maintain the bonds of medieval society. Vassals swore oaths when they pledged allegiance* to their lords, and knights took oaths when they were dubbed*. People also took oaths when they testified in court.

Oaths often were used in medieval law as a form of proof to establish the truth or falsity of an accusation. This form of proof, known as a compurgation or wager of law, was found mostly in Germanic law. With a compurgation, an accused person could establish his or her innocence by taking an oath and having supporters take oaths swearing to the character of the accused. Such oaths did not attest to the truth of evidence, however, since the oath takers, or compurgators, often had no direct knowledge of the facts and did not offer evidence. The idea behind such oaths was that God would allow compurgators to complete their oaths successfully only if justice was on their side.

Since compurgations did not involve any examination of evidence, there usually were two legal issues the court had to consider: the number of oath takers and the complexity of the oath. These two factors were determined by the seriousness of the charge and the reputation of the defendant. Over time, oaths became very complex in their wording, and a single mistake in swearing the oath could cause the defendant to lose the case. By the 1100s, some oaths had become so difficult that people preferred battle to the swearing of an oath.

The use of compurgation as a means of proof gradually declined. By the late 1200s, English royal courts preferred to rely on the opinion of a jury rather than on the swearing of oaths. In the 1200s, jury trials became the rule, although compurgations were still used until the early 1600s in matters involving debt. (*See also* **Law; Trials.**)

Ockham, William of

ca. 1285–1347
English theologian and philosopher

* **theology** study of the nature of God and of religious truth

* **philosophy** study of ideas, including science

* **heresy** belief that is contrary to church doctrine

William of Ockham was one of the greatest thinkers of the Middle Ages. He made important contributions in many areas of study, including theology*, logic, philosophy*, and science. Although his ideas troubled many people during his lifetime, after his death his work attracted many admirers, and his ideas were particularly influential from the late 1300s to the early 1500s.

Born in England, Ockham studied and taught at Oxford University until 1324, when he was summoned to the papal court at AVIGNON to answer charges of heresy*. While there, he studied papal writings and became convinced that the pope, John XXII, had become a heretic. In 1328, Ockham fled Avignon and settled at a FRANCISCAN convent in BAVARIA. He remained there for the remainder of his life and devoted himself to writing.

Ockham's ideas were guided by several basic principles. Among the most important was a deep faith in the absolute power of God. In Ockham's view, nothing other than God is absolutely necessary, including the physical and moral laws of the world. Ockham's philosophy was marked by nominalism, the idea that only individuals exist and that abstract concepts such as classes or natures exist only in the human mind. His philosophy was also characterized by scientific empiricism, the idea that certain principles are known through the senses and through feelings rather than through reason. This concept marked a significant break with medieval SCHOLASTICISM, which emphasized the importance of reason in understanding the world.

In theology, one of Ockham's most controversial ideas concerned transubstantiation, the conversion of the bread and wine during the Mass into the body and blood of Christ. Ockham believed that the body and blood of Christ were not produced out of the substance of bread and wine. Rather, he believed that the body and blood of Christ took the place of the space previously occupied by the bread and wine. This idea went against the more generally accepted views of the time, including those of ARISTOTLE, Thomas AQUINAS, and others.

Ockham's most famous principle was in the field of logic. It held that the best explanation for something is the simplest explanation. This principle is called Ockham's razor because it shaves away unnecessary elements. Scientists still apply this principle when they study natural phenomena. (*See also* **Mass, Liturgy of; Universities.**)

Odoacer

**ca. 433–493
Germanic barbarian
"king" of Italy**

* **mercenary** soldier who fights for payment rather than out of loyalty to a lord or nation

* **imperial** pertaining to an empire or emperor

Odoacer, once a general in the armies of Attila the Hun, joined the Roman army as a mercenary*. He rose to a position of command and was involved in a rebellion against the Roman commander, Orestes, in 475. After the rebellion, the troops elected Odoacer king. Orestes was killed, and his son, Romulus Augustulus, the last emperor of the Western Roman Empire, was deposed and exiled. Zeno, the emperor of the Eastern Roman Empire, reluctantly recognized Odoacer's authority in Italy and gave him the title of patrician, or member of the ruling Roman aristocracy. Odoacer, however, considered himself king.

During his reign, Odoacer distributed land to his troops, maintained the old Roman administration, worked closely with the Senate, and cooperated with the Roman Catholic Church. At first, his domain was limited to Italy, but he later secured SICILY from the VANDALS. Odoacer's successful reign frightened the emperor Zeno, who asked the OSTROGOTHS and their king, THEODORIC, to go to Italy and restore it to imperial* rule. Between 489 and 493, Theodoric regained most of Italy for the empire. In 493, after several defeats, Odoacer agreed to share authority with Theodoric. Theodoric had other plans. At a banquet to celebrate this agreement, Theodoric killed Odoacer and had his followers massacred. He then established an Ostrogothic kingdom in Italy. (*See also* **Huns; Italy; Migrations, Germanic.**)

Ordeals

See *Trials.*

Oresme, Nicole

**ca. 1320–1382
French philosopher,
mathematician, and
theologian**

* **liberal arts** seven traditional areas of knowledge—grammar, rhetoric, logic, geometry, arithmetic, astronomy, and music

* **theology** study of the nature of God and of religious truth

* **cosmology** study of the nature of the universe

* **philosophy** study of ideas, including science

Nicole Oresme was one of the most brilliant and original thinkers of the 1300s. Born near the city of Caen in Normandy, he studied the liberal arts* at the University of Paris and theology* at the College of Navarre. After completing his studies, Oresme rose steadily in the ranks of the church, eventually becoming bishop of the city of Lisieux in 1377. His career in the church was helped by his faithful service to the French royal court.

As a scholar, Oresme was noted for his translations from Latin into French of some of the works of the ancient Greek philosopher Aristotle. A man of enormously varied interests, he also wrote his own works on theology, mathematics, physics, cosmology*, magic, money, and astrology. Oresme was probably the first author to write anything of scientific importance in the French language.

In his work, Oresme tried to use reason to explain natural events. He also criticized medieval beliefs in magic and the supernatural. At the same time, however, he did not think that a person's Christian faith should be analyzed in the way philosophy* examines other ideas about right and wrong. He believed that the truths of religious faith are certain, and therefore superior to, the uncertain truths of philosophy or science. (*See also* **Aristotle in the Middle Ages; Astrology and Astronomy; Mathematics; Universities.**)

Osman I

ca. 1254–ca. 1326
Founder of the
Ottoman dynasty

* **dynasty** succession of rulers from the same family or group
* **nomad** person who wanders from place to place to find food and pasture
* **principality** region that is ruled by a prince

O
sman was an Islamic chieftain who conquered most of western ANATOLIA (the Asian part of Turkey) in the early 1300s. He founded the dynasty* that built the Ottoman Empire and that ruled Turkey and much of the Islamic world until the early 1900s.

Osman's rise began with the Mongol conquest of central Asia. The Mongols forced Turkoman nomads*, who had migrated to Anatolia from central Asia, to push farther west. Osman was one of several Turkoman chieftains who ruled independent principalities*. From his territory on the border of the Byzantine province of Bithynia, he and his followers raided Byzantine territory in the early 1300s. After Osman defeated the Byzantines at the Battle of Baphaeon in 1301, he brought the Bithynian cities under his control one by one, until only the most strongly defended remained in Byzantine hands. After Osman's death, his son Orkhan established a government that turned Osman's nomadic principality into a permanent Islamic state. (*See also* **Byzantine Empire; Islam, Conquests of; Mongol Empire.**)

Ostrogoths

* **imperial** pertaining to an empire or emperor

See map in Migrations, Germanic (vol. 3).

* **Arianism** heretical Christian belief that denied the divinity of Jesus Christ

T
he Ostrogoths (East Goths) were one branch of the Goths, a Germanic people that migrated to western Europe during the early Middle Ages. The other branch of the Goths was the VISIGOTHS (West Goths).

The Ostrogoths emerged as a group of related tribes during the 300s in the region north of the Black Sea. In 375, they were defeated by the HUNS and became part of the Hunnish Empire. Following the death of Attila, king of the Huns, in 453, the Ostrogoths revolted and regained their independence. Soon after, they received permission from the eastern Roman emperor to settle in imperial* lands in eastern Europe.

By the late 400s, the Ostrogoths had gained in numbers and power, and they began to pose a serious threat to the Eastern Roman Empire. In an attempt to solve this problem, Zeno, the Eastern Roman emperor, authorized the Ostrogoths to go to Italy and overthrow ODOACER, a Germanic king who had ruled there since 476. The Ostrogoths conquered Italy between 490 and 493, and their king, THEODORIC, became ruler.

During Theodoric's reign, much of Italy's imperial prosperity and splendor were restored. An able and just ruler, Theodoric satisfied his Italian subjects and maintained peace with his neighbors. He adopted the system of Roman administration, cooperated with the Senate, and maintained a good relationship with the Roman Catholic Church. Cities were rebuilt, monuments were restored, and new buildings were constructed. Theodoric also supported a revival of learning. Yet, while they lived together peacefully, the Ostrogoths and the Italians remained distinct populations, each governed by its own laws.

After Theodoric's death in 526, the Ostrogothic kingdom in Italy faced increasing problems and unrest. One problem concerned religion. Most Ostrogoths embraced Arianism*, a heretical Christian belief, and this brought them into increased conflict with other Christian kingdoms. Internal conflicts, particularly about who would take over the throne, also deeply divided the Ostrogoths. The Byzantine emperor, JUSTINIAN I, took advantage of this situation and seized the opportunity to reestablish imperial control in Italy. Beginning in 534, Byzantine armies took the offensive against the

Ostrogoths. After a long and bitter struggle, the Ostrogothic kingdom collapsed, its last city falling to the Byzantines in 561. Thereafter, the Ostrogoths rapidly faded from history, leaving little impact on the institutions or the culture of Italy. (*See also* **Byzantine Empire; Italy; Migrations, Germanic.**)

Oswald von Wolkenstein

ca. 1377–1445
German poet and composer

Born into a noble family in the medieval German region of Tyrol (in present-day Austria), Oswald von Wolkenstein was a celebrated poet and composer. According to an autobiographical song, he ran away from home at age ten, learned ten languages, and mastered several musical instruments. Widely traveled, he visited Prussia, Russia, the Holy Land, and North Africa.

In 1415, Oswald entered the service of the emperor SIGISMUND of the HOLY ROMAN EMPIRE. For the remainder of his life, he continued to be politically active. He joined the Portuguese in a successful expedition against Muslims in North Africa, became involved in a political plot against Duke Frederick IV of the Habsburgs, and participated in a disastrous crusade against the followers of Jan HUS. His activities landed him in prison several times.

While engaged in politics, Oswald also composed songs and poetry. Among his works were tender love songs, sarcastic songs about prison, and rustic court poetry. The themes of his works range from piety to pornography, and they provide a fascinating view of his era. Oswald's works follow the musical and poetic principles of his day, including styles and forms inherited from the minnesingers*. His most original songs resulted from his travels, his imprisonments, and his financial woes. In addition to his great need for attention and respect, he wished to remain famous long after his death. He fulfilled this wish by commissioning the Italian painter Antonio Pisanello to paint his picture. The famous portrait shows a stern man with an empty eye socket. (Oswald had lost an eye in his youth.) (*See also* **Courtly Love; German Language and Literature; Habsburg Dynasty.**)

* **minnesinger** German poet and musician, especially of the 12th to 14th century, who performed songs of courtly love

Otto I the Great, Emperor

ruled 936–973
German king and emperor

Otto I, founder of the German kingdom, did more than anybody else to make Germany the strongest European state of the 10th and 11th centuries. He was the only medieval German king to be called "the Great."

Otto continued the work begun by his father, Henry I, the duke of Saxony. The dukes of other important German territories—Franconia, Swabia, and BAVARIA—had named Henry king when they were faced with attacks from Danes, SLAVS, and Hungarians. However, Henry was little more than a military chief. Otto was determined to make Germany more than just a military confederation. He put down revolts by German dukes and ruled his region with a firm hand. He replaced German tribal rulers with supporters and family members and took over the rule of the duchy* of Franconia. Otto made partners of the German bishops, who were the best-educated people of the day. He relied on them to administer his realm in exchange for land and privileges. Whenever the post of bishop

* **duchy** territory ruled by a duke or a duchess

became vacant, Otto filled it with one of his own men or a relative. For example, he made his brother, Bruno, the archbishop of Cologne. Otto's close alliance with the bishops helped make Germany the most stable and best-governed country in Europe for more than a century.

Rebellious German dukes formed alliances with foreign enemies, forcing Otto to spend the early part of his reign in constant warfare. In the west, he fought the Franks and brought the kingdom of Burgundy under German influence. In the east, he defeated the Slavic Wends, threatened Poland, and established supremacy over Bohemia. Otto's victory over the Magyars, at the Battle of Lechfeld in 955, was his greatest triumph because it ended the Magyar threat to western Europe.

The symbolic high point of Otto's reign came in 962, when the pope crowned him emperor in Rome. Every German king after Otto regarded it as part of his office to seek imperial* coronation by the pope. Otto's close relationship with the Papacy caused him to spend the last years of his reign extending his rule into Italy. Otto's strong leadership laid the foundation for German kingship and the Holy Roman Empire. (*See also* **German Language and Literature; Germany; Hungary.**)

* **imperial**   pertaining to an empire or emperor

Otto III, Emperor

980–1002
German king and emperor

Otto III was crowned king of Germany at age 3 and emperor at age 16. Although he lived to be only 22, he was one of the greatest medieval emperors.

After his father, Otto II died, the young Otto was crowned king in Aachen on Christmas Day in 983. While in Rome for his coronation as emperor of the Holy Roman Empire in 996, he met the two men who were to have the greatest influence on him—Archbishop Gerbert of Rheims and Bishop Adalbert of Prague. Gerbert, the leading scholar of the time, became Otto's teacher. Adalbert convinced Otto that his most important duty as emperor was to convert the people of eastern Europe to Christianity.

In 1000, Otto traveled to Poland to give the Polish leader Boleslaw I the Brave the rank of ally of the empire. Then the following year, he and Gerbert (by then Pope Sylvester II) established an archbishopric* in Hungary and authorized the crowning of that country's first Christian king, Stephen I of Hungary. The Christianization of Poland and Hungary was Otto's most lasting contribution to the history of Europe. (*See also* **Germany.**)

* **archbishopric**   church district headed by an archbishop

---

Otto of Freising

ca. 1114–1158
Bishop and historian

Otto of Freising was one of the greatest historians of the Middle Ages. Born into the highest ranks of the German aristocracy, Otto was a bishop and the author of two important works: a history of the world and a book about the emperor Frederick I Barbarossa, who was his nephew.

Otto was the 5th of 18 children born to the daughter of the German emperor Henry IV. After completing his studies in Paris, he returned to Germany, where he became a monk in the Cistercian order. He was made an abbot around 1137, and, soon after that, he became bishop of Freising (near Munich), a position he held for the rest of his life.

Otto's reputation as perhaps the greatest medieval historical thinker rests on his work *History of the Two Cities,* which he wrote between 1143 and 1146. The work discusses human history in terms of the relationship between St. Augustine's "two cities"—the community of the faithful (City of God or City of Christ) and the community of the damned (City of the Earth or City of the Devil). Otto divided world history into three phases. In the first phase, the faithful are a minority living under heathen* rulers. In the second, Christians are freed from their oppression. In the third, the faithful are completely freed from their earthly bonds at the Last Judgment.

* **heathen** not believing in the God of the Bible

Otto did not finish his second work, *The Deeds of Frederick Barbarossa.* By the time of his death, he had written about Frederick's family, the Hohenstaufen dynasty*, and Frederick's reign to 1156. Otto's secretary, Rahewin, continued the narrative to 1160. In this final work, Otto praised Frederick for establishing peace in Germany and creating a new harmony between church and state. (*See also* **Augustine in the Middle Ages, St.; Germany; Historical Writing.**)

* **dynasty** succession of rulers from the same family or group

Ottomans and Ottoman Empire

* **booty** prizes of war

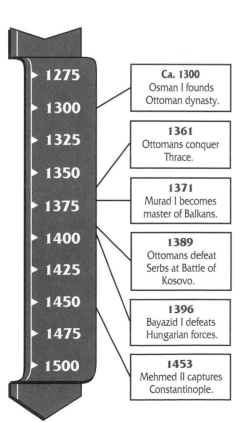

1275	**Ca. 1300** Osman I founds Ottoman dynasty.
1300	
1325	**1361** Ottomans conquer Thrace.
1350	
1375	**1371** Murad I becomes master of Balkans.
1400	**1389** Ottomans defeat Serbs at Battle of Kosovo.
1425	
1450	**1396** Bayazid I defeats Hungarian forces.
1475	
1500	**1453** Mehmed II captures Constantinople.

The Ottomans were a Muslim Turkish people originally from central Asia who lived in northwestern ANATOLIA (also known as Asia Minor). From about 1300, the Ottoman dynasty ruled over a principality in the northwestern part of the Anatolian peninsula that grew into a great empire which bears its name and which lasted until 1922. At its greatest extent, the Ottoman Empire included Anatolia, the Balkans, Crimea, HUNGARY, and parts of SYRIA, ARABIA, and North Africa. As rulers of many diverse peoples and cultures, the Ottoman state was the last great Islamic Empire. Shortly after its defeat in World War I (1914–1918), the Ottoman Empire was dismantled and its culture was absorbed in the modern state of Turkey.

Beginnings and Growth.   The name *Ottoman* derives from OSMAN I, a chieftain who headed a tribal principality in the northwestern corner of the Anatolian peninsula. From his base within the weakened empire of the SELJUK Turks, Osman successfully waged military campaigns against other principalities in Anatolia and brought them under his control.

Osman was able to extend his power even farther into enemy lands with the help of ghazis, Muslim volunteers who were eager to fight for Islam. These mounted warriors often came from far away to join Osman in his raids. In return, Osman rewarded his military companions with a share of the booty* taken from conquered peoples. During the course of Osman's rule (1288–1326), the ghazis became a privileged group within the Turkish tribal society. They established influential families whose members became leaders in the Ottoman army.

Later, during the reign of Sultan MURAD I, the young military recruits who served in the sultan's army evolved into an elite corps of foot soldiers called Janissaries. These Janissaries were usually prisoners of war or Christian slaves whose parents had to turn them over to the sultan as payment of tribute. The young recruits were then converted to Islam and subjected to the strict discipline of the Ottoman army. Janissaries quickly

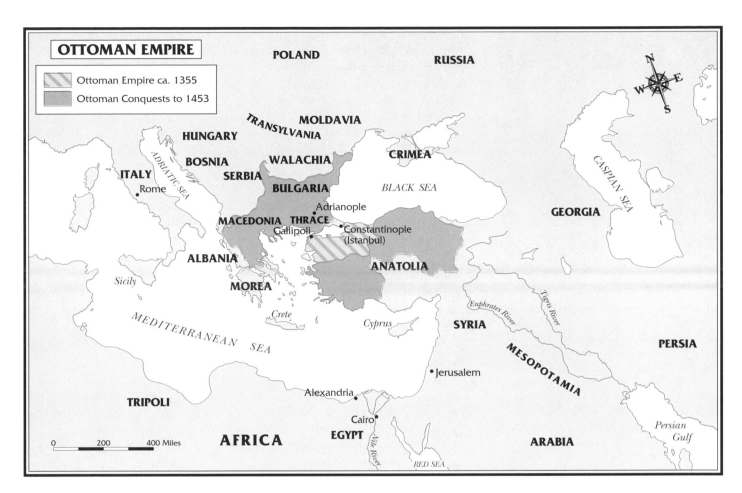

By the mid-1400s, the Ottoman Empire had expanded to cover territory around the northeast Mediterranean Sea and the Black Sea. In 1453, Constantinople, the capital city of the Byzantine Empire and the most splendid city of the Middle Ages, was captured by the Ottomans, who changed the city's name to Istanbul and made it the new capital of their own empire. The Ottoman Empire continued to expand into Europe, Syria, Arabia, and Africa until the late 1600s.

---

* **sultan** political and military ruler of a Muslim dynasty or state

became instrumental in the military successes of the Ottoman army. Eventually, their influence in the empire became so great that they had the power to force weak sultans* from the throne and to raise their own supporters to positions of power.

By 1400, the Ottoman army was organized into two parts—recruits from the peasantry and the standing army. The standing army, which included the Janissary corps, was under the direct command of the sultan and comprised the professional elite from whom the sultan chose his leaders.

Expansion into Europe. While the Ottoman military elite and volunteers established villages in abandoned Byzantine lands, they were always eager to acquire new land. Faced with the threat of the Mongols in the east, the Ottomans pushed westward. Their success was hastened by the erosion of central authority in lands held by the Byzantines. A series of military campaigns in the west brought them into Europe.

In 1352, Ottoman forces crossed the Bosporus, the narrow strait of water that separates Europe and Asia Minor, and established their presence on European soil. In 1361, they seized the former ancient Roman city of Adrianople and thereby gained undisputed possession of Thrace. The advance of the Ottomans into Europe and their threat to Constantinople alarmed Pope Gregory XI. When the Turks reached the Adriatic coast opposite Italy, the pope declared that Italy was under threat and called for a CRUSADE to push the Turks back to Asia Minor. The pope's

Mehmed II, called "the Conqueror," was sultan of the Ottoman Turks at the time of their invasion and conquest of Constantinople in 1453. Mehmed rebuilt the city as the new capital of the Ottoman Empire and changed its name to Istanbul. Mehmed, like other Ottoman sultans, was an absolute ruler. But as the primary lawgiver of Islam, he was responsible for the welfare and prosperity of those he ruled. This portrait of Mehmed II was painted by Gentile Bellini shortly before the sultan's death in 1481.

* **crusader**   person who participated in the holy wars against the Muslims during the Middle Ages

* **sultan**   political and military ruler of a Muslim dynasty or state

* **principality**   region that is ruled by a prince

* **annex**   to add a territory to an existing state

* **succession**   the transmission of authority on the death of one ruler to the next

failure to raise a crusader* army and the Ottoman victory over the Serbian army that tried to recapture Adrianople in 1371 allowed Sultan Murad I to strengthen his grip on the Balkans. From that time forward, the princes of SERBIA and BULGARIA, together with the Byzantine emperor John V PALAIOLOGOS, recognized the Ottoman sultan* as their overlord. It had taken just 70 years for the Ottoman principality* to become an empire.

Their success in the Battle of Kosovo and in the Balkans strengthened the Ottomans' control of Asia Minor, so that the only two powers able to challenge Ottoman power were Hungary and VENICE. Under Bayazid I, the Ottomans in 1396 defeated Hungary, then established control over Albania, and later challenged Venetian influence in Morea.

Bayazid I also threatened Venetian naval supremacy when he annexed* the western Anatolian principalities in 1389–1392 and took over and reorganized their naval forces. He turned Gallipoli into a strong navy base, which the Venetians tried to destroy three times—in 1416, 1429, and 1444. However, the Ottomans had to wait until the end of the 1400s to challenge the Venetian navy on the open sea. The growth of the Ottoman navy in the 1400s played an important role in the rise of the Ottoman Empire.

In 1453, the Ottomans achieved their goal of conquering the Byzantine Empire when they captured Constantinople, the Byzantine capital and center of Byzantine civilization for more than 1,000 years. The Ottoman sultan who invaded the city, MEHMED II THE CONQUEROR, then proceeded to rebuild the city as the new and lavish capital of the Ottoman Empire. The Ottomans renamed the city Istanbul. In the 20 years following the fall of Constantinople, the Ottomans brought the Balkan territories of Serbia and BOSNIA under their control. Mehmed could rightfully claim that he was truly sultan of two lands—Asia Minor and the Balkans.

Ottoman Rule.   The Ottoman sultan who headed the empire was the absolute ruler of a highly centralized, military state. The sultan's government was often referred to as the "Sublime Porte," a reference to the place where the ruler heard complaints and conducted government business. In the tradition of Turkish-Mongol khans, any one of the sultan's sons could succeed him to the throne, and the son who gained the upper hand usually came to be recognized as his father's successor. As a result of this practice, whenever an Ottoman sultan died or became seriously ill, a power struggle erupted among his sons. Sometimes the struggle developed into a full-fledged civil war with brother killing brother. Disputes over succession* made it possible for enemies of the Ottoman Empire to take advantage of the discord.

Although the Ottoman sultan was an absolute ruler whose word could raise the position of a humble person or lower that of a noble person, his responsibilities were great and numerous. Since he was the primary lawgiver of Islam, he was responsible for the welfare and prosperity of the entire community under his rule.

At the top of the Ottoman social hierarchy were the ruling military bureaucrats who helped the sultan rule the empire. They owned most of the land and resources, such as mines and farms, and controlled the

* **artisans** skilled craftspeople

On Guard

In the Ottoman capital of Istanbul, the elite Janissaries stood on duty inside the sultan's palace in a special courtyard assigned to them. Their rank was shown by the amount of richness in their clothing and headgear. Like other members of the court, Janissaries wore brimless caps around which they wrapped a turban, with each rank wrapping its turban in its own distinctive way. Unfortunately, court life corrupted the Janissaries. Their proud history came to a dramatic end in the early 1800s, when the reigning sultan had them all massacred.

empire's trade. The broad lower base of the social structure was made up of merchants, farmers, and artisans*, all of whom paid taxes to support the state. While their financial burden was great, members of this group had prospects of upward social mobility. A simple decree of the sultan could dramatically raise an individual or group within the ranks of Ottoman society.

The Ottoman state was one of the most tolerant in the history of Islam, as became evident after it gained control of southeastern Europe and the SLAVS, Greeks, Albanians, and other Balkan nationalities who lived there. While non-Muslims (Christians and Jews) had to pay an extra tax, they were free to practice their religion and to move about Ottoman lands. In addition, the state protected their lives and property.

In cities such as the Bosnian capital of Sarajevo, each non-Muslim community lived in its own quarter organized around its district church or synagogue. Although Muslims, Christians, and Jews lived in separate districts, they worked and traded together without discrimination. Ethnic and religious tensions sometimes resulted in violence, but the Ottoman government kept order by stationing Janissaries in cities to protect non-Muslims. (*See also* **Islam, Conquests of; Islam, Religion of; Islamic Art and Architecture.**)

Outlaws and Outlawry

Outlawry is the act of placing a fugitive from justice outside the protection of the law. It may be the oldest punishment in the world. It was common in societies that had a weak central government and little or no law enforcement. Outlaws were hunted down and killed.

The VIKINGS who invaded England probably introduced outlawry into ANGLO-SAXON law. It was applied to men who fled rather than stand trial for felonies (serious crimes). Women could not be outlawed, but a similar procedure, known as waiving, was applied to them. The earliest references to outlawry in England are from the early 900s.

The process of outlawry began in the county court when a victim made an accusation against somebody. If the accused person failed to appear in court to answer the charges, the sheriff ordered the accused to appear at one of the next four sessions of the county court. Any suspect who failed to appear after the fourth time was declared an outlaw and was sentenced to death. Because the outlaw had defied the laws of the community, the community had the responsibility of hunting him down. Helping an outlaw flee or hide from the law was also a crime, punishable by death. An outlaw whose innocence was established was inlawed, or brought back under the protection of the law.

After the NORMAN conquest, the kings of England became more involved in the pursuit of outlaws. Lists of those who were suspected of serious crimes were drawn up and circulated. As outlawry became commonplace, its harsher features were eased. Outlaws could be killed only when they resisted arrest, and they were punished with loss of property and imprisonment rather than death. Outlawry continued to be part of the English criminal code until 1938. (*See also* **England; Law; Trials.**)

Ovid

See *Classical Tradition in the Middle Ages.*

Palaiologos Family

* **aristocrats** people of the highest social class, often nobility

* **coup** sudden, and often violent, overthrow of a ruler or government

The Palaiologos family was the last family to rule the BYZANTINE EMPIRE, and members of the family did rule it for almost two centuries. Although Michael VIII Palaiologos was the grandson of the Byzantine emperor, he was not next in line to inherit the throne. He came to power in 1258 when the empire's most powerful aristocrats* staged a coup*. At the time, the Byzantine court was located in northern Greece because an army of western Europeans had captured CONSTANTINOPLE in 1204. Michael regained Constantinople from the Western invaders in 1261 and made it once again the Byzantine capital.

During the rule of the Palaiologos family—from 1261 to 1453—the family tried to defend the empire from enemies on two sides. Europeans from the west wanted to reunite the two Christian parts of what had once been the Roman Empire, while the Turks to the east wanted to extend their control over western Asia.

The Palaiologos family allowed Byzantine aristocrats to wield great power and gave large parts of the empire to members of the royal family, who ruled their regions as if they were independent states. This practice weakened the empire and may have contributed to its downfall. During the reign of Andronikos II Palaiologos, from 1282 to 1328, the Turks conquered much of the peninsula that the ancients called Asia Minor and that is now known as Turkey. The fall of Constantinople to the Turks in 1453 marked the end of the Palaiologos dynasty. (*See also* **Byzantine Literature; Christianity; Mehmed II the Conqueror; Ottomans and Ottoman Empire.**)

Palestine

See map in Crusades (vol. 2).

* **pagan** word used by Christians to mean non-Christian and believing in several gods

Palestine—called the Holy Land by Christians—was ruled during the early Middle Ages by the Greek-speaking BYZANTINE EMPIRE. In the 630s, the Muslims conquered Palestine. Later, during the CRUSADES, the region became a battleground for Christians and Muslims. Throughout much of the Middle Ages, Palestine suffered from neglect, political instability, revolts, and warfare.

Byzantine Rule. During the Byzantine period, Palestine was divided into three provinces. Palaestina Prima, the central part of the country, included the city of JERUSALEM. Palaestina Secunda, in the north, included the Sea of Galilee. Palaestina Tertia, in the south, included parts of present-day Israel and Jordan.

At the beginning of the Middle Ages, Palestine was inhabited by Jews, Samaritans, and pagans*. Christians accounted for a minority of the population. Although the Byzantine authorities often persecuted Jews, pagans, and some Christian groups, Byzantine interest in Palestine's religious and commercial roles resulted in increased population, economic prosperity, and the construction of many new churches and monasteries.

This Spanish manuscript illumination from the 1200s shows Spanish and Muslim merchants trading at the port of Acre in Palestine. Such trade might have included the export of olive oil, fruit, and glass. Imported items might have included spices and jewelry. Luxury items were imported and sold to Jewish, Christian, and Muslim pilgrims visiting Jerusalem and other sites in Palestine.

Muslim Rule.   Except for a brief period of SASANIAN rule, the Byzantines ruled Palestine until the 630s. By 636, the Arabs had forced the Byzantines to retreat and had taken control of SYRIA.

The Muslims tightened their hold on Palestine by capturing Jerusalem in 638, after an eight-month siege, and, in the early 640s, they also captured the fortified ports of Ascalon and Caesarea. The Arabs guaranteed the Christians of Jerusalem the right to life, freedom of worship, and the right to keep their property, churches, and monasteries in exchange for the payment of a poll tax.

At the end of the 600s, the UMAYYAD caliph* Abd al-Malik and his son built two impressive Muslim buildings on the Temple Mount—the Dome of the Rock and the al-Aqsa Mosque—that helped make Jerusalem a center of religious importance in Islam.

In the 700s, Palestine became a province, ruled first from Baghdad by the ABBASIDS and then from Egypt by the FATIMIDS. During this period, it declined through neglect and constant warfare. In the 1100s, European Christian kings ruled several states in Palestine. From the 1200s until the early 1500s, Palestine was ruled from Egypt by the AYYUBIDS and then by the MAMLUKS, who were responsible for building a number of magnificent mosques* and other buildings, some of which are still standing.

Palestine's main export was olive oil, but fruits, fruit products, textiles, and glass were also exported, mostly to Egypt. Imports included spices as well as luxury items and jewelry. These items were sold to the Jewish, Christian, and Muslim pilgrims from all parts of the world who visited Jerusalem and other sites in Palestine. (*See also* **Caliphate; Christianity; Islam, Conquests of; Islam, Religion of; Islamic Art and Architecture; Judaism; Pilgrimage.**)

* **caliph** religious and political head of an Islamic state

* **mosque** Muslim place of worship

Warfare and Decline

During Palestine's early years under Muslim rule, the population fell sharply because of almost continuous war. Soil erosion was another problem for dwellers in Palestine's semidesert climate, where fields and gardens had to be irrigated. In one area northwest of Jerusalem, 193 out of 293 villages were abandoned after the 600s, mostly because of soil erosion.

Papacy, Origins and Development

* **apostles** early followers of Jesus who traveled and spread his teachings

See map in Papal States (vol. 3).

* **imperial** pertaining to an empire or emperor

* **secular** nonreligious; connected with everyday life

* **cleric** church official qualified to perform church ceremonies

The papacy refers to the office of the bishop of ROME, who is also known as the pope. The special role of the pope within the Roman Church is based on two ideas. The first idea is that Christ considered Peter to be the first among the apostles* and charged Peter with the task of leading the church after his death. The second idea was that the popes, as bishops of Rome, were successors to Peter in his role as the first bishop of that city. These two beliefs gradually led to the development of the papacy as the central and most powerful institution of the church.

The Early Papacy. During the first century of Christianity, the church in the West was administered by bishops in various Christian communities. At the same time, the Christian community in Rome was rising to a position of prominence within the broader Christian community. There were several reasons for this. As the center of the Roman Empire, Rome had special political and cultural significance. In addition, the early persecutions of Christians in Rome left the city with an exceptionally large number of martyrs—people who were honored for giving their lives for their faith. As a result, Rome became the model for other Christian communities, and its bishops were seen as having a special dignity and authority.

Between the late 100s and the mid-200s, several Roman bishops played important roles in the development of the papacy and the city. They did this by asserting their own power over the broader church on various issues, such as penance and baptism. By 325, the bishop of Rome had clearly established a precedent for claiming prominence within the church. Also in the 300s, the title *pope* came into use for all bishops of the church, including the bishop of Rome. (It was not until the 1000s that this title was used exclusively for the bishop of Rome.)

The authority of the Roman bishop was greatly enhanced in the late 300s and the 400s. In 378, the emperor Gratian supported the claims of Pope Damascus I to exert authority over the other bishops of Western Christendom. Two years later, Emperor Theodosius I recognized the bishop of Rome as a special guardian of the faith. Pope Leo I took advantage of a decline in imperial* authority in the West to increase Roman authority. He adopted the trappings and titles of monarchy, and he received a declaration from the emperor in 445 giving him absolute authority over the church in the West. Leo took the title *pontifex maximus* (greatest bishop) and claimed special authority as sole heir to the apostle Peter.

One of the most important popes of the early medieval period was GREGORY I THE GREAT. Elected pope in 590, Gregory provided Rome with both secular* and religious leadership. In secular matters, he reorganized the administration of Rome, secured its defenses, and negotiated with the LOMBARDS. As religious leader, he encouraged MONASTICISM and missionary work, exerted complete control over the church in central Italy, and settled religious controversies in Africa, Spain, Gaul, and elsewhere. Gregory was especially admired by Christians in England, and English clerics* became enthusiastic supporters of the papacy. English missionaries helped spread this dedication to the papacy throughout northern Europe.

Pope Sylvester I is seen here receiving the Donation of Constantine. The emperor is bestowing the crown, Lateran Palace, and rank of imperial cavalry commander on the pope, who offers his blessing. The Donation of Constantine was a document in which the emperor endowed the Roman Church with temporal as well as spiritual authority. Probably written in the 700s, the document was accepted as genuine during the Middle Ages but is now known to be a forgery. It was sometimes used by popes as a claim that Christian rulers owed them allegiance.

Political Support for the Papacy. In the mid-700s, the papacy in Rome received important political support. The popes established themselves as spiritual and political leaders after 800 through alliances with new emperors in western Europe.

Political support for the papacy during this period was demonstrated in two significant events. One was the so-called Donation of Pepin, a gift of lands in Italy to the papacy in 756 by PEPIN III, the king of the FRANKS. Pepin's gift made the popes secular rulers over territories in central Italy, a region that later became known as the PAPAL STATES. The other was the Donation of Constantine. This was a decree drafted in the late 700s, which claimed to be based on a decree by the emperor Constantine in the 300s (although no such document was still in existence). The Document of Constantine granted rule over the Western Roman Empire to the papacy. In addition, it gave the pope an imperial palace in Rome, the imperial crown, and command of an imperial cavalry. From the 8th century onward, popes considered themselves to be the intermediaries between the old Roman emperors and the medieval heirs to imperial authority. Beginning with the coronation of CHARLEMAGNE by Pope Leo III on Christmas Day in the year 800, the popes in Rome claimed the right to crown the emperors, thus bestowing imperial authority on the monarchs. In return, the emperors protected the papacy against external threats. This relationship between popes and emperors continued throughout most of the 800s.

A Period of Declining Power. Beginning in the mid-800s, the authority and prestige of the papacy declined dramatically. Popes became pawns in factional strife among Italian aristocrats*. They rose to power and were removed from power by the nobility and secular rulers. Between 882 and 984, eight popes died violently, including one who died in prison. Christians, accustomed to viewing the pope as a spiritual leader and a source of imperial authority, considered the decline of the papacy a major disaster.

* **aristocrats** people of the highest social class, often nobility

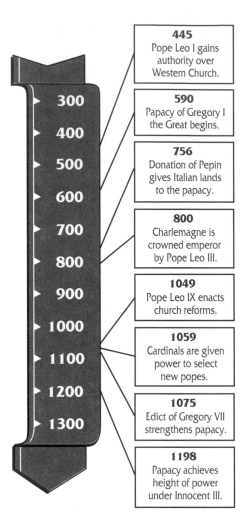

445
Pope Leo I gains authority over Western Church.

590
Papacy of Gregory I the Great begins.

756
Donation of Pepin gives Italian lands to the papacy.

800
Charlemagne is crowned emperor by Pope Leo III.

1049
Pope Leo IX enacts church reforms.

1059
Cardinals are given power to select new popes.

1075
Edict of Gregory VII strengthens papacy.

1198
Papacy achieves height of power under Innocent III.

* **secular**   nonreligious; connected with everyday life

* **investiture**   act of installing a person in high office, such as a bishop

* **ordeal**   means of determining guilt or innocence by requiring the accused person to undergo a painful or dangerous test

* **depose**   to remove from high office

The popes were eventually rescued from this situation by the intervention of western emperors.

During the 900s, German emperors, including OTTO I and OTTO III, appointed their own candidates to the papal throne. Their purpose was to ensure that the pope would support the German dynasty and to reduce rivalries among the nobility. Although the papacy survived, the popes functioned primarily as figureheads with little or no independent authority. Before long, however, the papacy regained its strength and acquired unprecedented power.

Ascendancy of Papal Power.   The papacy entered a period of great vitality in the 11th century. This was due in large part to the role of the popes in the movement to reform church practices. As the popes gained leadership in this movement, they reestablished their authority and control over church issues.

Reform popes concentrated on moral problems and on the political problems of secular* control. To keep papal elections out of the hands of aristocratic factions, Pope Nicholas II enacted a new policy in 1059 by which only the cardinals could choose a new pope. He also reformed church law to address issues of morality among the clergy. Pope GREGORY VII addressed moral issues such as SIMONY (the buying or selling of church offices and holy orders), but his fundamental goal was to free the papacy and the church from lay control. In 1075, Gregory issued a papal decree that set forth several basic principles. Among these were the principles that only the pope could depose bishops, convene church councils, and issue church law. Gregory's stand against lay investiture* led to one of the major conflicts between the church and the state—the Investiture Controversy. This conflict between papal and imperial forces over authority was bitterly fought with both pen and sword.

The papacy of Gregory VII marked a turning point in papal power. Under Gregory, papal claims to power reached a high point, even though these claims were not yet put into effect. Gregory set forth policies that enabled later popes to win the power that Gregory sought but never attained.

Among the most sweeping claims to authority were those made by Pope Innocent III, who held the office from 1198 to 1216 and under whom the papacy achieved the summit of its power. Innocent interfered in secular affairs in England, southern Italy, and France as well as in the HOLY ROMAN EMPIRE. In 1215, he called the Fourth Lateran Council—the largest council of the church since the Council of Nicaea. At this council, the essentials of Roman Catholic doctrine were established, and disciplinary measures were taken to enforce church rules regarding marriage and confession. In addition, clergy members were forbidden to preside at ordeals*.

The wide claims of the church and its interference in secular affairs in the 13th and 14th centuries brought many problems. FREDERICK II, the Holy Roman Emperor from 1215 to 1250, resisted the church's growing power. As a result, the pope tried to depose* him, an act that plunged Germany into civil war. The French were more successful in resisting papal influence. King PHILIP IV THE FAIR, who ruled from 1285 to 1314, supported efforts to dethrone one pope and put significant pressure on later popes

to support French policies. From 1305 to 1376, the popes resided in Avignon, where this pressure from the French was intense.

After the popes returned to Rome in the 1370s, problems broke out among the cardinals*. Various factions elected different popes and created a schism. For a while, there were two, even three popes. Many clergy became conciliarists—those who insisted that a council be called to end the schism* and that this council should have greater authority than the pope. A council did bring the schism to an end in the early 1400s. But conciliarism was rejected as a whole, and a strong papacy was reestablished. At the end of the Middle Ages, however, the papacy was far weaker in relation to secular monarchies than it had been in the 13th century. (*See also* **Cardinals, College of; Christianity; Church-State Relations; Coronation; Monasteries; Monasticism.**)

* **cardinal**   high church official, ranking just below the pope

* **schism**   deep organizational split, usually within a religious body such as the church, when members disagree about matters of belief

Papal States

* **imperial**   pertaining to an empire or emperor

The Papal States were lands in central and northern Italy under the direct control of the popes. During the Middle Ages, the status of these lands remained largely unclear as a result of border disputes, claims by rival states, violent internal disorders, and intervention by imperial* powers.

The nucleus of the Papal States consisted of huge estates in and around ROME, many of which had belonged to the popes since the 300s. Up through the mid-700s, this area was controlled by the BYZANTINE EMPIRE. Gradually, however, the church extended its rule over the papal lands, largely because of opposition to imperial taxes, the increasing political and military weakness of the Byzantines, and the Byzantines' inability to defend the area from the LOMBARDS. Faced with the Lombard threat, the popes sought and received help from the FRANKS. The Franks drove the Lombards from the papal lands in 756, and this marked the true beginning of the Papal States.

From the beginning, the political situation in the Papal States was marked by fierce struggles for power between Roman nobles and clergy. Also evident was the influence of external powers, most notably the Franks. For a long time, the Byzantines exerted influence as well. Insecure conditions in the 800s and 900s caused the rural population of the Papal States to establish new fortified centers, most of which fell under the control of the local nobility. At the same time, many church estates became fragmented, and church control over them also passed to the nobles. As a result, the nobles gained an increasingly tight hold on the church, and in the 900s and 1000s the papacy itself was controlled by various noble families.

In the 1000s, the popes relinquished control of parts of southern Italy to the NORMANS, but they strengthened the feudal ties that bound the Normans to them. For the rest of the Middle Ages, feudal law was a strong element in papal-state policies. The area of the Papal States was expanded in the early 1100s when it received large tracts of land from MATILDA OF TUSCANY. Rival claims to this land, however, led to a long period of struggle between the popes and the Holy Roman Emperors. The most important development of the 1100s was the rise of the Italian

The Papal States, the lands administered directly by the pope, expanded greatly in the 1200s. The political authority of the papacy was challenged constantly throughout the Middle Ages.

PAPAL STATES IN THE 1200s

Papal lands

* **secular** nonreligious; connected with everyday life

COMMUNES, especially the commune in Rome. The emergence of a permanent and well-organized secular* government in Rome posed a grave threat to papal power and led to disputes and conflicts for the remainder of the century.

In the 1200s, papal power increased in large areas of Italy as a result of treaties with the Holy Roman Empire, which ended much imperial interference. In southern Italy, however, papal power was shared with the French ANGEVINS, who ruled the kingdoms of Naples and Sicily. From 1309 to 1417, the Papal States were in chaos because of the move of the papacy to AVIGNON and the Great SCHISM that resulted. In 1414, the government of the Papal States had virtually collapsed. With the election of Pope Martin V in 1417 and his return to Rome in 1420, efforts were made to govern the Papal States in a more uniform and centralized manner. The difficulties in accomplishing this were great, however. Although the government of the Papal States tended to become more organized and effective in the years that followed, regional divisions in the late medieval period allowed the papacy only limited opportunities for asserting government power. The Papal States were finally annexed by Italy in 1870, although a small remnant—Vatican City—still exists in the city of Rome. (*See also* **Italy; Papacy, Origins and Development.**)

Paradise, Idea of

* **rabbinic** pertaining to rabbis, the Jewish spiritual leaders and persons authorized to interpret Jewish law

Medieval Jews, Muslims, and Christians all spoke of a concept of paradise. Muslims and Christians in particular emphasized paradise as an ideal place where the righteous abide after death.

For Jews, the terms for paradise and hell are Gan Eden (Hebrew for Garden of Eden) and Gehinnom. Gan Eden and Gehinnom are believed to have existed even before the world was created, with Gan Eden at God's right hand and Gehinnom at his left. Jewish teaching about life after death is not systematized, and life after death is variously referred to as the "Days of the Messiah" and the "World to Come." In some rabbinic* literature, the righteous and wicked enter Gan Eden and Gehinnom only after the Resurrection and Last Judgment. In other literature, the dead take their places immediately after death.

Many medieval Jewish writers give more detailed descriptions of Gan Eden and Gehinnom. Some tell of the seven sections of paradise and hell to which souls are assigned, according to either their good works or their evil deeds on earth. Generally, Gan Eden is pictured as a place where the Messiah, together with the souls of the righteous, awaits the Day of Redemption. The most extensive account of paradise and hell in Hebrew literature was written in the 1200s and the 1300s by poet Immanuel ben Solomon of Rome. His account includes the idea of a section in Eden for pious non-Jews as well as Jews, which corresponded to the Jewish teaching of the time.

According to the Islamic QUR'AN, paradise is the "garden of eternity," a beautiful place of comfort and ease, and a place that had unimaginable magnificence as well as simple earthly pleasures. Those who believed in Islam and performed good works would be led to this place by MUHAMMAD after the Day of Judgment. These righteous people would live there forever surrounded by their families and rewarded with sumptuous luxuries. The highest rewards, however, were the vision of God and his divine approval.

For medieval Muslims, the garden was thus the dominant symbol of paradise. Islamic poets, mystics, and theologians produced detailed descriptions of paradise, often visualizing it as a vast and beautiful walled garden with flowing streams, shade trees laden with ripe fruit, and people dressed in elegant clothing. The garden's many delights included rivers of milk, wine, and honey; winged horses made of ruby; marvelous fragrances; and gold-embroidered clothes and silver bracelets. Most of the people in paradise were Muslims, and Arabic was the only language spoken.

The idea of paradise as a garden inspired medieval Muslims to create their own magnificent gardens on earth, with exquisite fountains and running water, shade trees, and fragrant flowers. Such gardens were built throughout the Muslim world, and they became an important feature of Islamic culture.

The concept of paradise was more abstract to medieval Christians. Paradise was linked with the idea of "heaven," the ultimate abode of the faithful. Similar to Islamic beliefs, heaven was considered a place of light, peace, and restoration. But far more important than the physical characteristics of this paradise was the idea that heaven consisted of the vision of God, and that this would bring the faithful immeasurable and inexhaustible happiness and joy, as well as wisdom, immortality, and sanctity.

As the Islamic idea of paradise influenced behavior on earth, the Christian idea of heaven also affected earthly culture. This was most evident in the construction of churches. Medieval churches expressed a vivid belief in the reality of heaven, with decorative carvings of saints and angels, biblical scenes, and images of Christ. Soaring interior spaces and the colored light from stained glass windows helped create an otherworldly atmosphere. The church entrance itself became the entrance to paradise.

One factor that influenced the Christian understanding of paradise was the widespread devotion to saints. Pilgrimages* to holy shrines were symbolic journeys toward heaven. Christians also believed that heaven was partially attainable on earth through the spiritual journey of monastic life. The monastic emphasis on prayer and asceticism* was essentially a turning away from the present world to the next. (*See also* **Christianity; Gardens; Glass, Stained; Islam, Religion of; Judaism.**)

* **pilgrimage**   journey to a shrine or sacred place

* **asceticism**   way of life in which a person rejects worldly pleasure and follows a life of prayer and poverty

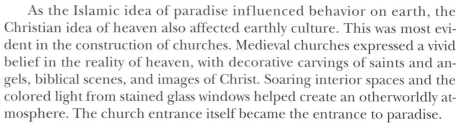

Paris

 See map in Carolingians (vol. 1).

D uring the Middle Ages, Paris became the French royal capital and an important European cultural center with a university that attracted students and scholars from across Europe.

Early History.   Paris began when the Romans established a small outpost on an island in the Seine River that was once inhabited by the Parisii tribe of ancient Gaul. The island became known as the Cité. (It is the center of modern Paris.) The city suffered a series of attacks by Germanic tribes in the late 200s and 300s, and the Roman defenders built walls around the Cité.

Legend states that in 451, when Attila and his HUNS surrounded Paris on their march through Europe, a young woman named Geneviève (422–500) begged Attila not to destroy the city. Shortly afterward, Attila and his barbarian army turned south instead of entering the city. Paris was spared, and Geneviève became the patroness of the city.

CLOVIS, the leader of the FRANKS, chose Paris as his capital. After his death, however, the city played an insignificant role in the history of the MEROVINGIAN and CAROLINGIAN dynasties that followed. Most activity in Paris was centered in the city's abbeys. Paris came under attack in the late 800s, when the VIKINGS sailed up the Seine River many times to pillage and burn the city. Viking warriors besieged Paris for a year in 885–886.

* **abbey**   monastery under the rule of an abbot or abbess

Royal Capital and Cultural Center.   In 987, Hugh CAPET became king, beginning the Capetian dynasty that would rule France for more than three centuries. The Capetian family lands centered on Paris, and the city once again became a political, economic, and administrative capital. In the 1000s, the principal abbey on the Right Bank section of the city was restored, and the Right Bank began to thrive as a marketplace.

In the 1100s under King LOUIS VI, the city continued to flourish. The population grew and prospered, and the city continued to expand from the island to the banks of the Seine. Students attended schools that sprouted on the Left Bank. Louis VI was a patron of SUGER, abbot of St. Denis, who sponsored additions to the church of St. Denis in the new Gothic* style. The building of the city's best-known medieval landmark, the

* **Gothic**   referring to a style of architecture developed in northern France and spreading through western Europe from the 1100s to the 1500s, which was characterized by pointed arches, ribbed vaults, thin walls, large windows, and flying buttresses

This miniature from the *Trés riches heures* of the duke of Berry, from the early 1400s, shows peasants working in the fields outside the walls of Paris. In the background is the Île de la Cité, with the Royal Palace and the Sainte Chapelle.

great cathedral of NOTRE DAME DE PARIS, was begun in 1163 and was completed more than a century later.

PHILIP II AUGUSTUS, who reigned from 1180 to 1223, made Paris into a great royal capital. It was the center of the royal domain, which Philip extended into other parts of France through warfare and advantageous marriages. To defend his capital, Philip built walls around the Right Bank and the more sparsely settled Left Bank. The city's population grew rapidly, as people settled within the walls. By the end of Philip's reign, about 60,000 people lived in Paris. Philip improved the city by draining the marshy streets and paving the principal roads with stones. He also built a hospital and a central market.

Paris's university helped to make it a great cultural city. Early in the 1100s, most learning took place at the cathedral school of Notre Dame on the Cité, under such scholars as Peter ABELARD. After Abelard quarreled with his former teacher, he left the Cité and set up a school on the Left Bank. Soon he was joined by other teachers and their students. Schools sprang up on the Left Bank in rented halls and rooms. Paris's fame as a center of liberal arts* learning attracted students and scholars from all parts of Europe.

* **liberal arts**   seven traditional areas of knowledge—grammar, rhetoric, logic, geometry, arithmetic, astronomy, and music

* **theology**   study of the nature of God and of religious truth

* **hostel**   lodging place or inn

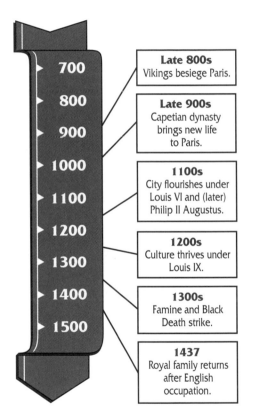

700	**Late 800s** Vikings besiege Paris.
800	**Late 900s** Capetian dynasty brings new life to Paris.
900	
1000	**1100s** City flourishes under Louis VI and (later) Philip II Augustus.
1100	
1200	**1200s** Culture thrives under Louis IX.
1300	
1400	**1300s** Famine and Black Death strike.
1500	
	1437 Royal family returns after English occupation.

The university that emerged on the Left Bank consisted of four schools: theology*, LAW, MEDICINE, and the arts. The hostels* where students lived came to be known as "colleges." One of the most important of the early colleges was founded in 1257 by the royal chaplain, Robert de Sorbon. His name was eventually applied to the theology school and then to the entire university. Today, a part of the University of Paris is better known as the Sorbonne.

During the long reign of St. LOUIS IX, from 1226 to 1270, Paris was the cultural capital of Europe. French nobles built palaces in the city to be near the king and his court. Parishes and religious communities built new Gothic churches throughout the city. Crafts and trades thrived, and the university reached the height of its fame with the help of such renowned scholars as BONAVENTURE, ALBERTUS MAGNUS, and Thomas AQUINAS.

Decline and Revival.   The 1300s and 1400s were a time of misery for the people of Paris. France was affected by the series of political, economic, and natural disasters that struck northern Europe. Population growth among the peasants, combined with a shortage of new land to farm, forced many country people into the city looking for work. By 1300, the population of Paris was between 100,000 and 120,000.

The first natural catastrophe to affect the city was the poor wheat harvest in 1314, which caused a severe FAMINE. Further suffering was caused by the HUNDRED YEARS WAR with England, which brought economic hardship to all of France. Then, in 1348, the BLACK DEATH struck western Europe, killing about half the people of Paris.

However, Paris's low point came in the early 1400s, when the city was occupied by a force of English and BURGUNDIANS for 17 years. Violence, looting, and hunger followed, and Paris was devastated and desolate. In 1433, a chronicler reported that wolves were roaming the deserted streets at night.

The French royal family returned to Paris in 1437 after the English occupation, and the fortunes of the city began to improve. Within 20 years, Paris was thriving again, although during the rest of the Middle Ages the French kings spent little time in the city. (*See also* **Cities and Towns; France; Gothic Architecture; Jews, Expulsion of; Fairs; Migrations, Germanic.**)

Parish

A parish was a community served by the medieval church. The parish became the basic organization through which the church carried out its mission to care for souls. It was one of the most important centers around which medieval life revolved.

Early Middle Ages.   After CHRISTIANITY was legalized in the Roman Empire in the 300s, the church spread beyond its city base into rural areas. The bishops in charge of urban parishes built rural churches and staffed them with priests, deacons, and minor CLERGY.

These rural parishes expanded the range of their religious activities until their officials gained the right to perform all Christian services, which included baptisms, Mass, last rites for the dying, funerals, and preaching. Between the 300s and the 600s, rural churches were established throughout most of Europe. Other rural parishes (especially in IRELAND) formed around MONASTERIES.

In addition to the churches that were founded by bishops and monasteries, private chapels and churches also emerged in the early Middle Ages. Local landowners built these chapels on their estates to provide a place for their family and workers to worship. These churches were called proprietary, or private, churches. Their religious services were conducted either by a clergyman from a neighboring parish church or by a private CHAPLAIN.

During the CAROLINGIAN period, owners of proprietary churches sought to earn money from their churches by selling priests the right to serve the church and by charging people to attend the services. By treating the churches as private property to be bought, sold, and rented, the owners took control of parishes, thereby reducing the authority of the bishops. Private ownership of churches caused widespread corruption in the 900s and the 1000s.

Late Middle Ages.   The economic and social revival that began in 11th-century Europe led to a rapid increase in the number of parishes. Population growth and the extension of Christendom* through conquest, colonization, and missionary activity created pressure for new churches. Old parishes were divided, and new ones were established to serve the newly conquered, colonized, and converted areas. Churches were supported by the tithes* of all parishioners and by gifts from the wealthy.

A reform movement soon developed that sought to free the church from feudal control. The reformers challenged the proprietary church system and greatly reduced the domination of parish life by landowners. By 1300, the parish system was more securely under the control of bishops. The bishops in turn appointed clergymen called rectors to take charge of the parishes.

Conflicts developed when members of religious orders—especially the mendicant* orders, such as the FRANCISCANS or the DOMINICANS—offended parish rectors and bishops by coming into their areas to preach, teach, and collect money. The zeal and training of these monks greatly impressed local parishioners. Many rectors and bishops resented the success of these mendicants, and the result was discord in many parishes. (*See also* **Benefice; Cathedrals and Churches; Church-State Relations; Monasticism; Sacraments; Simony.**)

* **Christendom**   name for all the Christian nations of the world

* **tithe**   payment or gift of a tenth of one's income for support of the church

* **mendicant**   begging; depending on charity for a living

Parliament, English

During the Middle Ages, the advisory councils of the English kings evolved into an institution that helped the king rule his kingdom. That institution has been known as parliament since the mid-1200s.

Kings generally called parliamentary meetings to gain the military, financial, and moral support of their subjects. When a king and his advisers decided that it was time for a parliament, royal clerks sent out writs of

Kings called meetings of parliament in order to help raise money for war, collect taxes, draft laws, answer petitions, and settle judicial disputes. This engraving from a manuscript of the 1300s shows King Edward I presiding over parliament. At his right is Alexander III, king of the Scots. At his left is Llywelyn ap Gruffydd, Prince of Wales.

* **abbot** male leader of a monastery or abbey. The female equivalent is an abbess.

* **burgess** a representative of a borough

* **borough** medieval town with special duties and privileges, such as sending representatives to parliament

* **earl** governor of a region in Anglo-Saxon times. The term was later used for a noble title.

* **chancellor** official who handles the records and archives of a monarch

* **abdicate** to give up the throne voluntarily or under pressure

summons to earls, barons, bishops, and abbots*. Writs were also sent to sheriffs, instructing them to have their counties choose two to four knights from each and two or more burgesses* from specified boroughs* to attend the meeting. Commoners, however, were only gradually included in parliament. Only about a dozen of the first 70 parliaments held after 1258 (when the institution first achieved recognizable form) included representatives of England's common people. The business of these early parliaments—especially in the reign of EDWARD I, from 1272 to 1307—was mostly raising men and money for war, collecting taxes, drafting laws and statutes, answering petitions and complaints, and settling judicial disputes.

Growth of Parliament.   The reign of King EDWARD II, from 1307 to 1327, was a turning point in the history of parliament. Several months after the death of his father in July 1307, Edward II's first parliament met in Northampton to grant him money so that he could travel to France to marry his 12-year-old fiancée, Isabella, daughter of the French king. Parliament also gave him money for his coronation, which took place on February 25, 1308.

In 1310, under pressure from his earls*, Edward appointed 21 lords to reform the laws of the realm. After more than a year, they produced the Ordinances of 1311, which Edward agreed to accept and publish throughout the kingdom. The Ordinances sought to give parliament control over the appointment and dismissal of royal officials. The document allowed the king to appoint his own chancellor*, treasurer, chief justices, and household officers but suggested he do so "by the counsel and assent of his baronage, and this in parliament." Nor was the king to undertake war or make changes in the coinage without the barons' advice, again "in parliament." The barons also recommended that the king hold a parliament at least once a year "in a convenient place."

The frequent use of the phrase "and this in parliament" in the Ordinances of 1311 showed that parliament was growing in importance. Edward II and his supporters, however, controlled the parliament of 1322, which enacted a law called the Statute of York. This law overturned the Ordinances of 1311 on the grounds that they limited royal power. The statute declared that any ordinance the king's subjects made that limited his power "should be null." However, it did acknowledge that matters pertaining to the king, the kingdom, and the people should be dealt with "in parliaments."

Edward abdicated* in 1327, and parliament ratified the act "by the unanimous consent of all the earls and barons, and of the archbishops and bishops, and of the whole clergy and people." It "unanimously agreed" that EDWARD III should succeed his father. The 48 parliaments that met during the long reign of Edward III, from 1327 to 1377, showed a spirit of cooperation between the king and parliament. Parliament supported the king's wars. By using commissions and committees, the members of parliament became more active and effective in the governmental process.

Parliament in the Late Middle Ages.   The role of parliament in king making grew in the 1400s. Anyone who seized royal power used parliament

The Highest Court

Parliament was more than a council of advisers for the king or a law-making body. It was also the highest court in England. In 1305, parliament tried a man for treason. On another occasion, several officials of Oxford Castle were summoned to parliament to explain a student riot that had taken place near the castle. Charges were also heard against cities. The towns of Salisbury and Winchester, for example, were tried by parliament for allowing a hostage to escape.

to ratify his right to rule. During England's political struggles in the late Middle Ages, parliament was used in this way by Henry IV, Edward IV, RICHARD III, and Henry VII. Parliament also continued to serve as the kingdom's high court for settling the most difficult issues of the realm.

At the end of the Middle Ages, parliament consisted of three groups: the Lords Spiritual (archbishops, bishops, abbots, and other clergy); the Lords Temporal (dukes, earls, viscounts, and barons); and the Commons (knights and gentlemen from the counties and burgesses from towns or boroughs). The largest parliaments counted more than 600 members. Over time, parliament was divided into an upper house for the Lords and a lower house for the Commons. When the Commons acquired its own meeting place in WESTMINSTER ABBEY, its independence from the Lords was recognized. The Commons succeeded in gaining control over parliament's money bills—those bills and laws that determined how the kingdom's money would be spent. This triumph paved the way for the eventual emergence of the Commons as the more powerful of the two houses. (*See also* **Clergy; Count, County; England; Germany, Representative Assemblies; Law; Nobility and Nobles; Shire.**)

Passover

See *Feasts and Festivals.*

Paston Family and Letters

* **scribe**   person who hand-copies manuscripts to preserve them

The Paston letters are a large collection of documents written in the 1400s by three generations of an English family that lived in Norfolk. The core of the collection is about 780 letters written by and to family members, but there are also other documents, such as wills and petitions.

The author of the earliest letters was the founder of the family's wealth, William Paston I (1378–1444). From a humble background, he became a successful lawyer in Norwich and London and acquired large amounts of land, including a manor that remained in the family for 300 years. His wife, Agnes Berry, the daughter of a Hertfordshire knight, also inherited a good deal of land.

Their oldest son, John Paston I (1421–1466), and his wife, Margaret, wrote many of the letters. (Margaret's letters are written in more than 20 different kinds of handwriting. This discovery suggests that she herself could not write or at least found writing difficult and had to use scribes*.) Three other sons and a daughter also wrote some of the letters. The oldest sons of the third generation, John II (1442–1479) and John III (1444–1504), wrote about 70 letters each.

The great majority of letters are about obtaining, managing, and defending family property. Some of the letters discuss important events of the day, such as the murder of the duke of Suffolk in 1450 and the recovery of King HENRY VI OF ENGLAND from insanity in 1454. The letters are an important source of information about daily life and the English language as it was used in the 1400s. (*See also* **English Language and Literature.**)

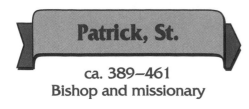

Patrick, St.

ca. 389–461
Bishop and missionary

* **Briton** person who inhabited Britain before the Anglo-Saxon invasions

St. Patrick is one of the most mysterious figures in early Irish Christian history. Much of what is known about him is enhanced by legend. According to his own account, Patrick was a Christian Briton*. His father was a church deacon, and his grandfather was a priest. Patrick lived at his father's home until he was captured in a raid when he was about 16. He spent six years as a slave in IRELAND, but his ordeal only strengthened his religious faith. Following his escape, he returned home and was reunited with his family. There he decided to return to Ireland as a missionary. (One biographer maintained that Patrick studied in Europe before returning to Ireland.)

In 431, Pope Celestine I sent a mission to Ireland under Palladius, a bishop and writer. Palladius soon died, and Patrick was quickly made a bishop and sent to Ireland as Palladius's successor. In 432, Patrick converted the king of Tara, an Irish kingdom, to Christianity.

Patrick faced his first major challenge when he revealed to a friend a sin he had committed in his youth. The friend told Patrick's superiors about the sin, raising doubts about Patrick's fitness. Patrick defended himself in a document called the *Confession,* which shows his unhappiness that the accusation called into question all the good work he was doing in Ireland. In his *Confession,* he stated his belief that God had chosen him for the mission to which he joyfully dedicated his life. Patrick spent more than 30 years traveling through Ireland, where his preaching helped to convert scores of people to Christianity. (*See also* **Celtic Languages and Literature; Missions and Missionaries, Christian.**)

Peace of God, Truce of God

* **excommunicate** to exclude from the rites of the church

* **synod** church council

The Peace of God was a movement that bishops and church councils in southern and central France started in the late 900s as a protest against constant fighting and widespread lawlessness.

The church instituted the Peace of God to protect churches, clergy, peasants, and poor people from violence. Anyone who broke the peace could be excommunicated*. The Peace of God was part of a larger religious revival that brought about an increase in the worship of saints' RELICS and the belief in miraculous cures. In many areas, authorities incorporated the aims of the peace movement into local laws. As a result, violators faced civil penalties as well as excommunication.

The Truce of God was an offshoot of the peace movement. Its purpose was to protect unarmed people from violence by prohibiting fighting at certain times, such as during Lent or on Sundays. In 1027, a church council at Toulouges called for knights and soldiers to lay down their weapons from Saturday night until Monday morning. A synod* of bishops meeting at Arles 15 years later extended the Truce of God from Thursday night to Monday morning. The Peace of God and the Truce of God helped advance the idea that Christians should never fight against other Christians.

Although the Peace of God and the Truce of God were not universally respected and violations were frequent and often went unpunished, they helped establish the important new idea that knights, soldiers, and the lords who employed them were responsible to society for their actions. (*See also* **Chivalry; Crusades; Excommunication; Feudalism; Knights, Orders of; Warfare.**)

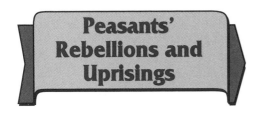

Peasants' Rebellions and Uprisings

See
color plate 14,
vol. 1.

* **artisans** skilled craftspeople

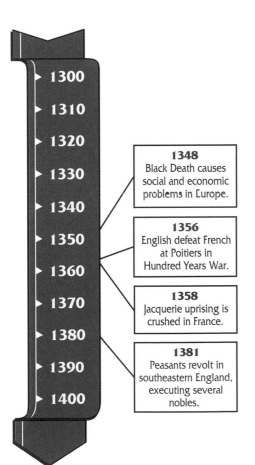

1348
Black Death causes social and economic problems in Europe.

1356
English defeat French at Poitiers in Hundred Years War.

1358
Jacquerie uprising is crushed in France.

1381
Peasants revolt in southeastern England, executing several nobles.

The harsh demands that medieval landlords and kings made on their peasants and villagers were a source of discontent that sometimes led to open rebellion. Many lords were haunted by the fear of a peasant revolt. King HENRY I OF ENGLAND was said to have had nightmares in which overburdened villagers attacked him with pitchforks. In the late Middle Ages, economic hard times and the frequent warfare waged by European states led to increased discontent among the peasants. Two of the largest peasant revolts of the late Middle Ages were the Jacquerie in France (1358) and the Great Rising of 1381 in England. But there were equally ferocious revolts in Spain, Hungary, Italy, and Germany.

Jacquerie. The French uprising began on May 28, 1358, in the village of St. Leu d'Esserent, about 25 miles north of PARIS. The revolt spread from village to village until it engulfed a large area around Paris, from Amiens in the north to Orleans in the south.

The rebels were called Jacques after Jacques Bonhomme (Jacques Good Man), a traditional nickname for a peasant. The revolt was joined by peasants, rural artisans*, wealthy villagers, clerics, and even minor royal officials. It was led by Guillaume Cale, who seems to have had military experience.

In early June, the Jacques attacked the fortified marketplace of Meaux, where a number of noblewomen, including the prince's wife, had taken refuge. Many rebels were killed in the attack. The nobles of Picardy—led by the king of NAVARRE, Charles II the Bad—crushed a large force of Jacques near Clermont after luring Cale into a trap. With the revolt now a lost cause, the authorities brutally subdued the peasantry, sometimes making little distinction between rebels and those who had not taken part in the uprising.

Historians now believe that the conditions for revolt were created by the pressures of the HUNDRED YEARS WAR, especially after the BLACK DEATH ravaged Europe in 1348, and the disastrous French defeat and capture of the French king John II at Poitiers in 1356. During four years of uncertainty, while the king was in captivity, roving bands of soldiers—English and others—roamed the French countryside intimidating villagers as they looked for food and work. Beneath all this turmoil was the deep hatred that many peasants and townspeople felt for the NOBILITY, who in turn regarded the peasants with scorn and fear. The Jacquerie was marked by suddenness and extreme violence. The rebels acted without warning against the privileged—including men, women, and children—in a surge of killing and destruction. The reaction of the nobility in crushing the uprising was equally violent and bloody.

English Peasants' Revolt. After the Jacquerie, the nobles of England feared a similar revolt. Their fears came true in 1381. The trouble began when villagers in southwest Essex attacked royal officials who had come to investigate widespread tax evasion. The uprising spread from Essex to Kent, Norfolk, Suffolk, Hertfordshire, Cambridgeshire, and parts of other counties in southeastern England.

The leader of the Kent rebels was Wat Tyler, who led a band into Canterbury, captured the sheriff of Kent, and destroyed property records. Meanwhile, the Essex rebels were plundering the sheriff's

John Ball was an English priest who had been excommunicated for preaching inflammatory sermons against the church. These sermons may have inspired Wat Tyler's rebels. On their march to London in 1381, they freed Ball from the archbishop's prison. Ball, in turn, incited the crowds and urged the killing of lords and prelates. After the rebellion had been crushed, Ball was tried and executed.

Rebel Leader Wat Tyler

Nothing at all is known of Wat Tyler's life before the Great Rising of 1381. The events of that dramatic uprising, however, prove that he was a capable leader of men. Tyler's downfall came during the meeting between the rebels and King Richard II, when Tyler presented demands that Richard could not meet. A scuffle broke out between the rebels and the king's men. Tyler was killed. Seizing his chance, the young king called out to the confused peasants that he would be their leader, and then he sent them home.

home, killing a government official, and destroying the manor of the royal treasurer. Then both groups marched off to London to meet with the 14-year-old king, RICHARD II, to help save him and his kingdom from "traitors."

On June 12 the young king was rowed down the Thames River in the royal barge to meet with the Kentish rebels near Greenwich. However, his courtiers would not let him go ashore for fear that the rebels would capture him. Sympathetic support from people along the way allowed the rebels to continue on to London and to enter the city. With help from some Londoners, the rebels destroyed the Savoy palace, home of the king's unpopular uncle, JOHN OF GAUNT, duke of Lancaster.

King Richard with his entourage sought protection in the Tower of London. He again, however, agreed to talk with the rebels and met the Essex group east of the city. After Richard agreed to pardon the rebels and promised to end SERFDOM in Essex and Hertfordshire, many of the rebels went home with guarantees that were later canceled. The king also gave the rebels permission to seize traitors and to bring them to him. That same day the rebels entered the Tower and seized the chancellor, the treasurer, and John of Gaunt's physician. They took the three men to Tower Hill and executed them. On June 15, after Richard met with the remaining rebels, he succeeded in leading them away from London.

The English rebellion was much less violent than the Jacquerie. The English rebels did not attack lords indiscriminately. In fact, very few lords (and no women and children) were put to death. The suppression of the uprising resulted in far fewer deaths among the rebels than was the case in France. (*See also* **England; France.**)

Pedro IV the Ceremonious

1319–1387
King of Aragon and Catalonia

* **chronicles** record of events in the order in which they occurred

Pedro IV was the scholarly ruler of the northern Spanish kingdoms of ARAGON and CATALONIA from 1336 to 1387. The culture and learning he promoted at his court during his long reign paved the way for the advances in literature, history, law, and science that took place during the reigns of his successors.

Pedro's support for the translation of scholarly works from Latin, Arabic, and Hebrew into the Catalan language laid the foundation for the creation of the body of Catalan literature that followed. He also supported the study of ASTROLOGY. Like many medieval people, Pedro regarded astrology as a science that could forecast human destiny through the study of planetary movement.

Pedro reorganized the royal library, commissioned architects to build splendid royal tombs, and paid close attention to such practical matters as palace and dockyard construction. He encouraged the creation of new universities and helped students study law and theology in foreign universities. Pedro's special interest was history. He collected chronicles* from other countries, especially those from France and Castile, and supervised the work of his court historians. He also wrote his own court chronicles of the history of Aragon and Catalonia from 1319 to 1369.

Pedro died in BARCELONA in 1387, but his influence lived on after him in the advances in science, law, and history that had begun during his reign. (*See also* **Arabic Language and Literature; Castile; France; Hebrew Literature; Latin Language.**)

Pepin III the Short

714–768
King of the Franks

After defeating the Lombards in Italy in the 700s, Frankish king Pepin III the Short donated their cities to the pope. This "Donation of Pepin" became the Papal States. Pepin is shown here with his son, Charles, later known as Charlemagne, who would become one of medieval Europe's greatest rulers.

Although Pepin III, known as Pepin the Short, is best remembered today for being the father of CHARLEMAGNE, he established the kingdom of the FRANKS by expanding its borders and forming a partnership with the popes in Rome that shaped the future of both that kingdom and the PAPACY. Pepin's father, CHARLES MARTEL, had defeated Muslim invaders from SPAIN, but it was during Pepin's reign that they were pushed back across the Pyrenees Mountains that divide France and Spain. Pepin had inherited from his father the title of "mayor of the palace," which he shared with his older brother, Carloman. Evidence of the brothers' ambitions became apparent when they began calling themselves "dukes and princes of the Franks." In 743, the brothers put the MEROVINGIAN Childeric III on the throne as a puppet king to ease the concerns of the other Frankish leaders.

After Carloman retired to the monastery at Monte Cassino, Pepin decided to declare himself king. He sent two Frankish church leaders, an abbot and a bishop, to Rome to gain the support of Pope Zacharias I. In November 751, at an assembly of Franks in Soissons, Pepin was acclaimed king. Representing the pope was the Anglo-Saxon monk Boniface, who anointed* Pepin. This was the first anointing of a Frankish king.

Meanwhile, the pope had ambitions of his own that needed Pepin's support. Pope Stephen II wanted to be independent of the BYZANTINE EMPIRE and the LOMBARDS, who were expanding their territory in Italy. In a show of support for Pope Stephen, Pepin led his army to Italy, where he defeated the Lombards and presented the keys of the Lombard cities to the pope. This gift, known as the "Donation of Pepin," gave the pope a

* **anoint**   to put holy oil on a person at a religious ceremony or coronation

wide strip of land in central Italy that became the PAPAL STATES. A Byzantine representative protested, but Pepin stood by his action.

Encouraged by Boniface, Pepin instituted many church reforms in his kingdom. He introduced sweeping changes in procedure and organization that helped make the church more orderly and its CLERGY more disciplined. (*See also* **Boniface, St.; Carolingians.**)

Peter the Hermit

died 1115
Preacher

* **Holy Land**   Palestine, the site of religious shrines for Christians, Jews, and Muslims

* **Byzantium**   ancient city that became Constantinople; also refers to Byzantine Empire

P eter the Hermit was a spellbinding preacher with a special ability to inspire poor and uneducated peasants. He organized a peasant army and played an active role in the First CRUSADE.

For many centuries, Peter the Hermit was mistakenly believed to have been the person who persuaded Pope URBAN II to call for the First Crusade. According to legend, Peter received a letter from heaven prophesying that Christians would defeat the Turks and recover the Holy Sepulcher, the site in JERUSALEM where Jesus was believed to have been buried. Although it was later established that Peter did not influence Pope Urban's decision, Peter did quickly rally support for the crusade by organizing a large army of peasants to go with him to the Holy Land*. After gathering forces in France and Germany, he led them through Hungary and Bulgaria into CONSTANTINOPLE. In August 1096, Peter led his followers across the straits to the Asian side of Byzantium*, where the group became uncontrollable and

Peter the Hermit provided spiritual support for crusaders during the First Crusade. This illumination from the 1300s shows Godfrey of Bouillon and his knights during the siege of Jerusalem in 1099. Peter the Hermit is seen on the left. Peter's preaching to the armies inspired them to capture the city.

began attacking Turkish positions. In several catastrophic battles, the Turks massacred Peter's followers, thus bringing the peasant crusade to its tragic end before it ever reached the Holy Land.

Peter survived these battles and went on to the Holy Land, where he continued to be an effective preacher and source of support to the crusaders*. His preaching during the siege of Jerusalem helped inspire the crusaders to capture Jerusalem in 1099. Peter is believed to have returned to Europe in 1101, where he died in 1115. (*See also* **Seljuks.**)

* **crusader** person who participated in the holy wars against the Muslims during the Middle Ages

---

Peter the Venerable

ca. 1092–1156
Abbot, theologian,
and writer

* **treatise** long, detailed essay

Peter was the highly respected ninth abbot of the Cluny monastery and author of a large body of treatises*, sermons, hymns, and a collection of letters that ranks as one of the most valuable of the Middle Ages.

Peter was 30 years old when he was unanimously elected abbot of the powerful monastery at Cluny, which housed between 300 and 400 monks. During Peter's 34 years as abbot, this monastic empire reached the height of its prosperity and influence over 2,000 monasteries. In addition to his leadership and writing skills, Peter the Venerable was admired for his lively personality and his warmhearted generosity toward other people. For example, after Peter Abelard was condemned at Sens in 1140, Peter treated him with sympathy and affection.

Peter commissioned a translation of the QUR'AN, and he wrote two treatises that reveal his extraordinary understanding of ISLAM. He insisted that Muslims should be treated "not by force, but by reason; not in hatred, but in love." It was this mixture of confident faith plus generosity toward others that made him so forceful, influential, and admired. (*See also* **Abelard and Heloise; Latin Language; Monasteries; Monasticism.**)

Petrarch

1304–1374
Italian poet and scholar

Francesco Petrarca, known as Petrarch, was one of Italy's greatest poets. He exerted enormous influence on the culture of his time and on that of the centuries that followed. This influence came partly from Petrarch's own writings, which other writers admired and imitated. His influence also came from his rediscovery of the writings of ancient Greek and Roman authors, which led him to play a major role in introducing educated Europeans of the late Middle Ages to the classics of the ancient world.

His Life. Petrarch was the son of a minor civic official in the central Italian town of Arezzo. His family moved several times while he was very young. This frequent moving established a pattern that was to continue throughout Petrarch's life, as he constantly searched for an ideal place in which to live and work.

Soon after the pope and the central government of the Roman Church moved from ROME to AVIGNON in southern France in 1309, Petrarch's father moved the family to Avignon in the hope of finding a position in the papal court. Young Petrarch began his studies at this time.

Petrarch is one of Italy's greatest poets. He studied classical Greek and Roman culture and was instrumental in introducing the classics of the ancient world to medieval Europeans. His works reflect a worldly, rather than spiritual, view. Petrarch's work has been said to mark the end of the Middle Ages and the beginning of the Italian Renaissance.

When he was 12, his father sent him to Montpellier, France, to study law. Petrarch continued legal studies in Bologna, Italy, until his father's death in 1326 forced him to return to Avignon. Petrarch wrote his earliest poems during his student years. One of them is a poem of praise for his mother, who died around 1318.

Petrarch and his brother enjoyed themselves for a few years, spending the money they inherited. During this carefree time, Petrarch caught sight of a beautiful young woman in church on Good Friday. Historians have been unable to discover her true identity, but Petrarch called her Laura. For years, his love for her was a source of inspiration for his poetry. The details of their real-life relationship (if any existed) remain a mystery.

In the years that followed, Petrarch became a minor church official and sought a position that would provide him with financial security and give him time to study and write. He traveled widely, spending time in Paris, Rome, and Belgium. On three different occasions, he lived near Avignon, but he also lived in various Italian cities, including Milan, Venice, and Padua. Petrarch's search for a permanent home ended in 1370, when he built a large house in the hills near Padua. His daughter—one of his several illegitimate children—lived there with him during his final years.

Petrarch died on the eve of his 70th birthday while reading the works of one of his favorite authors, the ancient Roman poet Virgil. According to legend, he was found with his head resting peacefully on an open volume of Virgil's poetry.

His Work.   Petrarch wrote hundreds of poems, essays, and letters. He wrote some of his poetry in LATIN and modeled it on the poetry of ancient Roman writers. Many of his Latin poems are short and concern such topics as the passage of time and his love for Laura.

A poem called *Africa* was more ambitious. It was Petrarch's attempt to write a long historical epic like those of Homer and Virgil. Although he never finished *Africa,* he won a prize for it and won a growing reputation as one of the leading poets of the age.

* **sonnet** fixed verse form of 14 lines; also a poem in this pattern

In addition, Petrarch wrote poetry in Italian. Many of the Italian poems are sonnets* addressed to Laura. In these poems, Petrarch claims that his love for Laura, who represented everything that was good and beautiful, led him to a greater love of God. The idea that human love can be a reflection of divine love was an important part of the medieval tradition of COURTLY LOVE. Petrarch's lyric poems, which were full of personal experience and feeling, were extremely popular and inspired the writing of a new, more personal kind of poetry.

Petrarch also wrote the *Trionfi (Triumphs),* a long philosophical poem about humanity's struggle to find truth and happiness. The *Trionfi* was probably inspired by the work of DANTE ALIGHIERI, an Italian poet who had been a friend of Petrarch's father and who composed a long epic poem about Hell, Purgatory, and Paradise called the *Divine Comedy.*

Petrarch also wrote essays about political, religious, and historical subjects. Several of his best-known works contained biographies of the leading figures of ancient Rome. *De vita solitaria (The Solitary Life)* described Petrarch's vision of the ideal life of a poet as one in which he or she could live alone far from the distractions of the city and devote himself or herself to prayer, study, and the contemplation of the beauties of nature.

Petrarch also wrote hundreds of carefully crafted letters to people throughout Europe. One scholar estimates that he wrote more letters than anyone else ever did. Covering a wide range of subjects, Petrarch's letters provide a vivid look at his times as well as a portrait of a thoughtful, creative scholar. (*See also* **Classical Tradition in the Middle Ages; Italian Language and Literature; Italy.**)

Philip II Augustus

1165–1223
King of France

During his long reign—from 1179 to 1223—Philip II Augustus strengthened the French monarchy. He expanded its territory and improved its government as well.

Philip's birth on August 21, 1165, was greeted with great joy and relief. The three marriages of his father, Louis VII, over a 30-year period had produced only daughters, who were unable to inherit the throne. In 1179, Louis suffered a stroke and decided to have 14-year-old Philip crowned in accordance with the long-standing French royal tradition of having a king's heir crowned while the king was still alive. Shortly before the ceremony, Philip became ill. Louis abandoned his own sickbed to travel to CANTERBURY in England. There he prayed for his son's recovery at the tomb of St. Thomas BECKET, his martyred old friend. Philip recovered and was crowned king of France in the cathedral at Rheims on November 1, 1179.

In October 1187, when the shocking news of the fall of JERUSALEM to the Muslims reached Europe, the pope called for a new CRUSADE. The English king, RICHARD I THE LIONHEARTED, responded to the papal appeal immediately, but Philip delayed leaving for the crusade because of the birth of his son, Louis, and his concern that his male heir might not survive past infanthood.

In July 1190, the two kings finally departed on the Third Crusade, which resulted in the siege and capture of the key port of Acre. Although Philip did most of the work and planning, Richard received all the glory. In late 1191, after the fall of Acre, Philip returned to France. Richard returned by way of Austria, where he was captured and turned over to the German emperor, who was Philip's ally. Richard was released only after the payment of a large ransom.

Although Philip fought against Richard over the latter's possession of French lands, it was not until after Richard's death that Philip captured Normandy from Richard's successor, King JOHN. He then drove the English south of the Loire valley. When English, Flemish, and German armies united against Philip, he defeated them at the Battle of Bouvines on July 27, 1214.

In addition to making France a strong military power, Philip enlarged the courts and created a central office for the permanent storage of royal records in PARIS. His government reforms strengthened the French monarchy and paved the way for its further growth in the 1200s. (*See also* **England; France.**)

Philip IV the Fair

1268–1314
King of France

* **bishopric** office of or area governed by a bishop

* **clergy** priests, deacons, and other church officials qualified to perform church ceremonies

* **excommunicate** to exclude from the rites of the church

King Philip IV's attempt to curb the power of the church in France brought him into serious conflict with the PAPACY. Philip's confrontation with Pope BONIFACE VIII in 1303 led to the election of a French cardinal as the new pope and the relocation of the papacy from ROME to AVIGNON, where it remained for most of the 1300s.

After Philip became king in 1285 following the death of his father, Philip III, he instituted several measures to strengthen royal rule and to expand its judicial and financial effectiveness. To gain greater control over the French church, he filled the bishoprics* with his supporters and levied taxes on the French clergy*, as well as his other subjects, to provide much needed money for the government.

In theory, the French clergy could not be taxed without the pope's consent. However, when the pope did not agree, Philip required local church councils to make "free gifts" to the monarchy. Like other European rulers, Philip sought to limit the authority of church courts. Since Philip protected clerical rights against the demands of feudal lords and town governments, the French clergy found itself depending on Philip even as it resented his policies.

In 1303, a crisis began when Philip arrested a bishop in southern France on a trumped-up charge of treason. When Pope Boniface VIII called for a council of French church officials to excommunicate* Philip, the king sent his representatives to Italy to arrest the pope and bring him to France for trial. The pope's arrest at the papal palace in Anagni sparked a local riot that led to the pope's release. However, the elderly pope died a few days later, quite possibly from the shock of the incident.

The death of Boniface ended the church's resistance to Philip. A year later, the Roman CARDINALS completely surrendered to Philip by electing a French archbishop as the new pope, Clement V. This new French pope established himself in Avignon, and the papacy remained under French control until it was finally restored to Rome in 1378. (*See also* **Aquitaine; Church-State Relations; France; Hundred Years War; Kingship, Theories of.**)

Philip of Valois

1293–1350
King of France

In 1328, Philip of Valois succeeded his cousin Charles IV as king of France because the French balked at being ruled by EDWARD III OF ENGLAND. Edward was the son of Charles's sister and was the closest heir to the French throne. Although Philip reigned for 22 years, his right to rule was constantly challenged, and he was never free from having to defend his title.

Philip's reign began with his victory over Flemish rebels at Cassel. He soon became involved in the HUNDRED YEARS WAR, which broke out between France and England in 1337. The conflict began badly for Philip, with defeats at sea that gave the English control of the channel between the two countries. In 1346, the English defeated Philip's forces at Crécy, and the following year they captured Calais. In addition to these military setbacks, the BLACK DEATH struck France in 1348, killing half the population. When Philip died in 1350, France was in a state of economic and military disaster. (*See also* **England; France; Warfare.**)

Pilgrimage

See map in Crusades (vol. 2).

* **Holy Land**   Palestine, the site of religious shrines for Christians, Jews, and Muslims

A pilgrimage is a journey to a holy place, and those who make such journeys are called pilgrims. During the Middle Ages, pilgrimages were important events in the religious life of Christians, Jews, and Muslims.

For all three religions—Christianity, Judaism, and Islam—the city of JERUSALEM was a holy city and a destination for pilgrims. For Jews, it was of central importance as the city of David and the site of Solomon's temple. For Christians, the city was sacred as the place where Christ died. In Islam, Jerusalem is the third holiest city, after MECCA and MEDINA.

Access to Jerusalem's holy places for Christian pilgrims became an issue after the SELJUK Turkish Muslims took control of the Holy Land*. In the late 1000s, Pope URBAN II called on the Christians of Europe to "liberate" the Holy Land from the Turks, thus launching the CRUSADES, a series of fierce battles between Christians and Muslims for control of Jerusalem and the Holy Land.

Christian Pilgrimages

For Christians, the idea of pilgrimage was based on three important aspects of their belief system. First, many Christians felt that their life on

earth was a preparation for eternal life. Therefore, when they made the long and arduous journey of a pilgrim, they were enacting the soul's difficult journey through the trials and tribulations of earthly life.

Second, Christians believed that the bones and other RELICS of saints were sacred objects, blessed by God, that could perform miracles, such as curing disease. For this reason, many Christian pilgrimages included visits to the various shrines* that held these relics.

Third, making a pilgrimage was a way to atone for one's sins. In fact, some pilgrimages were imposed as punishment for wrongdoing. Other pilgrimages were undertaken voluntarily by people who wanted to make amends for sinful acts or who believed that a pilgrimage would increase their chances of going to heaven. The difficulty of the journey was considered a form of penance, or payment for past sins.

Although the custom of making pilgrimages was as old as Christianity itself, during the Middle Ages pilgrimages became more common than ever. The judicial pilgrimage (punishment for a crime), which was introduced in Ireland in the 500s, was soon widespread throughout Europe. Judicial pilgrims walked barefoot and were bound in iron chains. Murderers had their murder weapons chained to them.

The increase in pilgrimage activity in the 11th century was accompanied by the construction of many new shrines and churches. One French chronicler reported that the world seemed to be covered with "a shining white robe of churches," and medieval roads were crowded with pilgrims. Pilgrims belonged to every social class—from kings to beggars. Pilgrimages were especially popular with knights, whose lives as warriors required them to commit violent acts for which they sought forgiveness.

Pope Urban II made pilgrimages more attractive in the late 1000s by linking visits to certain shrines with the granting of INDULGENCES, which excused sinners from part of their penance*. As more and more indulgences were granted, pilgrimages to these shrines became increasingly popular. Pilgrims visited these shrines to receive forgiveness for their sins and to shorten the time they had to spend in PURGATORY before ascending to heaven.

Pilgrimage Destinations. Christian pilgrims earned the greatest reward by visiting Jerusalem, a primary destination for Christians from as early as the 200s. By the 1000s, Jerusalem had become the destination of mass pilgrimages from Europe to the Holy Land. In 1033, and again in 1064, thousands of Christians went to Jerusalem to visit the scenes of the last days of Christ's life and to pray and walk in Christ's footsteps. Pilgrims also prayed at the tombs of the many Christian saints who were buried there. Pilgrims returned home with packets of soil from Jerusalem as relics* of their visit to the Holy Land.

Pilgrims also returned with bottles of water from the Jordan River, where Christ was baptized by John the Baptist. A visit to the Jordan was such an important part of a pilgrimage to the Holy Land that in 1172 one German visitor claimed to have counted 60,000 pilgrims on the river's bank. Many of the pilgrims bathed in the river in the belief that the bath was a sort of second baptism and a symbol of spiritual rebirth.

The second most popular pilgrim destination for medieval Christians was ROME. Not only was Rome the residence of the pope and the

* **shrine**   place that is considered sacred because of its history or the relics it contains

* **penance**   task set by the church for someone to earn God's forgiveness for a sin

* **relic**   object cherished for its association with a martyr or saint

Most Christian pilgrimages in the Middle Ages involved visits to the shrines of saints. This illumination from the 1400s shows pilgrims making a journey to Canterbury to visit the shrine of St. Thomas Becket. It comes from a manuscript of *The Siege of Thebes,* by English writer John Lydgate. In the story's prologue, the author imagines himself riding to Canterbury and meeting Chaucer's pilgrims, who ask him to tell the story of Thebes.

* **martyr**   person who suffers and dies rather than renounce a religious faith

headquarters of the PAPACY, it also was the place where Peter and Paul, the two greatest martyrs* of the early church, were buried. Rome also had an outstanding collection of saints' relics. St. Peter, who was believed to possess the keys to heaven, was especially popular in northern Europe. His shrine in Rome was a major attraction for pilgrims visiting the city. It was especially favored by criminals because of the legend that a prisoner's shackles would break after a visit to the shrine.

Rome's popularity as a pilgrimage destination increased in the 600s and the 700s, when the Arab conquests of the Holy Land made access to it more difficult for European pilgrims. Rome gained still more importance as popes gave Roman churches the power to grant the largest indulgences. In the 1200s, however, Roman pilgrimages declined because of the political turmoil and warfare in Italy.

The third great medieval Christian shrine was SANTIAGO DE COMPOSTELA in northwestern Spain. Dedicated to St. James, this shrine was especially popular with pilgrims from France, who reached the shrine along a road called the *camino de Santiago.* The bishops of Santiago and the Order of Cluny made sure that the bridges, inns, and hospitals along the route were well maintained. By the 1100s, so many pilgrims were traveling to Santiago that other smaller shrines sprang up along the way.

During the Middle Ages, Christians made pilgrimages to hundreds of shrines. Some were famous throughout Christendom, but many others were known only locally. Sometimes the reputation of a shrine changed. For example, the tomb of St. Thomas BECKET in CANTERBURY, England, attracted many pilgrims starting in the late 1100s. The popularity of the site

The Punishment of Frotmund

In medieval Europe, people who committed serious crimes were sometimes sentenced to a life of unending pilgrimage. In 850, a nobleman named Frotmund was ordered to become a perpetual pilgrim after killing his father. With his hands bound in iron chains, he traveled from shrine to shrine in Rome, Jerusalem, and North Africa, to Rome again, back to Jerusalem, and then back to Rome a third time. Finally, at the church of St. Marcellin in France, Frotmund's chains broke. This was considered a sign of God's forgiveness, and Frotmund's long pilgrimage ended.

* **patriarch** head of one of the five major centers of early Christianity: Alexandria, Antioch, Constantinople, Jerusalem, and Rome

varied during the later Middle Ages, but it was still sufficiently popular in the 1300s to become the focus of CHAUCER's *Canterbury Tales.*

Russian Pilgrimages. The practice of making religious pilgrimages arrived in Russia in the late 900s after KIEVAN RUS was converted to Byzantine Christianity. The chief destinations of medieval Russian pilgrims were the great cities of CONSTANTINOPLE and Jerusalem and famous monasteries, especially the ones on Mount Athos in Greece. Constantinople (present-day Istanbul, Turkey) was the capital of the BYZANTINE EMPIRE, the headquarters of the Byzantine Church, and the residence of the patriarch* of Constantinople, who was the head of the church. The city also had many splendid churches, such as HAGIA SOPHIA, and fine collections of relics.

However, after Constantinople fell to the Turks in 1453, Russian Christians no longer traveled to that city. Instead, they increased the number of pilgrimages they made to holy sites inside Russia. Monasteries in Kiev, Moscow, and northern Russia became popular destinations.

Changing Attitudes. By the late Middle Ages, the practice of making pilgrimages came into question, and church officials began criticizing pilgrims. In western Europe, complaints were heard about the high cost of feeding and housing hordes of pilgrims. Some church leaders were concerned that pilgrimages were becoming breeding grounds for strange cults and religious sects. In the late 1400s, the church ended one pilgrimage after its leader preached social revolt. By the late Middle Ages, many people who went on pilgrimages no longer seemed to take them seriously. Pilgrimages lost their spiritual inspiration, as people began treating them as sight-seeing adventures similar to modern tourism.

Jewish Pilgrimages

The chief destination of Jewish pilgrims was Jerusalem. In 135, however, after the second Jewish revolt against Roman rule in PALESTINE, the Roman emperor Hadrian forbade Jews to live in Jerusalem or even to visit that city. His ban remained in force for the next five centuries. Although some Jews managed to slip into Jerusalem during this period, most Jewish pilgrims visited other sites in Palestine—places associated with important events in Jewish history. After the Muslims conquered Palestine in the mid-600s, Jews resumed their pilgrimages to Jerusalem.

Jewish pilgrims from the Mediterranean region went to Jerusalem, usually in autumn, which coincided with ancient Jewish customs surrounding the Feast of the Tabernacles. In Jerusalem, they visited and prayed on the Temple Mount. This was where the Temple of Solomon had been built and where the Second Temple stood until the Romans destroyed it in 70. Some of the pilgrims were keeping vows they had made in a time of crisis when they had asked for God's help and had promised in return to make a pilgrimage to Holy Jerusalem.

Muslim Pilgrimages

Since medieval times, one of the duties of every faithful Muslim has been to make a pilgrimage to MECCA, the Arabian city that was the home of the prophet MUHAMMAD. This pilgrimage is called a hajj, and those who make it are honored with the title hajji. Because the hajj takes place at a particular date on the Muslim calendar, many thousands of Islamic pilgrims converged on Mecca simultaneously. In the Middle Ages, they traveled to Mecca by caravan. Large caravans assembled for the long journey in CAIRO, DAMASCUS, Niger, and other Muslim lands in western Africa. Muslims from Africa reached Arabia by crossing the Red Sea by boat.

This great annual event, which brought together Muslims from all over the world, created a vast network of trade and communication. Merchants sold their wares along the way, and students had an opportunity to meet Islamic scholars from many different countries. Many pilgrims wrote accounts of their journeys. The most famous of these was the one written in the late 1300s by IBN BATTUTA.

Rituals in Mecca.   Muslim pilgrims wore special robes and performed rituals—praying and bowing at specified sites in Mecca. Each pilgrim walked seven times around the Kaaba*, one of the holiest sites in Islam. Only Muslims were allowed to enter this holy place.

The pilgrimage to Mecca included several group ceremonies, such as the sermon preached to the huge crowd that gathered at Arafat (the mountain on the outskirts of Mecca where Muhammad had a divine vision). Another ceremony required pilgrims to hurl rocks at three pillars of stone that represented Satan. Sheep, goats, and camels were sacrificed, and the meat was given to the poor and needy. Before they left Mecca, Muslim pilgrims cut off their hair and made a final circuit around the Kaaba.

Other Islamic Pilgrimage Sites.   Some Muslim pilgrims combined the hajj with a visit to the nearby city of MEDINA, Muhammad's burial place. Others went to the large mosque* in Jerusalem. The Shi'ites, a Muslim sect that, after a dispute concerning the caliphate*, broke away from the main body of Islam, made the hajj to Mecca. But they also had their own pilgrimage sites, mostly in IRAN and IRAQ. (*See also* **Christianity; Islam, Religion of; Islamic Art and Architecture; Jewish Communities; Judaism; Knights, Orders of; Travel and Transportation.**)

* **Kaaba** large stone shrine covered with black cloth. It was a place of worship for pagan Arabs and became the main Islamic place of refuge and protection in Mecca.

* **mosque** Muslim place of worship

* **caliphate** office and government of the caliph, religious and political head of the Islamic state

Pillars of Islam

See *Islam, Religion of.*

Pisa

See map in Italy (vol. 3).

Pisa was an important trading center in central Italy in the region of western TUSCANY. For many years, the port was able to compete with the larger Italian cities of GENOA and FLORENCE. Then, in the late Middle Ages, the city declined.

Located near the mouth of the Arno River near the Mediterranean coast, Pisa prospered in Roman times from its location on the Via Aemilia, the coastal road to Rome. In the late 900s and the 1000s, Pisa became well-known when its fleet joined the struggle against the Muslims in SICILY and

The cathedral of Pisa was consecrated in 1118. The campanile or bell tower, also called the leaning tower, was begun in 1173 but not completed until 1370. The bell tower, built on unstable soil, began to sink and lean after only three stories were completed. Today the structure is nearly 17 feet off the vertical position. The tower continues to lean a fraction of an inch further each year.

* **patriarch** head of one of the five major centers of early Christianity: Alexandria, Antioch, Constantinople, Jerusalem, and Rome

* **booty** prizes of war

* **consecrate** to declare someone or something sacred in a church ceremony

southern Italy and competed with Genoa for control of two nearby islands, Corsica and Sardinia.

In 1080, the city leaders of Pisa persuaded the German emperor Henry IV to recognize the city government. In 1099, during the First Crusade, Pisan ships appeared off the coast of Syria. This was the first significant European fleet to appear in the East. The fleet's presence enhanced the position of the archbishop of Pisa and helped him become the patriarch* of JERUSALEM. As an effective advocate of Pisan interests, he helped Pisa establish trading rights in Acre, Tyre, and other eastern Mediterranean cities.

The early confidence and ambition of Pisa's residents can be seen in its cathedral, which was begun in 1063 at the very start of Pisa's most prosperous period. Paid for and decorated with booty* taken from the Muslims, the cathedral was consecrated* in 1118. The architect of the cathedral, Buscheto (also called Buschetus), was one of the first medieval architects to be remembered by name.

Pisa continued to grow and splendid buildings were erected, such as its famous leaning tower, which was begun about 1173. In the 1200s, when Pisa served as the main port for Florence's wool trade, its population more than tripled, reaching about 38,000. However, the constant competition with Genoa for dominance in the western Mediterranean was a drain on Pisan resources. After a series of expensive and inconclusive wars between the two rivals, Genoa decisively defeated the Pisan navy in 1284. Pisa's naval power and maritime commerce never recovered from the defeat.

In the 1300s, Pisa suffered from feuds and factional conflicts, and, in 1348, the BLACK DEATH nearly wiped out the city. After its conquest by Florence in 1406, Pisa declined rapidly. By 1427, its population had shrunk to 7,400. (*See also* **Cities and Towns; Commune; Crusades; Guelphs and Ghibellines; Trade; Warfare.**)

Plagues

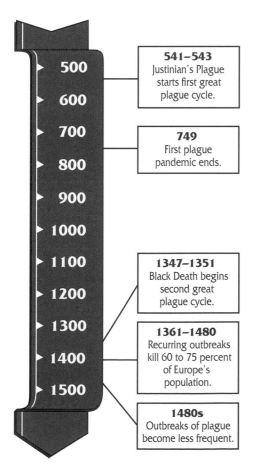

See map in Black Death (vol. 1).

* **epidemic** disease that affects a large number of people or animals

* **pandemic** outbreak of a disease over a large geographic area and occurring over a long period of time

541–543 Justinian's Plague starts first great plague cycle.
749 First plague pandemic ends.
1347–1351 Black Death begins second great plague cycle.
1361–1480 Recurring outbreaks kill 60 to 75 percent of Europe's population.
1480s Outbreaks of plague become less frequent.

500
600
700
800
900
1000
1100
1200
1300
1400
1500

Outbreaks of infectious diseases (called plagues) that spread rapidly through various regions devastated life in the Middle Ages. Plagues played an important role in determining the growth of medieval populations. Sometimes plagues killed up to half of the people in a given area of Europe or the Islamic world.

Types and Causes

Plagues occur when a disease is introduced in a part of the world where people have not yet had time to build up an immunity to it. When this happens, the disease suddenly bursts onto the historical stage by killing thousands of people. One factor that contributed to plagues in the Middle Ages was the expanding system of trade and travel that had been established in the ancient world, especially by the Romans. They had created a network of sea routes that connected India, Arabia, and the Mediterranean world. Travel to and from distant places had become quicker and easier. However, the same ships that carried goods and travelers from one port to another also carried disease. In this way, diseases from Africa and Asia reached Europe and spread among people who had no immunity to them.

From the 100s through the 600s, at least three new diseases reached Europe and the Near East. One was smallpox, which raged throughout Europe from 165 to 180. Probably carried to Europe by Roman soldiers returning from western Asia, smallpox continued to be a major killer throughout the Middle Ages, especially in the 1300s and the 1400s. Particularly fatal to children, smallpox proved to be the deadliest of the diseases that Europeans later carried to the Americas.

The second new disease that reached Europe was measles. At the height of one of the measles epidemics* in the 250s, the disease was estimated to have caused the deaths of 5,000 people in Rome on a single day. Its initial appearance in Sicily and North Africa cut down a significant portion of the population. Some historians even think that measles epidemics were a major cause of the decline and fall of the Roman Empire. During the Middle Ages, measles was primarily a disease that killed children.

As important as smallpox and measles were for the Middle Ages, they were insignificant compared with a third disease called plague. It was a complex series of infectious disease strains caused by the bacteria *Yersinia pestis* that originated in eastern Africa and southern Asia. Plague occurs in several forms, but the most common is bubonic plague. Carried by fleas and rats, bubonic plague was the cause of the mass deaths that ravaged Europe and the Islamic world again and again during the Middle Ages.

Europe

During the Middle Ages, bubonic plague occurred in cycles called pandemics*. Pandemics cover vast geographic areas and last for many years. The individual outbreaks of plague that recur every 3 to 20 years within a pandemic are called epidemics.

The bubonic plague that struck the medieval world in two great pandemics was truly deadly. No other infectious disease matched it. Historians estimate that only about half of all the people who ever contracted the

Death visits the printshop in this woodcut detail from *La grande danse macabre,* printed by Mathias Huss in France in 1499. The allegory of danse macabre, or dance of death, became popular in art and literature in the later Middle Ages, especially after the horrors of the Black Death. Death is pictured as skeletons that rise up and lure people randomly to their graves, often by dancing with them.

disease survived. This plague served as a major restraint on population growth through much of the Middle Ages.

First Pandemic.   The first medieval pandemic of plague originated in East Africa and was carried down the Nile River into EGYPT and the eastern Mediterranean. Because the first outbreak of this plague occurred in 541–543 during the reign of the Byzantine emperor JUSTINIAN I, the epidemic was called Justinian's Plague.

The plague struck quickly and with devastating effect. In the Byzantine capital of CONSTANTINOPLE, it killed 200,000 people (about 40 percent of the city's population) in a 4-month period. One Byzantine historian wrote: "During these times there was a pestilence, by which the whole human race came near to being annihilated." The scope of Justinian's Plague was so great—it hit central and southern Asia, North Africa, Arabia, and Europe as far north as Denmark and as far west as Ireland—that many were convinced that the whole world was dying. By 544, Justinian's Plague had killed between 20 and 25 percent of Europe's population.

New epidemics of plague occurred every 10 or 12 years for the next 200 years. By the time the first great plague pandemic had run its course (around 750), Europe's population was about half as large as it had been in 540. Medieval Europeans had no scientific explanation for the sudden arrival and devastating effects of plague. Many were convinced that it was a punishment sent by God.

Second Pandemic.   For the next six centuries, Europe remained fairly free of epidemic diseases. During that time, Europe's population rose to approximately 80 million people or more.

However, the growth of the MONGOL EMPIRE in the 1200s and the invasions and migrations that followed carried bubonic plague from southern China into central Asia and from there into Russia. By 1346, plague had broken out on the shores of the Black Sea, and the following year it struck Europe.

This epidemic—called the BLACK DEATH—ravaged Europe until 1351 and in just four years killed between 25 and 45 percent of its population. In some areas of Europe, the death rate was as high as 75 percent. Farms lay barren for lack of workers to till the fields, and crops rotted in the fields without people to harvest them. Trade and travel diminished, and entire districts were depopulated. The effects of this destruction lingered for decades. The Black Death was the greatest natural disaster ever to hit Europe.

As bad as the Black Death was, it was only the beginning of a second great plague pandemic. Another epidemic occurred in 1361–1362, and another followed in 1369. Plague became a part of everyday life, with each new generation seeing at least two or three epidemics. Attempts to curb the outbreaks led to new laws governing public health and sanitation. In the 1360s and 1370s, LONDON officials banned the practice of dumping the refuse from slaughterhouses into the streets and in the river from which the city drew its drinking water. During the 1400s, Italian cities introduced quarantine laws to keep sick people from having contact with the healthy. These measures probably helped control other diseases, but they had little effect on plague. The epidemic of 1479–1480 was one of the deadliest since the Black Death, killing 10 to 15 percent of those who had survived earlier outbreaks of plague.

The second plague pandemic lingered on past the end of the Middle Ages, with outbreaks occurring into the early 1700s. After the 1480s, however, the epidemics of the second pandemic were less frequent and less severe. That allowed the population of Europe to begin to grow again.

Islamic World

The effect of bubonic plague was as devastating in the Near East as it was in Europe. Justinian's Plague of 541–543 marked the beginning of a centuries-long pandemic in the Near East as well as in Europe. By the 750s, at least 38 more epidemics occurred in Egypt, SYRIA, IRAQ, and North Africa. Syria suffered the most during the pandemic.

The Black Death, which launched the second plague pandemic, began in the Islamic world in 1348 when plague broke out in Egypt. That same year, plague struck Arabia for the first time, infecting the holy city of MECCA. The disease spread slowly, but fatally, inland from the coastal cities, killing many thousands of people in Turkey, Syria, and North Africa.

The second plague pandemic proved to be even deadlier in the Near East than in Europe since its epidemics were more frequent and more severe. In addition to bubonic plague, the Near East suffered from another type of plague called pneumonic plague, which usually kills nearly all those infected. In Muslim towns and cities, entire neighborhoods were left desolate. In the countryside, some villages completely disappeared.

The problem worsened when people seeking to flee the infection carried the disease with them to previously uninfected areas. In addition,

The Plague in Literature

Medieval writers such as Petrarch, Boccaccio, and Chaucer wrote about plague and its deadly effects. In a sermon delivered in Florence in 1496, the preacher recalled Petrarch's images from 150 years earlier: "There will not be enough men left to bury the dead. So many will lie dead in the houses that men will go through the streets crying, 'Set forth your dead.' And the dead will be heaped in carts and on horses; they will be piled up and buried. Men will pass through the streets crying, 'Are there any dead? Are there any dead?'"

people in many areas suffered from starvation during epidemics because peasants who had worked the land had died or had left. Historical chronicles describe people forced to abandon all activities other than burying the dead and searching for food. Although the second plague pandemic ended in Europe in the 1700s, it continued in the Islamic world well into the 1800s. (*See also* **Death and Burial in Europe; Famine; Hospitals and Poor Relief; Medicine.**)

Plato in the Middle Ages

P lato (429–347 B.C.) was a philosopher of ancient Greece whose ideas had a powerful effect on the intellectual and cultural life of the Middle Ages. Christian, Jewish, and Islamic thinkers studied Plato, although most medieval scholars had limited access to Plato's writings. These writings consisted of dialogues, which were conversations between various characters who discuss such topics as justice, truth, love, and knowledge.

Plato was important during the Middle Ages not only because of the concepts set forth in his dialogues but because he represented the essence of philosophy—the idea that people can arrive at an understanding of life and the universe through the process of rational thinking. Some medieval thinkers found this idea exciting and challenging. Others, however, believed that all knowledge was contained in the BIBLE and Christian doctrine, and that an interest in Plato and other pagan* philosophers posed a threat to the Christian faith.

Plato in the East.   All 36 of Plato's dialogues were known in the BYZANTINE EMPIRE, the Christian Empire of the East. However, since the Byzantine Church was suspicious of secular* philosophy, Plato's writings were treated as examples of ancient pagan literature rather than as worthwhile inquiries into the nature of God and reality. In the 1000s, a scholar named Michael PSELLOS, who revived the study of philosophy in the Byzantine Empire, wrote several books on Plato's ideas.

At about the same time, Islamic scholars were studying Plato's work. After the dialogues were translated into Arabic, they influenced those Islamic scholars who wrote about science, law, and metaphysics*. Jewish philosophers in the Islamic world, who wrote most of their own works in Arabic until the 1100s, also studied Plato's dialogues. They tended to be influenced more by the work of Plato's student, Aristotle.

Plato in the West.   Until the 1100s, western European scholars knew Plato only through part of his dialogue called the *Timaeus*. This work expressed the idea that everything in the visible world is an imperfect copy of an ideal form that exists in the mind of God.

However, in about 1154, when the rest of Plato's works were being translated into LATIN, scholars began examining all of Plato's ideas. One lively field of medieval scholarship centered on the issue of whether or not secular learning had any value. Plato figured in this debate as the leading symbol of secular learning. Some church thinkers regarded his work as pagan and therefore untrustworthy, while others saw it as a secondary source of Christian truth.

* **pagan** word used by Christians to mean non-Christian and believing in several gods

* **secular** nonreligious; connected with everyday life

* **metaphysics** branch of philosophy concerned with the fundamental nature of reality

In the 1100s, a new phase in Platonic studies began when scholars at the cathedral schools in northern France claimed that Plato's ideas were harmonious with Christian belief. They argued that God gave the natural world and the power of reason to pagans and Christians alike, and that people who lived before the time of Christ, such as Plato, could perceive divine wisdom in the natural world.

In the late 1300s and the 1400s—after Aristotle came to be regarded as the most important philosopher of the ancient world—the study of Plato declined. However, in the late 1400s, Platonic studies revived after an Italian scholar, Marsilio Ficino, produced a new Latin translation of the dialogues. (*See also* **Aristotle in the Middle Ages; Christianity; Classical Tradition in the Middle Ages.**)

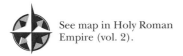
Poland

See map in Holy Roman Empire (vol. 2).

* **aristocrats** people of the highest social class

P oland is a flat, grassy land in north central Europe that SLAVS from the east settled and farmed. Bordered on the north by the Baltic Sea and on the south by the Carpathian Mountains, Poland is without natural barriers in the east and west. As a result, Poland's eastern and western borders have always been difficult to establish and maintain. The several rivers that flow north through Poland to the Baltic Sea have often served as boundaries. During the Middle Ages, the size of Poland's territory varied, widening and narrowing in response to political conditions.

Early Influences. The Romans never reached Poland, so they make no mention of the region in their histories. It is believed that by 700 the Slavic ancestors of the Polish people were farming the fields of Poland. (The name *Polonia* means people of the fields.) In the early medieval period, trade increased, fortified settlements multiplied, and self-governing villages gave way to rule by aristocrats*. One of the early aristocratic leaders was named Piast, and his descendants became the first kings of Poland.

According to the contemporary chronicler Widukind of Corvey, in 963 the Saxon count Gero made contact with "King Misaca (Mieszko), under whose rule the Slavs were living." Gero asked for help in pacifying the Veleti tribe, who lived between the Saxons and the Poles. Later, Mieszko agreed to pay tribute to the emperor of the HOLY ROMAN EMPIRE in return for keeping any Veleti lands Mieszko might conquer along the western bank of the Oder River. Mieszko also made an alliance with BOHEMIA by marrying Dobrava, the daughter of a Bohemian duke. She came to Poland along with priests and Christian literature. The conversion and baptism of Mieszko and his court in 966 paved the way for the Christianization of Poland and a new chapter in the history of medieval Poland.

Mieszko's baptism meant that Poland was now part of Christian Europe, and in return western Europeans recognized Poland as a respectable and civilized Christian state. The baptism also strengthened the claim of the Piast dynasty* to rule Poland. In 1025, Mieszko's son Boleslaw I was crowned the first king of Poland.

* **dynasty** succession of rulers from the same family or group

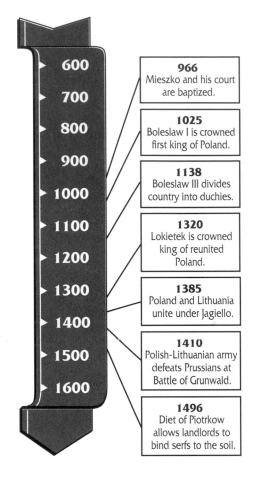

966
Mieszko and his court are baptized.

1025
Boleslaw I is crowned first king of Poland.

1138
Boleslaw III divides country into duchies.

1320
Lokietek is crowned king of reunited Poland.

1385
Poland and Lithuania unite under Jagiello.

1410
Polish-Lithuanian army defeats Prussians at Battle of Grunwald.

1496
Diet of Piotrkow allows landlords to bind serfs to the soil.

* **pagan** word used by Christians to mean non-Christian and believing in several gods

Many Poles were not eager to be ruled by a king, however, and many Polish nobles resented the growth of Piast power and harbored political ambitions of their own. Peasants were also restless, while the emerging towns and cities of Poland were only too willing to challenge central rule. To ease these political tensions, King Boleslaw III arranged in his will that Poland be divided into a series of duchies at his death, which came in 1138. Boleslaw hoped that the dukes and other factions of Polish society would cooperate with one another under a more decentralized form of government.

Outside Threats. The network of separate duchies was not strong enough to protect Poland against foreign threats. One such threat appeared in 1230, when the Teutonic Knights conquered Prussia and established on Poland's northwestern border a powerful crusader state that then went on to compete with Poland for control of the Baltic coast. In 1241, a new threat appeared when large numbers of MONGOL warriors on horseback put pressure on eastern Poland, and this pressure continued for more than a century.

Several attempts to reunify Poland were unsuccessful until a member of the Piast dynasty, Wladyslaw I "the Short" (also called Lokietek), was able to assert his authority and extend his political control in the early 1300s. His coronation as king of Poland in 1320 ended almost two centuries of political fragmentation.

Poland's size had diminished considerably during these years of fragmentation. Prussia occupied the whole of Pomerania, Bohemia expanded from the south into lands that had once been Poland, and the Mongols controlled the eastern lands. Lokietek recovered some of the lost territories, but his son, Casimir III, recovered lands that doubled the size of Poland. Casimir III, the only Polish king to be called "the Great," created a central royal administration and instituted laws that he applied throughout his kingdom. He also protected the rights of Jews in Poland and invited more to immigrate. His efforts to protect Polish peasants against landlords who took advantage of them caused him to be popularly known as "king of the peasants." When he died in 1370 at the age of 60, all of Poland mourned. However, since Casimir left no direct heir, Poland's unity was once again threatened.

Casimir's grandniece, who became Queen Jadwiga in 1384, married the grand prince of pagan* LITHUANIA the following year. He converted to Christianity and took the Polish name of Jagiello. With his new wife's encouragement and support, Jagiello effected the Christianization of his people. Jagiello united Poland and Lithuania under one crown.

Rise of Serfdom. The new dynasty's greatest threat was from Prussia. A year after war broke out in 1409, a joint army of Polish and Lithuanian forces decisively defeated the Teutonic Knights of Prussia at the Battle of Grunwald (Tannenberg). Although the diplomatic skills of the Prussians allowed them to hold onto much of their territory despite military defeat, Poland was able to regain eastern Pomerania by 1466.

In the meantime, Germans, Jews, and other non-Poles who had long been moving into Polish towns and cities established their domination over trade and commerce. The growing European demand for Polish grain increased the number and size of farms and the power of Polish landlords. The serfdom that was disappearing in western Europe increased in Poland after the Diet of Piotrkow in 1496 allowed landlords to bind SERFS to the soil. (*See also* **Agriculture; Christianity; Jewish Communities; Knights, Orders of; Trade.**)

Polo, Marco

1254–1324
Venetian explorer

See color plate 4, vol. 3.

Marco Polo was the most famous explorer of the Middle Ages. When he was still a teenager, he set out from VENICE for Cathay, the name medieval Europeans gave to China. By the time he returned 24 years later, he had traveled more extensively than almost anyone of his day.

During Marco Polo's lifetime, Venice was one of the leading trading centers in Europe, and the Polo family business was trade. Marco's father and uncle, Niccolo and Maffeo respectively, were experienced commercial travelers who had already been on a nine-year trip to Asia where they traded with chieftains of the MONGOL EMPIRE and met the Mongol ruler of China, Kublai Khan.

In 1271, when the Polos were planning to return to Asia, they decided to take young Marco with them. They sailed to the eastern Mediterranean port of Acre and then traveled overland through SYRIA, ARMENIA, IRAN, and central Asia until, in 1275, they finally reached Xanadu, the summer residence of Kublai Khan just north of the Great Wall of China.

Kublai Khan took an instant liking to Marco Polo. He appointed him inspector and sent him on various missions throughout China and southeast Asia. During his time in the royal capital of Cambaluc (present-day

Marco Polo spent many years traveling throughout China and southeast Asia as an emissary of Kublai Khan. When visiting India, he became impressed with the spices and jewels he saw there. Polo is shown with ruby hunters of Badakhshan in this miniature from a 1300s manuscript of his *Travels*.

Beijing), Marco Polo carefully observed the Mongol court and its ruler Kublai Khan. In 1292, Marco was ordered to accompany a Mongol princess to Persia where she was to marry the Mongol ruler of that country. In India, Marco was impressed by the abundance of jewels and spices in the region. His later descriptions filled European readers with wonder and a desire to acquire these treasures.

By 1295, Marco Polo was back in Venice. Although he was 41 and no longer a young man, his adventures had far from ended. When war erupted between Venice and its trading rival GENOA, Marco was captured in a sea battle and was imprisoned. While in prison in Genoa, he dictated the story of his travels in the East. After he was freed in 1299, Marco Polo returned to Venice, married, and lived for 25 more years.

The *Travels of Marco Polo,* written in a mixture of Italian and French, was a collection of his enthusiastic and picturesque tales of exotic people and places, vast cities, magnificent palaces, great riches, fantastic islands, and many things Europeans had never heard of, such as paper money, coal, and asbestos. His book fascinated medieval readers and inspired many adventurers to embark on explorations of their own. When Columbus left SPAIN in 1492 to sail westward across the ocean, he hoped to find the golden roofs of Japan as described (but never seen) by Marco Polo in his *Travels. (See also* **Exploration; Mandeville's Travels; Samarkand; Trade; Travel and Transportation.**)

Population of the Medieval World

The study of the population of the medieval world by historical demographers (scholars who study past populations) has led them to organize population trends according to periods. Demographers have concluded that in the period from 400 to 1000 the population level of medieval Europe was stable but low. From 1000 to 1250, the population of Europe grew rapidly, reaching high and stable levels from 1250 to 1350. Then, the population dropped sharply from 1350 to 1420, and it remained low but stable from 1420 to 1470. Toward the end of the Middle Ages—about 1470—Europe's population began to rise again, but slowly.

Population Studies. Historical demographers study numerous source documents to gain information about population. These documents include written records, such as CHRONICLES, surveys of manors* and estates, bills of sale and leases, and lists of births, marriages, and deaths.

The most famous survey of the Middle Ages is the DOMESDAY BOOK, which lists all the taxable property in England down to the last hog and sheep. King WILLIAM I OF ENGLAND ordered his officials to compile the survey to make sure that everybody paid a full share of taxes. As a rich source of information about English life in the 1000s, the Domesday Book is an invaluable resource for historical demographers.

Population levels remained low in the early Middle Ages for many reasons, including the abandonment of estates, barbarian invasions, FAMINE, and PLAGUE. By 800, the population of Europe was little more than 25 million. People in the early Middle Ages lived in tightly clustered settlements, or population "islands," surrounded by dense forests.

* **manor** farming estate, usually with a house for the lord and a village for the local farmworkers

Epidemics were a constant check on medieval population. During the Black Death of 1347–1351, between 25 and 45 percent of Europe's population died. The loss of this many people caused a great upheaval in the social order. It took about 150 years for the population of Europe to return to pre-plague levels. This detail from the *Triumph of Death,* a fresco painted by Italian artist Francesco Traini in about 1355, points out the inevitability of death.

 See map in Black Death (vol. 1).

However, from 1000 to 1250, people began moving outward from their enclosed communities into the forests, marshes, and wastelands, which they cleared and turned into farmland. Farms and villages sprang up in the countryside, and towns and cities flourished. The largest city in medieval Europe was PARIS, which, according to a 1328 survey, had a population of about 210,000. In northern Italy and FLANDERS—the most heavily urbanized regions of Europe—about 25 percent of the population was living in towns by 1300.

Population Disasters.   By 1300, Europe had a population greater than ever before. Between 1086 and the early 1300s, the population of ENGLAND increased from about 1.1 million to more than 3.7 million (the present-day population of Los Angeles). At its greatest point around the year 1300, Europe's population may have been as high as 100 million. During this time, landlords and merchants had most of the wealth and prospered, while poor peasants struggled to hold on to their plots of land. As rents soared and wages sank, the poor became poorer and the rich became richer.

In the early 1300s, a series of catastrophes struck Europe. Crop failures in northern Europe from 1315 to 1317 caused widespread starvation. The HUNDRED YEARS WAR, which began in 1337 between England and France, spread death and destruction over large stretches of the French countryside.

Then in 1348, the BLACK DEATH struck Italy and Spain and most of France. In 1349, it spread to the British Isles and Germany. Within a few short years, plague had wiped out one-third of the population of Europe—from Ireland to Russia and from the Baltic countries to Sicily. Entire towns and villages disappeared, and once heavily populated regions, such as PROVENCE in southern France, became wastelands. The survivors of the catastrophe were too poverty-stricken and malnourished to recover sufficiently to restore some regions. Europe's population continued to decrease into the 1400s and remained at a low level from 1420 to 1470. A period of high population growth did not begin until the 1500s.

Life Expectancy and Marriage Patterns. Demographers estimate that the average life span of medieval people was about 30 years, although before the Black Death struck Europe in the mid-1300s people had lived an average of 40 years. The average was brought down by the high death rate among infants and among mothers giving birth, as well as by the high death rate among children and young adults during times of plague. However, once past their youth, people might lead long lives, and those who lived through one epidemic* were likely to survive the next. In 1427 in the city of FLORENCE, almost 12 percent of the population was age 60 or older. Those who lived the longest tended to be wealthy people who were better fed.

Families with many children were common in the Middle Ages. During times of epidemics when death rates soared, especially among children, people tried to compensate by having more children in the hope that more of them would survive past childhood. More than 15 percent of the population in Florence in 1427 was age 4 or younger. Peasant families tended to be large out of necessity since many children were needed to help farm the land.

Medieval women often married in their teens, and men in their early 20s. Women lived longer than men, especially in towns and cities and among the NOBILITY. (*See also* **Agriculture; Family; Feudalism; Inheritance Laws and Practices; Land Use; Women, Role of.**)

* **epidemic** disease that affects a large number of people or animals

Portugal

Portugal is a small, narrow country located on the Atlantic coast of the Iberian peninsula, which it shares with SPAIN. During much of its early history, the region was fairly isolated from major events on the peninsula. Yet many of the cultural changes of the Middle Ages took root in this region. By the end of the medieval period, Portugal was at the forefront of exploration and discovery.

Early History. During the time of the Roman Empire, the area that became Portugal was firmly under Roman rule and the Roman way of life. Roman roads, aqueducts*, and bridges were built, and commerce in the region flourished. A network of towns developed that later grew into the Portuguese cities of today. The Roman language, LATIN, was spoken, and it later developed into Portuguese. The inhabitants of western Iberia adopted Christianity.

In the early 400s, Germanic tribes migrated into the Iberian peninsula in search of new land to farm. Among the first tribes to enter western Iberia were the Alans, the Suevi, and two branches of the VANDALS. They were followed by the VISIGOTHS, who eventually gained control over most of the peninsula. During the late 400s and the 500s, many of these

* **aqueduct** channel, often including bridges and tunnels, that brings water from a distant source to where it is needed

 See map in Aragon (vol. 1).

Germanic peoples converted to Christianity as a result of missionary activity, and churches and monasteries were founded in the region. By the late 500s, Christianity had become the religion of the entire peninsula, and the town of Braga emerged as an important center of Christian thought and culture.

Conquest and Reconquest.   In 711, Islamic armies swept into the Iberian peninsula from Morocco in North Africa and conquered all of the peninsula except for a small area in the north, which became the Christian kingdom of ASTURIAS. During the Muslim conquest, a widespread dislocation of population occurred. People abandoned the land and took refuge in fortified towns and castles. Fields went untended and crops withered. Soon, however, a slow retaking of the peninsula was under way, led by the kings of Asturias.

Over the next few centuries, Christians gradually reconquered Portuguese lands and incorporated them into the Spanish kingdoms of Asturias, CASTILE, and LEÓN. During this time, several noble families rose to positions of great power. By the mid-800s, the northern part of the region had its own governor and was referred to for the first time as "portuguese territory." In the early 11th century, Ferdinand I of León and Castile took control of the region. His death in 1065 and the subsequent division of his kingdom among his children set in motion a separatist movement that eventually resulted in the creation of the kingdom of Portugal.

Kingdom of Portugal.   During the early 1100s, civil war raged among various heirs to the territory that included Portugal. In 1128, one of these heirs, Afonso Henriques, gained victory at the Battle of São Mamede and took over the rule of Portugal. In time, Afonso began calling himself King Afonso I. During his long reign—from 1128 to 1185—Portugal gained independence from Castile and León and became recognized as an independent kingdom.

While Afonso ruled, the Muslims continued to hold much Portuguese land, and he waged continual war against them. One of his greatest victories against the Muslims was the conquest of the city of Lisbon in 1147. He also gained control—at least temporarily—of other important Muslim strongholds. Many of these were recaptured by the Muslims in the 1160s.

Afonso I initiated a strong tradition of monarchy in Portugal. He was aided by several factors, including the territorial compactness of his kingdom and the length of his reign. As part of his effort to create an independent Portugal, Afonso established a strong church in his kingdom that was separate from the major Spanish churches at SANTIAGO DE COMPOSTELA and TOLEDO. Ironically, the Portuguese church became the fiercest rival to royal authority, and bitter internal struggles for power occurred between the crown and the church throughout most of the medieval period.

Towards the end of his reign, Afonso I ruled jointly with his son and heir, Sancho I. When Sancho succeeded his father in 1185, he turned his attention to stabilizing his kingdom. To this end, he encouraged the resettlement of areas reconquered from the Muslims. He developed a variety of institutions to attract settlers to these abandoned zones and granted town

Port Wine

The Portuguese town of Oporto gave its name to one of the most popular drinks of medieval times: port wine. Grapes gathered in the Douro River valley, in which Oporto lies, were pressed and their juices were stored in wooden casks. Most ports were kept in a cask for two or three years. Some were stored for even longer periods. A 25-year-old bottle of port was not unusual. The business of making port wine and shipping it to foreign countries was a major Portuguese industry in the Middle Ages. The industry was controlled by guilds, which set regulations for every aspect of port production. Today, Portuguese law allows only wine bottled in the Oporto region to be called port.

Henry the Navigator was a Portuguese prince of the 1400s who played an important role in overseas exploration and colonization. At his headquarters at Sagres, Henry gathered mapmakers, astronomers, mathematicians, and ship designers, who helped him plan expeditions. The voyages Henry sponsored helped advance the study of geography and made Portugal a leader in navigation among European nations at that time.

* **excommunication** formal exclusion from the church and its rituals

* **interdict** papal decree that forbids an entire district from participation in the sacraments and from Christian burial

* **depose** to remove from high office

* **cortes** advisory parliaments of the Spanish kingdoms

charters and special privileges to settlers in frontier areas. He supported agricultural projects and encouraged immigration from outside the Iberian peninsula. During the first half of Sancho's reign, Portugal was plagued by clashes with its neighboring Christian kingdoms. Conflicts with the church also erupted over payments to the PAPACY and concerning the power and privileges of Portuguese bishops. These resulted in the first of a long series of excommunications* and interdicts* that plagued Sancho and his successors.

Consolidation of the Kingdom.   The kings who followed Sancho I sought to consolidate the gains of their predecessors, particularly in increasing royal power and making further headway against the Muslims. Afonso II ruled from 1211 to 1223. In the first year of his reign, he issued the first body of Portuguese law, which helped guarantee rights and property ownership, regularize the administration of justice, and eliminate abuses by both the clergy and the nobility. He also summoned the first CORTES, an advisory council of nobles and clergy. Although little fighting against the Muslims on Portugal's borders took place during his reign, Afonso II sent Portuguese troops to aid the kingdom of Castile in its struggle against the Muslims. The victory of the Portuguese and the Spaniards over the Muslims at the Battle of Las Navas de Tolosa in 1212 was considered to be the greatest Christian victory of the reconquest.

Sancho II, who ruled from 1223 to 1248, achieved notable military success against the Muslims. However, he was unable to restrain and pacify the restless Portuguese clergy and nobles, who were upset by the crown's efforts to consolidate its authority and to recover royal lands and income. Law and order in Portugal were breaking down, and conditions in the country had deteriorated. Murder, theft, rape, and arson were widespread, churches were sacked, and clergy members were assassinated. By 1242, the kingdom seemed to be nearing civil war. Finally, the church and the nobility deposed* Sancho and turned over the government to his brother, who became Afonso III.

Afonso III, who reigned from 1248 to 1279, renewed the policies of Portugal's earlier monarchs by asserting royal authority wherever possible. He also continued to drive the Muslims from their isolated strongholds in southwestern Portugal. Early in his reign, Portuguese forces pushed southward and retook the Algarve, the southernmost region of Portugal, freeing it from Muslim control. By the time Afonso's son Dinis took the throne in 1279, Portugal was free from the Muslim threat. Afonso also promoted greater participation in national life by towns and local officials. In 1254, for the first time in the nation's history, representatives of the cities participated in the cortes*. Laws were enacted to protect commoners from abuse at the hands of the privileged classes, and the economy expanded.

Later History.   Freed from the Muslim threat by the end of the 13th century, Portugal entered a new era of achievement. During the reign of Dinis I, from 1279 to 1325, royal authority was extended over the towns of the kingdom's border areas. All along the frontier, Dinis restored and reinforced the strongholds and castles and promoted resettlement. He also tried to bring various orders of knights, such as the Templars and Hospitalers, under his control. These knights had settled in Portugal in

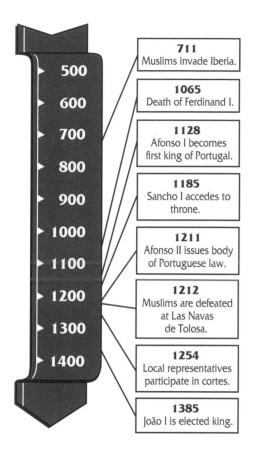

711	Muslims invade Iberia.
1065	Death of Ferdinand I.
1128	Afonso I becomes first king of Portugal.
1185	Sancho I accedes to throne.
1211	Afonso II issues body of Portuguese law.
1212	Muslims are defeated at Las Navas de Tolosa.
1254	Local representatives participate in cortes.
1385	João I is elected king.

earlier centuries to battle the Moors. To strengthen the economy, Dinis improved agriculture, reclaimed marshes and swamps, planted forests, and redistributed property. He encouraged foreign trade and established a navy to defend the nation's coast and to protect shipping. Under Dinis's enlightened rule, Portuguese scholarship and literature also flourished.

During the 1300s, the history of Portugal was marked by periods of internal strife, recurring conflicts with the kingdom of Castile, and the disintegration of society and the economy caused by the BLACK DEATH. Despite such problems, Portugal's monarchs were able to maintain the kingdom's stability and to retain their own authority. In 1385, the Portuguese cortes elected João I of Aviz as king, thus ending a brief struggle for succession. Shortly after João became king, Portuguese forces defeated the Castilians in two decisive battles—the Battle of Trancoso in June 1385 and the Battle of Aljubarrota in August of that year.

Much of Portugal's history in the 1400s revolved around the children of João I and their heirs. One of João's sons, Prince Henry the Navigator, played a significant role in overseas exploration and colonization. Through his guidance and efforts, Portugal boldly embarked on far-reaching exploration of the Atlantic and the west coast of Africa. These explorations laid the groundwork for the great age of exploration that began in the late 1400s and resulted in the discovery of the New World. (*See also* **Asturias-León; Castile; Exploration; Islam, Conquests of.**)

Postal Services

During the Middle Ages, the Byzantine and Islamic Empires had organized, government-run postal services. Europe had two informal systems of postal service—government couriers, and members of society who carried messages for others as they traveled from place to place.

The BYZANTINE EMPIRE had an intricate and sophisticated postal system established primarily to gather information. Having inherited an excellent network of roads from the ancient Romans, the Byzantines operated an express service that used saddle horses, two-wheeled carriages, and four-wheeled carts. Staging posts were located 8 to 15 miles apart between cities. Some posts were used as relay stations for changing teams of animals, and others served as rest stops for people as well as animals. The Byzantine state maintained its postal service at huge public expense. Although its use was restricted to official state business, the rich and powerful found ways to use the service for their own purposes.

The Islamic world also had a postal service called the *barid,* which was used to carry messages and goods and to gather information about neighboring states. When Europeans invaded the Middle East during the CRUSADES, Muslims used runners, riders on swift camels, visual signals, and pigeons to carry messages back and forth.

In Europe, governments employed couriers to carry a variety of messages. Diplomats were entrusted by their rulers to gather intelligence (secret information about enemies). Ambassadors at foreign courts often wrote to their kings about the size of foreign armies, weapons, and other useful subjects. Diplomatic correspondence—usually carried in a special pouch—included treaties, copies of other important documents, records of sensitive negotiations, and official letters. States often granted foreign couriers bearing diplomatic messages passes of safe-conduct, which insured their protection while they traveled on foreign soil. However, the countryside was dangerous, and sometimes couriers were held up and killed and their documents stolen.

Networks of communication were also formed by other members of society. Traveling monks and priests were sometimes employed as couriers. Travelers making PILGRIMAGES often carried messages for others, as did traders and merchants escorting their goods to and from distant parts of Europe. As FAIRS and MARKETS developed in the 1100s, long-distance business correspondence became part of the traffic between European cities and towns. Medieval universities used their own messengers to deliver mail to their faculty members. (*See also* **Cities and Towns; Diplomacy; Missions and Missionaries, Christian; Roads and Bridges; Travel and Transportation; Universities.**)

Prague

* **dynasty** succession of rulers from the same family or group

See color plate 3, vol. 2.

* **artisans** skilled craftspeople

The origins of the medieval town of Prague date from the late 800s when the Premyslid dynasty* established its seat at the Prague castle on the left bank of the Vltava River. From there, they governed Bohemia until 1306. The first written reference to Prague appeared in the work of the Saxon chronicler Widukind of Corvey in 929. In about 965, a Jewish merchant from Tortosa described Prague as a busy city where SLAVS, Russians, Muslims, Jews, and Turks traded goods. German and Jewish merchant settlements are mentioned as existing in Prague in the 1000s, and the first record of regular FAIRS in the region is from the early 1100s.

Prague experienced a cultural golden age during the reign of King Charles IV, from 1346 to 1378, when it became one of Europe's most splendid cities. In 1348, Charles expanded the city by founding the New Town next to the Old Town and a university. Named after himself, Charles University was the first university in central Europe. The king also built new churches, monasteries, fortifications, and a stone bridge across the Vltava River.

To make Prague a great center of European learning and culture, Charles invited artists, architects, sculptors, and writers to his court. Among them was the great Italian poet and scholar PETRARCH. During Charles's enlightened reign, the city prospered and artisans'* GUILDS gained importance. By the time of Charles's death, Prague was the largest European city east of the Rhine River, with a population of about 40,000.

The period of peace and prosperity ended in Prague in the early 1400s, when the city became embroiled in turmoil over the teachings of the Czech religious reformer Jan HUS. By 1419, the Hussites in Prague were in full revolt against churches, monasteries, and civil authority. The Hussite army and imperial troops battled each other until the Hussites were defeated in 1434. The physical and economic damage suffered during the Hussite uprisings took a long time to heal. Peace and prosperity did not return to Prague until the late 1500s, when the city regained its prominence as the residence of Emperor Rudolf II. (*See also* **Cities and**

One of the oldest synagogues in Europe, Altneuschul (the Old-New Synagogue), is located in Prague. It was built in the late 1200s to early 1300s. This interior view shows the synagogue's Gothic influences. The banner of the Prague Jewish community is also seen.

Towns; Heresy and Heresies; Holy Roman Empire; Kievan Rus; Muscovy, Rise of; Universities.)

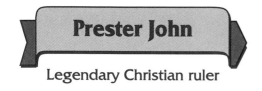

Prester John

Legendary Christian ruler

* **magi** ancient priests of Persia, who were believed to possess supernatural powers

Prester John (or John the Priest) was a legendary medieval ruler who was believed to have governed a fabulous Christian kingdom somewhere in the Far East, India, or ETHIOPIA. According to the legend, Prester John brought various Muslim forces in the region under his control and came to the rescue of the crusaders.

The power and prestige of Prester John was first acknowledged in the mid-1100s by the writer OTTO OF FREISING. Otto based his information on unconfirmed reports of a priest-king called John, who was said to be a descendant of the magi*. These reports claimed that John ruled a country in the Far East and that he led his army to victory over the Persians. Around 1165, a letter circulated in Europe that was allegedly written by Prester

Prester John was the legendary Christian ruler of a kingdom believed to be in the Far East, India, or Africa. Stories about him began to appear in the mid-1100s. Various attempts were made to find his kingdom, which supposedly had great wealth and power. Prester John is seen here in this detail from an atlas from the 1500s.

John himself. This letter, which was addressed to various European monarchs, described John as the ruler of an ideal place where everyone prospered and law and order prevailed. It was a land of enormous wealth, forests, crystal-clear waters, monstrous animals, and other marvels. At first, this kingdom was thought to be in Asia. But after almost two centuries of searching by European travelers, attention shifted to Africa, particularly to Ethiopia. Communication between Ethiopia and Europe began around 1400. As Europeans gathered more accurate information about that land, the legend of Prester John gradually disappeared. While it lasted, however, the story of Prester John gave Europeans a ray of hope for the Christian world at a time when much seemed rather gloomy and depressing.

Printing, Origins of

* **movable type** wooden or metal blocks with raised letters that were arranged to form words

The origins of modern printing are found in the late Middle Ages. The development of printing had a tremendous effect on medieval society, stimulating the growth of literacy (the ability to read and write) and the spread of knowledge.

The first press in Europe to produce printing with movable type* was that of Johannes GUTENBERG in Mainz, Germany. Gutenberg's press began printing around 1450, and by 1455 it had completed its first major work, a Latin Bible in two volumes. From Mainz, printing spread to other German cities and to Italy, which became the chief center of printing in the 1400s. Early printing in Italy differed in character from

Incunabula

Books printed before the year 1501 are called incunabula, from the Latin word for cradle and referring to the earliest stages of printing. Many incunabula contain no information about the printer or the date of publication. In recent years, however, accurate methods for dating types of paper and ink have enabled experts to identify and date these works more reliably. Incunabula are important sources for studying the technical development of printing.

* **humanistic** referring to a concern for human interests and values

* **vernacular** language or dialect native to a region; everyday, informal speech

* **typeface** individual design or style of type

* **archaic** characteristic of the language of the past

that of Germany. While early German printers usually produced Bibles or devotional books, Italian printers focused on classical and humanistic* texts.

By the 1470s, VENICE had become the most important center of printing in Europe, for both the production and the distribution of printed works. Printing first became a truly international craft in Venice, with printers of many nations working there. Soon, networks of international trade helped spread printing to other parts of Europe, although it was still concentrated in Germany and Italy. By 1480, the book trade was organized so efficiently that books printed in any country could be obtained easily throughout most of Europe. As a result, many printers often produced only those books written in their own countries.

At first, printing affected only a small circle of high church officials. It became apparent, however, that printing had the potential to reach a much wider audience. Unlike handwritten manuscripts, printed books could be mass-produced to reach large numbers of people. Soon printed books, often highly specialized, reached universities, churches, monasteries, governments, the nobility, and the professional classes (lawyers and physicians). Printers also reached other classes of society by producing works in inexpensive popular versions, often with appealing illustrations and text in the vernacular*. They also experimented with book design and typefaces*; the development of standardized typefaces was one of the most dramatic developments in printing. Books intended for individual use became smaller in size than those for institutions. To help guide new readers, printers included such features as indexes, titles, and headings.

The majority of books in the 1400s were printed in Latin. The role of vernacular languages became increasingly important, however, and this affected the languages themselves. Larger-scale distribution of texts in the vernacular led to the creation of standard forms for vernacular languages. Printers abandoned archaic* language and regional differences in favor of modern, urban forms of the language. With increased uniformity of the language, printers also developed a sense of responsibility for the quality of the text. Since various editions of a work were often produced, these texts could be compared for accuracy. Printers and editors attempted to ensure accuracy by bringing together superior sources, investigating the accuracy of manuscripts, and striving to improve their own editions. This concern for accuracy changed Western thinking in the 1500s, and it laid the foundation for the modern age. (*See also* **Books, Manuscript.**)

Prisons

During the Middle Ages, prisons served as places of confinement and sometimes as sources of income. Beginning in the late 800s, prisons were used to confine accused persons before their trial and sentencing. If found guilty, the accused were punished by death, mutilation, branding, or fine, but they did not serve prison sentences as they do today. From about the 1200s, prisons were also used to imprison debtors.

In the early medieval period, enemy soldiers were generally killed or enslaved. However, if the captured person was important enough, his captor might keep him in a castle until a sizable ransom was paid. If the captive did not fetch the ransom price, he might languish in a dungeon indefinitely. In addition to the military, the church had its own prisons for clerical offenders and heretics.

Imprisonment took many forms—from being confined in a tiny room or cage to being restricted to a region, town, or part of a building. Prisoners might also be held in stocks that restricted the movement of their arms and head or in chains attached to their hands and feet. Since prisoners were required to pay for their food and upkeep, jail keepers earned income by maintaining the jails. By the late 1200s, inmates could end their imprisonment by paying a fine.

Medieval people were fully aware of the horrors of prison life and generally regarded prisoners with sympathy. Religious orders of nuns, monks, and laypersons collected alms* to help prisoners. Many famous and important people were imprisoned during the Middle Ages, including the English crusader King RICHARD I THE LIONHEARTED and the French national heroine JOAN OF ARC. Some prisons became notorious—such as the Tower of London and the Bastille in Paris—because of their size, the treatment of inmates, or the fame or social position of their prisoners. (*See also* **Heresy and Heresies; Inquisition; Law; Torture; Witchcraft, European.**)

* **alms** money or gifts given to help the poor and suffering

Provence

* **dynasty** succession of rulers from the same family or group

Provence in southern France played an important role in the political, cultural, and religious history of the Middle Ages. Extending from the Rhône River in the west to the southern Alps in the east, and with the Mediterranean Sea its southern border, medieval Provence was subject to invasion and to competition between dynasties* that sought to rule the area.

In the 1200s, Provence was home of the TROUBADOUR poets who composed their songs in the Provençal dialect. A century later, Provence became the residence of the PAPACY during the 75 years the popes lived in AVIGNON rather than ROME.

Political History.   The region was settled by the ancient Greeks and later ruled by the Romans, who named their first Roman province in Gaul Provincia. The FRANKS who conquered Provence in the 500s faced the task of protecting it from the Muslims from SPAIN after they advanced into southern France. Beginning with the campaigns of CHARLES MARTEL against the Muslim invaders in the 730s, the region became a battleground between Christians and Muslims until the 970s, when William "the Liberator" of Provence finally drove the Muslims out of the region permanently.

After Provence was incorporated into the CAROLINGIAN Empire in the 800s, it became part of BURGUNDY in the 800s and early 900s and briefly was part of the HOLY ROMAN EMPIRE of the German emperor. After being part of the domains of the counts of TOULOUSE and BARCELONA in the 1100s, the counts of Anjou gained control of Provence through marriage in the 1200s. Provence remained under ANGEVIN control for more than 200 years, until the kingdom of France annexed* it.

* **annex** to add a territory to an existing state

An outstanding example of Provençal Romanesque architecture is the Palace of Justice in Poitiers. Begun in the 1100s, it served as the ancestral home for the dukes of Aquitaine and the place where they rendered judgments.

Religious Heritage. According to legend, the first Christians in Provence were Mary Magdalene and a group of her companions who, after being miraculously transported across the Mediterranean Sea in a raft, proceeded to convert the population. Certainly, Christians were in the area very early, as evidenced by the funeral monuments from the early 100s. The first known bishop was Marcion at Arles (ca. 254). In 314, the first of many church councils was held in Arles.

Provence became known for its MONASTERIES, beginning with the abbey* of St. Victor that was founded in Marseilles by John Cassian in about 416. Cassian composed the first set of instructions for monastic life in the West. St. Caesarius of Arles (who died in 542) also wrote a rule for monks and one of the earliest rules for nuns in western Europe.

* **abbey** monastery under the rule of an abbot or abbess

The abbey of St. Victor was influenced by the reforms initiated by the monastery at Cluny in Burgundy and succeeded in obtaining special privileges from Rome like those of Cluny. By the late 1080s, St. Victor was the center of a reformed monastic order with many houses in southern France and northern Spain. By the mid-1100s, the order of the CISTERCIANS was also established in Provence, followed by those of the DOMINICANS and the FRANCISCANS in the 1200s.

Provence also had a strong Cathar tradition. The CATHARS were Christians who were considered heretics* by the church. St. DOMINIC designated Provence as one of five provinces in which the movement should be eliminated. Although Provence was spared many of the destructive effects of the crusade that followed against the Cathars in France (called the Albigensian crusade), many Cathars fled to northern Italy.

* **heretic** person who disagrees with established church doctrine

Culture. The Provençal ROMANESQUE ARCHITECTURE of the area drew from the styles of the region of LANGUEDOC to the north and from the area's many Roman monuments. Examples of the Provençal style were the cathedrals at Arles, Marseilles, Aix, and Avignon. The Cistercian monasteries in Provence had their own distinctive style of architecture. In the 1300s,

Avignon developed its own papal GOTHIC ARCHITECTURE and introduced Italian artists to the papal court, who developed a French Avignon school of painting. Among the several masterpieces that have survived from Avignon are the *Burning Bush* by Nicolas Froment and the *Coronation of the Virgin* by Enguerrard Charonton.

Provençal poets perfected the tradition in poetry set by the troubadours. After the movement began in AQUITAINE, it soon reached Provence, where Raimbaut d'Aurenga (who died in 1173) was the earliest known practitioner. The courts at Orange and Marseilles quickly became major centers of patron* support for the troubadours. The wars in Languedoc and the conflict between the houses of Aragon and Anjou drove some of the poets into northern Italy, where the troubadour tradition began to take root in the 1200s. In the 1400s, there was a brief revival of Provençal art and literature before the area was united with the kingdom of France in 1486. (*See also* **Chivalry; Courtly Love; France; French Language and Literature.**)

* **patron**   person of wealth and influence who supports an artist, writer, or scholar